This account, penned by a noted British military historian of the late 19th century, remains one of the best narratives of a 19th-century battle yet published.

The Battle of Spicheren was fought in early August 1870, and like many of the battles in the opening phase of the Franco-Prussian war, could be termed an encounter battle. Fighting over very difficult terrain, German forces dislodged the French II Corps after a heroic defence.

Henderson not only drew on the General Staff works and other official sources available to military historians of the late 19th century - the value of his work is that he also utilised many other accounts, including regimental histories. He presents an extremely detailed narrative of the battle. Following a full discussion of the events of 6 August 1870, he also discusses the tactics of the battle, and training and other characteristics of the troops involved.

This reprint not only includes all of the maps from the original, but also features a new essay outlining the life and military writings of Henderson, by Duncan Rogers, as well as added illustrations and a bibliography of the Battle of Spicheren.

THE BATTLE OF SPICHEREN

AUGUST 6TH, 1870, AND THE EVENTS THAT PRECEDED IT

Lieut.-Col. G.F.R. Henderson
Professor of Military History, Staff College

New introduction and biographical essay about Henderson by Duncan Rogers

Helion & Company Ltd

Helion & Company Limited
Unit 8 Amherst Business Centre
Budbrooke Road
Warwick
CV34 5WE
England
Tel. 01926 499619
Email: info@helion.co.uk
Website: www.helion.co.uk
X (formerly Twitter): @Helionbooks
Facebook: @HelionBooks
Visit our blog at https://helionbooks.wordpress.com/

Published by Helion & Company 2009. New edition published 2025
Originally published by Gale & Polden Ltd, London, 1891, with the title *The Battle of Spicheren, August 6th 1870, and the events that preceded it. A study in practical tactics and war training*

Designed and typeset by Farr out Publications, Wokingham, Berkshire
Cover designed by Paul Hewitt, Battlefield Design (www.battlefield-design.co.uk)

ISBN 978-1-804518-50-2

British Library Cataloguing-in-Publication Data.
A catalogue record for this book is available from the British Library.

For details of other military history titles published by Helion & Company Limited, contact the above address, or visit our website: http://www.helion.co.uk

We always welcome receiving book proposals from prospective authors.

CONTENTS

LIST OF ILLUSTRATIONS

LIST OF MAPS

G.F.R. HENDERSON – HIS LIFE, WORK AND LEGACY

A NEW INTRODUCTION BY DUNCAN ROGERS

Blessed with a cheerful temperament, he brightened the lives of all with whom he was associated, and his letters display a spirit of playful tenderness towards those whom he loved, which is most attractive.
Field Marshal Lord Roberts, 1905[1]

INTRODUCTION

G.F.R. Henderson – Frank – 'Hender' – remains one of the few later nineteenth century British military theorists and historians whose work has remained continually accessible until the present day. In particular, his biography of Thomas J. 'Stonewall' Jackson of American Civil War fame has remained in-print nearly continuously since its original publication in 1898.[2] Although some of his writings about the development of the British Army, with suggestions for improving it, are chiefly of historical interest, the clarity, the accessibility, the organisation and general penmanship of his work mean that much of what he wrote remains vivid and relevant to today, paintings in words that have lost little of their colour since originally laid down by their creator. Such a combination of talents are rare in the military historian, such talents were recognised in Henderson's lifetime, and such talents have continued to enable readers of his works to gain much from them right up until today.

Certainly even during his lifetime Henderson's original approach to writing about military history and military institutions was noted. In particular, he originated a school of thought that emphasised the psychological factors in war, in contradistinction to writers such as E.B. Hamley[3], whose *Operations of War* reduced the actions of generals and armies to, at times, the most abstract of diagrammatic reasoning. Henderson

1 Malcolm (ed.), *The Science of War* (London, 1905), p. xxxviii.

2 *Stonewall Jackson and the American Civil War*. First published in 1898, even a cursory check of the British Library's catalogue reveals around 20 different printings.

3 Sir Edward Bruce Hamley (1824-93), an artilleryman by training, and veteran of the Crimean War, was also a well-known reviewer for journals such as *Blackwood's Magazine* and *The Edinburgh Review*, as well as Professor of Military History at the Staff College (1859-65), later becoming its Commandant (1870-77). He wrote *The Operations of War Explained and Illustrated* (first published 1866), which enjoyed phenomenal success on an international level.

breathed fresh air into British military thought and writing, just at a time when the triumph of Germany in all matters military seemed assured, and when French military theoreticians, such as Henri Bonnal, were also becoming known on a wider stage. Above all, Henderson was quick to deduce tactical and other developments and foresee with a remarkable degree of accuracy their likely effect on future military operations. This ability to divine possible outcomes due to a tremendous grasp of military knowledge combined with a very humanistic personality (that in itself must have played a role in his emphasising the psychological factors in war) placed Henderson above many of his contemporaries, and displayed talents which were spotted by men of higher rank than he – Viscount Garnet Wolseley[4], for instance.

Certainly, Henderson touched the lives of those he came into contact with, as just a selection of quotations from those who knew him demonstrate …

> … whether in the lecture-hall or in the field, the extraordinary qualifications of Colonel Henderson as an instructor were equally conspicuous. He showed great clearness of thought and perception, simplicity and correctness of demonstration, a practical mind that discarded at once methods impracticable in war, and untiring industry and patience.[5] (Lieutenant-General Sir Henry Hildyard, Commandant of the Staff College 1893-98)

> The influence of such a man must bear good fruit, and the more widely his writings are read, and the more closely his teachings are followed, the more successful will be our would-be commanders and the better it will be for England when again she is forced to go to war.[6] (Field Marshal Lord Roberts)

> His kindly nature and broad sympathies won for him the sincere affection of those who had the privilege of working with him, or under him. He exercised a deep influence over those with whom he was brought into contact, and the traces of his work at this College, to which he devoted the best years of his life, can never be effaced.[7] (Colonel H.S.G. Miles, Commandant of the Staff College 1898-99, and 1900-03)

Early life

Henderson was born 2 June 1854 at St Helier, Jersey, eldest of 14 children to the Rev William George Henderson (1819-1905), later Dean of Carlisle, and his wife Jane Melville (died 1901), daughter of John Dalyell of Lingo, Fife. Henderson's father had been appointed headmaster of Victoria School, Jersey in 1852.

In 1862 the family moved to Yorkshire when the Rev Henderson was appointed headmaster of Leeds Grammar School. It was there that Frank received his education.

4 Garnet Wolseley, later first Viscount Wolseley (1833-1913), rose from a lowly background to become commander-in-chief of the British Army in 1895. A controversial figure, historians continue to debate his reputation, and remarkably, a comprehensive modern biography remains to be written.

5 Quoted in Malcolm (ed.), *op. cit.*, p. xxix.

6 *Ibid.*, p. xxxviii.

7 Quoted in Lieut.-Colonel R.M. Holden, "Lieut.-Colonel G.F.R. Henderson, C.B. in Memoriam", *The Journal of the Royal United Service Institution*, Vol. XLVII, No. 302 (April 1903), p. 375.

Seemingly popular at school, one of his friends at the time wrote, "As a boy he possessed many of the qualities which go to make a great leader, and I can readily believe that his personality acted largely in his influence as a teacher."[8] At school Henderson won the English prize for his essay 'Alexander the Great', whilst he was particularly fond of cricket, as well as football and drama.

He later won a history scholarship to St John's College Oxford, and an exhibition from his school, however he did not graduate, and in 1876 went to Sandhurst. Reading between the lines, it seems Henderson devoted more time to physical activity than study, and by doing so disappointed some of those close to him.[9] His father had intended him for a career in the church, but Frank was set upon the military, and duly entered Sandhurst in 1877.

Early years in the army and marriage

Henderson spent a year at Sandhurst, during which time he was captain of the cricket eleven. He was gazetted Second Lieutenant in the old 65th Foot (York and Lancaster Regiment) at Dinapore on 1 May 1878, at the age of 24, which was unusually old at the time. However, he spent only a brief time in India before returning to England, and was promoted Lieutenant in the 84th Foot on 24 June 1879, being stationed at Dover, and later Ireland.[10]

In 1882 he sailed with his Battalion from Dublin on 5 August in the *Nevada* to take part in the Egyptian campaign, writing to his mother at the time,

> The route has not yet actually arrived, but we are nearly all packed and ready to start ... It is a great bore for us being kept in suspense like this. Of course it is all right for us fellows, we have the voyage and all the excitement and novelty to look forward to, but it is sad work for the women ... I hope we shall do our duty and come back safe and sound.[11]

Henderson and his unit reached Alexandria on 17 August, the Battalion forming part of Major-General Sir Gerald Graham's Brigade, 1st Division. During the voyage he had displayed what would become his trademark inquiring mind, telling his mother "I have been improving the shining hours by learning Arabic, but it is a difficult language to master."[12]

Frank saw active service during the campaign, commanding a half-company at El Magfar (24 August) and Tel-el-Mahouta (25 August), and a company at both Kassassin (28 August) and Tel-el-Kebir (13 September), where he was first into an enemy redoubt, an act of bravery which attracted much attention, the more so since he survived unscathed. For his sterling service during the brief campaign, Henderson received the 5th Class of the Order of the Medijideh, the Egyptian medal and clasp, the Khedive's Star, a mention

8 Quoted in Malcolm (ed.), *op. cit.*, p. xiii.

9 Roberts writes, "At the University Henderson somewhat disappointed those who expected him to devote himself entirely to study." Malcolm (ed.), *op. cit.*, p. xiv.

10 The 84th Foot was the sister battalion of the 65th, both forming the York and Lancaster Regiment.

11 Quoted in Malcolm (ed.), *op. cit.*, p. xv.

12 *Ibid.*, p. xv.

in despatches and a brevet majority.[13] Perhaps as importantly for his future prospects, his exploits had attracted the attention of the expeditionary force's commander, Sir Garnet Wolseley.

Following Arabi Pasha's surrender the day after the Battle of Tel-el-Kebir, Henderson returned to England. He did hope to join the new gendarmerie of the Egyptian army, but was to be disappointed.

In 1883 he married Mary Joyce, of Galway; the couple had no children. The first two years of their marriage were spent on a tour of duty with Henderson's regiment in Bermuda, and Halifax, Nova Scotia. During this time he lived the life of a typical subaltern when off-duty, playing cricket, and fishing. He was also beloved by his men, known for the attention and care he paid to the soldiers under his command, and indeed former NCOs of Henderson continued to correspond with him long after he left the Regiment, Lord Roberts noting "His consideration and his absolute fairness in his dealings with his men endeared him to them; he heartily joined in their games, at which he was always the most skilful, and the soldiers trusted him as they will always trust and follow a man in whom they thoroughly believe."[14] He was also rapidly developing a passion for reading, reflecting and writing about military history, as Lieutenant-Colonel Holden commented,

> At that time there were few military libraries abroad. In Gibraltar, Bermuda, and Nova Scotia were the relics of Government libraries, but the books were of ancient date. In Henderson's quarters, however, were to be found well-thumbed volumes of standard military works, which he had ordered from England at his own expense.[15]

It was during his sojourn in Bermuda that Henderson first became actively interested in researching the American Civil War, and began to consider writing a history of this conflict. His wife and he also made a trip to the battlefields of Virginia to study them at first hand, Lord Roberts noting "this he did to such good purpose that when he later paid them a second visit, his knowledge of the ground and his grasp of the circumstances under which the various battles had been fought, excited the astonishment of men who had themselves taken part in the stirring events of which he afterwards gave the world such a graphic description in *Stonewall Jackson*"[16]. However, in the short term, he was to be frustrated in his efforts to devote further time to writing, as the poor pay of a lieutenant allowed him little freedom. Consequently, in search of a role that would allow him greater leisure time to pursue his burgeoning military studies, and an increase in salary, Henderson joined the Ordnance Department as a Deputy Assistant Commissary General in January 1885.

Service in the Ordnance Department, the publication of *The Campaign of Fredericksburg*, work begins on *The Battle of Spicheren*

Henderson would serve in the Ordnance Department for five years, being stationed at Woolwich, Edinburgh, Fort George (Scotland), and Gibraltar. He was promoted

13 The brevet majority was obtained on promotion to captain in 1886.

14 *Ibid.*, p. xix.

15 Holden, *op. cit.*, p. 376.

16 Malcolm (ed.), *op. cit.*, p. xvi-xvii.

Captain on 2 June 1886, thereby obtaining the brevet majority awarded to him in the wake of the Egyptian campaign.

Henderson's first station was at Fort George, Scotland, where he began to set his military history writings in order, continuing to focus on the American Civil War and Franco-Prussian War. In his off-duty hours he was also keenly interested in the burgeoning volunteer movement, at that time extremely popular in Britain, even playing cricket with his local unit. At a more serious level, however, Henderson was passionately keen for the volunteers to improve both their practical and theoretical knowledge. Rather like Napoleon, he believed that short of combat experience, the best way to become acquainted with the great principles of war was to thoroughly acquaint oneself with the past experiences of the great generals. Henderson believed in particular that the lessons of the 1862 Campaign of Fredericksburg as they related to the British volunteer officer emphasised the need for responsibility of leadership at lower levels within a unit, and discipline. Unlike many of his professional colleagues, Henderson had the greatest regard for the fighting quality of the American soldiers during the Civil War, and felt that their performance demonstrated how volunteers in Britain could function on a future battlefield.[17]

In 1886 he published his first book, *The Campaign of Fredericksburg*. This title was intended for the instruction of volunteer officers, indeed it was subtitled *A Tactical Study for Officers*.[18] Henderson published it anonymously, the book being credited to 'A line officer'. In his preface, the author explained why he had selected Fredericksburg as a suitable campaign for the study of volunteer officers:

> This campaign has been selected, amongst other reasons, as having been fought by two armies very largely composed of unprofessional soldiers. The lessons it teaches, the shortcomings it reveals, are likely, therefore, to be of exceptional interest and value to that class of officers to whose consideration I ventured to recommend them.[19]

In fact, sales of the book were extremely good, for it attracted a wider audience than that intended, bearing all the hallmarks of Henderson's writing style – accessibility, clarity and fresh interpretations offered in a balanced and judicious manner. As Jay Luvaas has written,

> ... to those concerned with the education of the British officer this book had a unique appeal. Written with an intelligence and insight unusual for such literature and filled with thoughtful observations on the military significance of the campaign, it

17 See Luvaas, *The Military Legacy of the Civil War: The European Inheritance* (Chicago, 1959), pp. 171-174, for a careful analysis of Henderson's links between the Fredericksburg campaign and its implications for the British volunteer movement.

18 The book's full publication details are *The Campaign of Fredericksburg November-December 1862. A study for officers of volunteers* by a line officer (London: Kegan Paul, Trench & Co, 1886). It had reached a third edition by 1891.

19 Quoted in Malcolm (ed.), *op. cit.*, p. xx.

> represented a skilful blending of personal knowledge of the terrain, careful study of the available sources, and a lively, readable style.[20]

Shortly after publication of the Fredericksburg book Frank turned to his next project – this book, a study of the Battle of Spicheren during the Franco-Prussian War, August 1870. Wanting to utilise the best sources available, as he had done when writing his first book, yet only having a superficial knowledge of German, he undertook to learn that language more thoroughly, his persistent thirst for knowledge being another of his notable characteristics. Again, the author intended the book to be of value for the instruction of volunteer officers, remarking that the ground over which it was fought bore strong similarities to the terrain that could be expected to be fought over during any potential invasion of England. At the time he was writing, no definitive study of the battle had been produced in any language. When considering Henderson's research, it is wise to remember that he was writing before the French official history had made a profusion of important documents available, and indeed a number of years before several very important studies were published regarding the operations on that day, particularly those by Cardinal von Widdern, Maistre and the German General Staff's volume on III Corps in the series *Kriegsgeschichtliche Einzelschriften*.[21] In 1887 Henderson commented "Spicheren is getting on but slowly. I have a mass of material which has to be unravelled and put into order and decent English – not an easy job, especially when the military problems have to be solved as well. I cannot say I work with lightning rapidity; it is hammer, hammer, hammer, and chaos reigns supreme."[22]

Henderson was fascinated by the Franco-Prussian War, and by the lessons he believed it imparted. In particular, he felt that the success of German arms highlighted the necessity for initiative and acceptance of responsibility at all levels within an army. During the writing of this book, Henderson displayed that incisive ability to cut to the heart of a problem, as demonstrated by his explanation of why the Germans triumphed:

> At no single point did the Prussians show themselves superior in courage or hardihood to their opponents. They did not, like their opponents, rely on natural attributes or martial spirit alone. Officers and men had received the highest training, both of mind and body, that was possible in peace. It was this training which turned the scale.[23]

In 1887 Henderson was transferred to Gibraltar, and experienced a difficult time. He felt marooned, or possibly that his career was becalmed, strongly desiring an appointment at Sandhurst, and it was this desire that drove his military history writing forward. Nevertheless it seems that for a period of time in Gibraltar he seriously considered leaving the Army. Fortunately, his study of Fredericksburg came to the attention of Lord Wolseley, and as soon as that officer discovered the identity of the author, the desired appointment followed in January 1890. Wolseley had visited the Confederate Army during the Civil War, and a copy of Henderson's book had been forwarded to him

20 Luvaas (1959), p. 170.

21 For full details of these titles see the section on Further Reading near the end of this book.

22 Quoted in Malcolm (ed.), *op. cit.*, p. xxi-xxii.

23 Henderson, *The Battle of Spicheren* (Aldershot, 1891), p. 300.

by Colonel Frederick Maurice, at that time Professor of Military Art and History at the Staff College, Camberley. Initially, his appointment was as an instructor in topography, Henderson later becoming an instructor in tactics, military administration and law.

Sandhurst and publication of *The Battle of Spicheren*

Frank remained at Sandhurst until December 1892, finally beginning to find an outlet for his great talents. In 1891 his book on the Battle of Spicheren was published[24], the present-day Oxford Dictionary of National Biography describing it as "a masterly study in breadth and detail".[25] It is hard to disagree with this assessment. Henderson had taken the time and trouble to track down a wide array of sources, fully utilising French and German regimental histories, for instance. This ensured that his account was far more than a simple regurgitation of official accounts, which was the principal fare served up in English regarding this war up to that time. Henderson's was a new account worthy of being read by any professional officer, of any army. It was lucidly written, encompassed both strategic and tactical level analysis, and allowed him to develop further than he had in his study of Fredericksburg his theories on the science and art of war.

A practical man, he chafed at the limitations imposed upon him, however, at Sandhurst. His duties were in theoretical instruction alone. As an instructor, or 'usher', his official duties were limited to interacting with the cadets in the classroom rather than in the field. Parades were for the officers, not the instructors, the latter being looked down upon. Firmly believing that theory and practice should be integrated, he emphasised the importance of demonstrations in the field to support the theory he was teaching to cadets. Breaking with tradition, he obtained permission to take cadets out skirmishing and patrolling, albeit probably not as much as he would have wished. Later in his career he was to argue passionately that the titles of 'Professor' and 'Instructor' should be abolished at Sandhurst, smacking too much of theory and limiting practical applications. His advice was followed.

Henderson also continued to enjoy sports and physical exercise, and was popular with both the staff and cadets, seeming to have an easy affability that won him many friends. Lt Col Holden wrote,

> It speaks a great deal for Henderson's personality that … he was one of the most popular men at the College. His tact, his cordial bearing, and his love of sport endeared him to the cadets, upon whom his influence was conspicuous. He interested himself in them in and out of study, and they were frequent guests at his house. He played cricket with them, and was generally requisitioned as umpire or referee in any sport or game requiring accuracy of observation, quick decision, and persistence of opinion.[26]

24 G.F.R. Henderson, *The Battle of Spicheren, August 6th, 1870, and the events that preceded it: a study in practical tactics and war training* (Aldershot: Gale and Polden, 1891). A second edition appeared in 1909.

25 Wessels, "Henderson, George Francis Robert (1854–1903)", *Oxford Dictionary of National Biography*, Oxford University Press, Sept 2004; online edn, Jan 2008.

26 Holden, *op. cit.*, p. 377.

Despite the artificial limitations imposed in his post, he found his employment congenial, and benefited from the time it allowed him to continue his military historical researches. His reputation as a writer continued to grow, and he contributed both to *The Times* and *Edinburgh Review*. Around this time he wrote, "I have more offers of articles than I can accept, the new *Military Magazine* offers me a guinea a page for anything I like to write. It is cheering, but I shall stick to 'the *Edinburgh*'. The worst of it is that it is such hard work".[27] His rigorous schedule was, however, also beginning to take its toll, and it was at this time that he first began to suffer from the ill-health that would eventually lead to his premature death.

In 1890 Frank had begun work on what was to become his greatest book, or as Lord Roberts called it, "A labour of love, and … a monument of his industry and originality" – *Stonewall Jackson and the American Civil War*.[28] This work would take up the majority of his spare time until its publication eight years later. He also found time to create, edit and contribute to the *R.M.C. Magazine*. Interestingly, Holden comments that after only a few months this was ordered to be discontinued by the War Office, "presumably as too progressive".[29]

In December 1892 Henderson's time at Sandhurst came to an end when he took up an appointment as Professor of Military Art and History at the Staff College, Camberley, having been chosen to succeed the incumbent, Colonel Frederick Maurice, by none other than Maurice himself.

The Staff College and publication of *Stonewall Jackson and the American Civil War*

Henderson's tenure at the Staff College, from December 1892 until December 1899, was crucial both for himself and the Army, working as he did with the best officers within the system. As usual, he was not content to work within established modes, but pushed boundaries. He continued to emphasise practical outdoor work, and his battlefield tours, especially those of the Franco-Prussian War, became the stuff of legend. He certainly brought all his undoubted qualities to bear in the appointment, realising the responsible and influential position he held. His capacity for hard work was displayed to the full, Lieutenant-General Sir Henry Hildyard, Commandant of the Staff College during the greater part of Henderson's professorship, recording,

> The amount of work he got through was enormous: the preparation and delivery of most carefully thought-out lectures on 'Military History', from which were drawn valuable lessons on every aspect of strategy and tactics. Whole days were spent on the ground working out and criticising tactical schemes. No practical point, whether in connection with the tactical use of ground, the aspect of fire, or the framing and conveyance of orders, being ignored. In all these exercises, whether in the lecture hall or in the field, the extraordinary qualifications of Colonel Henderson as an instructor were equally conspicuous. He showed great clearness of thought and perception, simplicity and correctness of demonstration, a practical

27 Quoted in Malcolm (ed.), *op. cit.*, p. xxvi.

28 Malcolm (ed.), *op. cit.*, p. xxvii.

29 Holden, *op. cit.*, p. 377.

> mind that discarded at once methods impracticable in war, and untiring industry and patience.[30]

Hildyard, appointed in 1893, was a man in Henderson's mould, and swept out the final vestiges of pedantry that remained at Camberley, commenting, "We want officers to absorb, not to cram".[31] Henderson's predecessor at Camberley, Colonel Frederick Maurice, wrote to him soon after the former took over his chair,

> The able men who would make good Staff Officers benefit greatly; so do those who have strong character or practical experience of war to guide them; but from the ruck we have turned out, I fear me, some cranks and not a few pedants. I am sure that under the new regime you will succeed where I have often failed.[32]

Certainly, the new regime under Hildyard, with Henderson in the front rank of those assisting him, dispensed with the old system of accumulating knowledge as a means of preparing for paper examinations, and instead tested students to a greater degree by asking them to solve all manner of military problems, from strategy and tactics to details of organisation. In short, it aimed to stimulate and stretch the students, rather than overwhelm them with mere facts. Henderson was aware of both the strongpoints and limitations of the Staff College when he noted that it contained

> ... no cauldron in which folly might be transmuted into wisdom, or ambition purged of the vanity which is as dangerous to soldiers as to angels. But it could make good men better, broaden their views, strengthen their powers of reasoning and improve their judgment.[33]

During his time at Camberley, a large number of future Great War generals were taught by Henderson, including Haig, Allenby, Capper, Hunter-Weston, and Hubert Gough. The future Field Marshal Sir William Robertson wrote that such future generals "... would readily admit that such successes as attended their leadership were largely due to the sound instruction and inspiring counsel which they received from their old tutor some twenty years or so before. Of the different causes which are alleged to have given us the victory over Germany, not one should be assigned a more prominent place than the influence and teaching of Henderson at the Staff College".[34]

It may be that Henderson overworked himself. His attention to detail when marking papers was unwavering. Nevertheless, he appears to have been a gifted tutor, fair-minded

30 Quoted in Malcolm (ed.), *op. cit.*, p. xxix.

31 Quoted in Luvaas (1959), p. 185.

32 Quoted in Godwin-Austen, *Staff and the Staff College* (London, 1927), quoted in Luvaas, *The Education of an Army: British Military Thought, 1815-1940* (London, 1965), p. 210.

33 Quoted in Bond, *The Victorian Army and the Staff College 1854-1914* (London, 1972), p. 169.

34 Quoted in Bond, *op. cit.*, p. 159. Brian Bond then noted wryly, "Whether or not the Professor would have been entirely enthusiastic about the qualities of generalship displayed by his former students between 1914 and 1918, Robertson's statement is important testimony to the formative influence of the Staff College and its most distinguished teacher in the 1890s."

and generous in sharing his knowledge and opinions without dogma or inflexibility. In this regard, Lord Roberts's testimonial is worthy of mention:

> Soon, like all others with whom he came in contact, I succumbed to the spell of Henderson's most fascinating personality … Henderson's success as a lecturer was great. Gifted with a finely modulated voice, and an easy but impressive delivery, his cheery pleasant manner of speaking, absolutely free from any symptom of pedantry or attempt at forced eloquence, added charm to the intellectual appreciation with which an intelligent audience listened to his lectures. His style was simple and clear; he marshalled his facts with ease, and enforced them with a wealth of illustrations drawn from his wide reading, and from those facts he deduced with impressive directness the lessons he wished to convey."[35]

Such indeed is also an admirably clear exposition of Henderson's style and ability to communicate complex information to both his listeners, and his readership.

Another commentator also picks up on Henderson's apparent attraction, noting "The students respected his great brain power, and his extraordinary capacity for work, his strong views on discipline and the absolute fairness of his methods. His personality fascinated them [the students], as, indeed, it fascinated all who came within its spell."[36]

All this time, Frank was hard at work on his *magnum opus*, *Stonewall Jackson and the American Civil War*. This was undoubtedly a labour of love, and he expended a prodigious amount of energy on it. A letter he wrote to Stonewall Jackson's topographer, Jed Hotchkiss, demonstrates the careful and inquiring mind which Henderson brought to bear on this topic. In this letter, Henderson listed those factors which he believed would be of interest to professional soldiers, and volunteers, in Britain, should Hotchkiss pen his own account of the Civil War:

> What may seem trivial details to you will be exceedingly interesting to soldiers and also to our large army of enthusiastic volunteers. I am now going to be impudent, and suggest what points we should like to hear about particularly.
>
> 1. The characters, demeanours, and appearance of your generals.
> 2. The character of the troops and of their fighting, and of their discipline.
> 3. The nature of the entrenchments and breastworks constructed.
> 4. The way in which the fighting in woods was carried out and the precaution taken to maintain order and direction.
> 5. The way intelligence of the enemy was obtained, and the country mapped. I would suggest you give an example or two of the … maps …
> 6. The methods of the Confederacy marksmen – the efficiency of their fire and the manner in which it was controlled by their officers – or otherwise. The more military your book is the better it will go down over here, as, owing to our number

35 Malcolm (ed.), *op. cit.*, p. xxxi.
36 Holden, *op. cit.*, p. 377.

> of volunteers and our constant little wars, the people generally understand and enjoy all details connected with the grand art of killing one's fellow man.[37]

In terms of his development as a military historian, this book was a considerable step up from his previous efforts. It aimed at combining matters of grand strategy, as well as all other apparatus of military history, in addition to portraying Jackson not only as a soldier, but also as a living and breathing man, frequently aiming to put the reader alongside Jackson, the man, as he made his decisions. In short, it breathed life into a legend, and by doing so, developed a little more of that legend. It also allowed Henderson to continue to demonstrate his keen interest in the psychology of war, and of the great captains of military history. Published in 1898[38], within a few years it could be accurately stated that it would live on in literature, Lieutenant-Col Holden divining that "…it has already been invaluable in rousing in young officers a desire to study strategy, and appreciate the teachings of military history at its true value. It has been well described as three books in one – a biography, a history of a military campaign, and a treatise on the art of war."[39] General Sir Henry Brackenbury wrote of it in *Blackwood's Magazine* in December 1898,

> I rise from a close study of it profoundly impressed. As a soldier, the story of these campaigns, of that great warrior, has stirred my blood. As an old Professor of Military History, I uncover my head to the author, and tender him my grateful thanks.[40]

Henderson's biography of Stonewall Jackson was immediately recognised as a vastly important book, and a major contribution to military history, and even if it does sometimes border on hagiography, nevertheless it has retained its place as a core title concerning the American Civil War – no mean feat considering the vast outpouring of literature about that conflict in the past century or so.

In 1899, Henderson also produced a brief yet noteworthy study of the Battle of Wörth, fought on 6 August 1870 during the Franco-Prussian War – the same day as the Battle of Spicheren.[41] That he had lost none of his former interest in this conflict is evident in the comments of the Secretary of the Royal United Service Institution, Lieutenant-Col R.M. Holden:

> One of the most agreeable of his duties was the personally conducted tours over European battlefields, which will be long remembered by those who had the good fortune to take part in them. His cheery method of conveying his wonderful and intimate knowledge of the details of the battles fought on the ground visited,

37 G.F.R. Henderson to Jed Hotchkiss, 13 October 1895, Hotchkiss Papers, quoted in Luvaas (1959), p. 175.

38 G.F.R. Henderson, *Stonewall Jackson and the American Civil War* (London: Longmans, Green and Co., 1898, 2 volumes).

39 Holden, *op. cit.*, p. 380.

40 Quoted in Holden, *op. cit.*, p. 380.

41 G.F.R. Henderson, *The Battle of Wörth, August 6th, 1870* (Yorktown, Surrey: W. Webb, 1899). A second edition was published by A. Bradford of Camberley in 1911.

> more particularly the great battlefields of the Franco-German War, made a deep impression. Every incident appeared to be recorded in his retentive memory; he described the actions in a happy conversational manner that compelled the interest of his hearers, and rendered the tour round the battlefields one of the most enjoyable features of the Staff College course.[42]

Throughout his tenure at Camberley Henderson also regularly contributed to the *Edinburgh Review*, as well as writing papers for the Aldershot Military Society, Dublin Military Society and the Royal United Service Institution. He was very much involved in the latter institution, being a member of its Council, serving on the Journal and Library Committee, and lecturing there frequently. He was also the regular correspondent on foreign manoeuvres for *The Times*, and contributed articles on war, strategy and tactics to the 10th edition of the *Encyclopedia Britannica*.

Yet the world outside Camberley had change in store for Henderson. By late 1899, the initial phase of the Second Anglo-Boer War was going badly for the British, and he was to find himself invited to fulfil an important and influential post, as Lord Roberts' Director of Intelligence in South Africa.

The War in South Africa, and Henderson's final years

Lord Roberts'strategy in South Africa was heavily influenced by that recounted by Henderson in his study of Stonewall Jackson, Roberts writing,

> Bearing all this in mind, when appointed to the chief command of the Army in South Africa, I determined that the wisest thing to do, both from a military and political point of view, was to march on the capitals of the Orange Free State and the Transvaal, and so to break up their combination … It will be seen from this what a high opinion I had formed of Henderson's abilities. I was convinced that he was well fitted for Staff employ in the field, and that, given the opportunity, he would be able to turn his knowledge to practical account – I therefore applied for his services.[43]

When Roberts sailed on the *Dunottar Castle* for South Africa to revive Britain's flagging fortunes, he took Henderson with him, the latter being made a half-pay Lieutenant-Colonel, from his old regiment, the York and Lancasters, on 23 December, as well as being made a full pay special service officer on the same day. When he reached South Africa in January 1900 he took up his appointment with the local rank of colonel. However, Frank's health was poor, and had been before he even accepted Roberts' request. Reflecting on the reasoning behind his decision, he wrote "It was far better to accept. I could not have stood waking up every morning and thinking that I was one of the few soldiers who were doing nothing for the country; I should never have felt like a man again."[44] Despite his fragile health, Henderson brought his customary energy and talent to bear on his role, reorganising and expanding his department, and supplying Roberts with skeleton maps of the Orange Free State, as well as discovering,

42 Holden, *op. cit.*, p. 379.

43 Malcolm (ed.), *op. cit.*, p. xxxv.

44 Quoted in Malcolm (ed.), *op. cit.*, p. xxxvi.

in something of a coup, maps of the Transvaal that had been produced for the Boer Government. He even planted misleading newspaper articles to deceive the enemy as regards the British plan of campaign. He also acted as a close adviser and confidant of Lord Roberts and accompanied him during the victorious Paardeberg campaign. In all but name, he acted as Roberts' Chief of Staff. At the camp on the Modder River he was reacquainted with many of his former students from his days at Camberley, who eagerly sought out his valued advice and companionship. However, Henderson did not witness Cronjé's surrender on 27 February 1900, as his health had broken down due to malaria and exhaustion, and he was sent home to England to recuperate. For his service in South Africa he was mentioned in dispatches, and on 29 November of that year would be made a C.B.

By late August, Henderson's health had improved sufficiently for him to join the War Office, taking up the post of an Assistant Adjutant-General on the 25th of that month. Initially his work there involved revising the infantry drill book, Henderson being responsible for the tactical portion. He died before his work on this was complete, leaving behind a manuscript so comprehensive and groundbreaking that it was issued with a new title, *Combined Training* in 1902. It was typical of Frank's adherence to a belief in what could be termed a holistic approach to war – theory and practise linked, and the individual arms-of-service linked, too. Later, he was tasked with writing the official history of the war in South Africa. Certainly, there were few men amongst his contemporaries better qualified. Henderson seemed to relish the opportunity, and intended to bring both the broad brush and fine pen which had combined to such effect in his biography of Stonewall Jackson to bear on this project, too. In an effort to break away from the Government's grip on the official history, he had even arranged to have a commercial firm publish the volumes instead of the His Majesty's Stationery Office, with its "dreary format".[45] In autumn 1901 he returned to South Africa to visit the battlefields, but his health failed him again, and tortured by malaria he was back in England by February 1902. As the cold of an English winter approached, Frank was sent to Egypt to continue his recovery, all the while continuing his work on the official history. He duly completed the first volume, dealing with the antecedents of the war, but fell seriously ill, and died at Aswan, Egypt, on 5 March 1903. Following the embalming of his body, he was buried with military honours at the Roman Catholic cemetery in Cairo, where a memorial to him can still be seen. There is a certain symmetry in the fact that his military career, and life, ended in the same country where it had seen its baptism of fire a mere 21 years previously.

Following his death it was decided that politics should be omitted from the official history of the South African War, so his volume was – and remains to this day – unpublished. In particular, it was felt that Henderson's work should be abandoned because of his less than charitable assessment of the former Boer leaders, and that publication of such judgements could make the ongoing peace negotiations harder to achieve. During his final years he had contemplated – indeed had begun to plan – writing a life of Robert E. Lee, which was to be a sequel to his life of Stonewall Jackson. Indeed, Lee's family had begun collecting material for this. A life of the Duke of Wellington was

45 Luvaas (1965), p. 188.

also under consideration, to which Henderson had "... amassed a considerable quantity of material".[46]

Henderson's legacy

During his lifetime Henderson was acknowledged as a gifted lecturer, tutor, military historian and author, as well as possessing a kind and extremely likeable personality. "Rarely," Jay Luvaas has written, "has publication led to such rapid promotion, even in an academic atmosphere".[47] He influenced a whole generation of British officers, although he cannot be compared to – as he sometimes erroneously has been – von Moltke of the Prussian General Staff, as the institutions and *milieu* in which the two men functioned were quite different. It should also be remembered that Henderson died in what could be described as the midpoint of his career, and that the theories he was possibly developing were still very much in their formative stages. It is impossible to guess where his considerable energies would have been directed had he lived – that he would have continued to leave a mark on any role that was assigned to him is, however, indisputable.

In a tribute to Henderson in the *Royal United Service Institution Journal*, the secretary of that organisation, Lieutenant-Colonel Holden, wrote:

> In him the King has lost a faithful soldier, the country a loyal servant, and the Army a writer and historian of great ability, a strategist whose reputation was not confined to England, and a man whose intellectual influence was enormous. The knowledge that he possessed it was his great object to apply to the advantage of his country and the Army.[48]

Holden also echoed similar remarks about Henderson's nature when he recorded that "he was a man of a fascinating and modest nature, and a firm friend; without an enemy himself, he spoke ill of no man".[49]

Henderson broke with established British military thought, as exemplified by Hamley, by emphasising the importance of psychology in war. Hamley's work, Henderson wrote, was

> ... an aid to study not to practice. In the description of Campaigns the keynote, that is, the aim of the commander seems often wanting ... Thus the student has read a great deal about rectangular bases, re-entering frontiers, parallel and transverse obstacles, but he had heard little of great principles; if he is set to solve a strategic or problem he finds that he has no clear idea of what to do or how to do it. Again Hamley deliberately omitted all reference to the spirit of war, to moral influences.[50]

46 Holden, *op. cit.*, p. 381.
47 Luvaas (1959), p. 171.
48 Holden, *op. cit.*, p. 381.
49 *Ibid.*, p. 382.
50 Henderson's "Strategy and its teachings: a lecture", *Journal of the Royal United Service Institution*, July 1898, quoted in A. Smirnoff, "A Tribute to the memory of Colonel G.F.R. Henderson", *The Army Quarterly*, Vol. XVII, No. 2, January 1929, p. 339.

Much of Henderson's time spent studying military history focused on the American Civil War. He linked the large numbers of volunteers and civilian conscripts of this conflict with a potential British Army on a major war footing, as in these remarks made in 1894, which eerily foreshadow Kitchener's armies of the Great War:

> If I see in the future an English general at the head of an army far larger than that which drained the life-blood of Napoleon's empire in the Peninsula, if I see our colours flying over even a wider area than in the year which preceded Waterloo, you may think that I am oversanguine; but to my mind the possibility exists, and with it the probability that the forces which are employed will be constituted, at least in part, as were the armies of the American Civil War. Our men will not all be regulars. They will come straight from civil life, and to civil life they will return. The habits and prejudices of civil life will have to be considered in their discipline and instruction, and officers will have to recognise that troops without the traditions, instincts, and training of regular soldiers, require a handling different from that which they have been accustomed to employ.[51]

Henderson was also a firm believer that operations in which entrenchment played an important role were likely to become a major feature of the future battlefield, extolling the view that Grant's 1864 operations in the Wilderness were the best indicators of such.[52]

There is a certain irony that Henderson's very success in opening up the lessons which could be drawn from the American Civil War to the British army induced a dogmatic approach, with the years following his death witnessing a flood of books that were little more than sets of cramming notes for officers' examinations. "By writing to drum facts into the heads of candidates for promotion, the authors of these cram books succeeded only in eclipsing the main lessons Henderson had tried to teach."[53] Such a flood of books not only focused on Jackson's Shenandoah Campaign, but also other aspects of the Civil War, as well as the Russo-Turkish War, and the Franco-Prussian War. This imitation of Henderson ignored the very individual and original approach to the study of military history that had brought him such success. The mere accumulation of facts was not enough. As Liddell Hart amusingly wrote, "…to be able to enumerate the blades of grass in the Shenandoah Valley and the yards marched by Stonewall Jackson's men is not an adequate foundation for leadership in a future war where conditions and armament have radically changed".[54] Yet the very debate caused by this particular short-term legacy itself stimulated the theory and practise of military history in Britain during the years preceding the Great War.

It was one of Henderson's greatest qualities that he possessed a flexible mind that allowed him to approach the writing and study of military history with an open mind, and not to hammer into his analysis of specific battles and campaigns pet theories at the expense of depth and breadth of knowledge. As Smirnoff correctly pointed out, the

51 Quoted in Luvaas (1959), p. 177.

52 See Luvaas (1959), p. 180.

53 Luvaas (1959), p. 188.

54 Liddell Hart, *The Remaking of Modern Armies* (London, 1927), pp. 170-171, quoted in Luvaas (1959), pp. 188-189.

opposite approach, that of almost making a fetish of one-sided military criticism, was typified by the great Schlieffen:

> He could not conceive waging war except by planning a double envelopment *à la* Hannibal, and, in analysing the campaigns of Napoleon and Moltke, he invariably criticised those great leaders if they failed to follow his pet idea.[55]

Henderson, indeed, could be said to have died before he had truly become an exponent of any particular theory of war. Rather, he wrote lucidly and with an open mind about the principles of war as he saw them, in particular the importance of morale and psychology. Perhaps his lack of adherence to an inflexible set of rules for the art of war is one of the reasons why his work has survived so well. As Jay Luvaas has commented, "Henderson had used military history as a means to stimulate independent thought rather than to provide specific patterns or lessons".[56] As Smirnoff correctly divined, "His outlook on the art of war, free from any pedantic teaching or preconceived theory, will make his name go down to posterity."[57] It was in this open-mindedness, and his desire to combine the theoretical with the practical to assist his students' reasoning, that lay his genius as a teacher. As Cordonnier wrote,

> Instructed in this way, the student when left to himself in the silence of his library, will become his own master, thereby strengthening his soul by experience ... Little by little the doctrine will become conscious from subconscious and from theory it will transform into practice.[58]

Henderson's approach to tutoring is exemplified by this passage in his paper on 'Strategy':

> It is not sufficient, any more than in the study of any other business, merely to place before the tiro a general summary of the maxims by which he is to be guided. He must convince himself of their scope and value by constant reference to apt illustrations. A study of the campaigns of his famous predecessors must be active and not passive; he must put himself in their place, not content with merely reading a lively narrative, but working out every step of the operation with map and compass; investigating the reasons of each movement; tracing cause and effect, ascertaining the relative importance of the moral and the physical, and deducing for himself the principles on which the generals acted. It is probable that he will only discover what has been discovered already. But the value of the discovery will not be in the smallest degree diminished. Far from it; for knowledge that is gained by hard labour and independent effort is of high worth, and much more likely to be permanently absorbed, than that which comes in by the ear.[59]

55 Smirnoff, *op. cit.*, p. 338.

56 Luvaas (1959), p. 208.

57 *Ibid.*, p. 340.

58 Cordonnier, *La Methode dans l'Etude de la Strategie* (Paris, 1912), quoted in Smirnoff, *op. cit.*, p. 340-341

59 Malcolm (ed.), *op. cit.*, pp. 48-49.

Henderson's greatest legacy was that his work has remained assiduously studied, debated, critiqued, read and enjoyed continuously for over 100 years since his untimely death, and his reputation continues to enjoy the esteem and respect that it so richly deserves.

List of sources

Bond, Brian, *The Victorian Army and the Staff College 1854-1914* (London: Eyre Methuen, 1972)

Henderson, Lieut-Col G.F.R., *The Battle of Spicheren. A study in practical tactics and war training* (Aldershot: Gale & Polden, 1891)

Holden, Lieut-Col R.M., "Lieut.-Colonel G.F.R. Henderson, C.B. in Memoriam", *The Journal of the Royal United Service Institution*, Vol. XLVII, No. 302 (April 1903), pp. 375-382

Luvaas, Jay, *The Military Legacy of the Civil War: The European Inheritance* (Chicago: The University of Chicago Press, 1959)

Luvaas, Jay, *The Education of an Army: British Military Thought, 1815-1940* (London: Cassell, 1965)

Malcolm, Captain Neill, D.S.O. (ed.), *The Science of War. A Collection of Essays and Lectures 1892-1903 by the late Colonel G.F.R. Henderson, C.B.* (London: Longmans, Green, and Co., 1905). Includes an important memoir of Henderson by Field Marshal Lord Roberts.

Smirnoff, Alexander, "A Tribute to the memory of Colonel G.F.R. Henderson", *The Army Quarterly*, Vol. XVII, No. 2, January 1929, pp. 335-341

Wessels, André, "Henderson, George Francis Robert (1854–1903)", *Oxford Dictionary of National Biography*, Oxford University Press, Sept 2004; online edn, Jan 2008

PREFACE

Military history teaches us that, generally speaking, success and disaster depend on the application or neglect of certain tactical principles. These principles are few in number and simple in theory; they are the basis of drill, the guiding spirit of all manœuvres; every soldier is more or less familiar with them, but, if there is one fact more conspicuous than another in the records of war, it is that, in practice, they are as readily forgotten as they are difficult to apply. The truth is that the tabulated maxims and official regulations which set forth the rules of war go no deeper than the memory; and in the excitement of battle the memory is useless; habit and instinct are alone to be relied upon.

The habit of acting in accordance with sound principles is developed only by experience. Experience assists us to recognise instinctively what is sound and what is dangerous, what need not be feared and what must not be overlooked. Personal experience of war is, however, given but to few, may be purchased at too great a price, and in point of view is often circumscribed.

"Wars are of rare occurrence," says Gizycki, "the exception and not the rule, so that the officers' training takes place not in war but in peace – and personal experience of war is always one-sided, and that in a variety of ways. In the first place, every man's experience is confined to the narrow circle of his own activity, which, as a rule, is in a different sphere in every new war in which he takes part."

"Such experience, it is true, is more comprehensive in preparation as a man rises in rank; but the superior officer misses much which only the subaltern officer experiences. The subaltern officer is mainly occupied with the troubles that have to be overcome with the rank and file; the superior officer with the friction that arises in the distribution of orders and the conduct of the larger units. But even within the same limited sphere, individual experiences of war differ entirely one from another. One man has only been present at successful actions, another only at a defeat, a third has never been under fire at all; one was in the advanced guard which was struggling with all its forces to win the day, another only arrived on the battle field when the enemy's strength was almost broken."

It is nevertheless possible, by appropriating the experience of others, to find an efficient substitute for practical acquaintance with almost every phase of active service. But if we would make this alien experience our own, it must be dealt with systematically. It is not sufficient to read or to listen to the account of a campaign or battle. A cursory glance at a variety of incidents leaves little behind. To gain from a relation of events the same abiding impressions as were stamped on the minds of those who played a part in them – and it is such impressions that create instinct – it is necessary to examine the situations developed during the operations so closely as to have a clear picture of the whole scene in our mind's eye; to assume, in imagination, the responsibilities of the leaders who were called upon to meet those situations; to come to a definite decision and to test the soundness of that decision by the actual event. The intellect is thus brought into collision with reality, and the contact is little less impressive than practical experience.

If, having formed our plans to meet an emergency which actually happened, we find, on turning to the relation of the facts, that the neglect of some precaution on our part, or the occurrence of some event which we ought to have foreseen, would have ruined our scheme, the rebuff to our judgment will not be readily forgotten. Our first instinct, when we next confront such a situation, theoretically or practically, will be, to provide against the recurrence of such a misadventure. The first advantage, then, of such a system of self-instruction, is the training of the judgment to act instinctively on sound principles. The student is confronted with a succession of problems, the solution of which – such is the nature of war – is complicated by the intervention of many untoward incidents; fresh factors are introduced at every step and thus, habit of quick resolution, together with a comprehensive *coup d'œil*, and the power of bringing under consideration everything that may affect the working out of any plan we may have conceived, of observing the effect such and such a manœuvre will produce and the precautions that must be adopted to ensure its execution, will gradually be developed. The tactical examinations for promotion, at least for the higher ranks, no longer mere tests of memory, have, of late years, taken the more practical shape of trials of the capacity for speedy and sound decision, the quality most essential to a soldier; and the surest means of acquiring and improving this capacity is the system here advocated.

2nd: – An acquaintance with the devices which others have adopted in order to avoid violating, or to apply tactical principles, will, if it does not supply an exact model, at least suggest the way in which such devices may be modified to meet circumstances with which we may be confronted.

3rd: – A knowledge of what has already taken place helps us to anticipate what will occur in the time to come. Realising, although only through the eyes of others, the phenomena of the battle-field, they will not appear altogether novel and bewildering when we are called up to face them; we may meditate on the best means of checking or avoiding their disturbing influence, so that they will not find us unprepared. "It is in the novelty lies the danger," writes Colonel Hale, "for the danger of novelty is surprise, and surprise is the deadliest of foes. Reduce to a minimum the chances of surprise; let a man be always prepared, and it loses half its danger."

4th: – The study of actual operations teaches us the strength of the other arms, the manner in which they can best render support to our own, the circumstances in which they most require support; in a word, it helps us to understand how artillery, cavalry, and infantry, may be best combined to achieve a definite purpose, and in this respect the personal experience of any regimental officer is of little value.

5th: – As the principal duty of the officers of today, at least of the regular forces, is the instruction of their men, the deeper the knowledge of the instructor with what his men have to be trained for, and the clearer his insight into the difficulties he and they will have to encounter, the sounder will be his work.

Lastly: It is only from the experience of others – and this is the true definition of military history – that we can obtain knowledge of the more startling and decisive aspects of the breech-loader battle. The effect of fire, the intense strain on the nerves produced by a protracted engagement, the dispersion of units, the tendency and the temptations to straggling and disorder, the moral effect of flank attacks and turning movements, the difficulty of transmitting orders, and, more than all, the importance and influence of ground, with these, not all the experience and exercises of peace can afford more than the most superficial acquaintance. If we would realize them, we must have recourse to history.

If it be conceded that the study of actual operations is essential, and we are anxious to discover the principles which are applicable to the more recent developments of war, it is evident that we must turn to those campaigns which have been fought under conditions of armament as nearly as possible analogous to the present.

Although, owing to late improvements and inventions, the effects of musketry and artillery will be certainly intensified in the battles of the future, the rapid and long-ranging fire of infantry and of rifled cannon will be then, as in 1870, the chief factor of the fight. Nor will the introduction of smokeless powder, of an effective shrapnel, and of a magazine rifle with a flatter trajectory, have so altered – except in so far that they will have increased – the difficulties of leading and the conduct of troops as to lessen the value of the great engagements of the Franco-Prussian War as most reliable guides to the situations and exigencies of the future.

Moreover, the history of the war of 1870–71 is accessible in such detail, not only in the account compiled by the Prussian General Staff, but in German and French regimental histories, in the narratives, of individuals, of soldiers who witnessed or who actually took part in the events they describe, or of correspondents who were present with the armies, that it is possible to follow the movements of brigades, battalions, companies, and even sections, through every incident of an engagement.

The mass of literature that relates to the battle of Spicheren has been carefully examined; the movements of even single companies and sections have been traced, and in the following pages, therefore, the student has presented to him numerous situations, with the surrounding circumstances in such detail, that, even if he aspire to no more than the leading of a single company, he is in possession of the knowledge requisite not only for the conception of a definite plan of action, but also for testing the wisdom of his resolution.

The volumes issued under the superintendence of the Prussian General Staff form the basis of the whole narrative. So frequent are the extracts that they are not always marked as quotations; but their statements have been amplified, and in some cases corrected, by reference to the Regimental Histories, and to the observations of non-combatants.

A consideration of the battle will also prove of use to those who are interested in the land defence of England, for the ground over which it was fought is in many respects similar to the range of heights which intervene between London and the Channel. There are the same steep hill-sides, covered, as is often the case in Kent and Surrey, with woods, and with the same open plateaux and deep gullies behind the crest. Volunteer officers, whose brigades and regiments have been detailed in case of invasion to occupy portions of this line, will do well to study the manner in which the Spicheren position was defended and attacked.

In the censure or praise bestowed on the commanders, an endeavour has been made to follow Napier's example, and to justify the verdict by showing how the received maxims and established principles of war, were violated or adhered to. Military critics have often been reproached with being over liberal with their censure, but this charge applies only to those who write history merely. A work which professes to teach cannot avoid showing up errors, however excusable.

It is scarcely necessary to add that if it is to be beneficial, the study of military operations must be thorough. "We must seek to place ourselves entirely in the position of the actors; we must work upon the bases of the materials and information which the leader in the case before us had at his disposal; we must try and work for ourselves, not superficially, but entering into the minutest detail, with the map and the compass in our hand, taking into careful account the conditions of time and space."

To assist the reader in following this suggestion, a series of problems for his solution, indicated by numerals in the text, will be found in Appendix III. These should be dealt with when arrived at without further reference to the letter-press.

INTRODUCTION

Fought on the 6th of August, 1870, Spicheren was one of the earliest engagements of the Franco-German war.

Little had as yet occurred to shake or strengthen the morale of either army, and the merits of the systems under which each had been organized and trained were then, for the first time, fairly tested. From a consideration, therefore, of the incidents of the battle, it will not be difficult to arrive at a just conclusion as to the relative efficiency of these systems. A sketch of them will precede the account of the actual combat; and this, with a brief relation of the events which led to the collision, and some account of the temper and discipline of the troops, should give the reader a clear understanding of the various forces which influenced the issue. Armies are bodies of extreme sensibility, affected by a variety of circumstances; and, unless the study of warlike operations is accompanied by a knowledge of the moral and physical condition of the combatants, no useful deductions can be drawn.

Moreover, if we except the action at Weissenburg, fought on the 4th of August, and the battle of Woerth, fought also on the 6th of August, Spicheren was the first great engagement under the new conditions of breech-loader *versus* breech-loader.

CHAPTER I
THE MOBILIZATION AND CONCENTRATION OF THE ARMIES

On the evening of the 14th of July, Napoleon and his advisers had resolved on war. His formal declaration was not presented at Berlin until the 19th; but on the 15th, the mobilization of his forces had been ordered, and the regiments which were to form the Field Army immediately moved forward to the frontier.

The French message of defiance had named but a single State.

The quarrel was with Prussia, and with her alone. But Prussia was no isolated kingdom. The principalities and duchies of North Germany were her vassals, those of South Germany her allies.

But Saxony and Hanover in the north; Baden, Bavaria, Wurtemburg and Hesse-Darmstadt in the south, had leagued with Austria against her in 1866. The memories of their defeat were still green in 1870, and Napoleon had some ground for hope that the treaties imposed after the crowning victory of Sadowa, would be as eagerly repudiated as they had been reluctantly subscribed.

Italy, also, was bound by ties of gratitude to the sovereign whose arms had restored Lombardy to her dominion in 1859; and both Denmark and Austria were now offered an opportunity of repaying the debt of vengeance they had incurred in '64 and '66.

The French Emperor, therefore, when he so suddenly rushed into war appears to have done so in the expectation of finding allies beyond the Rhine, to have believed that his first success would raise the standard of revolt in Dresden and in Hanover; that it would be no difficult task to bind the South Germans to neutrality, and that Austria and Italy would ultimately lend him active aid.

It would serve no useful purpose to inquire whether, as regards the three European Powers, these expectations were justified—they certainly, were never realised; but, astute as he undoubtedly was, Napoleon was far from comprehending the vitality of that spirit of pride in their common nationality which lies in the heart of every German people. Smouldering indeed during the fratricidal war of 1866 it was still unquenched, and the first threat against the integrity of the Fatherland fanned it into sudden and enduring flame. Prussia was not loved, it is true, beyond the Maine, but France was the hereditary enemy. The Southern States stood staunchly to their bonds. Saxon and Hanoverian soldiers ranged themselves beside the Prussian eagles, to show themselves in the days to come as strong in friendship as once in enmity; and the gauntlet so recklessly cast down was picked up by the strong hand of a United Germany.

By the treaties of 1866, the supreme command of the German forces was vested in the King of Prussia. Ordered to mobilize on the 15th July, they were the next day organized into three distinct Field Armies and a Reserve.

The First Army, composing the Right Wing, under General von Steinmetz.

The Second Army, composing the Centre under Prince Frederick Charles.

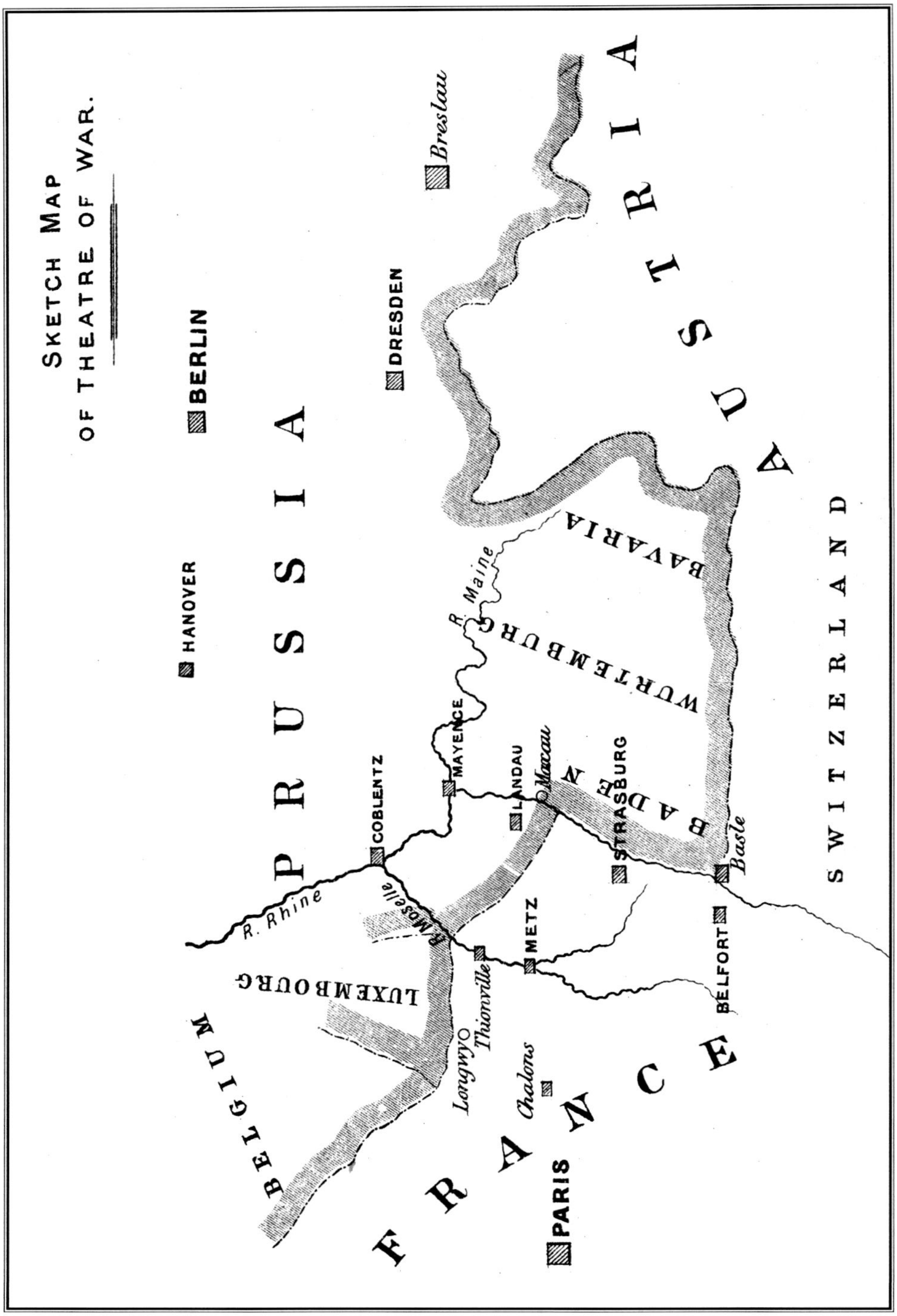

Sketch map of the Theatre of War

The Third Army, composing the Left Wing, under the Crown Prince.

The Reserve at the disposal of the King.

The strength of the whole force, when the reserve men had come in, would amount to 480,000 men, with 1,584 guns.

The Chief of the Royal Staff was General von Moltke, the same great soldier who held that post in 1866.

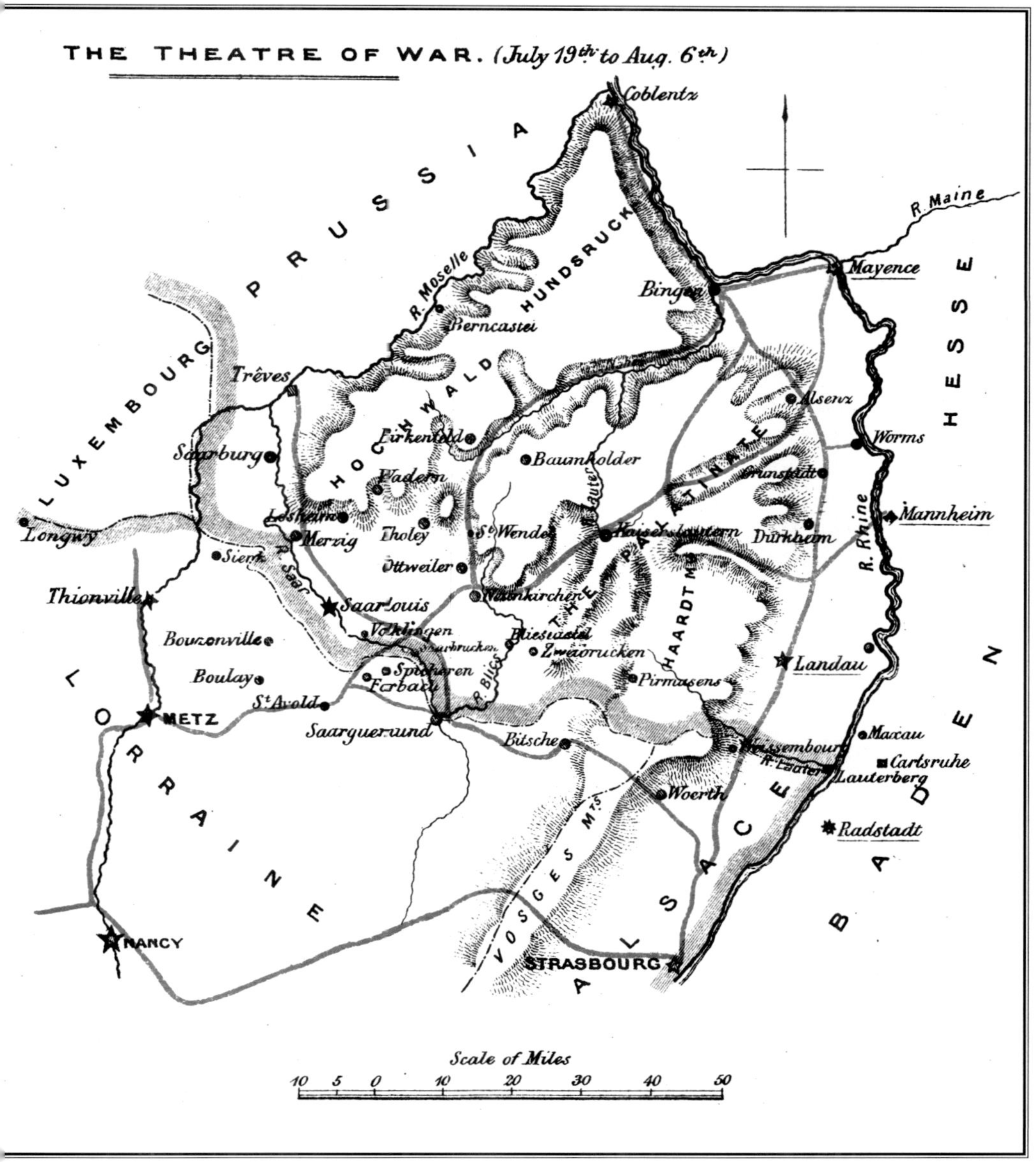

The Theatre of War

Napoleon, with Marshal le Boeuf as "Major-General," Chief of the Staff, led his troops in person.

The French Field Army, named at the outset "The Army of the Rhine," consisted on paper of 336,000 men with 240 guns. Of these, 300,000 men were expected to be eligible for active operations.

The German Field Armies, that is, the contingents of the north and south combine, out-numbered, therefore, that of France by 184,000 men and 660 guns.

On the 20th July the concentration of the French regiments on the frontier was generally completed. The Corps d'Armée were organized and assembled, awaiting only their reserves and matériel.

The frontiers of the rival powers were contiguous from the borders of Luxembourg to the town of Basle, a distance of 220 miles.

The portion which concerns the campaign about to commence was the upper half, between Longwy and Lauterburg. On reference to the map it will be seen that between these towns the line of demarcation runs almost due east and west, leaving the then French provinces of Lorraine and Alsace to the south, and the district called by the Germans the Palatinate to the north. From the border of Lorraine, the Rhine is from 60 to 80 miles distant; whilst a few miles on the German side of the frontier and parallel to its general direction, flows the River Saar, the natural, although not the actual, boundary between the French province and the Palatinate.

The latter district is generally hilly and well wooded; and the western portion, the Hochwald and the Hundsruck, is especially rugged and capable of defence.

The Vosges Mountains, running a little east of north from Belfort to the Rhine, cut the frontier between Bitsche and Weissenburg almost at right angles, interposing between the two great fortresses of Metz and Strasburg; and as they approach the Rhine, spreading out into numerous spurs, across which, pass the roads and railways which connect Paris and Berlin.

Between the northern portion of this range, the so-called Haardt, and the Rhine, extends a strip of open country, which below Worms, is highly cultivated, gently undulating, and for the most part free from forest.

The breadth of the level country is twenty miles. If we follow the direct road from the Rhine to Metz, the capital of Lorraine, two-and-thirty miles of mountain have to be traversed before we emerge on another comparatively open tract, roughly speaking some fifteen miles square, extending from Homburg at the foot of the Haardt to Saarbrucken on the Saar. This tract is bounded on the west by the rugged Hundsruck, on the east by the main chain of the Vosges. Ottweiler, Zweibrucken, Saarlouis and Saarguemund mark the four corners of the square; Neunkirchen and Saarbrucken the centre of the northern and southern sides.

The Army of the Rhine was divided into eight Corps, located as follows

1st & 7th, in Alsace, forming the Right wing.
2nd, at St. Avold, }
3rd, at Metz, }
4th, at Thionville, } in Lorraine, forming the Left Wing
5th, at Bitsche }
The Imperial Guard at Nancy, in second line }
6th, at Châlons, in third line.

The strength of the Left Wing, with which we have to do; amounted on the 20th July, to 100,000 men, to be augmented by the reserves to 150,000. Of its five Corps d'Armée, the 2nd, 4th & 5th, 60,000 strong, had already assembled within a few miles of the frontier.

Aware of the preponderating strength of the German forces – for the army of Prussia alone was larger than that of France – Napoleon had determined to balance his inferiority in number by rapid movement and skilful strategy.

Without waiting to mobilize his regiments on a peace-footing, and but partially equipped for active service, assembled round Metz and Strasburg. As soon as their reserve men and matériel had come in, he proposed to bring together his right and left wings, 100,000 and 150,000 strong respectively; and crossing the Rhine at Maxau, 48 miles below Strasburg, to thrust himself between the North and South Germans; to bind the latter to neutrality, and then to turn against the Prussians. At the same time, the navy was to threaten a descent on the Baltic provinces, and retain part of the Prussian force in that distant quarter. A design, sound enough in strategy, but depending for success on a mobilization and concentration more rapid than that of the enemy.

"It was necessary," says Napoleon, "to assemble in a few days, on points already determined, not only the requisite number of men, but the essential accessories, such as engines, the supply trains, the ammunition columns, the bridging matériel, the gun boats to protect the passage of the Rhine, and lastly the supply of biscuit, indispensable to a large army marching united."

On the 21st July the Left Wing began its movement. The 2nd Corps d'Armée pushed forward from St. Avoid an infantry division and a brigade of cavalry to Forbach, four miles within the frontier, and supported this force by a second infantry division at Bening, six miles in rear.

On the 24th, the remainder closed in upon the centre:

The 3rd Corps from Metz to Boulay.

The 4th Corps from Thionville to Bouzonville.

The 5th Corps to Saarguemund, leaving a division at Bitsche.

The Guard from Nancy to Metz.

On the same day the great concentration of the German troops began. The regiments had already left their barracks; and in accordance with a project drawn up in the winter of 1867–8 by General von Moltke, which not only laid down the organization of the field force and the areas of concentration, but forecast with remarkable accuracy the numbers, design, and dispositions of the French. It was at first intended that the Army Corps composing the three Field Armies should take post at the following rendezvous:

The First Army, 70,000, the line Saarlouis-Merzig.

The Second Army, 130,000, the line Volklingen-Zweibrucken.

The Third Army, 131,000, the line Landau-Rastatt.

The Reserve, 63,000, Mayence.

In order to watch Austria and the Baltic Coast, three Army Corps, 90,000 men, in addition to the foregoing, still remained in Prussia.

The French and German frontier marched, as has been said, from Longwy to Basle. To the north, Luxembourg and Belgium; to the south, Switzerland, interposed, and the contingency of their neutrality being violated by the weaker belligerent was held by the German staff to be remote.

Nor had they reason to fear that invasion would come from the southern portion of the frontier, for had the French chosen such a course, the direct road from the Rhine to Paris would have been left free to the enemy; and moreover, von Moltke had foreseen that the strategic purpose of Napoleon, did he determine on attack, would be to strike in between the north and south, and to drive the allied stated asunder.

The river Maine, forming the boundary between North and South Germany, joins the Rhine at Mayence, and it was evident that to achieve his purpose the enemy would have to cross the river somewhere in this neighbourhood. The point where attack was to be expected being thus determined, the next step was to select positions for the three Field Armies which would both baffle such an operation, and, at the same time, serve as an advantageous starting point for invasion; for, be it noted, an active offensive was the main-spring of von Moltke's plans. Relying not only on numerical preponderance, but also on the knowledge that, thanks to their superior organization, the mobilization and concentration of the German Field Armies could be effected before that of the French, he was not disposed to surrender the manifold advantages of the initiative. His project pointed out that if the French made full use of their railways to concentrate as rapidly as possible on the frontier – and there was little doubt but that they would adopt this line of action – their troops would disembark at Metz and Strasburg, the nuclei of the great railways which connected Paris and the Eastern provinces. Three lines converged on Metz, and two on Strasburg. It was therefore confidently assumed that, at the outset, the larger portion of the French army would assemble in Lorraine.

Now the key-note of the German offensive was this: to seek out the main force of the enemy and attack it. This force would be met in Lorraine.

The concentration therefore, of the First and Second Armies, supported by the Reserve, opposite Metz, on either side the great road and railway from Paris, by way of Saarbrucken, to the Rhine, placed the bulk of the German forces opposite the bulk of the French. Again, this road and railway were the easiest line for the invasion of France, for they passed the obstacle of the Vosges Mountains in German territory, and were the shortest and most direct routes to the French capital.

But, whilst an invasion of France was uppermost in von Moltke's mind, every eventuality had been considered. The positions he proposed that the three Field Armies should occupy were, as will be seen, as favourable for defence as for attack.

The First Army, concentrating on the line Saarlouis-Merzig, would hold a rugged district, easily defended. It was protected on the right flank by the neutral territory of Luxembourg, and on the left by the Second Army. If called upon to assume the offensive, it was to act in concert with the latter.

The Second Army, concentrating on the line Volklingen-Zweibrucken, was the most advanced. If attacked by superior numbers from Metz, it would fall back through the mountains on the Reserve, and accept battle in a favourable position, already selected, in front of Mannheim. Here it could be reinforced by a portion of the Third Army from Landau; whilst the First Army operated against the enemy's flank and rear. Should it, on the other hand, advance into Lorraine, the First Army secured its right, whilst the Third would hold fast, or, if strong enough attack any force that might have assembled at Strasburg on its left.

If the French assembled in great force at Strasburg, the Third Army was to concentrate on the right bank of the Rhine instead of on the line Landau-Rastatt. Here it could be rapidly reinforced by the Reserve from Mayence. The weight of such a force on their communications with Strasburg, would compel the French, after they had passed the river, to arrest their march into South Germany, and to disengage towards the north. At the same time the First and Second Armies would sweep forward into France. Invasion, however, on the part of France, was held improbable. To combine the Metz and Strasburg forces would be a work of time, and it was absolutely certain that long before such a conjunction could be affected the German troops would have seized the initiative, and have begun their advance.

If, lastly, the French, without waiting to mobilize, were to make a sudden irruption from Lorraine before the Germans had time to concentrate; the project showed that 150,000 men at most would be available for such a movement, and that during the march of this force to the Rhine there would be time to assemble a superior body of troops in order to oppose the passage of the river.

The German position, it will be seen, was comparatively central; and here the whole of the Field Armies were to be massed, not blocking directly every avenue of approach, but so placed as to threaten the flank of each line of advance, thus barring them as effectually as if drawn up across them. And at the same time, if by greater rapidity of mobilization and concentration, they were enabled to begin their forward march before the enemy moved, they were drawn so closely together that his inferior numbers would in all probability be attacked, when met with, by a vastly superior force. "In the Palatinate," wrote von Moltke, "we stand on an interior line of operation to the two groups of the enemy. We are in a position to act against either of them, or against both simultaneously, provided we are strong enough. This concentration protects the Upper as well as the Lower Rhine, and permits of an offensive operation in the enemy's country, which, if resolved upon in time, will probably anticipate every attempt on the part of the French to set foot on German soil."

The march of the French battalions to the frontier had been hailed with acclamation by the Press, and from its incautious freedom the Germans received early and accurate information of the enemy's movements. Not only was the position of each army corps thus discovered, but their strength was calculated; whilst on the other hand, the French remained in absolute ignorance of what was passing beyond the frontier.

As already stated, the possibility of that portion of Napoleon's force which had thus rapidly assembled at Metz, suddenly crossing the frontier, without waiting to mobilize, and invading the Palatinate, had been foreseen. Had such an irruption been made, the Army Corps of the German First and Second Armies might have been caught, had the first dispositions been adhered to, in the act of concentrating on their respective lines; and attacked in the act of converging from widely separated points upon the rendezvous, have been defeated piece-meal. In accordance, therefore, with the advice laid down in the project of '67–68, the Second Army, on the news of the advance of the French battalions to the frontier, was at once ordered to assemble at Mayence and Mannheim on the Rhine, instead of on the line, of Volklingen-Zweibrucken; which was only five-and-twenty miles within the frontier: whilst the garrisons of the towns upon the Saar, 11,000 strong, were directed to prevent reconnoitring parties crossing this frontier-stream, and if compelled to fall back before superior forces, to remove the rolling stock, and to temporarily destroy the railways. No other change was made. It was thought better to surrender the Palatinate without a struggle, than to forego by a forward movement of partially equipped and hastily assembled: troops, the advantage of meeting the enemy with the combined force of a superior army, well prepared and at full strength.

On the 28th, Napoleon joined his Guard at Metz. Seven days had now elapsed since his troops had assembled on the order, and it was evident that he was awaiting the completion of the work of mobilization ere he moved.

On the 29th he proceeded to St. Avold, 16 miles from the Saar, and met his generals in council. To them he unfolded his designs. He had already abandoned his project of crossing the Rhine at Maxau. There was now no hope of binding the South Germans to neutrality; their armies had assembled, and the voice of their people was strong for war. More than all, the cloud, which had hitherto veiled the Prussian movements, had lifted for a moment, and a rumour that the enemy was gathering, in strength at Mannheim and at Trêves exercised an irresistible force upon the strategy of the French. An advance from Lorraine to Maxau or to Strasburg would have exposed a flank to attack from Trêves and Mannheim and have laid open the road to Paris. To that road Napoleon was now bound. But he, nevertheless, still held to his offensive purpose but without making any attempt to combine the Armies of Alsace and Lorraine. They remained 60 miles distant from each other, on either side the Vosges Mountains. Nothing was done to shorten the gap between them, and opposite that gap, so placed that a forward movement would sever the communication between the two, was gathering a mass of nearly 400,000 foes. Napoleon's new plan was as follows; – under the command of Marshal Bazaine, three Corps d'Armée, the 2nd, 3rd, and 5th, were to cross the Saar, the river which formed the natural boundary between Lorraine and Palatinate; at Saarbrucken whilst the 4th Corps, making a show of advancing against Saarlouis, an insignificant fortress, was to cover their, left flank At the same time, McMahon was to move forward from his position near Strasburg, covering the right.

The river Saar was held by the Prussians merely as a line of observation. The force cantoned along its banks was but a slender one, maintained with the object of gaining, information, of giving timely warning of invasion, and of breaking up the roads and railroads in case of retreat, whilst the main body gathered on the Rhine, 60 to 8 miles in the rear.

The Saar itself is an inconsiderable stream, and there were many points of passage.

The valley of the river above and below Saarkbrucken is screened on either side by rolling and well-timbered hills. In both the French and the German border province are numerous roads; and the main line of communication between Paris and Berlin crossed the river at Saarbrucken, and connected by a line or rail and a splendid highway the towns of Mannheim on the Rhine and Metz on the Moselle.

9 battalions and 8 squadrons, drawn from both the First and Second Armies, a force of not more than 11,000 men watched the Saar from Trêves to Bliescastel, a distance of 60 miles. Beyond Bliescastel the duty was taken up by regiments belonging to the Third Army. About 1,200 cavalry were available for the surveillance of this extensive line but boldly crossing the frontier and penetrating far into French territory with numerous small patrols, this significant force gained valuable information as to the positions of the hostile divisions and proof of their unreadiness for immediate action. The French, on the other hand, had after July 24th no less than 19 regiments, or 76 squadrons, available for the like duties:

At Forbach	2 regiments	}
At Bening	2 regiments	}
At Rohrbach	1 regiments	} 19
At Saarguemund	3 regiments	}
At Thionville	4 regiments	}
At Boulay	7 regiments	}

The reconnaissances effected, however, by this imposing array of horsemen, although numerous enough, were carried out without energy or enterprise. They were undertaken, as a rule, in conjunction with infantry and artillery, and the combined detachments were unable either to move rapidly or to conceal their approach. The same villages were visited at the same hours, and by the same roads; and the enemy's patrols, made aware by the country people of the time and route at and by which the French were to be expected, easily avoided them. No attempts were made by small parties to pierce the hostile lines. Nor was this powerful force of 8,000 men able to prevent the approach, at all hours and at every point, of the Prussian scouts. At the French Head-Quarters, therefore, the most absolute ignorance prevailed as to the points of concentration and the whereabouts of the Prussian Army Corps. No single item of intelligence was permitted to filter through the line of the outposts on the Saar. The German Press maintained a discreet silence as to military movements, and Napoleon's staff had to rely for their information on the columns of the English newspapers, or the reports of double-dealing spies. The leaders of the French Corps d'Armée, along the frontier, who had each of them four regiments of cavalry at least attached to their command, appeared to have been fettered in their employment by instructions from Head-Quarters. Thus, General Frossard, commanding 2nd Corps, the advanced guard of the Metz force, was ordered by Marshal Bazaine, in temporary charge of the left wing, to reconnoitre from St. Avoid, but only as far as the frontier, and without compromising any important detachment.

Such instructions were certainly misleading. No hard and fast limit should have been drawn, the frontier was but an artificial barrier, and it should have enjoined instead, that the touch with the enemy should be obtained and kept at all costs. Accurate information would at this juncture have been well worth the loss of even a brigade of cavalry. At the same time an injunction not to compromise strong detachments need not have been construed to include small patrols. Yet it was so read by Frossard, who ordered his troopers to avoid engagements even with hostile scouts, and by this measure carefully avoided a sure means of gaining intelligence by the capture of prisoners; and, also, by offering no obstacle to their progress, opened a path into the centre of the French lines to the enemy's patrols. It is sufficiently apparent that from the Chief of the Staff downwards, Napoleon's officers were ignorant that to act as the eyes and ears of the army, to screen it from observation, to secure it from surprise and to discover the dispositions of the enemy, is the first duty of cavalry. It is a grave reflection on the capacity of the corps commanders, that on the 26th July, five days after the concentration had been completed, Marshal Le Boeuf had occasion to issue the following instructions: "Let your cavalry be seen. It, must reconnoitre the whole of the Saar, and must not fear even to cross the frontier." It is extraordinary enough that in any army which relied so much upon the traditions of the great Napoleon and his marshals, these instructions should not have been anticipated, and it is still more extraordinary that when issued they should never have been executed.

The truth is that, in the first place, the generals were ignorant of the science of war. They knew the names of the great French victories, but they had not studied how they were won. And in the second place, the cavalry were ill-trained. The business of reconnaissance, of covering the front, so efficiently performed in the wars of Napoleon, was a lost art in France. Maps too were wanting of the Franco-German border. Had they been provided, moreover, neither officers nor men had been taught to read them; and without systematic instruction in this art, cavalry, in a strange country, is practically useless. Again, as regards the men and horses in the ranks; the French mounted troops were at a disadvantage. 156 reserve men and a number of horses were required at the outbreak of war to complete the establishment of each regiment. In Germany, on the other hand, where it had been generally recognised that to re-instruct the reserves, and

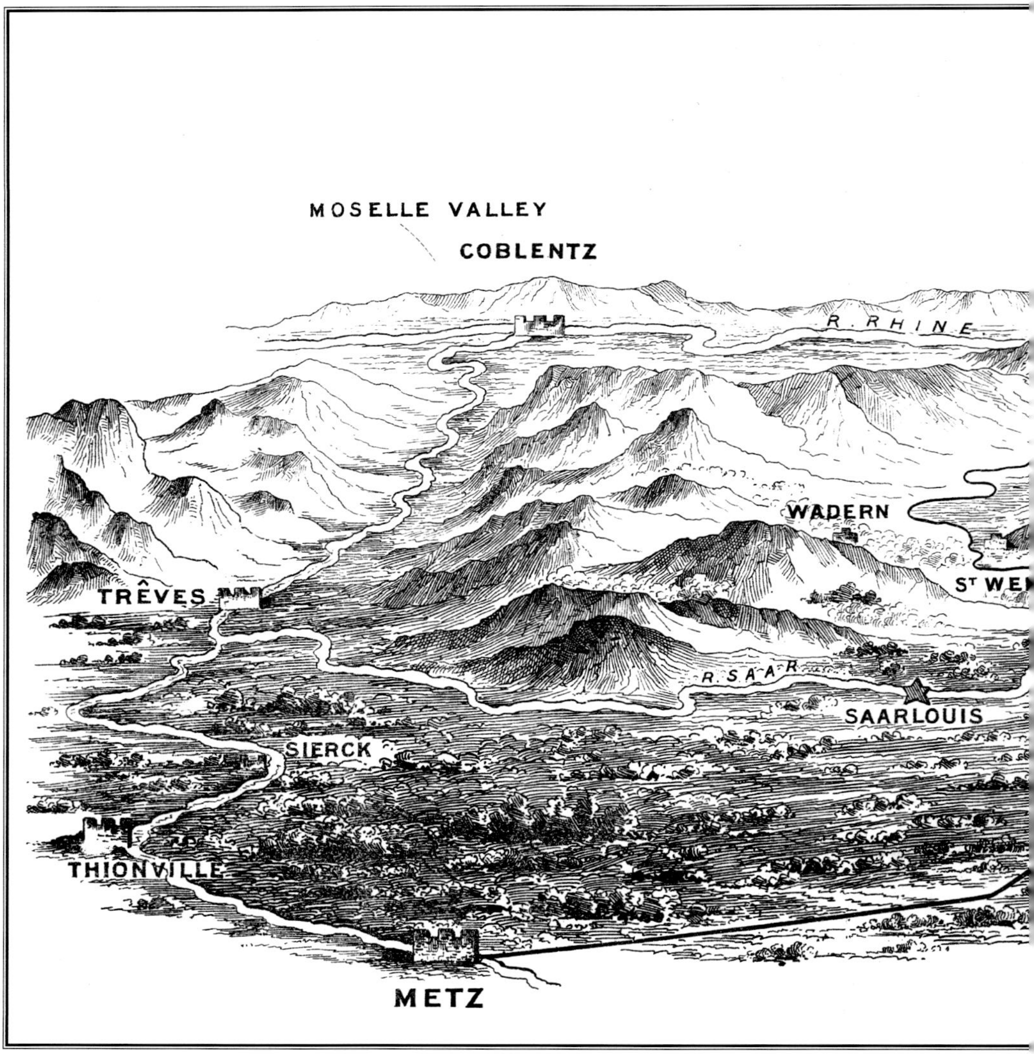

Relief map of Lorraine and the Palatinate

to train fresh horses, several weeks were necessary, the peace strength of the regiments was greater than that for war, five squadrons against four. The fifth squadron, on the order to mobilize, was left behind as a depôt for the regiment. It was formed by the recruits, the young horses, and the reserves. Thus, only trained soldiers and seasoned horses took the field. "Previous to 1866," says von Borbstaedt, "the cavalry was completed with horses purchased in the country, but the experience of that year's campaign proved but too plainly how difficult it is to inure such 'country' horses, even when most carefully selected, to the work demanded for cavalry in the field, and to accustom them to the change of food."

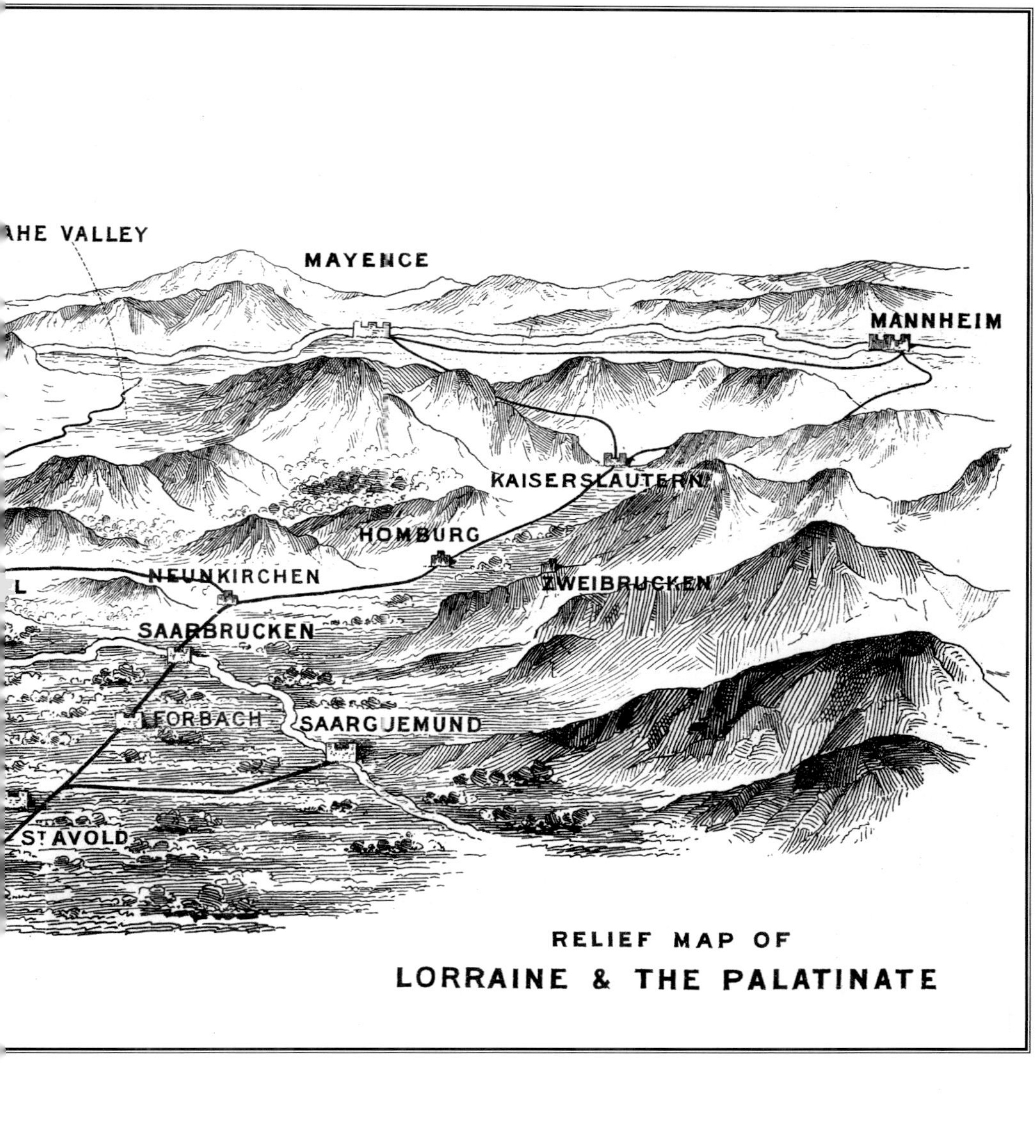

It is at least doubtful, had the ranks of the German squadrons in 1870 been partially filled with reserve men and, requisitioned horses, whether they would have been able to carry out so thoroughly their exacting duties.

But, notwithstanding the uselessness of their cavalry, the French authorities were not without intelligence, inaccurate as it was, of the German movements and dispositions. They knew that the Saar was weakly held. It was reported that the VIII German Army Corps, 40,000 strong, was near St. Wendel; and as already stated, information was to hand that large masses of troops were gathered near Mannheim and at Landau. But either of these localities was 20 miles further from St. Wendel than was St. Avold, the centre of the French line, and an opportunity, therefore, of engaging with superior numbers on German soil an isolated portion of the Prussian army appeared to present itself.

This information, however, on which Napoleon based his plan, was misleading. On the 29th July, the day on which he held his council of war, the VIII German Army Corps was still north of the Moselle; nor, within a radius of 50 miles from Saarbrucken, did there stand a single complete division of German troops. In fact, von Moltke had taken every precaution not to expose any isolated portion of his armies to collision. On the 29th, as if in anticipation of Napoleon's resolve, a telegram from the Royal Head-Quarters was received by General von Steinmetz, commanding the First Army, to which the VIII Army Corps belonged, instructing him not to advance beyond the line Wadern-Saarburg – a hilly country, well adapted for defence, and 46 miles distant from St. Avold.

Napoleon's scheme of attack, however, was destined never to be tried; and not from more accurate information, but from his own lieutenants, came its death blow.

Those whom he had called to council at St. Avold declared that the army was as yet incapable of offensive movement. The regiments were much under strength; and even had the ranks been full, the equipment and supplies necessary were in every case deficient. In fact, the army was not yet mobilized.

To quote the German Staff History: "There was a dense accumulation of men at the different depôts (scattered over the whole of France), but no means of causing a speedy outflow of them. The railways, although taxed to the utmost, could neither transport the reserves to the depôts nor thence to the troops. Mistakes in forwarding reinforcements to regiments on the march (as were the French regiments, generally speaking, from July 16th to 29th) were unavoidable; a great number of reserves were disembarked at places where no one knew the temporary position of their regiments. In certain districts where the lines were blocked, the further transport of the reserves was stopped … and in the confusion and haste with which everything had to be pushed on, they joined their regiments, as might be expected, deficient of the necessary equipment. Many of them were without cooking utensils, water-bottles, or *tentes d'abri*."

The regimental and divisional transport were also incomplete. Horses, ambulances, vehicles, sick-bearers, veterinary surgeons, and commissariat officials, were not forthcoming. A considerable part of the artillery harness was found to be useless. Some of the ammunition columns had not yet been organized others were incompletely equipped, and, lastly, although large consignments of maps had been forwarded to the troops, they comprised only German territory; there; were none whatever of the districts where the Corps d'Armée were cantoned.

Lastly, Napoleon had expected, on his arrival at the front, to find 150,000 men with the eagles in Lorraine, in Alsace 100,000. The highest estimate of the numbers present at the end of July admits but 129,000 in Lorraine, and 57,000 in Alsace.

In the face of this evidence it is impossible to assert that the opposition of the French leaders to an immediate offensive was unfounded, or that Napoleon was unwise in yielding to their protests.

But, whilst surrendering, or rather postponing his project, he took no precautions to secure his forces from attack. After the council of war had broken up, Marshal Le Boeuf wrote to McMahon, commanding in Alsace, to the effect that no forward movement would take place for eight days. Now, during this interval, it was quite possible that the enemy might seize the initiative, and that the French might find themselves suddenly assailed by superior numbers. The dearth of information, and the impossibility of procuring it, laid them open to surprise. Measures should have been taken, as von Moltke had done, to occupy positions strong for defence. Moreover, vigorous attempts should have been made to break through the thin line of the German outposts on the Saar, and to gain, at all costs, accurate intelligence of the designs and whereabouts of the hostile masses. As it was, the inactivity of the cavalry still continued, the scattered positions of the divisions rendered them liable to be overwhelmed in detail; and from the end of July to the 6th of August the French army presented the extraordinary spectacle of the weaker army disseminated from Thionville to Belfort, a distance of 220 miles as the crow flies, without reliable information of the dispositions of an army more than double its strength, and which was already concentrated on a line, from end to end, from Wadern to Rastadt, not more than 100 miles in length, and but seven days' march at farthest from the French cantonments. Students of military history will recall the several instances where the great Napoleon, well instructed as to his adversary's dispositions, won the first move of the game by concentrating his whole available force against a scattered and extended line; notably in Italy in 1796; upon the Maine in 1806, and upon the Sambre in 1815.

The German movements up to the end of July need mot detain us long. The army was mobilized; that is, each unit, from the squadrons up to the pioneer company, had been made up to its full strength and had received its equipment for war, by the 23rd of July. On the following day began the transport of troops to the rendezvous assigned to the three Field Armies; and, by the 1st of August, the various corps of the First and Second Armies stood as follows:

FIRST ARMY

VII Corps	Trêves
VIII Corps	Wadern
3rd Cavalry Division	Still concentrating

SECOND ARMY
(Now reinforced by the Reserve)

III Corps		}
IV Corps		} On line Alsenz-Grunstadt
IX Corps		}
X Corps	Bingen	} Still concentrating

Guard West of Mannheim }
(Saxon) } West of Mayence
XII corps }
5th Cavalry Division } On line Martinstein-Durkheim
6th Cavalry Division }

THIRD ARMY
5 Army Corps, and 1 Cavalry Division, on left bank of the Rhine

IN PRUSSIA
I Corps (Coming up to reinforce First Army.)
II Corps
VI Corps
1st Cavalry Division: (Coming up to reinforce First Army)
2nd Cavalry Division
25th Cavalry Brigade
17th Infantry Division

The whole of these troops were completely equipped; although some of the regiments and batteries and a portion, of the supply train had not yet reached the rendezvous. It will be well to pause a moment, and to ask how it was that, the Germans, 16 days after the declaration of war, were able to achieve this great result with 12 Army Corps, whilst their adversary with but 8 was still in such a deplorable state of unreadiness. The answer to this question involves a sketch of the systems of mobilization and concentration which obtained in either country. Territorial organization was the fundamental principle of the German system. To each Army Corps a Province was permanently assigned, to each division of the Army Corps a district of the Province, to each brigade of the division a large town or group of villages in that district There the regiments had their quarters; thence they drew their recruits, there the men settled when discharged to the reserve, returning in most cases to their own homes.

To clothe and equip the reserves when called upon for service, a full supply of all necessaries was kept in the regimental stores. Each division possessed its own Commissariat Staff, with a full complement of waggons, at its own Head-Quarters; and each corps and battalion its own ammunition carts, baggage waggons and ambulances. And, as each unit was kept intact and complete (except in strength) during peace, each Army Corps, division, and brigade, had, generally speaking, its own staff officers, already intimately acquainted with the troops they would lead in war.

The arrangements for calling out the reserves, and forwarding them to their regiments, were committed to certain officials in each district. Thus each Army Corps had in its own territory every requisite for mobilization. Every single article necessary to complete equipment was at hand. Every single officer and soldier, every civilian official and reserve man, knew exactly what he had to do when the order to mobilize was published. "The Prussian system of mobilization, which has been gradually extended to the whole North German and, finally South German Armies, so completely answers every demand that can be made on it, that it only requires a simple order to mobilize, with the specification of the date on which the first day's work has to commence, to set in perfectly harmonious movement the colossal machinery, without rendering it necessary to lose time in asking one single question from below or to issue a further instruction from above."

The order for the mobilization of the field forces was issued on the night of the 15th July; on the 19th the transport of the reserves to their regiments commenced; and by the 23rd the regiments were at full strength both in men, and matériel, and perfectly ready to enter on a protracted campaign.

Chiefly from political reasons the territorial system had not been established in France; nor had the regimental system been so far developed as to give each battalion the means of fitting itself speedily for the field. The depôts did not contain all the necessary equipment; and many of the regiments were serving at a distance from their depôts: Nor were the Corps d'Armée – the few that were already organized – independent agents. All administration was centralized at Paris. The matériel of the whole army, with the exception of the greater part of the soldiers' kits was retained at a few places in time of peace. The transport waggons were accumulated at Vernon, Paris, Satory, and Châlons; the camp equipment at Paris and Versailles. On the order to mobilize, long and minute instructions had to be drawn up in Paris and issued to every officer concerned. For the supply of the most trifling article of equipment a ministerial order was necessary. The branches of the administration were overwhelmed with demands, with questions, with complaints. Rapid distribution to the regiments from their depôts or from the great central arsenals proved a work of extraordinary difficulty; and the arrangements for causing the assembly of the reserves were but imperfect. As the regiments were not territorial, that is, raised and serving each in its district, but migratory, the men were recruited from all parts of France, and on discharge to the reserve dispersed to every quarter of the Empire. In very many cases the men had to be conveyed from their homes to the depôt; to be clothed, and when clothed from the depôt to the regiment. "In some instances, therefore," says Colonel von Borbstaedt, "many a soldier had travelled over one half of France before he arrived at his destination." Napoleon himself has recorded how reserve men, living at Strasburg, and whose regiments were already in Alsace, were first sent to their respective depôts; perhaps in the South of France or even in Algeria, to be clothed, and then transferred to Alsace to join the ranks. Moreover, at the outbreak of hostilities, only four Corps d'Armée existed, those of Châlons, Lyons, Paris, and the Guard. Not one of these, however, had its stores under its own charge, or its departmental services already organized; and the four others that were created had to be supplied with regiments, batteries, staff-officers, and administrative officials, drawn from every garrison in the Empire, utterly unacquainted with each other, and without the *esprit de corps* which animates every permanent military organization.

The transport of the troops to the theatre of war, involving, if it were to be rapidly completed, as systematic preparation as the mobilization, had been worked out in Germany with the greatest care and the most minute arrangement. Each Army Corps required between 60 and 70 trains for the conveyance of its men and matériel to the rendezvous, .and there were 12 lines of railway available. It was found possible to despatch 12 trains by the single lines, 18 by the double.

On a single line, therefore, an Army Corps could be forwarded in 5½ days, on a double line in 3½. Estimating the speed of the trains at 15 miles an hour, including stoppages, the distance traversed would be 360 miles in 24 hours.

The railway lines, however, had not been constructed with a strategical purpose, that is, with a view to the concentration of troops at certain specified localities; each line therefore had not the same amount of transport demanded from it. For instance, while each of the two Bavarian Army Corps had a line of railway to itself, the six corps of the Second Army had four lines between them, in the latter case, therefore, the same line was in some instances used by two and even three Army Corps:

The work of transport could not consequently be completed until the tenth day, the 2nd of August, when 380,000 men, fully equipped for war, were concentrated on or near the Rhine. Forethought, system and experience alone enabled this stupendous operation to be so successfully carried out. Immediately the transport of the troops began all other traffic was stopped. The requisite platforms and sidings had been already provided. The soldiers had been practised in embarking and disembarking, and in packing waggons with speed and order. A special section of the general staff was charged in peace with the task of formulating schemes for the despatch of the troops to any possible theatre of war. The exact locality of concentration, had, as in von Moltke's project, already been pointed out. To each regiment had been issued a time-table giving the hour and place of departure and arrival, and the size and number of the trains told off for its conveyance. There remained but to notify the day on which them movement would commence.

In France, on the other hand, no such system existed; hence the extraordinary confusion and mistakes which have already been recounted. "The error," says the German Staff History, "was committed in assuming that the concentration of the army by rail could be acted with order and precision without a very thorough and comprehensive preparation. Moreover, in the absence of any sound and previously worked-out plan for the conveyance of stores to the troops and to the fortresses near the frontier, and to the lack of military supervision along the lines, the transport of supplies and matériel were thrown completely out of gear." "At Metz," says Home, "nearly 7,000 railway carriages were blocked together in a solid mass none of the people at this spot knew what the waggons contained; ammunition, food, clothes, arms, entrenching tools, pontoons, and hospital arrangements, being mixed together in a confused mass. The railways immediately in rear of the army were blocked and useless, and the waggons, containing the things that were really needed, could not be got at."

"The Emperor," says the pamphlet attributed to Napoleon himself, "had flattered himself that he had it in his power to anticipate the Germans in mobilization and concentration; but he erred, as did all the world, in cherishing the illusion that by means of the railways, the concentration of so many men, of horses, and materiel could be carried out with the necessary order and precision, without the work having been regulated a very long time in advance by a vigilant administration."

CHAPTER II
THE CHARACTERISTICS OF THE ARMIES

Since the Crimean expedition in 1854–55, there had been three European wars. In 1859, France, allied with Piedmont, had attacked Austria in Lombardy, and by the victories of Magenta and Solferino had confirmed the prestige she had won on the shores of the Black Sea.

In 1864, Denmark, after a brief struggle, had yielded her southern provinces to the combined forces of Austria and Prussia. Over their prize the allies quarrelled, and two years later, on the field of Sadowa, Austria was decisively defeated.

Minor enterprises, in Africa, China, Mexico, and Italy, had meanwhile employed the arms of France. In these, as in her conflicts with more powerful foes, she had been uniformly successful; and in the eyes of the world, notwithstanding the startling triumph of Prussia in Bohemia, she was still the first of military nations. Yet the downfall of Austria had been more complete in '66 than '59. Sadowa was a more brilliant victory than Solferino. These facts were not disputed; but the disparity of armament (for the breech-loading needle-gun had proved a weapon far more effective than the Austrian muzzle-loader) was held accountable. The fact that thorough training, skilful strategy, sound tactics, and superior organization, had played as important a part, was, if suspected, disregarded.

France, especially, affected to think lightly of the Prussian success. Nevertheless, always jealous of warlike renown, from the very morrow of Sadowa, she had made up her mind that Prussia must be humbled. Her pride could brook no rival. And, on her side, Prussia, since the defeat of Austria, had plainly manifested that she no longer acknowledged France as arbiter of the destinies of Europe.

The conflict, therefore, was inevitable, and had been long foreseen by both. But whilst the one bent all her energies to the task of preparation the other was idle, looking only to the laurels which crowned her eagles. The army that bore blazoned on its colours the long roll of Napoleon's victories, had little to from a single German State. Never since the days of Rossbach had Prussia, single-handed, been a match for France. But was her rival, the old Prussia, the Prussia of Ligny, Jena, and Auerstadt? In her blind self-confidence she never troubled to inquire. In absolute ignorance of her system of short service and large, reserves, of her high standard of practical training for war, the French nation believed that the national force of Prussia was but a Landwehr or Militia, led by pedantic and inexperienced officers. Against the veterans of France, more familiar with the hardships of the campaign than the routine of home service, and armed with the deadliest of modern weapons, it was proudly assumed that the valour of these half-trained levies would avail but little. To increase the numbers, therefore, or to improve the efficiency, of the army, but little was done. Reform was thought unnecessary; and the training, organization, and tactics of 1859, were held to be adapted to the era of universal breech-loaders, of enormous reserves, and of rapid mobilization, which had dawned since Solferino.

Yet there were those who doubted. Napoleon himself and more than one of his marshals were alive to the fact that great changes were taking place in the art of war, that Prussia had become a most formidable rival, and that France was weaker than of yore. A pamphlet which declared in 1868, that the soldiers were no longer the men of the Crimea and Italy, that discipline had deteriorated, that the military establishment was far too small and the tactics antiquated, bore the signature of one of the ablest French Generals. For an hour France was stirred. But the Emperor dared not acknowledge the truth of the criticism. The nation was soothed by judicious flattery and the man who had fearlessly published the unwelcome truth saw parasites and time-servers preferred before him. Never was warning a more prophetic or more unheeded. Yet it is scarcely just to blame the nation or the army. The nation was subservient to the Sovereign; the army was commanded by his creatures. The Imperial Court and the existence of the Imperial party in the state, exercised an evil influence upon the troops. The personal adherents of the Emperor, and not the ablest soldiers, monopolized the higher commands. Preoccupied in intriguing for further favours, these courtiers generals had neither time nor inclination to exchange the luxurious life of the Imperial circle for the study and the camp. Following the example of their superiors, many of the staff and regimental officers were idle to a degree, indifferent to all save their personal interests, and luxurious even to effeminacy.

But an army is dependent for its morale and efficiency on the impulse it receives from above; it is an accurate reflex of the character of its chiefs. Such was the case in France. Vanity, thoughtlessness, and indolence reigned in high places. The men who should have corrected error, themselves created it; and the army was rotten to the core. And yet, to all outward appearance, it was a magnificent force. The soldiers were well drilled, and the parade manœuvres of all arms had lost none of their elasticity. The Guard was the most imposing corps in Europe. Foreign critics were loud in their praises of the artillery, and allowed that the infantry were the most agile and intelligent of skirmishers; whilst the English Government, about to re-organize its commissariat service, had taken for its model the French Intendance.

To those who, so long as the regiments could defile in even lines upon the Champs de Mars, and execute the attack of imaginary enemies upon the plains of Chalons without confusion or irregularity, believed that the troops were well trained for war, all this was satisfactory enough. But to those who held that something more was necessary than showy exercises and a knowledge of drill, the system of instruction seemed absurd. War was not taught at all, and veterans of the Crimea and Italy said openly that the day France took the field all that had been learned in peace would have to be forgotten.

Practical training and musketry were neglected; and other critics than those above mentioned, silent but observant, for to them the moral power of the French Army was a matter of the deepest moment; who looked upon it as a possible foe, and spared no pains to discover its defects, congratulated themselves that infantry, whose formations were vicious and who could not use their rifles – artillery, who had not been taught to shoot and whose weapons were inferior – cavalry, skilled in all movements of the parade-ground but ignorant of the duties of reconnaissance – an administrative system, efficient enough in peace, but unsuitable for war – lacked, as an army, the most essential elements of strength.

That the French soldier possesses a quick intelligence and a special aptitude for his calling, not even the most prejudiced of his detractors can deny. But he must have leaders who can use his warlike qualities, and in 1870 these were wanting. The majority of the officers did not study, and no pains were taken to instruct them. That something more is demanded than exact drill and high courage to make war successfully, they did not understand. "The war of 1866," – it is one of themselves speaking, – "had taught them nothing. The Minister of War had published a resumé of that campaign. Those whose curiosity induced them to read it saw nothing but what was pitiable in the Prussian tactics. Their strategy, they said, 'was vicious, and it was only to be hoped that if it came to war, the same tactics and strategy would be employed as in 1866.'"

Moreover, a breach had opened between officers and men. It had been visible in 1859. At Magenta and Solferino the cry had been heard, "*Les epaulettes en avant*". It was never the habit of French officers to interfere with their men in camp or in quarters. The privates were dependent for their comfort and well-being on the sergeants and corporals: With their food, clothing, and instruction, the officers were not required to concern themselves, under the Second Empire less than ever; and save in the Guard and Algerian regiments alone, the commissioned ranks had but little knowledge of, or sympathy with the privates, the privates little respect or affection for their officers.

Nor had the frequent political changes of the century, the instability of successive rulers, and the discontent of a large portion of the nation with the existing régime, failed to produce a baneful effect on the temper of the troops. Where the Government was not respected, where it was the universal habit to criticize and to condemn, not only the actions, but the very right to exist, of every authority, military discipline could not well escape untainted. It had perceptibly weakened since 1854. The irregular life of Algerian cantonments had also tended to relax its bonds. Brave and intelligent as they were, the French soldiers of 1870 lacked that habit of unquestioning obedience which alone gives valour and skill their due reward.

Yet the army was not without its characteristics of strength. The thirst for glory, the pride in tradition, the confidence in the invincibility of France, gave promise that the dash and daring of her officers would be as conspicuous as ever on the battle field. That promise was not belied. Furthermore, the Emperor had not been altogether heedless of the developments of the past few years. Something he had accomplished towards raising the standard of efficiency; but he had to contend with much obstruction. Despite his successful conduct of the '59 campaign, he was but an amateur in war. His opinions weighed little with his ministers, and not greatly with his marshals. Strenuous were his efforts in 1867 to introduce a new artillery armament. But a council of generals (although reports of the accurate practice of the Krupp cannon were laid before them,) declared, without a dissentient voice, that the French field-gun had no superior. In the gigantic reserves of Prussia, moreover, he recognised an element of strength for which France had no equivalent. With the help of Marshal Neil, his most capable adviser, an act was passed for the formation of a national army; but on the death of that minister was tacitly repudiated by the Government, preferring a small budget to a strong line of defence; and although the *cadres* still appeared on the returns of the military establishment, the gorgeous uniforms of the bourgeois officers were almost the only token of the existence of the Garde Mobile.

Again, Napoleon had followed the progress of the Secession War with interest, and had not altogether missed its lessons.

One, of the most prominent of these was the value of temporary breast-works, and since 1867, his soldiers had been instructed in the construction of entrenchments. But, on the whole, his influence as Commander-in-chief was not for good. He was incapable of wielding at one time, like the great founder of his house, the civic sceptre and the marshal's baton. Save in some few instances, he left the care and instruction of his troops to irresponsible subordinates, and in their choice he was unfortunate. And so the French Army, without a leader to correct abuses or to maintain its *moral*, whilst those of other nations were fast improving, lost little by little its former vigour. It would be easy to point out other circumstances which assisted to destroy efficiency; the want of homogeneity in the corps of officers, one third of whom were taken from the ranks; the impaired authority of the non-commissioned officers; the antagonistic spirit which had arisen between the civilian and the soldier; the contempt with which the profession of arms was regarded by the bourgeois; the attacks on the very existence of the army by the peace-at-any-price party; the ridicule of the theatre and the press. But, although these and other evils existed, it was not to them alone that the successive defeats of 1870 were due. The primary cause was that spirit of which Arnold wrote: "If there be, as perhaps there are, some physical and moral qualities enjoyed by some nations in a higher degree than others, yet the superiority is not so great but that a little over-presumption and carelessness on the one side, and a little increased activity on the other, and still more any remarkable genius in the generals or in the government, may easily restore the balance, or even turn it the other way. It is quite a different thing, and very legitimate, to feel that we have such qualities as will save us from ever being despicable enemies, or from being easily defeated by others; but it is much better that we should not feel so confident, as to think that others must always be defeated by us."

In Prussia as in France the Sovereign was Commander-in-chief. In the one case it was an evil, in the other incalculable benefit. Himself a soldier inferior to few in experience, for his service dated back to 1807 and included the War of Liberation, King William of Prussia had made his army his peculiar care. He had been the soldier first, the statesman afterwards; or rather, he had been true to his conviction that the prosperity of Prussia depended on her physical strength. In his choice of advisers he was more than fortunate. The times indeed were favourable. The universal liability to military service, the social precedent given to the soldier, made the sword the most honourable of professions. The greatest and most ambitious minds were attracted to it, for no other calling offered the same rewards. But, at the same time, it was by no simple turn of fortune that these were found in the councils of the King. No great general, whether his achievements have been conspicuous in the field or in the business of organization, who has been either supreme himself or has been allowed a free hand in the selection of his assistants, has been without capable subordinates and loyal support. And this fact is no fortuitous coincidence, but the sure indication of a mind beyond the common, possessing quick and true perception of character and the power of drawing to itself natures of the same mould as its own.

Little marvel is it therefore, that with great minds to conceive improvements and reforms, and the strong will of the ruler to push them through, the military machine of Prussia was well nigh perfect, and the system of training and organization superior to any that has existed since the days of Rome's ascendancy. Discipline was strict but not severe. In educated men – for universal service brought them in numbers to the ranks – who appreciate its importance and in those of humbler position who were carefully taught its necessity, habits of subordination were rapidly confirmed. And discipline was hereditary; its traditions were handed down from father to son, in the same manner as the liability to bear arms; its influence was paramount, not in the army alone, but in every branch of the public service, and in every institution, from the school and the university to the railway and the factory. The nation was on the side of authority, and those who rebelled found no sympathy in their comrades or elsewhere. The belief – conscious or unconscious – was universal that, to hold its place among the nations, Germany must be strong; and a nation of soldiers knew, that without strict discipline military strength does not exist. The system of military training for many years previous to 1870 had been more thorough than that of any other European nation in modern times. War was made familiar. Great manœuvres had been practised since the days of Frederick. Somewhat artificial before 1850, these annual exercises had since become a close representation of war. "When the summer drills are over," wrote General Brackenbury, "the men who have hitherto practised their work in battalions, brigades; and divisions, are assembled in corps, and made to manœuvre against each other exactly as in war, except that their weapons are not loaded. Every department has to perform its own functions, while the talents of individual officers are tested. All things necessary in war are practised. Outpost and intelligence duties, patrols and reconnaissances, billeting and bivouacking."

At the larger manœuvres too, in which every regiment of the army took part at least two years out of three, and which lasted for a month or six weeks, the reserves rejoined the colours, and the battalions took the field, on the war-establishment.

Nor was the system either then or now, for it still obtains, limited to the exercises of Army Corps, divisions and brigades. In these the commanders and the staff receive their special training, and the three arms learn to work in conjunction; but, in the neighbourhood of their own quarters, the regimental officers and men are constantly exercised over broken ground, where, as far as possible, situations which might occur in battle are rehearsed; and the yearly programme of each battalion embraces equal periods of drill, musketry and tactics.

So highly is practical knowledge esteemed that the promotion of the officer depends, not on his theoretical attainments, but on his capacity for conducting operations in the field. And he finds instructors in his immediate superiors. The battalion is the tactical school. From the chief who superintends the whole, down to the sergeant who takes his squad into the fields, and there explains the duties of sentry and patrol, all are incessantly engaged in the work of practically teaching in peace what is requisite in war.

Careful *individual* training is the foundation of the Prussian efficiency. Every officer and man is made intimately acquainted with his duties on active service, for they are thoroughly instructed not in squad, company, or class, but each man by himself, in every detail of their trade. It may be noted, at the same time, that this individual training is not so much enjoined with the view of making the soldier more apt in independent or individual fighting, as of enabling him to do his best in combination with his comrades.

When Prussia took the field in 1866, her troops had less experience of war than those of any other nation. Their knowledge was theoretical; but their rapid and decisive victories proved conclusively, that troops trained as they were may be the most formidable of enemies, and that the general principles which regulate tactics can be so learned in peace that they will be followed instinctively in war.

Under her system, far more is effected than in inculcating discipline, in moulding skilful strategists and expert fighters. The intelligence, which has not only framed her institutions, but watches to preserve them in their integrity, works assiduously for the formation of individual character. Every rank is given its own responsibilities. The instruction and well-being of the men are committed wholly to their immediate commanders; here every officer, commissioned or non-commissioned, is left to himself he is compelled to use his intelligence, for his own advancement depends on the efficiency of his men; and *habits of decision and self-reliance are thus confirmed*. Again, little less remarkable than the knowledge of their profession possessed by all, and the smoothness of the mechanism of the military system, is that spirit of confidence in themselves, their training and their leaders, of loyalty to king and country, which pervades every rank of the Prussian Army. The soldier is treated as an intelligent being, a fit recipient of patriotic ideas and lofty sentiments. He is brought into contact with them from the day he joins the colours, and throughout his service his mental and moral training is considered as important as his physical.

It may be well to notice that practice in battle-exercises by no means occupies the greater portion of the soldier's time. The greatest precision is demanded in close order and this can only be attained by a long and arduous course of training. How great was the influence in the war of 1870 of this mechanical accuracy and of the habits of subordination, and attention thereby engendered, on both discipline and marching, it is difficult to estimate

It has already been stated that the bonds of union between the French officers and men were but slight. The non-commissioned ranks had been encouraged to usurp the prerogatives of their superiors; and had become responsible for duties which should have been the chief care of the company officers. And not only did the sergeants encroach upon the functions of these officers, but the battalion commander and adjutant absorbed the control of the minutest detail of instruction and administration, depriving the captains of the charge of their men, and of all opportunity of winning their respect and confidence.

The German system is in marked contrast. The higher authorities consistently maintain the high position of the company commander, and crush every attempt to curtail his prerogatives or to lessen his responsibilities. From the first day the recruit falls in upon the barrack square he is under the eye of his captain. The whole of his military knowledge, his rewards and his advancement, he owes to the officers of his own company. For the economical administration of his command, for its comfort and well-being as well as its efficiency, the captain bears the sole responsibility. On the bonds thus created between officers and men may be cited the opinion of a well-known Prussian author: "The captain is the only officer between whom and the soldier a personal relation exists in peace time. He knows every individual soldier in the most intimate manner, and the soldier on his part is well aware that his captain so knows him. It is upon this relation that the uncommon influence rests, which he, above all other officers, has over the individual soldier as well as over the whole company." In the French Army this uncommon influence, the root of the Prussian discipline, was altogether lacking.

In the first place, the system was one of centralization; individual initiative and independent action were discouraged. Within the tactical unit, the battalion, battery, or regiment of cavalry, all responsibility was vested in the hands of the commanding officer and his staff. Subordinates had merely to obey orders and to move in the authorized grooves. The commanding officers were likewise under strict and unceasing supervision, exercising their functions on lines laid down for them; and the supervisors themselves were closely controlled from Paris.

"If the habit be once acquired," wrote Colonel Maurice, so long ago as 1872, "of being never entrusted with authority; in even a limited degree, of leaning always on the mere dictation of others, it becomes extremely difficult for any man in later life to shake himself free from it, and either willing to assume responsibility, or – for the two things almost universally run together – to delegate power. Yet for the present conditions of war, a readiness to assume responsibility if necessary, a knowledge when to assume it, and a capacity for giving orders without dictating them, are more needful than all theoretical training, and, if we, are to believe those who have seen recent fighting, than all practical experience."

Secondly, the chief business of the army was drill; drill pure and simple. The drill they practised had, it is true before the introduction of the breech-loader, been the best preparation for battle, for the majority of the manœuvres were those employed before the enemy; but it had not been recognized that this was no longer the case.

Lastly, there was no training for battle whatever.

If they had acquaintance with the history of war the military chiefs had not reflected on it. They had not grasped the fact that the soldiers of Napoleon, of whose skill and powers they believed themselves the heirs, possessed something more than drill, discipline, and a warlike activity of thought; that they did not spring into being the expert warriors they were, but that a long probation and much experience developed their extraordinary efficiency.

To supply the place of that probation and experience nothing was done. It was held that the training of a barrack-square was sufficient to make her officers skilled leaders; that there was no necessity to supplement it by instruction in the art of war; and that the capacity for independent action should be rather repressed than fostered. It was traditionary in the army that, in the field, individual intelligences must have free play and parade-ground manœuvres be discarded. Against over-drilled soldiers like the Russians and Austrians their loose and independent methods of fighting had been successful. These methods, however, the military chiefs expected would be improvised. The soldiers knew enough of war to understand that confusion was inevitable. But their leaders had neither accustomed them to confusion, nor set themselves to evolve order out of disorder. And so, in 1870 the French met troops better trained for fighting than themselves, to whom the confusion of battle was no novelty, who had been practically taught how to make the best of it, and whose manœuvres were even more rapid than their own.

We have now to give some attention to each arm of the service, and to remark the various circumstances which affected their action in the field.

THE INFANTRY

In the Prussian, army much care was given to musketry training; great stress was laid upon the value of individual instruction, of accurate shooting at short range, and of economy of ammunition. Each infantry soldier fired nearly 130 rounds a year. The French, on the other hand, underrated the effect of a high average, and expected great results; which were never realized except against close and deep formations, from the long range fire of masses of men.

The "small book" of a French soldier, picked up at Woerth, showed that, in 1866, he had expended 14, in 1867, 20 rounds, and in both years had ranked as a "first class shot." In 1868 and 1869, he was quartered in Algeria, and during that period never fired at all. The German infantry was still armed with the famous needle-gun; the French with the Chassepôt; and of these the latter was in every way superior. The material and workmanship of the barrel were more satisfactory, the trajectory was flatter, the weight less, and the action of loading performed with greater rapidity and ease. Eleven shots could be delivered in a minute. It was sighted for 1,200 metres, the needle gun for only 600. Assiduous practice and a less cumbrous equipment rendered the Prussian soldiers stouter marchers than the French. In the field King William's troops were content to bivouac or to occupy the villages. The French soldier was weighed down by a heavy cooking apparatus, an enormous kit, and a portion of the *tente d'abri*, of which the burden and the shelter was shared by four men. Campaigning under the powerful sun of Africa, Mexico and China had made the soldiers less hardy than those of the Republic and the First Napoleon. A roof had come to be considered an absolute necessity, even in a temperate climate and mild weather, and because it was dangerous in Algeria, where villages are far between, to sleep *à la belle etoile*, the men of the Army of the Rhine were encumbered, in the midst of summer and in a thickly populated country, with the useless addition of their canvas shelters.

The French infantry regiment consisted of three battalions; the battalion, on the war strength, of 6 companies of 130 men. One or more companies skirmishing, the remainder deployed in line, or massed in column, was the ordinary formation for attack. The skirmishers merely covered the advance of the main-body; and it was the main body with the bayonet that was expected to carry the position.

The battalion was the tactical unit, the smallest body to which independence of action was allowed; and the companies executed all movements at the command of the battalion leader.

The Prussian infantry regiment also consisted of 3 battalions; the battalion, on the war strength, of 4 companies of 250 men.

The company was divided into 3 sections, or züge, of 80 rifles each. When in line it was formed into two divisions; standing side by side, of 3 ranks each. When in column it was formed of 3 sections, one behind the other, at a distance of 6 paces. The rear section was called the skirmishers, or marksmen's section, and composed of the best shots. In line, this section formed the third rank.

The company column therefore, presented six ranks to the enemy on a front of one section; and when the skirmishers were out, four ranks the same front.

In the attack, the battalions advanced either in line of company columns at deploying intervals (80 paces), each company furnishing its own support and reserve, assigning a section to each; or, with two company columns in front, furnishing the skirmishers and supports; the remainder following as a half-battalion, generally in line of company columns, in reserve. The company was the tactical unit and therefore semi-independent. Between the major commanding the battalion and his four captains there was no intermediate grade. As in quarters, so in the field, the latter were allowed considerable latitude. They mounted on parade. In the attack the major gave general directions, pointed out the objective, leaving it to his captains to carry them out as they judged best.

The official instructions for attack, which were in force in 1870, have been condensed as follows. (It will be observed that the conditions of the new fighting were so accurately forecast, that the principles then put forward are those which regulate the tactics of the present):

"Dwelling on the power imparted to the defence by the breech-loader, they asserted that a good, steady infantry was hardly to be assaulted in front, unless at the same time attacked in flank. But still the offensive was brought into the foreground, and the principal task of tactics was represented to be that of carrying out the infantry attack successfully; if not at the first rush, yet by perseverance, a clever use of the ground and of the situation.

"It was recommended, then, as a general rule, to direct your movements against the enemy's flanks, or if that were not possible, at least to threaten them. The battle should, it was said, be opened by dense clouds of skirmishers, who, advancing at a run, should get as near the enemy as possible before they opened fire."

"Supports were directed to place themselves as close as possible behind the line of skirmishers. Then little by little, the latter would push forward firing, close up to the enemy, when, after a hot fusilade, the reserves combined with the first, or first line alone, according to circumstances, would be led forward to the assault."

The offensive was the mainspring of the Prussian tactics. In the invasion of France it was imposed upon them by the fact that they were assailants and superior in numbers. It had been strongly advocated, as the surest means of defeating the French, in a remarkable pamphlet by Prince Frederick Charles; and their chiefs adopted it without hesitation, for they could trust their officers to let no opportunity escape them. If a weak point existed in the line of defence – and such points exist in every line of defence – it would be rapidly discovered where all were resolute in seeking it. "The assailant triumphs," writes von der Goltz, "if he gains the upper hand at a single spot: the defender only when he is victorious all along the line." The French held the contrary opinion, and believed the best means to utilise the breechloader was to remain on the defensive until the moment should be ripe for a general counter stroke upon the shattered enemy. The policy of this course was urged in the official instructions, and had been impressed upon the minds of officers and men.

Unfortunately, this idea was not at all in consonance with the national characteristics and traditions. That the French fight well on the defensive, the stubborn battles of the last phase of the Peninsular War, as well as those of 1870, sufficiently prove, but their greatest victories have been won by the impetuosity of their attack. "A constant offensive," said Marshal Bugeaud, "is vital to the efficiency of the French soldier." If the defence is to be decisively successful; it must be combined with attack, it must be active not passive. Such was doubtless the intention of the authorities, but so enamoured were they of the prospect of crushing the assailants with the fire of the Chassepôt, that they left in the background the importance of the counter stroke, and appear to have taken for granted that it would be easily improvised. But the sudden change from the defensive to the offensive, – that is, to a general offensive, which wrests the initiative from the enemy, compels him to suspend his attack, and transposes the rôle of the combatants – is the most difficult of tactical operations. Throughout the whole range of military history examples are rare. Except by the greatest captains it has never been successfully executed; and in not one single engagement, even when they were superior in numbers, was it successfully executed by the French commanders of 1870.

It may be well to remember that amongst English-speaking generals there are two who are regarded as the greatest exponents of defensive tactics, Wellington and Lee. And yet, when they waited to receive attack, how seldom were they able to crush a repulsed enemy by a general counter-stroke. Salamanca and Waterloo are the only instances; these alone were decisive victories, and, in the latter case, after they arrival of the Prussians, numbers were all against the assailant. It is true that at Vimiero, Sir Arthur Wellesley was only prevented by untoward circumstances from pursuing Junot into Lisbon, but in every other defensive action, fought either by Wellington or Lee, with the exceptions above noted, the enemy was allowed to withdraw unmolested.

Instructions which gave prominence to the defensive, exalting it at the expense of the attack, had a prejudicial effect. The predilection for the defensive influenced disastrously the tactics of the whole campaign. The generals, waiting until the enemy should be shattered by the Chassepôt, let false manœuvres, made sometimes at the very outset of the battle, pass unpunished, and before the wished-for consummation arrived, their flanks were turned and the battle lost, The truth is that no general, before entering upon a campaign, can decide upon the method of his battles. If he wishes for victory, at one time he must act on the defensive; at another, he must attack. Even to defend a country from invasion the commander of an inferior force must be prepared to strike. The strategical defensive is, no doubt, generally, although not invariably, compulsory on the weaker of two belligerents; but no leader dare neglect opportunities for assuming the offensive; for, as an almost universal rule, it is by the offensive alone that decisive results are won.

More attention had been given in France than in Prussia to the construction of field-entrenchments. The utility of such works, under certain circumstances, was not disputed by the German leaders, but they were held to be out of place in offensive battle, as tending to check the *élan* of the troops. And yet, whenever a post was carried, such as a farm or village, it was the constant practice of the Prussians to put it at once into a state of defence and hold it as a rallying point.

The French infantry carried 90 rounds per man, the Prussian 80, and in both armies the reserve ammunition was conveyed in battalion carts.

Field manœuvres were not unknown in France. Her Republican armies at the close of the last century imitated and improved upon the exercises of Frederick the Great; and General Dumouriez was the first to pit division against division. Napoleon the First neglected them, relying on his own genius and the experience of his troops; even at the great camp at Boulogne, the army assembled for the invasion of England was never called upon to execute other movements than those of ordinary parade. Under the Third Napoleon they had been revived, but were confined to the attack of a skeleton enemy in accordance with a previously arranged programme, a system affording the minimum of instruction to the generals and staff, and exciting neither the interest nor the thinking powers of the officers and men. In the summer months of 1870, a smaller number of regiments than usual had assembled at the Châlons Camp, the annual scene of the manœuvres, but siege exercises only had been carried out.

The utility of tactical instruction of smaller units, of battalions and companies, was not recognised in France; moreover, officers who did not study would have made but indifferent teachers.

THE CAVALRY

In 1866, the Prussian cavalry had failed to answer expectation. In the shock of battle it had indeed proved superior to the famous horsemen of Austria; but reflecting on the experiences of the campaign, the Head-Quarter Staff came to the conclusion that the organization of the regiments was faulty, and that their tactical employment had been too limited. Intelligence of the hostile movements had been often wanting, the front ineffectively covered, and touch with the enemy often lost. In the years that intervened between the defeat of Austria and the invasion of France, this arm was thoroughly reformed. A more practical, although less economical, system of organization sent only well-instructed men and seasoned horses to the front. Instruction in map-reading was made more thorough, theoretically in the barrack rooms, and practically in regimental exercises and at the manœuvres; and the youngest trooper knew how to gather intelligence, what to report, and how to find his way in an unknown country.

To each infantry division a regiment of cavalry was attached, which provided escorts and orderlies, maintained communication with neighbouring bodies of troops, and when on the march or in cantonments proved a secondary screen for the division, in rear of the independent division of horsemen who covered the general front. The latter was composed of two or three brigades; and each brigade of two regiments. To them were assigned the duties of collecting intelligence by keeping touch of the enemy, of concealing the march of the armies; the battle field, of engaging the hostile horse, and of supporting their own infantry by charging the enemy's guns and riflemen; after victory or defeat, of following up the pursuit or covering the retreat.

On the outbreak of the war, two squadrons of cavalry were attached to each division of French infantry, and to each Corps d'Armée a division of two brigades of two regiments each, or 2,400 sabres. Reserve divisions were also organized, which remained at the disposal of the Commander-in-Chief.

We have already seen that Napoleon had grasped the lesson which, to superficial observers, appeared the most important of the Secession War. But he had failed to observe one of equal weight, the excellent use made by the American leaders of their mounted regiments. "Little was said," writes Colonel von Borbstaedt of the French official instructions, "about the movements of cavalry acting as a veil to an army, and guarding it against surprise, and training in patrol duties was much neglected, except in a few light regiments."

In fact, the duties of reconnaissance, of securing the repose of the other arms while encamped, and of preventing hostile interference with their movements, were expected to be carried out by the weak divisional cavalry, whilst the larger units were retained in rear of the infantry, and their employment was limited to actual battle. The divisional cavalry, even had it been properly instructed, would have found it quite impossible to have performed the rôle laid down for it, for, as a general rule, its whole available strength was frittered away in providing escorts and orderlies.

Lastly, the French squadrons seldom reached the war establishment. The sudden mobilization of the whole force of the country threw the arrangements for supplying remounts completely out of gear; horses had to be handed over to the artillery, and the authorized complement was never present with the regiments.

The regiments of both consisted of four squadrons each. The Prussians numbered 150 sabres, the French about 130.

THE ARTILLERY

The German artillery was armed with a serviceable steel breech-loader, firing a common shell with a percussion fuze. The batteries allotted to the horse and light field artillery were nine-pounders; to the heavy field artillery, sixteen-pounders. That this arm, like the cavalry, had not played its proper part in 1866, but had allowed the needle-gun to reap the laurels of the campaign, had been promptly realized. The Austrian guns had been employed with greater boldness and with better judgment. Their practice was more accurate, and in every engagement they had rendered the hard-pressed infantry the most valuable support.

The marvellous improvement and influence of the Prussian artillery in 1870 was a tribute to the genius of the chiefs who suggested and enforced reform; and to the capacity both for learning and instruction which existed amongst the officers.

France had disregarded the lessons of 1866. Her artillery was far inferior in matériel to the Prussian armament, and her officers clung to antiquated tactics. The training of the personnel was insufficient, and steady and accurate shooting was not taught. Her bronze muzzle-loaders threw a common shell, with, a time fuze available at two ranges only, at 2,800 and 1,500 metres; at all other distances it was supposed to burst on contact. A few shrapnel, with fuzes which should have ensured their bursting at four ranges between 500 and 1,300 metres, were carried by the light batteries, but the fuzes were so defective that these powerful shells were of little use.

The horse and light field-batteries were nine-pounders; the heavy, sixteen-pounders, with a small proportion of twenty-four.

THE MITRAILLEUSE

Any record of the French armament would be incomplete without a notice of this famous machine gun. So great was the mystery that surrounded it before the war – for even the army knew little of its construction and nothing of its working – so exaggerated the stories of its destructive properties, that the soldiers and the public expected from this novel weapon the most extraordinary results.

The shortsighted policy, however, of the Emperor and his advisers, prevented its proper development. It was their intention that the unexpected appearance of a strong and terrible weapon would surprise and demoralize the enemy. The trials of its capabilities had been carried out with most profound secrecy; and when its adoption had been approved, the batteries were carefully locked away in the arsenals, and no examination of their mechanism was permitted.

On the outbreak of hostilities, detachments of artillery; with the necessary teams, were sent to take the arm over; but in the few days that intervened before the first engagements, there was no time to instruct the gunners in their new duties. Combined in batteries, the mitrailleuses were attached in the field to the divisional artillery. But the question of their tactical employment had never been threshed out. They were used as field guns; and owing to their shorter range (1,800 yards), were utterly unable to cope with the Prussian cannon. In positions where it was possible to conceal them until the enemy's artillery fire was masked by the advance of his infantry, on more than one occasion they did extraordinary execution.

Despite the secrecy maintained by the French authorities, the Prussian staff was well aware of the fact that a machine gun had been introduced into the armament of France. Machine guns of American and Belgian patterns were examined in model at Berlin, but it was decided that, whist demanding nearly as many horses and as much apparatus as a field gun, as artillery they were useless, and, as adjuncts to the needle gun, unnecessary.

THE STAFF

It has already been stated that the promotion of the Prussian officer does not depend upon his theoretical attainments, but on his capacity, practically tested, of conducting operations in the field. But the study of theory is not therefore neglected. However extended the experience of any individual officer, however constant his practice, there must still be situations, so various and so constantly changing are the phases of the battle and the campaign, of which he cannot possibly have personal knowledge. If he would master every move of the game, the devices, tricks, and stratagems, wherewith to foil his adversary's cunning, he must not only saturate his mind with the principles of the tactical art, but he must widen his own experience by drawing on the experiences of others, particularly on those of great and successful soldiers. He must learn, too, what to avoid, what rules cannot be violated with impunity, when and why certain manœuvres are impracticable.

Unless he has this knowledge, his practice in the field will fail. So thoroughly is this appreciated in every rank of the Prussian army, that the military chiefs are content to leave the study of theory to the discretion of the regimental officers, and the system has answered expectation.

At the same time, at the outset of his career, every officer is required to spend a portion of his service at one of the many war schools, and is there thoroughly grounded in the elements of his profession; but, when he has once taken up the duties of his rank, he is exempted, not from the necessity of study, but from the necessity of theoretical examination. Furthermore, if he is ambitious of staff employment, or solicitous of advancement of any sort whatever, he is compelled to devote himself to the acquisition of professional acquirements, for on the reports of his superiors regarding his industry, zeal, and intelligence, his future career depends.

Enough has been said already on the high aim of the system of administration and instruction in Prussia, and it has been shown that the object is not merely the acquisition of knowledge, but the formation of character, and the development of initiative.

Trained in this practical manner, it follows that the Prussian regimental officers are efficient and self-reliant soldiers; and it would seem easy to select a sufficient number, who, with further instruction in a larger sphere of duties, would immediately become fitted for employment on the staff.

High, however, as is the general standard of education and knowledge, the regimental officer has to pass a probation of at least six years, – years of incessant application and frequent trials of progress, before he is finally admitted to the coveted position.

Three years' service is a necessary qualification before he can present himself for examination; and not only during his long probation, but also afterwards, he serves for certain periods in his own as well as the other branches of the army, thus renewing his acquaintance with regimental duties and routine.

The examination for entrance is not competitive; the course of study lasts three years, and not more than 30 per cent of those who complete it are permanently incorporated with that distinguished corps, which for more than twenty years was under the control of Count von Moltke; but the remainder are available for the expansion of the staff in a time of war, and to supply casualties. The great strategist of 1866 and 1870–1 more than once publicly declared, with just pride in the success of his own handicraft, that to her staff officers Germany owes much of her military supremacy; and Baron Stoffel, French attaché at Berlin before the war, reported to the Emperor – and he was a keen and impartial critic, as well as an able soldier – that in his opinion, the Prussian Staff was not only far superior to the French, but the most valuable element of her force.

In France, an entirely different system existed, which, since the downfall of the Empire and the reconstitution of the army, has found no apologists. Officers entered the staff corps at the age of 21, proceeding to it directly from the military schools. Their training was purely theoretical, their practical knowledge scanty in the extreme; and their severance from their regimental comrades a fruitful source of jealousy and misunderstanding.

THE TERM OF SERVICE IN 1870

In Prussia, 12 years service was exacted from the soldier, 3 years with the colours (in practice commuted to 2½ or even less); 4 years in the reserve, with legal obligation to two periods of duty, not exceeding 8 weeks each, 5 years with the Landwehr, with legal obligation to two periods of duty not exceeding 14 days each.

Men of superior education, on passing certain examinations, were free to engage as "one year volunteers." They might choose their own regiment and join at the age of 18 if they preferred to do so. The remainder joined at the ago of 20. The complement necessary to raise the field force to the war-establishment came from the reserves, men between 23 and 27 years of age.

The Landwehr, formed in distinct battalions, was composed of men from 27 to 33 years of age.

Of the annual contingent of conscripts not more than one half were called upon to take their places in the ranks; but the residue did not escape their obligations. In time of war, they were summoned to the Head Quarters of their district-regiments, and formed the Ersatz or depôt battalions. They were officered from the regular army, and in two months were considered fit for duty in the field. The Landwehr was officered by men who had retired from the regular army, and by those who had served at least a year in a regular regiment and had passed an examination.

In France the term was for five years, with four in the reserve; but re-engagements as substitutes were frequent. The reserves were never called up for training; many of them had never handled the Chassepôt; the second portion, consisting of 112,000, had only five months' experience of barrack life and discipline, and the Garde Mobile was simply raw material.

Perhaps one of the greatest differences, and as regards discipline and efficiency one of the most important, which existed between the French and German armies, was in the non-commissioned officers. In the former the sergeants and corporals had lost all authority, and were in no way superior to the men in the ranks; no inducement was offered to the best of them to prolong their service and they were often the ringleaders in mischief and indiscipline. In Germany, on the other hand the greatest pains had been taken to secure men of high character and experience. If he re-engaged for twelve years, a non-commissioned officer had a claim on many lucrative appointments under government; they were entrusted with much responsibility, and the officers were obliged to give incessant attention to their instruction.

As regards the German sergeants, the reflections of an experienced American general, attached to the Royal Head Quarters at the siege of Paris, are worth quoting. "I have commanded regiments of volunteers (during the Civil War) with not a non-commissioned officer in them equal to some of the non-commissioned officers in every German regiment; while I have seen many sergeants there who, in our service, would have been given colonels' commissions."

Every Prussian regiment of infantry consisted of three battalions, No. 1, No 2, and the Fusilier Battalion. These are indicated in the letterpress by Roman numerals and the letter F; for instance I/12, II/12, F/12. The Fusilier Regiments, of which two, the 39th and 40th, were engaged at Spicheren, number their battalions I, II, III.

In every battalion were four companies, numbered consecutively throughout the regiment; thus, No. 1 to No. 4 form the First Battalion; No. 5 to No. 8, the Second; No. 9 to No. 12, the Fusilier or Third Battalion. The companies are described by Arabic numerals, placed before the number of the regiment; for instance, 1/39, 5/39, 9/39. Batteries were formed into regiments, and numbered through the regiment; but light, heavy, and horse batteries were on separate lists. In the letter-press they are shown thus I/7, I/7, IH.A./7 indicating the First Heavy, the First Light, and the First Horse batteries of the Seventh Regiment.

The French infantry regiments of the Line were each organized in three battalions, numbered and indicated as follows, I/2, II/2, III/2. Both Jägers and Chasseurs (rifles) had but one battalion.

The Prussian corps consisted of two infantry divisions; the French of three in the 2nd and 4th, and of four in the 3rd Corps d'Armée.

In both armies each infantry consisted of two brigades, each two regiments or six battalions strong.

For the number of brigades in the cavalry divisions, and of batteries, in the divisions and the corps, reference may be made to the Order of Battle in the Appendix.

For the strength of battalions, &c., the reader is referred to Appendix I.

CHAPTER III
THE COMBAT OF SAARBRUCKEN

On the 29th of July, Napoleon, as, already recorded relinquished for the time his design of a general advance. But he dared not face the contingency that, in the meantime, von Moltke might seize the initiative, and throw the French on the defensive. Behind him was Paris, clamorous for conquest, and murmuring at delay. If by word or deed he had suggested that, instead of carrying on the war beyond the Rhine, France herself might have to submit to invasion, the revulsion of feeling would have brought about a tumult in the capital. Dreading his own subjects more than the enemy, he postponed the concentration of his widely severed wings, and resolved by a semblance of offensive operations to quiet the impatience of the mob. To Marshal Bazaine was assigned the command of seven infantry divisions which, with artillery and cavalry, were 60,000 strong. With these troops he was to seize Saarbrucken; whilst the 4th and 5th Corp d'Armée reconnoitred to the right and left, towards Bliescastel and Saarlouis. Saarbrucken, it was assumed, would not be surrendered without a struggle; and, did they attempt to defend it, the 40,000 Germans, reported present near St. Wendel, would be drawn into battle with a superior force. Moreover, it was expected that actual collision with the enemy would throw some light on his numbers and dispositions. In fact, this was the chief military end of he operation; and that such should have been the case is in itself a grave charge against the French Intelligence Department. Four Corps d'Armée were employed to gain the information which a single brigade of cavalry, skilfully handled might have easily obtained. The bridges across the Saar where it runs parallel to the frontier were closely guarded it is true, but that at Saarguemund was in their own hands. The necessary concentrations for this movement brought the French Corps and their divisions to the following localities on July 31st:[1]

2nd Corps	1st Division, S.W. of Forbach
	2nd Division, Oetigen
	3rd Division, Spicheren and Forbach
3rd Corps	1st Division, St. Avold
	2nd Division, Haut Homburg
	3rd Division, Ham sous Varberg
	4th Division, Boucheporn.
4th Corps	1st Division, Bouzonville
	2nd Division, Boulay
	3rd Division, Teterchen
5th Corps	1st Division Bitsche
	2nd and 3rd Divisions, Saarguemund

Imperial Guard, Metz

1 See map page 101.

The dispositions for the operation were as follows:

2nd Corps	To carry the Saarbrucken ridge, a low range of heights on the south side of the river, commanding the town, and occupied by the Prussian outposts.
3rd Corps	3 divisions to support the 2nd Corps. 1 division to demonstrate towards Volklingen on the left flank.

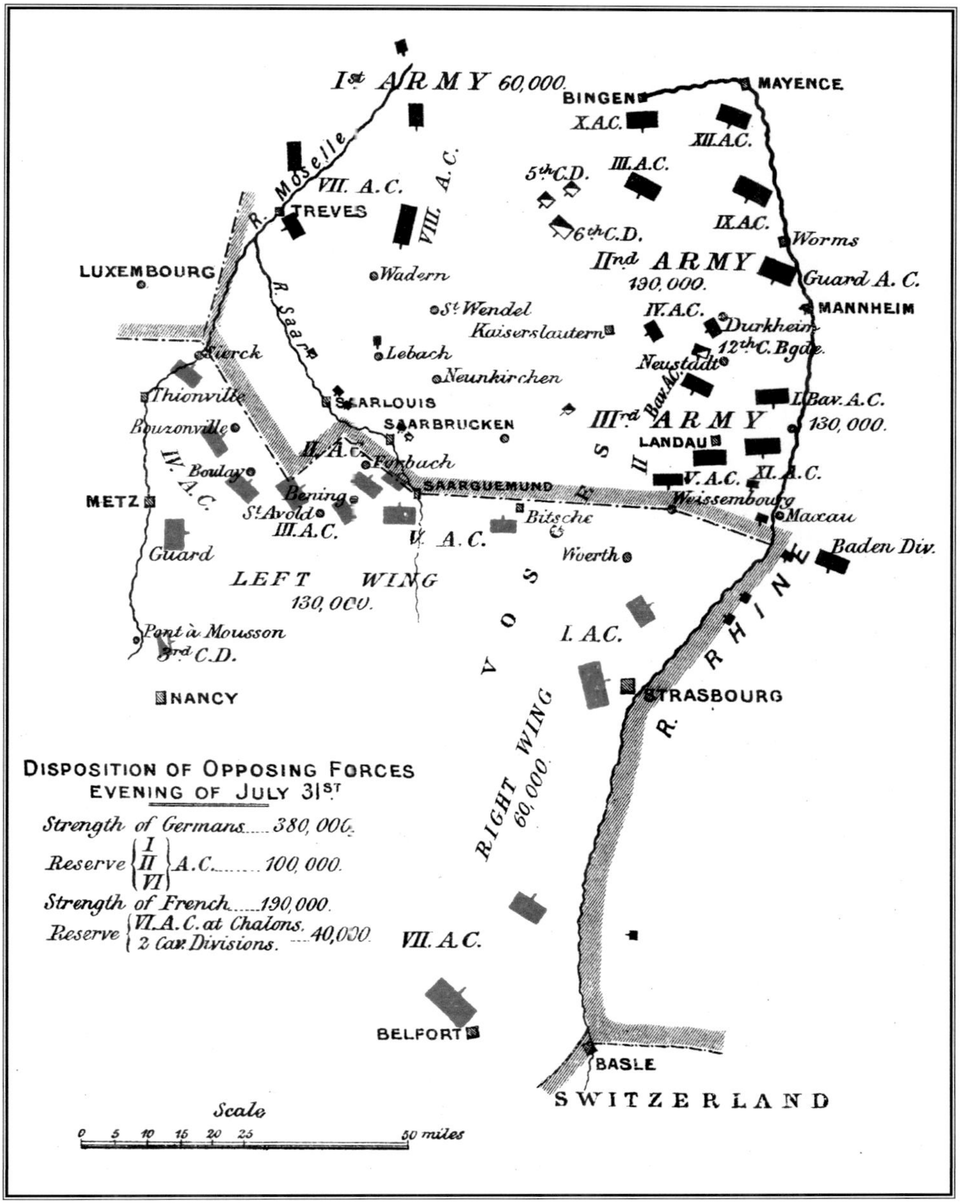

Disposition of opposing forces, evening of July 31st

4th Corps	To reconnoitre the little fortress of Saarlouis
5th Corps	To demonstrate from Saarguemund on the right flank towards Bliescastel.

The troops to advance at daybreak on August 2nd.

The combat which ensued, although at the time invested with a fictitious importance by the inflated despatches of Napoleon and the presence of the little Prince Imperial, is worthy of notice on one account alone. The garrison of Saarbrucken consisted of 6 guns, 450 sabres, and 3,250 bayonets. It was attacked by a complete Corps d'Armée, 25,000 men, with 90 pieces of artillery; but so skilfully was the slender force of Prussians handled, that the engagement affords a most instructive example of a rear guard action, and of a well conducted retreat before superior numbers. Moreover, the disposition of the troops during the preceding days is an excellent lesson in outpost duties.

THE PRUSSIAN POSITION BEFORE SAARBRUCKEN[2]

Rising twenty miles away in the Alsatian Highlands the Saar flows northward through the town of Saarguemund. Before reaching Saarbrucken, nine miles distant, the stream turns abruptly to the west; and, running parallel to the frontier, holds its course in that direction for more than seven miles. Leaving the village of Volklingen upon the right, it then inclines to the north-west; and passing through Saarlouis and Saarburg, joins the Moselle a few miles south of Trêves. The river is sluggish but not shallow; of an average width of 60 yards, and flows through a narrow valley whose high and undulating slopes are covered with extensive forests. Saarbrucken, on the left bank, is open and unfortified. Opposite to, and connected with it, by two stone bridges, is St Johann; the two together forming a thriving town of 20,000 inhabitants, the railway centre of a rich coal district. The twin city lies in the valley of the Saar, 200 feet below the crests on either hand; but while the hills stand close above Saarbrucken on the south, a long and gradual ascent leads from St. Johann on the north to the great Kollerthaler Forest, through which runs the road to Lebach and St. Wendel, the line of retreat of the Prussian garrison. At St. Arnual, a village 2,000 yards above Saarbrucken, where the river changes its course from north to west, a brook strikes the angle, flowing from the west. This watercourse drains an open valley, parallel to that of the Saar but narrower, which has been named the valley of St. Arnual. Between Saarbrucken and the St. Arnual Valley rises an isolated ridge, broken into four distinct crests. To the west, the hill on which was the drill ground of the garrison. Beyond a shallow cutting and above the Lower Bridge, the Reppertsberg. To the east, across a deep and narrow glen, the Winterberg, the highest point, its shoulder looking down upon St. Arnual and the angle of the Saar. Between the Winterberg and the Reppertsberg, standing back, and closing the head of the rift between them, the steep and wooded knoll which is called the Nussberg. On this ridge were posted the Prussian sentries. 150 feet below, at the foot of the terraced slopes on which they stood, for the bare hill-sides were carefully cultivated, lies the St. Arnual Valley, without hedge or wall to divide the little plots of cultivation which chequer its surface like the squares of a chessboard. 2,000 yards beyond, the level is checked abruptly by the woods which clothe with an almost unbroken sheet of foliage the steep slopes of the Spicheren Heights, the northern limit of the Plateau of Lorraine. The crest of the heights is 300 feet above

2 See map of battlefield of Spicheren.

the St. Arnual Valley and 150 above the Saarbrucken Ridge. On the plateau, hidden by the timber, were the French camps. Opposite the cutting between the Drill-ground Hill and the Reppertsberg, the crest strikes back at right angles to the south, and a deep re-entrant ascends very gradually, narrowing as it goes, towards Forbach. At the angle thus formed, a long and narrow spur, comparatively bare of trees, runs downward to the valley. This is the Rotherberg, so called from the patches of red earth and stone which scar its slopes, a feature insignificant in itself, for it is dwarfed by the wooded heights from which it springs, but famous in the annals of war. On the other side of the re-entrant, which has been called the Forbach Valley, a great tract of undulating forest stretches as far as eye can range. Along the western border of the valley runs the railway from Metz to Saarbrucken, concealed by deep cuttings and an extensive copse which half closes the mouth of the re-entrant. By this intervening belt of timber, the village of Stiring Wendel, in the centre of the valley, and the little town of Forbach, at the head, were hidden from the sentries on the Saarbrucken Ridge, only the spires of the churches and the tall chimneys of the Stiring Foundry being visible.

The great high road from the Rhine to Metz, crossing the Saar by the Lower Bridge, winds round the northern shoulder of the Reppertsberg, cuts the saddle between that hill and the drill-ground, dips sharply to the level, and, lined in 1870 by lofty poplars passes south over the undulations of the valley. Striking the Rotherberg, it turns, half-right, and beneath the shadows of the wooded cliffs of the Spicheren Heights, pursues its way to Forbach.[3]

The Saarbrucken-Spicheren Road, ascending from the Upper Bridge between the Reppertsberg and Nussberg, leads directly to the Rotherberg, and there inclining to the left and built on a strong embankment, winds round the precipitous bluffs the eastern face. The easier gradient gained it passes up the saddle, cuts the sky-line and is lost to view.

On either side the Saar, within the valley and close to the water's edge, are two excellent roads, forming the principal communications between the towns which stand on the river bank.

The St. Arnual Valley is seamed with bridle-paths and cart-tracks; but, level and unobstructed as it was, troops of all arms could manœuvre freely over its cultivated area. The harvest had been already gathered.

Two hundred feet below the western shoulder of the Drill-ground Hill, the railway crosses the Saar by a massive viaduct; and running alongside the line is a road which connects Saarbrucken with Stiring Wendel.

The line from Saarguemund to Trêves passes through St. Johann, running on the right bank of the Saar.

The railway station is on the northern outskirts of St. Johann; behind the centre of the Saarbrucken Ridge 3,000 yards distant on the Metz high-road, in the Forbach Valley west of Stiring Wendel, and close beneath the shadow of the Spicheren Heights, stood the French Custom House, and a little further south a tavern called the Golden Bremm. The frontier ran across the mouth of the valley, and a little to the north was the Prussian Toll House. Between the copse in front of Stiring Wendel and the viaduct was

3 See sketch of battlefield pages 126–127.

a large farm called Drathzug, and beneath the eastern shoulder of the drill-ground, the German Mill.

Such were the principal features of the country which lay within the observation of the Prussian sentries. Their view extended over the St. Arnual Valley and up the Metz High-road within a mile of Forbach, but the lofty beeches of the copse in front of Stiring Wendel allowed only a small portion of the Forbach Valley to be seen.

Directly to the front the thick woods which climb to commanding Heights of Spicheren effectually closed the view, but where the Rotherberg juts out between the heavy timber on either hand a narrow strip of the plateau was visible, and in the far distance the bare slopes of the Pfaffenberg, a commanding ridge, beneath which lies Spicheren Village, just one mile distant from the spur.

To the right front and flank the great forest which take its name from Saarbrucken, stretches to the horizon; but on the left, the roads on either side the river, are under observation from the Hallberg, a conspicuous hill opposite the Winterberg, forming the other portal of the gate by which the Saar breaks through the Saarbrucken Ridge.

The position was strong, forming a natural bridge head; but on the flanks the woods approached too close for security, and the garrison was compelled to exercise the greatest vigilance. The front of observation was restricted; the enemy was vastly superior in number, and, concealed by the forests, it was always possible that he might make a sudden dash upon the town.

On the 19th of July, the day war was formally declared, the garrison of Saarbrucken consisted of 3 squadrons of the 7th Uhlans, and the 2nd Battalion of the 40th (Hohenzollern) Fusiliers. This force had been hastily despatched from Trêves on the 17th, without waiting for its reserves; the infantry, therefore, numbered but 500 rifles.

Up to the 29th the following was the general disposition of the troops :

Cavalry

1 troop at St. Arnual	} Patrolling the river roads on the left flank.
1 troop at Brebach	}
1 squadron in support	North of St. Johann, on the Dudweiler Road, a mile in rear, furnishing patrols for the Forbach Valley.
1 squadron in reserve	At Dudweiler 3 miles in rear of the support; maintaining communication with the 5th Dragoons at Bliescastel, 11 miles east, and with the little garrison of Volklingen (1 Company, 69th Regiment), 9 miles west.

Infantry

7th Company	60 men on Drill-ground Hill. 60 men in support near the Lower Bridge, constantly patrolling the Saarbrucken Forest.
5th Company	In support, beyond the river, with a sentry on the Lower Bridge, a section on the viaduct, and a detached post, under a non-commissioned officer, at the Burbach Iron-works.
6th Company	On St. Arnual Road immediately below the Nussberg: maintaining a non-commissioned officer's picquet on the Winterberg, patrolling towards the Spicheren Heights, and supporting the cavalry in St. Arnual.

8th Company	In eastern quarter of St. Johann, supporting the cavalry at Brebach. Sentry on Upper Bridge, and constant patrols towards Brebach.

The bridges were barricaded 10 Uhlans were attached to each picquet as orderlies.

On the 19th the supporting squadron rode up the Metz High-road towards Forbach, for French cavalry had already appeared in that direction, and had taken prisoners the officials in charge of the Prussian Custom House at the mouth of the Forbach Valley. From information received from the country people it was ascertained that General Bataille's division of the 2nd Corps d'Armée was encamped between Forbach and St. Avoid.

On the night of the 20th, infantry patrols heard French reconnoitring parties moving on the Metz Road, and discovered that their scouts had visited Gersweiler, a village in the great Saarbrucken Forest to the right front.

On the 21st, a strong infantry patrol proceeded to this hamlet, and the Uhlan scouts brought the intelligence that hostile picquets were posted in the Forbach valley near Stiring Wendel. The post of 5th Company on the viaduct was doubled, so as to patrol more efficiently towards Stiring Wendel and Gersweiler. A company of the 69th from Saarlouis occupied Volklingen.

On the 23rd, French infantry advanced through the Saarbrucken Forest, and a skirmish broke out near the viaduct, the picquet being reinforced by the remainder of the 5th Company. Small parties were observed taking soundings above Volklingen, and a hostile detachment was reported posted at Gersweiler.

On the 24th, a cavalry patrol arrived from Saarlouis bringing news of the enemy's movements near Trêves and Thionville; and on the same night a detachment of 32 Uhlans and 20 riflemen, led by a subaltern, crossed the frontier, and tore up the rails of the Saarbrucken Saarguemund railway, at a point where it strikes the Bliesbrucken road.[4] Reports were brought in that 4,000 French and 28 guns had marched into Saarguemund, and that troops were advancing from St. Avold.

On the 25th, detachments of 5th and 7th Companies, with half a squadron of Uhlans, starting at 2.45 am, reconnoitred towards Gersweiler and the Forbach Valley. French posts were observed at the Golden Bremm, and on the Spicheren Heights. The cavalry penetrated the woods to beyond Ottenhausen.

On the 26th, infantry patrols, which had constantly, hitherto, both by day and night, explored the woods on the slopes of the Spicheren Heights, found them occupied above St. Arnual. Vedettes were seen at the foot of the Rotherberg, and a small camp in the Forbach Valley. The patrol furnished by the 7th Company which reconnoitred to Stiring Wendel was composed of a subaltern and 14 men. After sundown, three strong patrols proceeded to the frontier. On the 27th, a subaltern with 30 men of the 6th Company approached close to Stiring Wendel; another officer, with a patrol of the same strength penetrated the forest above St. Arnual, and ascertained that the enemy was present there in strength. The Uhlans again made attempt to destroy the railway near Reinheim, but were compelled to retire before a stronger force of hostile cavalry.

4 Little damage was inflicted, as the men employed knew nothing about demolition.

Men of the Prussian 40th Fusiliers explore the woods on the slopes of the Spicheren Heights, led by a local guide (Ruppersberg)

On the 28th, 44 reservists, fully equipped, arrived to join the 40th, and a strong reconnaissance was pushed forward by the French against the ridge. Two guns on the Rotherberg and two in the Forbach Valley covered the advance of two companies of infantry, whose approach was early discovered by the patrols. The Prussian supports reinforced the picquets and the enemy soon withdrew. The artillery alone opened fire, but although a score of shells fell upon the drill-ground, and a tavern called the "Bellevue," which stands close to the cutting, was struck, no casualties occurred amongst the troops. On the retirement of the French two sections of Fusiliers reconnoitred towards the Golden Bremm; a stronger patrol crossed the frontier after dark. Apprehensive that this demonstration might be the prelude to more serious operations, and determined to gain early information, the Prussian commander, Lieut.-Col. von Pestel, despatched at daybreak on the 29th three patrols, each composed of a few troopers and 80 rifles; one from St. Arnual, a second up the Metz high-road, a third towards Stiring Wendel. No signs of an immediate advance were, however, discovered. At night-fall strong patrols, of 120 men each, searched the St. Arnual Valley.

On this day the First German Army began its advance from the Rhine.

On the 30th the sphere of operations was enlarged, and Schoneck, a village in the Saarbrucken Forest to the east of Stiring Wendel, was visited by a detachment of the 40th Fusiliers. A patrol of 34 men made its way through the St. Arnual Forest, drove

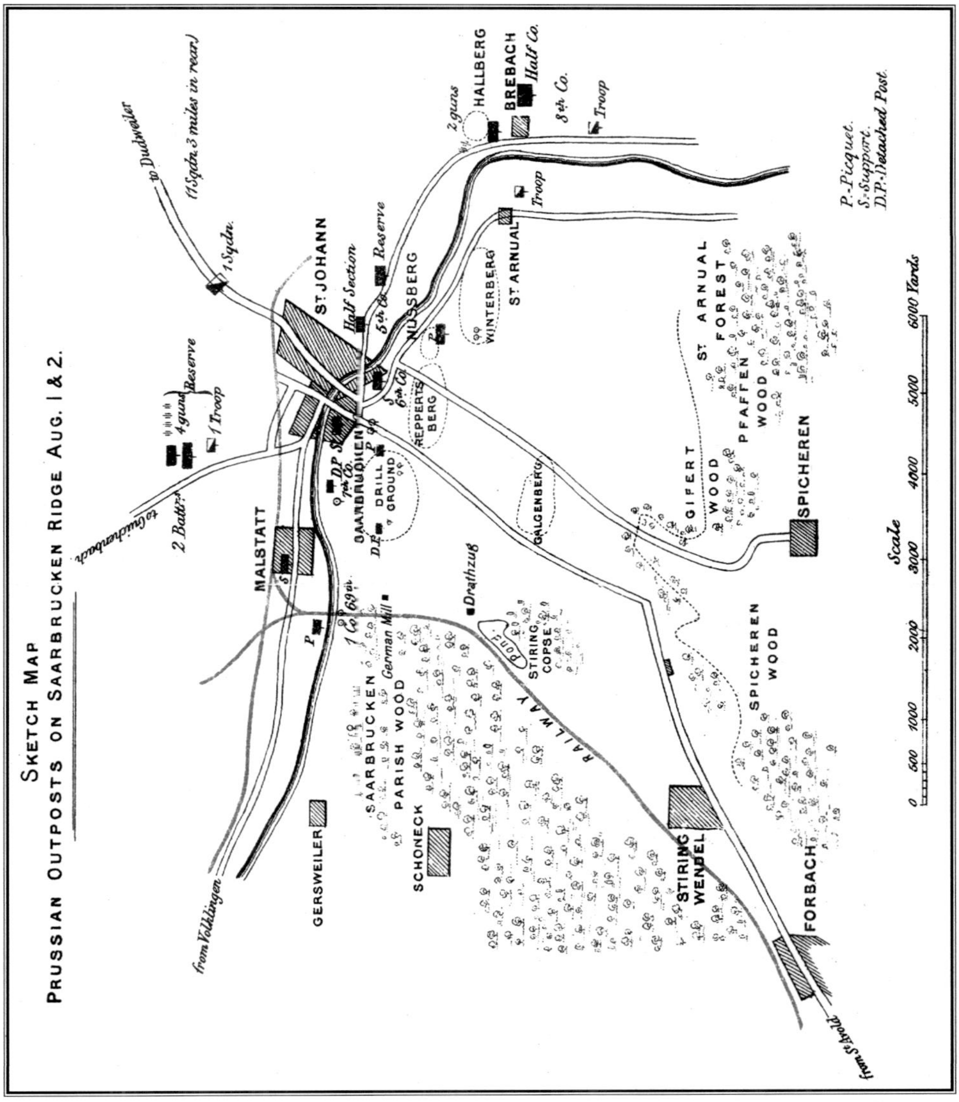

Battlefield of August 2nd, and outposts, August 1st

back a hostile picquet, and, favoured by the dim light of the early morning, obtained a comprehensive view of the interior of the plateau and of a large French camp. Working parties were observed from the ridge constructing entrenchments on the Rothberg. Strong reconnaissances were pushed down the river roads on the left flank, and a somewhat lively skirmish broke out near St. Arnual. The inhabitants of the district, moreover, reported that the enemy had thrown a bridge of boats between Grossbleiderstroff and Hanweiler, and that his cavalry had at length crossed the river.

The Second Army commenced its forward movement from the Rhine during the last day of July, and the first of August saw large reinforcements arrive at Saarbrucken. A company of the 69th Regiment from Volklingen relieved the picquet of the 40th at the Burbach Ironworks, whilst the 1st and 2nd Battalions of the Fusiliers, together with a light battery and a troop of the 9th Hussars, the whole under the command of Major General von Gneisenau, took post at Raschfuhl, a clump of houses on the hill side above St. Johann, covering the line of retreat. This force formed part of VIII Army Corps of the First Army, which had now begun to concentrate at Wadern, 20 miles in rear, and the Saarbrucken garrison may henceforth be considered as the advanced detachment of the First Army. Before this welcome addition of strength arrived, Lieut Col. von Pestel, hitherto commanding, had been instructed by a telegram from Head-Quarters to evacuate Saarbrucken, for no less than two Corps d'Armée confronted his tiny force. He reported, however, that the French were afraid of him, and requested permission to remain. von Moltke assented, and the Fusiliers and Uhlans, although menaced by a far superior force, still occupied the ridge and pushed constant reconnaissances across the frontier. The reinforcement permitted a more advantageous distribution of the outposts, but it is worthy of remark that, notwithstanding the force had now increased from one to three thousand rifles, not a single extra sentry was placed along the front; and although the strength and disposition of the picquets underwent alteration, the 2nd Battalion 40th, which had become thoroughly familiar with the ground and with the range of every landmark, was not relieved, despite the severity of the duties.

On the right a picquet of the 69th held the viaduct, with the remainder of the company as support in Malstatt. The 7th Company of the 40th occupied the Custom House above the Lower Bridge, sending a subaltern and 35 men to the drill-ground. Two double sentries, posted at intervals on the high-road, formed the connecting links by night between picquet and support. On the right shoulder of the hill, overlooking the approach from Stiring Wendel and also the sentry on the viaduct, a non-commissioned officer and 6 men (9 by night) were placed as a detached post, 800 yards distant from the picquet. A non-commissioned officer and 6 men were also stationed midway between the Custom House and the viaduct, in order to furnish immediate information of an attack on this important point. Constant patrols were sent out both from picquet and support in the direction of Drathzug.

In the centre, the 6th Company maintained a picquet on the Nussberg: 2 non-commissioned officers and 20 men, with a double sentry on the Winterberg. This party was reinforced by night by a subaltern and 20 men, thus forming a strong guard across the Saarbrucken-Spicheren road. The remainder of the company occupied a house near the Upper Bridge, 4 non-commissioned officers and 24 men being constantly employed on patrol, and a double sentry posted on the St. Arnual Road.

The left, beyond the river, was committed to the 8th Company: 120 men in Brebach Village and 120 at the foot of the Hallberg, ready to man either the strongly-fortified churchyard of the village, a breast-work which had been thrown across the railway, or a shelter-trench which had been constructed on a river bank.

The 5th Company lay in reserve between the Upper Bridge and the eastern entrance to St. Johann, with half a section (40 men), near the Lower Bridge.

The cavalry retained its former positions, leaving orderlies with each infantry picquet.

The 1st and 3rd Battalions of the 40th, with four guns, remained, at Rachspfuhl.

Two guns of the light batterery were posted on the lower slopes of the Hallberg, on the extreme left. Fear of jeopardizing their retreat over the narrow and barricaded bridges was evidently the reason that none were placed upon the ridge.

The detail of patrolling as given above must not be held to imply that the duties of the 2nd 40th, during the sixteen days they occupied the Saarbrucken Ridge, were an easy nature.

Besides the expeditions to the villages between the hostile lines, and the reconnaissance of the roads to front and flanks, constant communication was kept up between the different sections of the force. The work was unceasing and exacting. The heat of the weather was very great; and frequent alarms, raised by the firing of the patrols, or the exaggerated reports of the country people, disturbed the repose of the wearied soldiers.

At the same time the efforts of this slender force were not unrewarded. 50,000 French were held at bay, for the going and coming of the patrols, the presence of the picquets on the ridge, and the appearance at all hours of strong parties of infantry and cavalry, imposed so effectually on the enemy that it was believed in their camps and even at the Imperial Head-Quarters that Saarbrucken was occupied by a considerable force. Their reconnoitring parties were held in check; the mystery as to the German numbers and dispositions prevented any attempt to seize the river towns or even to destroy the railway and telegraph lines; and although the French soldiers were suffering from want of supplies, German citizens were saved from the unwelcome presence and requisitions of the foe.

An English officer, Captain Seton, of the 102nd Fusiliers, accompanied the 40th throughout the campaign in France. He has left a record of his observations, and it is interesting to note the points which impressed him at Saarbrucken. Whilst enlarging on the strength of the Prussian position, he notes the skilful dispositions made for the defence of bridges, the sparing use of sentries, the activity and frequency of the patrols, giving us to understand that the object of the Prussian commander was, without provoking the French, to appear perfectly confident, as if he were strongly supported. Whenever the alarm was sounded, and the troops were mustered to defend the position, he tells us that "every one, down to the privates, knew how to cover himself, either by availing himself of immediate natural advantages, or by bringing to his post whatever useful article, a log, a barrow, or such like, lay within his reach," and he adds that in every case an effective cross-fire was provided.

It seems an error not to have provided permanent cover for the picquets. A few earthworks would have still more effectually imposed upon the French. It is not improbable, however, that such a proceeding might have provoked attack.

In the frequent collisions with the enemy's patrols both Uhlans and Fusiliers suffered a few casualties, and it would appear that there was a good deal of unnecessary firing at vedettes and single scouts. At the same time, with strong parties working through thick, woodland, it was often impossible to disengage without a skirmish.

It may be added that from the observations of officers and men employed on reconnoitring duties and from the examination of the peasants and prisoners, valuable information was obtained and transmitted to Head Quarters. It is also important to notice that the dearth of supplies and transport in the French camps was common talk amongst the Prussian troops, and a strong impression had gained ground that it would be many days before the enemy would be in a condition to advance.

It did not escape the observation of the sentries that the reveillé was not sounded as usual in the French encampments on the morning of the 2nd of August, and towards 9 o'clock the cavalry scouts reported that a general and his staff were riding from the direction of Forbach as if for reconnaissance.

Nothing further, however, was discovered. The enemy's movements were completely screened by the woods, and the patrols, furnished to-day by the 9th Hussars in order that the French might be induced to believe that reinforcements had arrived, had been withdrawn, when suddenly, about ten o'clock, the sentries gave the alarm.

Advancing on both flanks, a strong force deployed along the whole length of the St. Arnual valley, followed by heavy columns of infantry and guns. As the Prussian picquet stood to arms, and watched the enemy's masses streaming down the Rotherberg, up the Forbach valley and the river road, they saw that the ridge was lost. But the order had been passed round that retreat was to be deferred until the flanks were turned. Every hour that the French advance might be delayed gave longer warning to the armies pressing forward from the Rhine.

The Uhlan vedettes before St. Arnual were the first to fall back, and as they trotted through the village, a message from the Nussberg informed the 6th Company that hostile infantry was issuing from the woods beyond the valley, and making for the Winterberg. St. Arnual was the first point threatened.

The picquet on the Nussberg extended along the crest of the Winterberg. 40 rifles were detached from the support to occupy the gully on the right, whilst the remainder doubled forward to St. Arnual. As this party took post amongst the scattered trees that clothe the lower slopes of the Winterberg, the head of a heavy column, debouching by the river road, broke into a long line of skirmishers across the stubble. The scouts were already out in front, and although the range was fully 1,200 yards, the Chassepôt bullets whistled shrilly past.

The two guns upon the Hallberg now opened, and from the shelter trench upon the river bank the fire of 80 rifles, although the distance was too great for effective practice, checked for the moment the advance of the enemy's right, but his battalions further to the left pressed rapidly forward against the Winterberg. Behind that hill lay the line of retreat to the Upper Bridge, and, fearing to be cut off, the captain of the 6th Company gave the order to withdraw by the Saarbrucken Road. A French field-battery came into action against the little force across the river, and the skirmishers, covered by its fire, swarmed into St. Arnual and began to scale the Winterberg.

The 7th Company of the Prussian 40th Fusiliers defend the area near the drill-ground and the "Bellevue" (Ruppersberg)

As its flank was now uncovered, the picquet on the height, after exchanging a brisk fire at long range with the French skirmishers, in its turn descended to the bridge, followed by the detachment occupying the ravine.

The 5th Company had taken post upon the Reppertsberg. By this time not only had the hill across the gully on their flank been carried, but the valley in front was filled with French. The brilliant sunshine glanced from ten thousand bayonets, and the blue and scarlet uniforms lent vivid colour to the animated scene. Deployed behind a waving line of skirmishers, which covered the advance with a rolling fire, a long array of battalions in close order stretched far to right and left. The tirailleurs pushed onward at a run. The foot of the ridge was gained and the red *kepis* of the foremost soon rose above the crest line. The ardour of the leaders had, however, led them too far forward, and the marksman's section, which had been drawn up behind the reverse slope of the ridge, dashed across the stubble and drove them down the hill. The supports followed quickly, and the whole company, extending along a hedge row, brought a heavy fire to bear upon the enemy immediately below, whilst the left section engaged the force upon the Winterberg, across the gully.

The 7th Company, upon the Drill-ground Hill was meanwhile confronted by an entire brigade of six battalions, with a second brigade close support. Troops were also observed descending the Rotherberg, from which a battery had already opened fire. The picquet had extended along the crest to the left of the road at the first alarm, and under the lofty poplars that fringed the hill in rear many of the inhabitants of Saarbrucken watched the brilliant spectacle of the French attack. So rapid was the advance that, when the support reached the heights, it came at once under fire. 40 men reinforced the picquet, and extended on the drill-ground; but the enemy had still 1,200 yards to traverse ere he reached the ridge and the Fusiliers made no attempt to reply to his brisk

The 5th Company of the Prussian 40th Fusiliers withdraws from the Reppertsberg (Ruppersberg)

but useless musketry. The remainder of the company was posted (under cover of the reverse slope), on the high road.

The hostile skirmishers had crossed the hollow at the foot of the hill, and their leading files were already climbing the terraced slopes, when a sudden burst of musketry was heard to the right rear. A force was endeavouring to turn the ridge from the Saarbrucken Forest, and had attacked the picquet on the viaduct. Almost at the same moment the Reppertsberg was abandoned. The 5th Company, enfiladed from the Winterberg, had been compelled to withdraw.

Although his left was now exposed, his right menaced, and overwhelming numbers were pressing heavily against his front, the leader of the 7th Company was determined to secure an unmolested retreat.

His men were instructed to reserve their fire until the enemy approached within 300 yards. Notwithstanding the storm of musketry to which they were exposed, the order was carried out with precision and effect.

The French advance was roughly checked. Their sharp-shooters halted and sought cover on the hillside.

The 5th Company had now reached the road below the ridge, the skirmishing section, on the crest above, holding back the pursuers with a steady fire, and even menacing by forward rushes the foremost groups.

In front of the 7th, the crowd of hostile riflemen rapidly increased, gathering strength for an onward rush; the musketry swelled to a heavier roar, but not until the whole of the 5th Company had reached the bridge was the order given to retire.

Covered by the heavy independent fire of the picquet, the support dashed down the further slope in two separate columns, and was followed in a few minutes by the last defenders of the ridge.

As the dark blue uniforms and spiked helmets vanished in clouds of smoke, the French infantry advanced on all sides, but with cautious movements, and when their loud *vivas* announced that the heights were won, the Fusiliers had almost gained the bridge. As the circle of fire closed round them and annihilation seemed inevitable, they had adroitly slipped away, gauging the moment to a nicety, and leaving but seven severely wounded men in the enemy's hands.

The barricades across the bridges were held by the 3rd Battalion of the 40th, which had been called up from Rachspfuhl at 11 o'clock.

Saarbrucken was now evacuated, but the French made no attempt to follow up their success, or to seize the town. Only a few scouts approached the bridges.

Two field batteries and one of mitrailleuses were then brought up to the ridge, and engaged the four pieces posted above Malstatt at a range of 2,200 yards. The duel was unequal, but by frequent changes of position the Prussian battery escaped destruction, and not until guns of a heavier calibre opened fire from the Reppertsberg was it driven to seek shelter in the Kollerthaler Forest.

Whilst this action was in progress and shells were bursting on the drill-ground, Napoleon and the little Prince Imperial ascended the ridge and rode forward to the poplars. Beneath their feet lay the river and the towns, and beyond, the long green hill with the darker forest creeping down its slopes. Save the guns near Rachspfuhl there was no appearance of the enemy, for the Fusiliers were hidden by the buildings; but whether suspicious that the woods beyond were full of men and that the retreat of the garrison was merely a ruse to draw them into an unequal conflict beyond the Saar, or whether still unready for a decisive advance, the French, although, so easily victorious, showed no disposition either to renew the fight or to attempt the passage of the river. They seemed, on the, contrary, apprehensive of attack, for the sappers were soon busy on the ridge, and by sunset a long series of shelter-trenches and epaulments crowned the northern crest. The towns were left unoccupied, and not a single patrol attempted to explore the country beyond St. Johann; a striking contrast to the activity of the late possessors of Saarbrucken.

At 2 o'clock, von Gneisenau ordered a general retreat upon Rachspfuhl. This was effected with little loss, although the retiring troops were assailed by artillery and mitrailleuses.

At this new position assembled 11 companies of the 40th and the company of the 69th from the Burbach Foundry. The latter had taken but little part in the action, but it had watched the right flank closely. The picquet on the viaduct had been slightly engaged, and a detached party had frustrated an attempt of the enemy's scouts to cross the river from Gersweiler.

From Rachspfuhl, the enemy's movements were plainly visible; but patrols were, nevertheless, sent out in every direction.

At 6 o'clock, French scouts were discovered by one of these in St. Johann, and another reported that a strong force was advancing from Gersweiler (part of Bazaine's Corps d'Armée). Fearing that his position might be turned from that point, von Gneisenau determined to withdraw. The battalion of the 69th from Volklingen and the Uhlans from Dudweiler had now come in. The Hallberg force was instructed to rejoin as soon as possible, and the remainder retired by the Lebach Road.[5]

After a march of 7 miles, the 2nd Battalion of the 29th Regiment, a squadron and a battery, were found at Guichenbach. The 29th was ordered to furnish the outposts, and the remainder bivouacked at Hilsbach, a mile in rear. The Hallberg detachment fell back on Dudweiler, and did not reach the rendezvous till the following morning.

During the afternoon, notwithstanding the retreat of the Prussians from the town, the French remained inactive. The whole of the 2nd Corps, with the exception of the cavalry and reserve artillery, encamped in the St. Arnual valley. As for the part played by the flanking divisions, that of Bazaine's Corps had engaged, with a strong body of infantry and 4 guns, a Prussian company holding the bridge at Volklingen, but made no serious attack: that of the 5th Corps advanced a force of cavalry, and occupied a village, some 7 miles north of Saarguemund.

The Prussian battery expended during the engagement 127 rounds, the 2nd Battalion 40th, 12,000 cartridges, about 12 per rifle.

The losses on either side were insignificant.

	Prussians			French		
	Officers	Men	Total	Officers	Men	Total
Killed	–	8	8	2	8	10
Wounded	4	64	68	4	72	76
Missing	–	7	7	–	–	–
	4	79	83	6	80	86

The French casualties appear exceedingly few in proportion to the ammunition used and the open ground over which they advanced, but the needle gun was ineffective over 600 yards, within which range few of their skirmishers approached. Moreover, the Prussian fire was maintained with a view of showing a bold front and making an appearance of strength, and not with any serious purpose of resistance. So skilfully was this accomplished, and so confident the attitude of the Fusiliers, that General Frossard, as well as his troops, believed that they had been opposed by a considerable force.

The English officer already quoted declared the commander's "project of display" was so thoroughly understood, and so adroitly carried out by his subordinates, that every company appeared a battalion at least. He was impressed with the steady shooting of the 40th. In spite of the numbers that threatened to overwhelm them, the men were cool and well in hand.

It would scarcely have been a matter of wonder had the contrary been the case, for many were young soldiers of but nine months' service, and one half the fighting strength had only rejoined the colours within the week. The reader also can scarcely fail to notice the skilful manner in which the withdrawal from the ridge was executed, each picquet holding its ground until its flanks were threatened, but avoiding unnecessary loss, and taking care to cover the retreat of the companies that had already fallen back. Although separated by wide intervals, the companies worked in exact combination, co-operating with the precision of a field-day.

At 6 o'clock, von Gneisenau had held his ground long enough to prevent the French pushing forward their reconaissances into the Kollerthaler Forest; he had discovered all

5 See map page 97.

he could of their intentions, he had been ordered to fall back, and the longer maintenance of his position could serve no useful purpose.

Although up to this time he had acted with judgment and resolution, it appears, reading between the lines of the Staff History, that he now committed a mistake.

On his arrival at Hilsbach, he found there Lieut.-General von Barnekow, commanding the 16th Infantry Division, to which the 40th belonged, who immediately made arrangements for regaining touch of the enemy. The capture of Saarbrucken appeared to point to the immediate advance of the French, and it was a matter of the greatest moment that early and full information of such a movement should be given to Royal Head-Quarters and the commanders of the armies. By removing the whole of his force, cavalry included, to Hilsbach, von Gneisenau had relinquished all chance of fathoming the enemy's intentions. We learn that by the next morning patrols had been sent out towards Dudweiler, Volklingen, and St. Johann, and that the outposts were pushed forward so as to watch the outskirts of the Kollerthaler Forest.

The French troops actually present at the engagement were four brigades of the 2nd Corps d'Armée, 18 battalions, and 4 batteries, under General Frossard. The remainder, (2 brigades and 10 batteries) of the 2nd Corps, as well as 3 divisions of the 3rd Corps, were held in reserve, and the greater part did not leave their camps.

On the intelligence being received that the French were advancing, the rolling stock was removed from St. Johann, and the railroad broken up (temporarily) in rear.

CHAPTER IV
THE FRENCH DISPOSITIONS FROM AUGUST 3RD TO AUGUST 6TH

The reconnaissance in force of August 2nd, announced in Paris as a brilliant victory, stilled for a time the impatience of the French people, but failed altogether to clear up the situation at the front. No attempt was made to follow the garrison of Saarbrucken as it retreated; and although the bridges over the Saar were in Frossard's hands, and his cavalry had free access to the northern bank, not one of his troopers crossed the river.

During the engagement, two strong detachments of the 5th Corps d'Armée had explored the roads leading north and north-east from Saarguemund; but their advance had been limited to seven miles, and, consequently, although one of them fell in with some Prussian dragoons, it is not surprising that no information was obtained as to the whereabouts of the enemy's main body.

By the morning of the 3rd of August, the strength of the German cavalry along the front had visibly increased, and from Trêves to Bliescastel, along the whole line, their activity was unceasing.

On the march and in their bivouacs, the French divisions were alarmed by the appearance of hostile scouts. By day and night, through the streets of every frontier village, rang the hoof-strokes of patrols; on every country road were to be seen the lances of the Uhlan; each commanding eminence was crowned by a vedette; and on the skirts of the French reconnoitring parties, imposing bodies of cavalry and infantry combined, single horsemen were often to be observed, who, when pursuit was threatened, disappeared in the forests. Each one of these troopers had something to report; and telegram after telegram flashed along the wires to the Royal Head-Quarters at Mayence, each containing no more than a scrap of information, but which, pieced together by von Moltke's Staff, gave an accurate picture of the French dispositions. And so the great strategist, by means of those solitary horsemen, kept his fingers on the enemy's pulse, watched his marches and his counter marches, his earth-works rising rapidly on the Saarbrucken Ridge, noted the indecision of his movements, the inactivity of his cavalry, the dissemination of his divisions, and waited imperturbably for the moment that would see the concentration of the German host completed.

Since von Gneisenau's rear-guard had vanished in the Kollerthaler Forest, not a single Prussian infantry soldier had come within the observation of the French outposts; but so constant was the going and coming of the horsemen, so unexpectedly did they appear at points that were miles within the frontier, that an uneasy feeling of insecurity spread through the French encampments. With what seems almost a foreboding of Weissenburg and Spicheren, the surrounding woods were regarded as something sinister; and when night had fallen, the imagination of the sentries peopled them with enemies, and heard within their sombre depths the sound of the Prussian trumpets and the tramp of marching men. The Emperor and his advisers, shrinking in irresolution before the veil which their own ineptitude had drawn between the frontier and the Rhine, shared the apprehensions of the soldiery. Attack was expected now from this quarter and now from that. Each trifling telegram was productive of the greatest excitement, and orders and counter-orders, following in rapid succession, harassed and demoralized the troops. Ignorant of the enemy's dispositions, swayed by every alarming rumour or by hopes based on insufficient information and false inferences, Napoleon was incapable of adopting any resolute plan of combination either for attack or defence.

It had been decided that L'Admirault's Corps from Boulay was to reconnoitre towards Saarlouis on the 4th. On the 3rd, however, intelligence was received from the Commissary of Police at Thionville that 40,000 Prussians had passed through Trêves and were marching on either Saarlouis or Thionville. L'Admirault was immediately informed that the latter fortress was threatened, but the reconnaissance, instead of being strengthened and ordered to embrace the Thionville district, was countermanded. Frossard was directed to fall back upon St. Avold if the Prussians appeared in greater force than reported. Marshal Bazaine, who was to have the command in case of attack, joined the 4th Corps at Boulay, and drew back Montaudon's division from Homburg to St. Avold; whilst Le Boeuf actually conceived the idea that, in order to protect Saarlouis, 40,000 Prussians, unsupported, were about to cross the Saar and to assume the offensive. Although the Chief of the Staff indulged in cheerful speculations as to the result of such an operation, he does not appear to have long cherished hopes of its execution, and the Imperial Guard was the victim of his premature conclusions. It was first ordered to leave Metz; then to remain in its bivouacs; then to advance to Volmerange, west of Boulay, and whilst this movement was in progress, to return once more to Metz.

Not many hours after Le Boeuf had confided to the leaders of the Corps d'Armée his inference based on the support of the Commissary of Police, and preparations had been made to receive the isolated band of Prussians with a far superior force at Boulay, fresh intelligence was received by the Imperial Staff. The alarm was now for the other flank. Von Steinmetz's Army, it was reported, was concentrated between Saarbrucken and Zweibrucken, supported by a corps of the Second Army, with the intention of marching on Nancy, south of Metz.

Two divisions of the 5th Corps were thereupon ordered to Bitsche; the Guard to Courcelles, 13 miles in rear of St. Avold, and a division of the 3rd Corps to Puttelange, covering the Saarguemund-Nancy road.

But the sun had not set before more startling and more trustworthy tidings came to hand. A French division, the outpost of McMahon's Army in Alsace, had been surprised and defeated by a far superior force at Weissenburg.

For the third time in twenty-four hours Napoleon changed his plans.

The whole of the 5th Corps was at once ordered to concentrate at Bitsche, and a division of the 3rd was despatched to Saarguemund. There was now no doubt that both wings of the long French line were seriously threatened, and the movement of the Prussians against the right wing should have enlightened the leaders to the fact that the enemy had already assumed the offensive.

Napoleon and his Staff at least realized that action of some kind was necessary. During the 5th of August, the Army of the Rhine was divided into two portions, the troops in Alsace being placed under McMahon, those in Lorraine under Bazaine; the

Guard being retained at the disposal of the Emperor. But the day passed without any instructions being issued, and it was not till the morning of the 6th that a despatch was addressed to Bazaine containing instructions for a junction with McMahon by the Saarguemund Bitsche road.

The orders for the 7th of August were as follows:

The 2nd Corps to Bitsche.
The 3rd to Saarguemund.
The 4th to Haut-Homburg.
The Guard to St. Avold.

Now the enemy's cavalry had already appeared at various points in the neighbourhood of the proposed line of march; and unless Napoleon had rejected as utterly untrustworthy the intelligence of the concentration of Prussian troops near Saarlouis and Zweibrucken, he must have been aware that the operation he was about to undertake was that most dangerous of operations, a flank march across the enemy's front. Moreover, ignorant as he was of the whereabouts of the German main-body, there was still sufficient evidence to show that large forces were present near the frontier; and, under the circumstances, he was bound to act with the utmost speed and resolution. Yet, as we have seen, it was not until the night of the 5th that he made up his mind to a definite design, that of combining with McMahon; and even then, the movement was not ordered to commence until the morning of the 7th, twenty-four hours later. An inferior force has, generally speaking, but one chance of success, that is, being concentrated itself and possessing early intelligence, to act against the extremity of the enemy's line or an isolated portion of his force. The less information, the greater the necessity for concentration. For an inferior force to attempt to cover several points of passage, is but to court destruction. To concentrate in a central position is the only hope; and had Napoleon, when the affair at Saarbrucken failed to reveal the Prussian dispositions, brought up his whole left wing to the neighbourhood of St. Avold, ready either for attack or defence as opportunity offered, or if necessary for retreat, the campaign would have probably opened in a less unfavourable manner.

There is this excuse for his delay. Part of the reserves were still *en route* to join their regiments at the front, and a sudden change in position would have thrown the arrangements for their transport and disentraining still further out of gear; moreover, like the rest of the world, he had as yet scarcely realized the possibility of an army more than 400,000 strong being mobilized and making several forward marches in the space of three weeks.

It is noteworthy, as betraying what seems almost absolute ignorance of the ordinary precautions of war, that, on the 5th and 6th of August, no orders were given by strong reconnaisances to discover whether the enemy's infantry were in a position to interfere with the flank march along the Saarguemund-Bitsche road. On the 7th of August, the day the march was to have begun, the foremost corps of the Second German Army was within ten miles of Bitsche.

Never was the helplessness of a general without information as to his enemy more strikingly illustrated; never was there a more conspicuous absence of activity and energy in the leaders of an army; never a more complete disdain of the lessons of military history as to the use of cavalry.

Général de Division Frossard, commander of the French II Corps (Rousset/*Histoire*)

We may also remark that, on the 5th of August, even Bazaine was left in ignorance of the Emperor's intentions; and that, on the 6th, none of the subordinate generals knew that the flank march was contemplated. When an army is not concentrated, or when the Commander-in-Chief is not in close communication, by telegraph or otherwise, with each of the different fractions, it is indispensable that he should give his subordinates a general idea of his intentions; and to do this he must have come to some decision as to what his actions will be in case the enemy assumes the offensive. On the 5th August, after the outpost of his right wing had been overthrown in Alsace, Napoleon should have instructed Frossard, commanding the outpost of the left wing, as to his conduct in case he was attacked. With such a warning as Weissenburg, it is inconceivable that he should have neglected to do so.

The withdrawal of Montaudon's Division from Homburg, close behind Forbach, on the 4th, and of a brigade of the 5th Corps from Grossbliederstroff to Saarguemund on the same day, so far uncovered the flanks of the 2nd Corps on the Saarbrucken Ridge, that Frossard, early on the 5th, considered it necessary to draw back a brigade of his 1st Division to Forbach and one of the 3rd Division to Spicheren. When the tidings of Weissenburg were received, even these dispositions appeared inadequate for security. The appearance of hostile patrols on front and flank, the reports of spies, and rumours in the town, convinced him that the Kollerthaler Forest concealed a Prussian army. Notwithstanding that his position was protected by the Saar, and that it covered the principal passage of that river, he suggested to Marshal Le Boeuf that he should be allowed to retire from the Saarbrucken Ridge.

"The Emperor has decided," was the reply, "that to-morrow morning, you are to withdraw your Head-Quarters to Forbach, leaving you to concentrate your divisions in such a manner that you may be able to draw back your Head-Quarters to St. Avold, immediately you receive an order from the Emperor to do so."

This despatch, be it noted, said no word as to what Frossard was to do in case he was attacked, and left it open to him to believe that he was bound to maintain his position at Forbach until he received explicit instructions to retreat. Had Le Boeuf added, "it is the Emperor's intention to join McMahon by the Saarguemund-Bitsche road"; or, "if you are attacked before you receive the order to retire, hold your ground and you will be supported by Bazaine"; or, "fall back slowly, retarding the enemy as much as possible, on Calenbronn" (a strong position, previously reconnoitred), the battle of the 6th would have been less disastrous.

On receiving the Emperor's approval of his proposition, Frossard resolved to anticipate matters by a few hours, and withdraw his divisions the same evening, leaving no rear guard whatever on the Saarbrucken Ridge. A large magazine had been established at Forbach, but no attempt was made to commence the removal of the supplies and matériel; a measure which Le Boeuf's telegram, speaking as it did of a further retreat upon St. Avold, fully justified. Moreover, the bridges over the Saar were left intact. Had they been destroyed the enemy's advance would certainly have been delayed; and the demolition of the viaduct, by rendering the railway useless for many days, would, as it turned out, have been of the utmost value to the French.

From the date of the decree assigning the command of the left wing of the Army of the Rhine to Bazaine, the Marshal shares the responsibility of the mishaps along the Saar. At the same time, it must be remarked that this delegation of authority bore the same halting and indecisive character as the rest of Napoleon's measures. McMahon and his colleague were only independent "in respect of military operations," terms vague enough to give rise to much misunderstanding. No special staffs were assigned to them, and both continued in command of their own Corps d'Armée.

Before this arrangement was come to, the troops of the left wing, under the instructions, or with the approval of the Emperor, had assumed the following positions:

2nd Corps	1st Division	Stiring Wendel& Forbach
	2nd Division	Oetingen
	3rd Division	Spicheren Heights
3rd Corps	1st Division	Saarguemund
	2nd Division	Puttelange
	3rd Division	Marienthal
	4th Division }	
	Cavalry }	St. Avold

4th Corps	1st Division	Teterchen
	2nd Division	Coum
	3rd Division	Ham-sous-Varberg
	4th Division	Boulay
	Cavalry	
Guard		Courcelles
3rd Cavalry Division		Faulquemont

The 5th Corps had been transferred to McMahon's command, but a brigade had been left at Saarguemund, as convoy to the baggage-train.

On the 5th of August an important reconnaissance was carried out by General L'Admirault, commanding 4th Corps d'Armée. His 3rd Division moved in the morning in the direction of Felsberg, where the fortress of Saarlouis came under observation. No hostile troops, save a few vedettes, were to be seen; and the country people declared that the fortress held but a small garrison, and that they had no knowledge of any considerable gathering of troops in the vicinity.

Bazaine, on receipt of this information, ordered L'Admirault to draw still closer to St. Avold, and to occupy Boucheporn and Boulay with two of his divisions on the 6th. His apprehensions of attack from Saarlouis were not, however, altogether dissipated, for the remaining division of the 4th Corps was still retained at Teterchen on the extreme left.

We may notice that on the morning of the 5th, the whole of the 2nd, 3rd, and 4th Corps were within 20 miles of Spicheren, the Guard at Courcelles being distant 28 miles; and that the whole force was within a day's march of the strong defensive line, of which Calenbronn was the centre.[1]

The total strength of these troops did not exceed 130,000 men.

1 See map page 97.

CHAPTER V
THE GERMAN ADVANCE TO THE FRONTIER

On the 29th of July, the greater part of the three Field Armies had already reached the Rhine:

The First Army, Coblenz.

The Second Army, Mayence and Mannheim.

The Third Army, Landau and Carlsruhe.

During the day, the First Army, which had already commenced its march, received orders, instead of occupying the line Saarlouis-Merzig, its original destination, to halt behind the line Wadern-Saarburg in order that, if the enemy be advanced, it might not be exposed to an isolated position. The arrival of Napoleon at Metz, and possibly intelligence of the Council of War summoned to meet him at St. Avold, was, in all probability, the origin of this change of purpose. The two Army Corps which formed the bulk of von Steinmetz's command, were, when these fresh instructions reached them, still north of the Moselle; the 3rd Cavalry Division had not yet come up, but the 7th Uhlans and the 9th Hussars, two divisional regiments belonging to VIII Army Corps, were watching the front between Trêves and Saarbrucken.

The Second Army, not yet entirely assembled, was at the same time ordered to concentrate on the line Alsenz-Grunstadt, six-and-twenty miles in advance of Mayence, and on the German side of the Haardt Mountains. On the 30th, the 5th and 6th Cavalry Divisions joined Prince Frederick Charles. These 8,400 horsemen were immediately despatched towards the frontier between Saarbrucken and Bitsche, with instructions to establish themselves a short day's march on this side of the frontier, and from thence to carry out constant enterprises against the enemy, finding and keeping touch with him. Two divisions of infantry were to follow in support.

The advance of the Second Army from the Rhine to the Saar, a distance of more than 80 miles, was by no means a simple operation. Between the line Alsenz-Grunstadt to the north east, and Neunkirchen-Zweibrucken to the south-west, and directly across the path of the troops, rises the Haardt, a spur of the Vosges, some 40 miles in breadth. Several good roads cross the first half of this rugged and forest-clad chain. Two on the right were assigned to the III and X Army Corps respectively; but the remainder, traversed by the IX, XII, IV Army Corps, and the Guard, merged into one at Kaiserslautern, halfway through the hills, and so continued as far as Homburg, three-and-twenty miles to the front. Four corps, therefore, had to make the passage of this long defile in succession: Moreover, the possibility had to be kept in view that the French might advance rapidly from Forbach, and the Prussians be thrown upon the defensive.

Now, although the mountains are of no great height, yet it was extremely difficult for the army, after leaving the line Alsenz-Grunstadt, to deploy for battle until the line Neunkirchen-Zweibrucken was reached, more than 40 miles to the front; and even then,

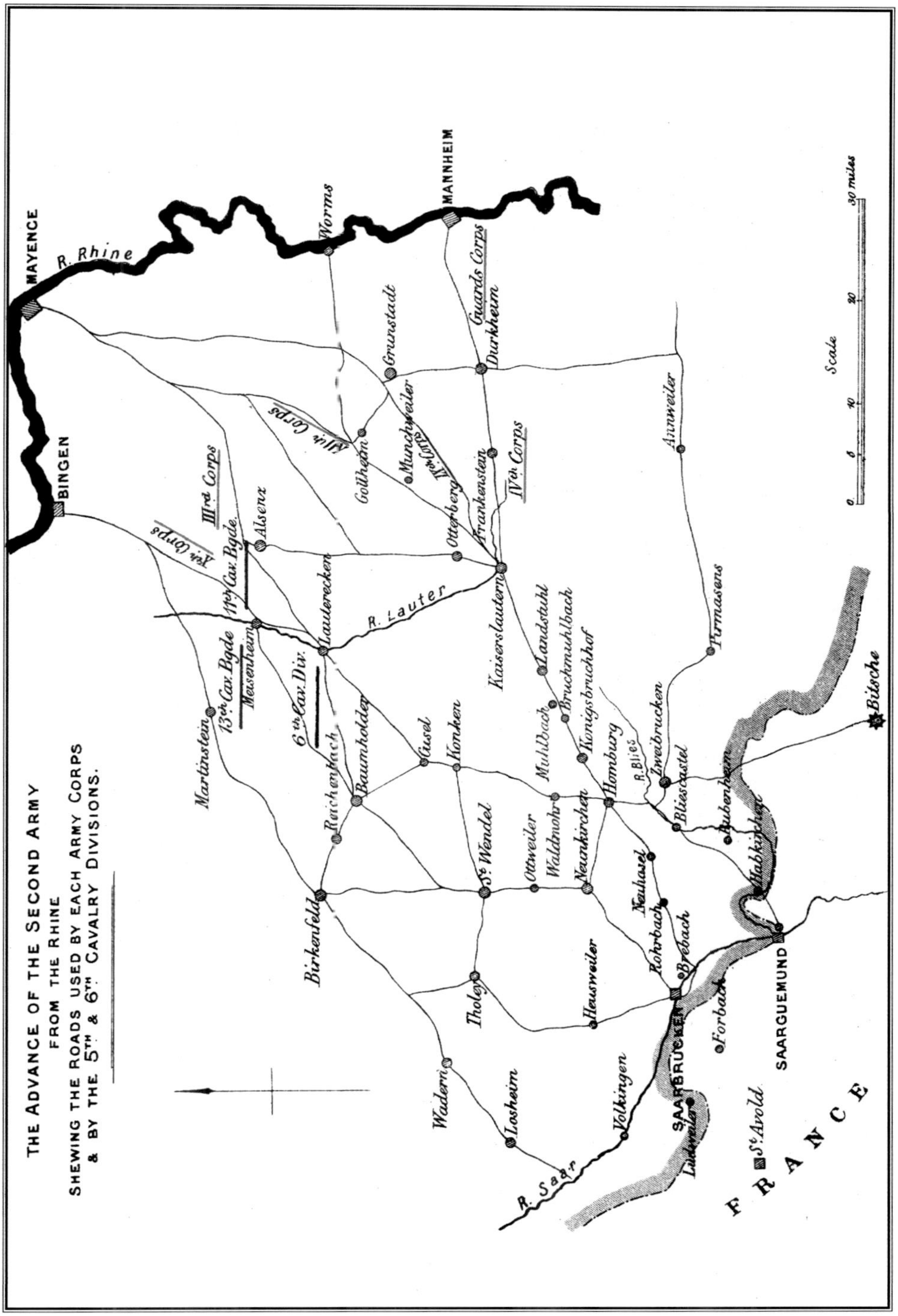

The advance of the Second Army from the Rhine

to deploy the four corps, following one another as far as Homburg on a single road, would be a work of time.

But the line Neunkirchen-Zweibrucken, on the far side of the hills, was but 20 miles distant from the French camps at Forbach and Saarguemund. It was evident, therefore that the Second Army could not advance from Alsenz-Grunstadt until the intentions of the French were ascertained; and further, that when the movement was once begun, it would have to be carried out with the utmost rapidity. Had the column – more than 120,000 strong – been attacked in the act of disengaging for the defile, a great disaster would probably have been the result.

The operations of the First and Third Armies were designed to facilitate the movement. The First, occupying the line Wadern-Losheim, was in a position to threaten the flank of the French, should they cross the Saar between Saarlouis and Saarguemund, in a manner they could not afford to despise; whilst the Third was to move immediately, in greatly superior numbers, upon the left wing of the enemy in Alsace – an operation which could not fail to have a great effect upon his plans.

On the 1st of August the III and IV Corps (Second Army), were pushed forward slightly in front of either flank of the line. Alsenz-Grunstadt, the former supporting the cavalry of the right wing and centre, which was about 15 miles to the front at Meisenheim, with the 5th Division; the latter, sending the 8th Division to join the cavalry of the right wing at Kaiserslautern.

On the evening of the 2nd, the 5th Division reached Offenbach, the 8th still occupied Kaiserslautern. Only the IX Corps, and the remaining divisions of the III and IV Army Corps had as yet arrived on the line Alsenz-Grunstadt. The cavalry had moved on to the line Tholey-Muhlbach, 20 miles to the front, where they had taken up connection with the First and Third Armies on the right and left flanks respectively. As early as the 31st, Prince Frederick Charles had been warned that, on and after the 2nd, the disentraining stations for those troops who had not already assembled, would be Birkenfeld and Kaiserslautern, both points more than 20 miles in advance of Alsenz-Grunstadt. They were already protected in some measure by the cavalry, by the two infantry divisions which had moved into the hills to support the horsemen, and by the First Army, which had occupied the line Wadern-Losheim on the 2nd; but in order to ensure their complete security, the commander of the Second Army decided to push forward the whole of III and IV Army Corps to Baumholder and Kaiserslautern, with advanced guards still further to the front. Both corps had received orders to reach the places specified on the 3rd.

During the 2nd, Prince Frederick Charles reported the tenor of these orders to von Moltke. The latter, thereupon, issued further directions, to the effect, that in the event of the enemy having already advanced from Saarbrucken and Saarguemund, the Third Army Corps was to remain at Meisenheim, the Fourth at Kaiserslautern. If, on the other hand, the enemy made no attempt to push forward, then the Prince's orders for the 3rd of August were to hold good; with the exception that the Fourth Corps was to move, on the 4th, to Landstuhl, ten miles to the front. No further movement of these two corps, forming advanced guards for either wing, was to take place until the remaining corps had closed up to within half-a-day's march.

Nothing was yet known of the engagement at Saarbrucken, and in consequence the following positions were taken up on the 3rd of August:

Lieutenant-General Baron Rheinbaben, commander of the German 5th Cavalry Division (Rousset/*Histoire*)

III A.C.	{ 5th Infantry Division	Konken
	{ 6th Infantry Division	Baumholder
IV A.C.	{ 8th Infantry Division	Bruchmuhlbach
	{ 7th Infantry Division	Kaiserslautern

Remainder either on, or in rear of, the Alsenz-Grunstadt position.

5th and 6th Cavalry Divisions, 15 miles in front of Konken and Bruchmuhlbach, with patrols on the Blies and Saar.

THE NEWS OF THE ACTION OF SAARBRUCKEN, AND MEASURES ADOPTED IN CONSEQUENCE

But during the day came the news that the French had advanced from Forbach and Saarguemund, and had seized the Saarbrucken Heights.[1] Prince Frederick Charles proposed, if the enemy continued his forward movement, to concentrate the Second Army on the line Alsenz-Grunstadt, slowly withdrawing the two Army Corps already pushed into the Haardt.

Very soon, however, it became evident that the attack on Saarbrucken was not being followed up. The cavalry, in accordance with their instructions, had already gained touch of the enemy, and their commander, General von Rheinbaben sent in the following information:

(1) A detachment of the enemy, consisting of all arms, in the course of the forenoon of the 2nd of August, had advanced as far as Rubenheim (5 miles south of Bliescastel),

1 It is curious that this news did not arrive till the 3rd. The telegraph was in working order.

and come into contact with patrols of the 5th Dragoons, but had retired in the evening across the frontier.

(2) A squadron of the 3rd Uhlans had moved, on the 3rd, *via* Brebach, upon St. Johann. A troop forced its way into the town, and captured seven French infantry-men.

(3 On the same day, a squadron of the 6th Cuirassiers also advanced towards St. Johann, and learnt that the enemy had been seen in Saarbrucken, but had not actually occupied the place.

(4) Two squadrons of the 3rd Hussars and 15th Uhlans pushed forward in the direction of the lower Blies, and were not fired upon until they arrived within five miles of Saarguemund.

Von Moltke thereupon came to the conclusion that the French, although they had a considerable force on the Saar and Blies, had no immediate intention of undertaking a serious offensive movement, and, on the evening of the 3rd, he sent the following telegram to Prince Frederick Charles:

> Wavering advance of the French leads us to anticipate that the Second Army can be deployed on the 6th instant, in front of the belt of forest near Kaiserslautern.
>
> The First Army is drawn forward to-morrow (August 4th), upon Tholey. Both armies should aim at a joint co-operation in battle. If rapid advance of enemy cannot be checked, concentration of the Second Army behind the Lauter, the First Army upon Baumholder.
>
> The Third Army crosses the frontier to-morrow at Weissenburg.
>
> A general offensive is proposed.

The line "in front of the belt of forest near Kaiserslautern," referred to in the first paragraph, was, as we learn from the orders issued by Prince Frederick Charles, that of Neunkirchen-Zweibrucken.

Should the enemy rapidly advance whilst the deployment of the Second Army was still in progress, the flank position of the First Army and the offensive movement of the Third were relied upon to check him. Should these fail, he was to be held in check in the mountain passes by the foremost detachments of the Second Army until the two leading Army Corps could take up a suitable position.

On the 3rd of August, the whole combatant force of the Second Army and the principal parts of the train were assembled; and from the 4th, although four of the Army Corps had for the present to obtain waggons for the second line of train by requisition, Prince Frederick Charles' troops were in complete readiness for active operations.

THE FIRST ARMY

Before we consider the manner in which the passage of the Haardt Mountains was effected by the Second Army, it will be well to relate the movements of the First Army up to the 3rd of August.

The VIII Corps, forming the left wing of von Steinmetz's command, and crossing the Moselle at Berncastel, reached the neighbourhood of Wadern and Birkenfeld on the 31st.

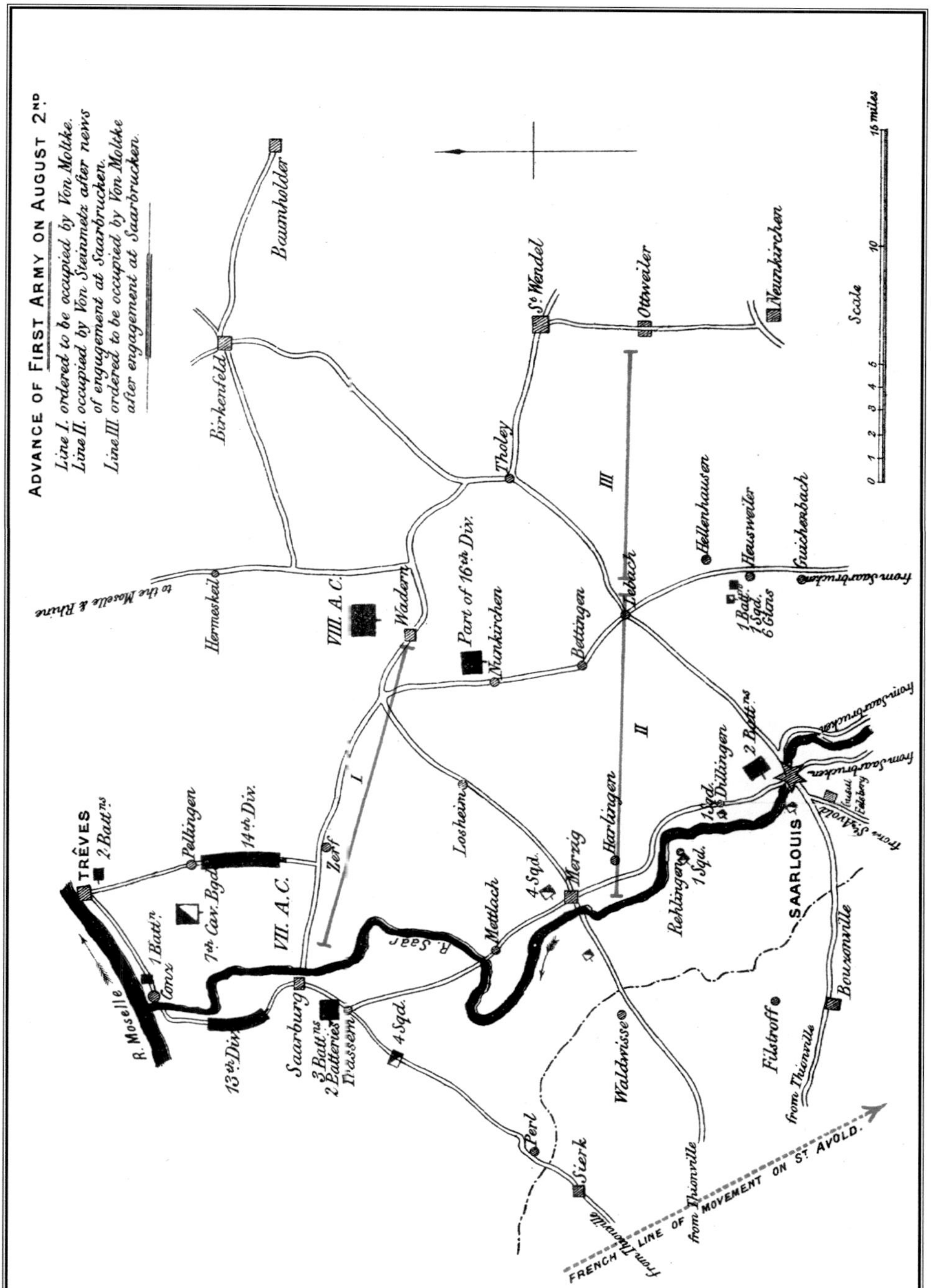

The advance of the First Army from Trêves

The VII Corps, leaving the Rhine on the same day as the VIII, marched on Trêves, within 20 miles of the frontier. Assembling there on the 30th, the vanguard, consisting of 4 battalions, 4 squadrons, and 2 batteries, pushed forward to Saarburg and Conz.

On the 2nd August the VII Corps wheeled to the left, and moved on Losheim, marching on either bank of the Saar. The line of advance was parallel to the French frontier, and threatened from Thionville and Sierck, 12 and 24 miles distant. Two roads were available, the one, used by the 13th Division, on the French bank of the Saar, crossing at Saarburg; the other, used by the 14th Division, on the German bank. Much precaution was therefore essential to cover this flank march, but it may be premised that the 9th and 7th Uhlans were already distributed in the river towns, and the efficient service of their patrols ensured early warning of danger. Moreover, their scouts had discovered that the enemy was also moving in an easterly direction from Thionville on St. Avold, that is, that he was already moving on a line parallel to the roads by which the VII Corps was to advance and in the same direction, and was therefore in no condition to interfere with the operation.

The VIII Corps having reached Wadern on the night of the 1st of August, was now in a position to support the VII, and the country was favourable for defence.

Before the march commenced, the 7th Cavalry Brigade (3rd Cavalry Division), moved out 5 miles south of Trêves. The advanced guard of the 13th Division occupied Trassem on the Thionville Road, and threw out cavalry to watch the frontier. A battalion was detailed to hold the bridge at Conz. Under cover of this screen, the division marched to Saarburg, 12 miles distant from Trêves, and there crossed the river.

The 14th Division, which, on the night of the 1st had bivouacked south of Bittburg, marched by the road on the right bank of the Saar to Zerf, leaving two battalions to garrison Trêves.

In rear of the two divisions the corps artillery reached Pellingen, but the trains still remained at Schweich, on the left bank of the Moselle. On the 3rd, the 13th Division advanced to Merzig. The advanced guard reached Haarlingen. A battalion on the left bank secured the flank, and cavalry watched the frontier between Saarburg and Sierck. The flanking detachment crossed the river at Mettlach, and removed a bridge which had been constructed there. The battalion at Conz was drawn forward to Saarburg.

The 14th Division marched southward to beyond Losheim, and drew in the two battalions from Trêves.

The 3rd Cavalry Division, 6th and 7th Brigades, took up its quarters between Losheim and Lebach.

The Corps Artillery reached Losheim. The trains remained at Schweich.

THE NEWS OF SAARBRUCKEN, AND MEASURES PROPOSED IN CONSEQUENCE BY VON STEINMETZ

The VIII Corps which had arrived at Wadern, its original destination, on the evening of the 1st, had meanwhile, in consequence of the news of the engagement at Saarbrucken, pushed the 16th Division as far as Heusweiler, 15 miles south of Wadern, and the 15th to Lebach, 5 miles in rear.

This change of position, approved by von Steinmetz, was initiated by General von Goeben, commanding the VIII Corps; and was dictated by the expectation of the advance of the enemy from Saarbrucken, and the determination to retard by a flank

General von Steinmetz, commander of the German First Army (Rousset/*Histoire*)

attack any attempt on his part to move against the Second Army. On the 3rd of August, therefore, the First Army occupied the line Lebach-Merzig; the 3rd and 5th Cavalry Divisions covering the front, the Head-Quarters of the former being at Heusweiler.

The Corps Artillery was at Lebach; trains at Wadern.

Now, according to the reports received from the cavalry patrolling the frontier, it might with certainty be assumed that the French were in process of concentrating round St. Avold. Although hostile troops had been observed between Waldwisse and Filstroff, on the 1st of August, the Prussian patrols had come across no large bodies of troops north of the Saarlouis-Bouzonville Road since that date. The commandant of the fortress of Saarlouis reported the presence of considerable bodies of troops in the frontier district near the fortress; and it was also said that 40,000 men, under Marshal Bazaine, were assembled round Boulay, and that there were large forces at Saarbrucken. The enemy had not, however, made any attempt as yet to cross the river. Even the telegraphic communication between St. Johann and the stations in rear was carried on without interruption; and from the inhabitants of the town the Germans received constant intelligence of the enemy's attitude at Saarbrucken. From these reports von Steinmetz inferred that the French main-body was about to move forward against the Second Army. He resolved, therefore, to draw as large a portion of the enemy's force as possible upon himself, and thus facilitate the projected movement of the Second Army through the mountains, and its subsequent deployment.

With this view, he proposed advancing on the 4th of August into the line Saarlouis-Hellenhausen, and thence, on the following day, despatching strong reconnaissances up the Bouzonville, Boulay, and St Avold Roads.

General von Goeben, commander of the German VIII Corps (Rousset/*Histoire*)

Now, as we already know, the 4th was the day fixed by the Royal Head-Quarters for the Second Army to commence the passage of the Haardt, and this operation could not be completed under three days, that is, not until the evening of the 6th.

The position of the First Army, on the line Lebach-Merzig was already somewhat precarious. It was completely isolated, and support could not be expected from the Second Army until the 7th. The line Saarlouis-Hellenhausen, a day's march nearer the frontier, was still more exposed, and calculated to provoke attack.

But von Moltke intended that neither the Second, much less the weaker First Army, should be exposed singly to a collision with the main forces of the enemy; and, when he authorized the advance of Prince Frederick Charles' troops, he was careful to provide against such a contingency.

THE MEASURES ORDERED BY VON MOLTKE

As von Steinmetz, on the evening of the 3rd, was on the point of issuing his orders for the occupation of the line Saarlouis-Hellenhausen, he received the following telegram from the Royal Head-Quarters:

> Wavering advance of the French leads us to anticipate that the Second Army can be assembled in front of the belt of forest near Kaiserslautern. If rapid advance of the enemy cannot be checked, concentration of the Second Army behind the Lauter.
>
> Co-operation of both armies in battle purposed, First Army from St. Wendel or Baumholder.
>
> His Majesty commands the First Army to concentrate towards Tholey on the 4th.
>
> Third Army crosses the frontier to-morrow at Weissenburg.

A general offensive is proposed.

In consequence of these instructions General von Steinmetz at once issued the following order:

> The First Army commences its advance to-morrow in the direction of Tholey.
> The VII Army Corps concentrates at Lebach; the VIII Army Corps with its 16th Division at Ottweiler, 15th at Tholey.
> 3rd Cavalry Division between Tholey and St. Wendel, northward of the Tholey–St. Wendel road.

On the 4th, therefore, the whole army moved to the north-west, away from the Saar. The front was already watched by the 5th Cavalry Division, and the position of the 3rd Cavalry Division was dictated by the necessity of forming a link between the two armies.

During the day, reports were received by von Steinmetz from Saarlouis, Trêves, and from the patrols of the VII Corps, that fresh concentrations of troops had taken place towards Sierck, and that the frontier north of Bouzonville was once more strongly occupied. That the right and rear of the First Army were threatened might have been inferred from this intelligence; but so clear were the reports of the cavalry, to the effect that for some days the French forces had been in process of assembling round St. Avold, that General von Steinmetz disregarded this demonstration; and, believing that it proceeded from Thionville, and was probably intended to cover other designs, contented himself with arranging for the reinforcement of the force at Trêves by garrison troops from Wittlich.

The apprehension, vacillation, orders and counter-orders, which the appearance of even a few hostile scouts gave rise to at the French Head-Quarters, are in marked contrast to the manner in which the German leaders rated at its true value every item of intelligence from the front, and to the boldness with which they acted; and, as a proof of the confidence and security which the presence of a well-trained and active cavalry ensures, the above incident is well worth attention.

GERMAN MOVEMENTS ON THE 4TH AUGUST[2]

On the same day, Prince Frederick Charles began his advance through the Haardt, and, at nightfall, the divisions of both the First and Second Armies were encamped in the following localities:

First Army

VIII Army Corps	16th Division – Steinweiler. Adv. Gd. Schiffweiler.
	15th Division – South of Tholey
	Corps Artillery – Dirmingen
VII Army Corps	14th Division – Lebach. Adv. Gd. 3 miles south
	13th Division – Bettingen. Adv. Gd. Huttersdorf
	Corps Artillery – Neunkirchen.

Trains – Wadern

2 See map page 97.

3rd Cavalry Division north of St. Wendel, in immediate contact with troops of the Second Army.

SECOND ARMY

First Line	
III Army Corps	5th Division – Neunkirchen, &Waldmohr (4 miles in rear)
	6th Division – Cusel
IV Army Corps	17th Division – Mühlbach
	8th Division – Konigsbruchhof (10 miles from Zweibrucken)
Second Line	
Guard	Frankenstein
IX Army Corps	Munchweiler.
X Army Corps	Lauterecken.
XII Army Corps	Göllheim

The 9th Brigade of the III Army Corps at Neunkirchen, was in close communication with the 3rd Cavalry Division (First Army) at St. Wendel. Of the second line, but one corps of the left wing had as yet passed Kaiserslautern. The head of the Guard was 16 miles in rear of the IV Army Corps, the advanced corps on the left flank. On the right, the X Army Corps was ten miles in rear of the 6th Division of the III Army Corps. But both the 5th and 7th Divisions were practically at the foot of the mountains, holding the mouths of the defiles. Did the French advance, the Second Army was thus in a position to retire to the Alsenz-Grunstadt line, covered by the III and IV Corps; and, as connection had already been taken up with the First Army, the co-operation of the latter from Baumholder was assured.

THE CAVALRY ON 4TH AUGUST

3rd Division at St. Wendel, linking First and Second Armies.

5th Division:	
Right	11th and 13th Brigades – Heusweiler, covering First Army
	11th and 17th Hussars towards Volklingen and Saarbrucken
6th Division	
Centre	14th Brigade – Rohrbach
	15th Brigade – Neuhasel
Left	12th Brigade of 5th Cavalry Division, with 5th Dragoons of Third Army attached, at Einod – 13th Dragoons at Pirmasens.

On the right, detachments crossed the Saar at Volklingen, and moved forward to Ludweiler, three miles south. A captain of the 11th Hussars succeeded in penetrating to Emmersweiler, within two miles of Forbach, and almost in rear of the French position. From there he descried infantry and baggage on the march towards St. Avold, and learnt that troops had been retiring in that direction since the early morning.

This reconnaissance showed the Prussians that the left flank of the French position behind the Saar extended no further than Saarbrucken; but, be it observed, it also gave rise to the opinion that the enemy was retiring, and that there would be no combat on the Saar.

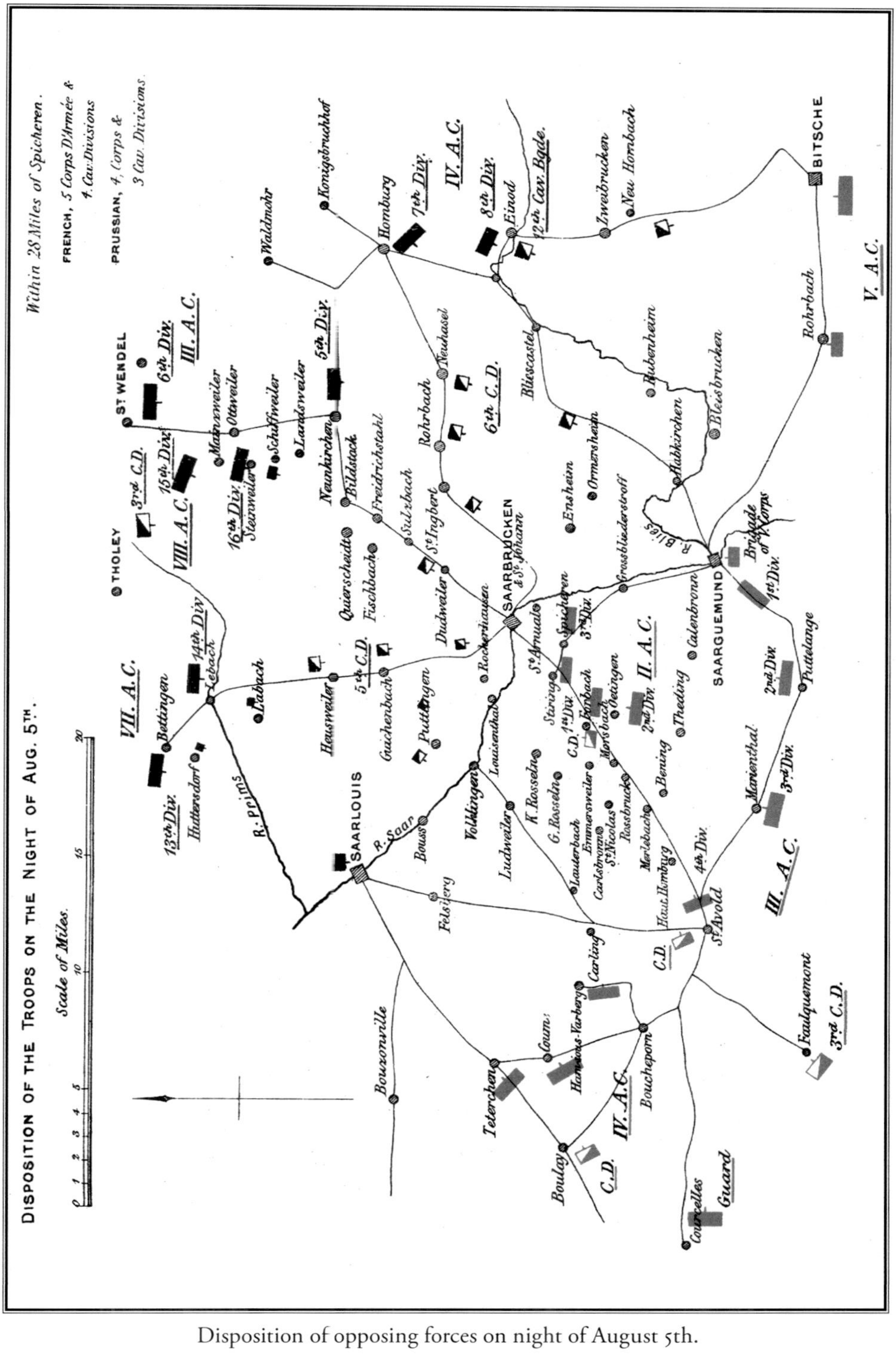

Disposition of opposing forces on night of August 5th.

The movements towards St. Avold, in reality, were merely unimportant changes within the position of Frossard's Corps, and the withdrawal of Montaudon's Division by Bazaine.

In the centre, some small reconnaissances showed that no essential change had taken place in the position of affairs on the Saar. A party of the 6th Cuirassiers found St. Johann unoccupied, but were fired upon from the Saarbrucken Ridge.

On the left, the frontier was crossed by five detachments, each consisting of several squadrons, some of which penetrated eight or nine miles into French territory. Wherever the enemy was met with he retired; and the 13th Dragoons, joined by a small detachment of Bavarian riflemen (Third Army) on waggons, ascertained the presence of a large hostile camp at Bitsche.

But before these reports had come to hand, enough information had been gathered to show that an attack on the part of the enemy was exceedingly improbable.

MOVEMENTS OF SECOND ARMY ON THE 5TH AUGUST

Prince Frederick Charles had, therefore, on the 4th of August, issued orders for the Second Army to continue the advance through the mountains, and deploy on the line Neunkirchen-Zweibrucken by the 7th.

Having extricated itself from the defiles, it was to be deployed on such a breadth of front as to be available for either a further advance or for battle.

The first line was to be formed by four Army Corps, one on each of the roads leading to the Saar. Two Army Corps were to form the general reserve in rear. The two cavalry divisions thrown out in front were to veil the movements of the infantry, and to reconnoitre those of the enemy; whilst, in case of battle, the First Army would co-operate from Tholey, and 255,000 men would be in readiness to meet the French.

The order did not lose sight of the unavoidable difficulties caused by four Army Corps, with all their trains, a moving from Kaiserslautern through a defile some 23 miles long. The second line of trains and the heavy baggage were to remain behind until the 7th, and on that day to move through Kaiserslautern by corps. On the night of the 5th of August, the following were the positions of the various corps of the Second Army:

First line	III A. C.	5th Division, Neunkirchen
		6th Division St. Wendel
	IV A. C.	8th Division, Zweibrucken
		7th Division, Homburg.
Second line[3]	X A.C.	Cusel
	Guard	Landstuhl
Third line[3]	X A.C.	Otterberg
	XII A.C.	Munchweiler

The First Army made no move.

The cavalry divisions remained in their old position.

On the right, the 11th Hussars (12th Brigade) made a reconnaissance by Volklingen and Ludweiler towards Forbach. They alarmed a hostile camp, observed troops moving partly by rail towards St. Avold, and the officer in command believed that he saw other indications of a diminution of the enemy's forces about Saarbrucken. The 17th Hussars

3 See map page 87.

(of the same brigade), who were pushed forward on the Lebach-Saarbrucken road, also remarked a decrease in the camp on the ridge beyond Saarbrucken. A subaltern with two men rode into the town and brought off two prisoners.

On the left, the patrols of the 6th Cavalry Division ascertained that the village of Habkirchen on the Blies, hitherto never left unoccupied by the enemy, had been evacuated; that a camp at St. Arnual had been abandoned, and that the other camps on the Saar and Blies were breaking up.

The patrols of the First Army learnt that guns had been withdrawn from the Saarbrucken ridge; and private information pointed to rearward movements of the enemy, to which the burning of St. Johann railway station, on the night of the 4th, was held to be the prelude.

There appeared, therefore, but little doubt that the enemy was falling back from the Blies and Saar. It was considered, however, at the Royal Head-Quarters, that the situation of affairs was not yet sufficiently clear.

A large French camp had been discovered at Bitsche upon the 4th; and, on the following day, reports were received from the cavalry of considerable traffic on the Saarguemund-Bitsche railway. This information seemed to point to an attempt on the part of the enemy's left wing to join McMahon; and a telegram from von Moltke reached Prince Frederick Charles, containing instructions for the raid of a large body of cavalry on the line of railway.

On the night of the 5th of August, von Moltke's leading idea was, for the Second and First Armies, so soon as the deployment of the former was effected, to remain in an attitude of expectation and hold fast the French upon the Saar, until the advance of the Third Army into Alsace should produce its effect. In the event of a decisive battle on the Lorraine frontier, the First and Second Armies would attack in front, while the Third Army would probably come up and attack in flank from the direction of Upper Saar. He intended, moreover, that the frontier should be crossed simultaneously by the First and Second Armies, on the 9th of August.

But stress must be laid upon the fact that on the evening of the 5th of August, General von Steinmetz was not cognisant of von Moltke's plans.

"As every day," says the Staff History, "might usher in some decisive result, the Royal Head-Quarters thought that no directions could be given extending beyond the immediate events. It was rather considered permissible and necessary, on this and subsequent critical occasions, to control the movements of the large units by definite orders, however much that arrangement might provisionally limit the independence of the Commander of the Armies.'

On the 6th of August, therefore, the leader of the First Prussian Army was aware that von Moltke contemplated a general offensive, but beyond this, he had no knowledge whatever of the purpose of the Commander-in-Chief. It will be seen, however, in the sequel, how the lack of instructions, and consequent misapprehension of the intentions of the Head-Quarters Staff, led to a collision, which, at the outset, bade fair to be disastrous to the Prussians. The truth appears to be that, to control the movements of vast masses of men, although divided into distinct armies, without admitting the leaders of those armies into the confidence of the Commander-in-Chief, and disclosing to them the general idea of the plan of campaign, is difficult in the extreme. Such armies are composed of numerous strong units, and lacking definite information as to the designs of the Head Quarters Staff, the leaders of units (especially in an army where a large initiative is allowed), are apt to form erroneous ideas, and to destroy the symmetry of the whole strategical design. In an army, on the other hand, where initiative is discouraged, a leader may find himself, as did Frossard on the 6th, confronted by circumstances which demand instant resolution, and allow no time in which to ask for orders. The result in either case is likely to prove disastrous. It goes without saying that due precautions should be taken with respect to secrecy, but there remains "the great necessity," to quote Lord Wolseley, "of fully and freely imparting to your subordinate commanders the aim and object of the operations to be undertaken."

On the 5th of August, the First Army Corps, already disembarked at Kaiserslautern and Birkenfeld, together with the 1st Cavalry Division, were assigned to the First Army, bringing the total of the First and Second Armies up to 320,000.

Front covered by the 5th and 6th Cavalry Divisions.

5 brigades: 14 regiments: 56 squadrons; with 4 squadrons of 5th Dragoons = 9,400 sabres.

31st July	Martinstein	to Durkheim	– 33 miles
1st August	Reichenbach	to Annweiler	– 42 miles
2nd August	Tholey	to Pirmasens	– 34 miles
3rd August	Eiweiler	to Pirmasens	– 34 miles
4th August	Heusweiler	to Pirmasens	– 34 miles
	Do.	do.	do.

5th August { Advanced patrols 18 miles to the front.
{ Two infantry divisions at Neunkirchen and Homburg respectively, about 5 miles in rear of main-bodies of the cavalry divisions.
{ About 260 sabres to the mile.

CHAPTER VI
THE BATTLE OF SPICHEREN

It was a lovely summer morning, cool and fresh after a night of rain, when the German outposts beyond the Saar broke up their bivouacs in the forest. Before the mists had cleared away von Rheinbaben's cavalry were pushing forward to the Saar, and when at 5 o'clock the infantry divisions of the First and Second Armies began their march, his squadrons were eight to ten miles ahead of the advancing columns, and his scouts already riding on the river bank.

Behind this screen of horsemen, a mass of 320,000 men, invigorated both by their onward movement and by the tidings of the victory at Weissenburg, was gradually advancing towards the Saar. After the lapse of more than half-a-century, France was once more threatened with invasion; and for the defence of her frontier province of Lorraine, Napoleon could muster no more than four Corps d'Armée, the 130,000 men that formed the left wing of the Army of the Rhine.[1]

When invasion was definitely decided on by the German Staff, it had been projected, as already mentioned, that the First and Second Armies should reach the Saar upon the 9th of August, maintaining until that date an attitude observant of the French left wing, and awaiting the result of the Crown Prince's attack on the enemy's right wing in Alsace. But this decision was modified by reports received on the 4th and 5th, of the enemy's withdrawal from the Saar. Consequently, on the evening of the 5th, instructions were sent from the Royal Head-Quarters for the raid on the Saarguemund-Bitsche railway; and the 5th and 6th Cavalry Divisions were ordered by Prince Frederick Charles to hang closely on the skirts of the retreating foe, and to report the probable direction of his rearward march. At the same time the following telegram was despatched by von Moltke to General von Steinmetz: "As the enemy appears to be retiring, the passage of the frontier is now open; but you should cross the Saar below Saarbrucken, as the road through the town belongs to the Second Army." This telegram was not received until the night of the 6th, and has therefore no bearing on the events of that day.

ORDERS FOR SECOND ARMY – MORNING OF THE 6TH

The Second Army had been originally timed to concentrate on the line Neunkirchen-Zweibrucken on the 7th. Until the direction of the enemy's retreat was ascertained, it was not considered judicious by von Moltke to accelerate the movement, or to alter the instructions already issued for the distribution of the troops upon the 6th. On the morning of that day, therefore, the following were the destinations of Army Corps:

III A.C. from St. Wendel to Neunkirchen, 14 miles 1 from Saarbrucken, with advanced guard (5th Division) to Dudweiler.

IV A.C. from Homburg to Zweibrucken, opposite Bitsche.

1 The 5th Corps (De Failly) was already on its way to join McMahon.

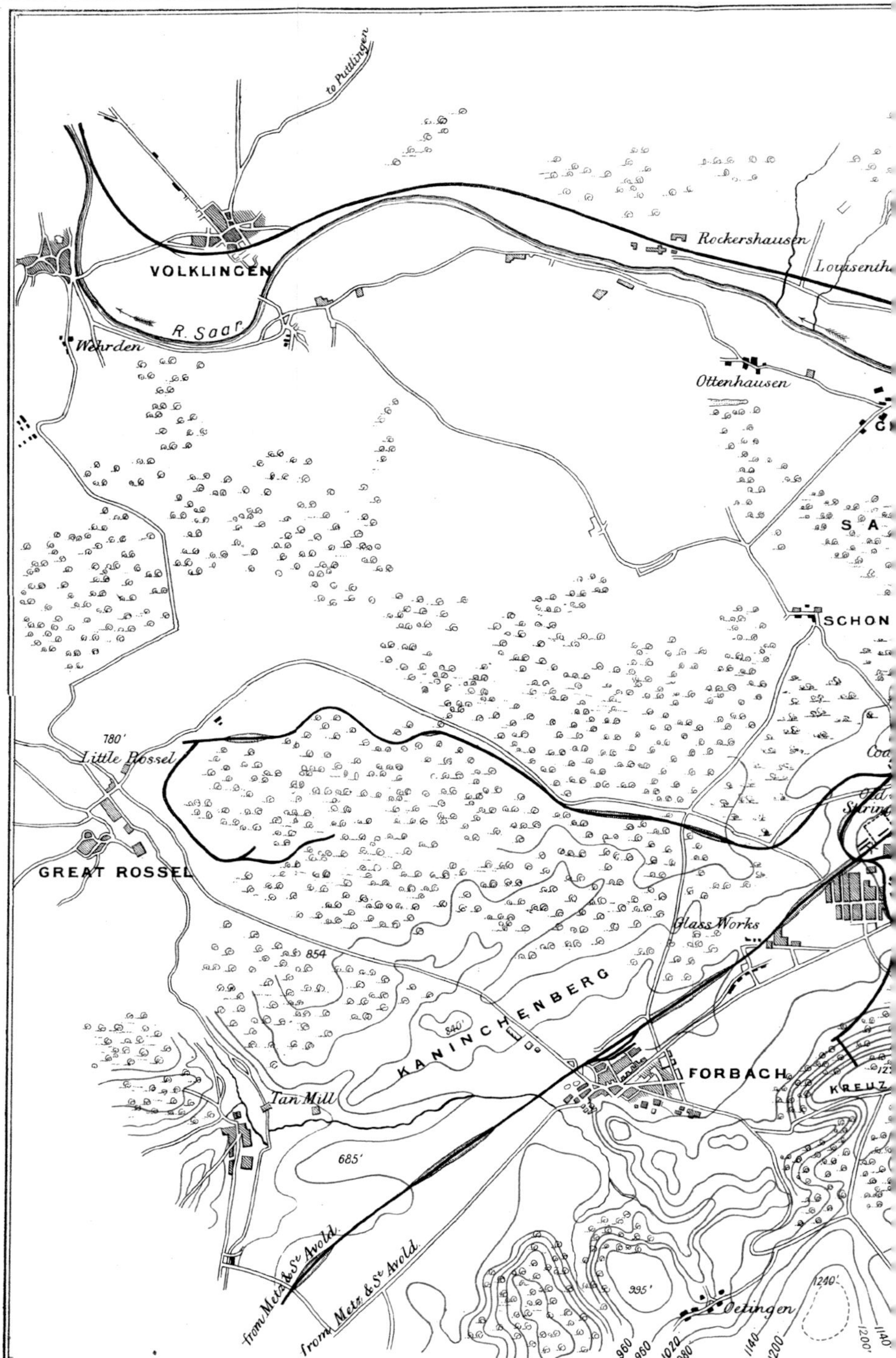

Battlefield of Spicheren

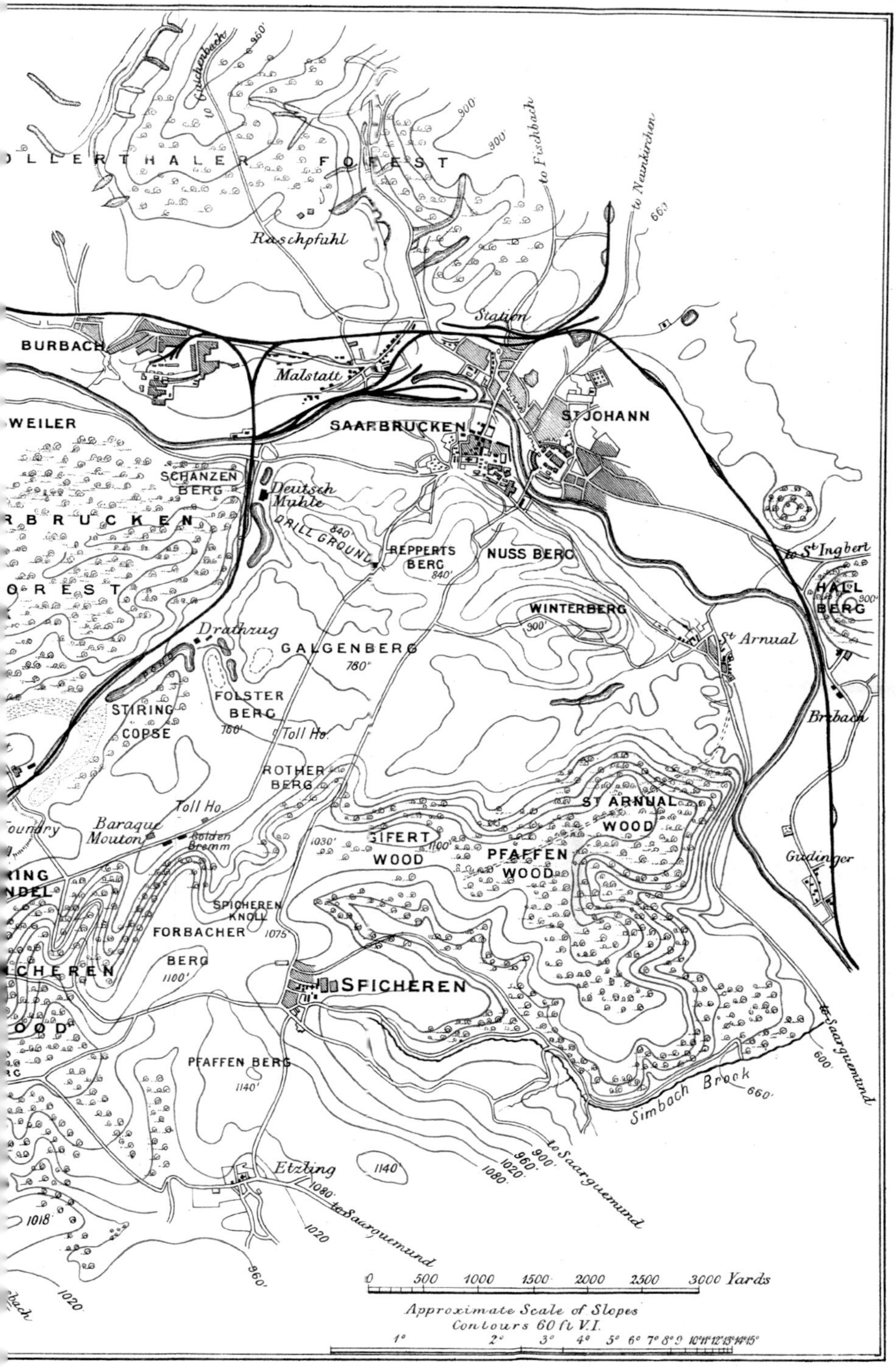
to Fischbach
to Neunkirchen
Raschpfuhl
Station
BURBACH
Malstatt
WEILER
SAARBRUCKEN
ST JOHANN
SCHANZEN BERG
Deutsch Muhle
DRILL GROUND
REPPERTS BERG
840'
NUSS BERG
to St Ingbert
HALL BERG
WINTERBERG
900'
St Arnual
Drathzug
GALGENBERG
780'
FOLSTER BERG
STIRING COPSE
Toll Ho.
Brebach
ROTHER BERG
ST ARNUAL WOOD
Toll Ho.
Baraque Mouton
Golden Bremm
1030'
1100'
PFAFFEN WOOD
WOOD
Gudinger
SPICHEREN KNOLL
1075
FORBACHER
BERG
1100'
SPICHEREN
to Saarguemund
PFAFFEN BERG
1140'
Simbach Brook
660'
600
Etzling
1140'
to Saarguemund
1080'
1020
960'
900'
to Saarguemund
1018
1020
960'
0 500 1000 1500 2000 2500 3000 Yards
Approximate Scale of Slopes
Contours 60 ft V.I.
1° 2° 3° 4° 5° 6° 7° 8° 9° 10° 11° 12° 13° 14° 15°

Guard A.C. from Landstuhl to Homburg

X A.C. from Cusel to Waldmohr (1 days' march in rear of III & IV A.C.)

IX A.C. from Otterberg to Landstuhl (12 days' march in rear of III & IV A.C.)

XII A.C. from Munchweiler to Kaiserslautern (13 days' march in rear of III & IV A.C.)

At an early hour, it was reported to the Head-Quarters of the Second Army by von Rheinbaben, commanding the 5th and the 6th Cavalry Divisions, that the French had evacuated the Saarbrucken Heights. At 8 am, therefore, Prince Frederick Charles gave orders, by telegram, for both divisions to keep close touch of the enemy; for the 5th Infantry Division (III Army Corps) to advance upon Saarbrucken; and for IV Army Corps to push an advanced guard to Neu-Hornbach. Not a word was said as to the advisability of an infantry attack upon the French rear-guard, or of an attempt to hold the enemy fast upon the Saar. It seems evident that the Prince was of opinion that until the issue of the approaching encounter between the Crown Prince and Marshal McMahon was known, any offensive movement on the part of the First and Second Armies would be premature; and further, that he deemed it desirable to postpone attack until the First and Second Armies had joined hands and it was possible to employ their whole strength, in the same field, against the inferior forces of the enemy. In a word, a powerful and combined effort, with many chances in favour of success, and in all probability decisive in result, was preferred to partial and isolated enterprises, where much would be risked and perhaps little gained.

ORDERS FOR FIRST ARMY – MORNING OF THE 6TH

On the 5th of August, General von Steinmetz had been warned to evacuate the St. Wendel-Saarbrucken road, leaving it free for the advance of the Second Army. The execution of this order necessitated a general shift of cantonments, for the villages near the highway had to be surrendered to the troops who were to march along it. In view, therefore, of the general offensive proposed by von Moltke, von Steinmetz resolved to push his army forward, south and west, withdrawing his left from the road, and to occupy a line advantageous either for the speedy passage of the frontier, or, should the French anticipate that operation by an attack on the Second Army, for striking the left flank of their advance. His Army Order, issued on the night of the 5th, may be thus condensed:

> The movement to the Saar commences to-morrow. VII Army Corps from Lebach to Guichenbach, advanced guards towards Volklingen and Saarbrucken. VIII Army Corps to Fischbach. III Army Corps of Second Army from information received, reaches Bildstock to-morrow. The Nähe Railway forms the line of demarcation between the VIII and III Army Corps as far as Landsweiler. 3rd Cavalry Division to Labach, 5 miles south-west of Lebach, covering the right flank of the army.

Now von Steinmetz, beyond the fact that a general offensive was proposed, knew nothing of the ulterior purpose of the Commander-in-Chief, and had even conceived an idea that was very far from the truth, expecting that to his own army an independent sphere of action would be assigned. Yet in the above order, he enjoined no movement that could in any way compromise von Moltke's plans; and, although convinced that the French were retiring, his intention was merely to assume a position of readiness within a day's march of the Saar.

But as the telegram directing him to cross the river *below* Saarburcken had not yet reached him, the VII Army Corps was ordered to push forward an advanced guard towards that town. It thus came to pass that on the morning of the 6th both the left wing of the First Army, and the right of the Second (III Army Corps) were moving by roads which met at St. Johann, and led to the same passage of the frontier stream.

The difficulty of retaining the control of enormous masses of troops in one hand is illustrated by the late arrival of von Moltke's despatch.[2] Had it arrived early on the 6th, the roads through the town and the bridges beyond would have been left free to the Second Army, and the risk of collision and confusion have been avoided. The distance from the Royal Head-Quarters at Mayence to those of von Steinmetz at Tholey was 65 miles, and the telegraph line was not continuous.

ADVANCE OF THE FIRST ARMY

VII Army Corps, which had been directed to march on the 6th, to Guichenbach, with advanced guards towards Volklingen and Saarbrucken, received the following orders from General von Zastrow:

13th Division, from Bettingen to Puttlingen; with outposts at Volklingen and Rockershausen.

14th Division, from Lebach to Guichenbach; with outposts at Louisenthal and above St. Johann.

VIII Army Corps marched on Fischbach and Quierscheidt, a little to the left rear of the 14th division. The 3rd Cavalry Division watched the right flank of the army along the river Prims. The front, from Bouss to St. Johann, was patrolled by the 5th Cavalry Division, with head-quarters still at Heusweiler.

The two divisions which formed the advanced guards of the First Army, marching abreast, moved in the following formations:

13th Division. – Lieutenant-General von Glumer

Advanced Guard	Van	2 squadrons, 8th Hussars
		2 companies, 7th Jägers
		II/55th Regt
	Reserve	I & F/55th Regt
		5L, 7th F. A. Regt
		2 companies, 7th Jagers
	Main body	II/55th Regt.
		73rd Regt
		13th Regt.
		2 squadrons, 13th Hussars
		6L, 5H & 6H, 7th F.A. Regt.
		l Baggage & Trains

2 See page 101.

14th Division – Lieutenant-General von Kamecke

Advanced Guard	Van	1 squadron, 15th Hussars
		III/39th Fusiliers
	Reserve	IL 7th F.A. Regt.
		I & II/39th Fusiliers. (8th Company with baggage)
		Sanitary detachment.
		1 Co. Pioneers, with light bridge train
	Main body	3 squadrons, 15th Hussars
		74th Regt.
		2L, 1H & 2H, 7th F.A. Regt
		I & F/53rd Regt. (2nd Batt. escort to Corps Artillery).
		77th Regt.
		Baggage and Train.

The composition of the advanced guards differed but little. That of the 13th Division included one-third of the infantry; that of the 14th, one-fourth. To both a light battery was attached, and the strength of the cavalry did not greatly vary.

The distances were probably much the same as those recommended by Verdy du Vernois; namely, 600 paces between the van and reserve of the advanced guard, and 1,000 paces between the advanced guard and the main-body of the division, the entire column thus occupying between six and seven miles of road. The distance differs somewhat to that laid down in the English drill book of 1889, where 1¼ miles is given as intervening between the head of the van-guard and the head of the reserve.

If criticism were called for as to the distribution of the various arms, it might be said that the bulk of von Kamecke's cavalry was placed too far forward, of von Glümer's batteries too far back. But, in the disposition of troops upon the march, as indeed in every other operation of war, local conditions are first of all to be considered. The work to be done, the character of the country, the strength, armament, position, and tactics of the enemy must be the basis of the calculation. A pedantic adherence to rule and theory is a fruitful source of disaster; and it is probable that the German commanders, trained as they are to regard the spirit rather than the form of regulations, were fully warranted in thus deviating from routine.

The strength of the Prussian advanced guards in 1866 and 1870, generally from one-fourth to one-third of the effectives of the columns, is said to have exercised a prejudicial effect on the conduct of the tactical operations. Very many battles in either campaign were begun by the commanders of the advanced guards upon their own initiative; and, in such cases, the action, small or great, had to be fought out in accordance with their view of the situation and on the lines they had laid down. The General-in-Chief, compelled to accept and work out the plan of battle devised by his subordinate, was thus deprived of all power of exercising his own skill and judgment, except in furthering that plan, and in feeding the fight from the reserve.

A man eager for action and distinction, finding himself in command of a strong advanced guard and beyond the control of his superior, was doubtless often strongly tempted to independent enterprise; and it may be that such temptation was sometimes yielded to without sufficient cause. But, on the other hand, the leaders of advanced guards achieved on more than one occasion decisive success, by engaging the enemy, when the situation clearly demanded it and there was no time to be lost, without hesitation and on their own responsibility. No German general would have acted as once did Ney in Portugal. In command of Massena's advance and in hot pursuit of Wellington, he came up with the enemy deploying for battle on Busaco ridge. "He had with him," says Napier, "40,000 infantry. A dark chasm separated the two armies, but Ney's military glance was sure. He instantly perceived that the mountain, a crested and not a table one, could hide no great reserves; that it was only half occupied, and that the allies were moving with the disorder usual on taking unknown ground. He wished, therefore, to attack; but Massena was ten miles in rear; the officer sent to him waited two hours for an audience, and then returned to Ney with an order to attend the Prince's arrival. Thus a great opportunity was lost. Scarcely 25,000 of Wellington's soldiers were in line." And this at a time, it may be added, when a single disaster would have led the British Government to have withdrawn their troops from the Peninsula.

To arrive at a just conclusion as to the proper strength for an advanced guard, we must consider the duties it is expected to perform:

(1) To clear the front of all hostile detachments.

(2) If the enemy be met, whether advancing or stationary, to seize a favourable position, and cover the deployment of the army.

(3) If the enemy is retreating or attempting a flank movement, to hold him fast; although to this rule there may be exceptions.

Under certain circumstances, when the enemy is at a great distance, or when a broad and bridgeless river lies between, the advanced guard cannot be called upon to carry out the more important – the second and third of these tasks and in such cases its strength may be diminished, or it may be formed of cavalry alone. But where there is the slightest probability that it may be attacked in force, or that it may have to hurl itself on the enemy's main-body, its strength and composition must be gauged by the numbers that may be employed against it, by the amount of resistance or of offensive power it may be called on to put forth. In the case we are considering, it was within the range of possibility that the French might suddenly advance across the still open bridges of Saarbrucken and Volklingen; and that the advanced guards would have to hold their ground until the main-body, not of the divisions only, but of the whole army, could deploy for battle. In the face of such a contingency it would have been imprudent to deprive them of the capacity for resistance which the infantry and artillery afforded.

The single disadvantage which arises from the great strength of an advanced guard is the temptation to independent action without adequate cause; but where Napoleon's maxim is adhered to, that the place of a commander is with his advanced guard, this objection disappears.

When, however, his troops form, as did the First Army, only a portion of the whole force, the position of the commander must be regulated by the facilities of communication with the supreme authority. If the march follows a line of telegraph, no difficulty can arise, and the expansion of the field-telegraph will, in the future, do much to simplify the question; but, if this resource does not exist, in order that instructions and reports may not be delayed, and strategic combinations thereby rendered tardy and uncertain, the commander will often be compelled to leave the conduct of his advanced guard to the discretion of its own leader. Under such circumstances, if collision with the enemy is a possible contingency, it is necessary that the advanced guard leader should be informed as to the general situation and the intentions of the Commander-in-Chief. Initiative is to be encouraged and demanded, but it is only fair to assist the man who is expected to exercise it, by giving him such information as may enable him to regulate his action in accordance with the broad design of the campaign. Had General von Steinmetz been enlightened as to the purpose of the Head-Quarter Staff of holding back the First and Second Armies until the Crown Prince had developed his attack, and also of concentrating in force against the main body of the French, and had he shared this knowledge with his corps and divisional leaders, all risk of a premature offensive, or of any action at variance with the plans of von Moltke, would have been avoided.

It has been stated that "If the commander of the whole were to accompany so considerable a portion of his force (*i.e.*, a strong advanced guard), there would seem little ground for allowing an important interval to separate it from the remainder. For if an engagement took place it would be an unquestionable advantage to have the whole at disposal from the outset," and instances have been cited to show, that if the enemy is met in superior force, this interval may be the cause of the advanced guard and the main-body being defeated in detail. But it may be remarked, firstly, that if the attack of the advanced guard is not unduly precipitate, this last danger will be obviated. Secondly, it is often possible that the enemy may suddenly advance; in which case it is necessary to cover the deployment of the main-body, and to give the commander, if he decide on assuming the defensive, latitude in his choice of a position, and time for its proper occupation. Thus, Prince Frederick Charles intended, if the French had advanced after the affair at Saarbrucken, to take up a position in rear of the Haardt, under cover of his advanced guard, retreating slowly through the mountains; the advanced guard being composed of cavalry, with strong infantry supports. Again, in the orders issued by Moltke on August 8th, we read: – "It is conjectured from the intelligence that has been obtained, that the enemy has retired behind the Seille and Moselle. The three armies will follow this movement … For the security of the march the cavalry is to be sent forward; supported by advanced guards, pushed well to the front, so that in case of necessity, the armies may have time to concentrate."

Thirdly, if the enemy stand fast, the commander requires time to make his dispositions for attack, and a screen is then of the utmost value. And lastly, when troops are on the march, the advanced guard forms the outposts, under cover of which bivouacs are occupied without disturbance or delay. At the same time, if it be absolutely certain that the enemy is either retreating or standing fast and it is important to attack him without delay, the interval may be advantageously reduced.

ADVANCE OF THE SECOND ARMY

The 5th Division of III Army Corps, advanced from Neunkirchen on Dudweiler at 5.15 am, in two columns.

9th Brigade – Major-General von Doering, by the Neunkirchen-Saarbrucken Road.

Advanced guard	1½ squadrons, 12th Dragoons
	48th Regiment
	3L. 3rd F.A. Regiment
	Sanitary Detachment

Main body
3rd Jägers
8th Grenadiers
2 squadron, 12th Dragoons
III H. 3rd F.A. Regiment
10th Brigade – Major-General von Schwerin, by the Neunkirchen-St. Ingbert Road
3rd & 4th squadrons, 12th Dragoons
12th Regiment
IV. & 4L, 3rd F.A. Regiment
52nd Regiment

Strength and distribution of the German Cavalry

Commencing from the right, the 3rd Cavalry Division, with head-quarters at Labach, covered the right flank of the First Army with 5 regiments; patrolling the Prims, communicating with the garrison of Saarlouis, and watching the course of the Saar as far as Bouss.

The 5th Cavalry Division had its head-quarters at Heusweiler.

The 11th Brigade, patrolled the Saar from Bouss to Volklingen, 3¼ miles.

The 13th Brigade, patrolled the Saar from Volklingen to St. Johann, 7¼ miles.

Four regiments appear to have covered the front; 2 were kept in reserve.

The 6th Cavalry Division had its head-quarters at Rohrbach.

The 14th Brigade, 3 regiments } extended from St. Johann to Bliesbrucken, 10½miles
The 15th Brigade, 2 regiments }

The 12th Brigade of the 5th Cavalry Division, 5 regiments, had its head-quarters at Einod, and secured the left flank of the Second Army, patrolling from Bliesbrucken to the neighbourhood of Bitsche, 10½ miles; whilst the 13th Dragoons at Bliescastel maintained connection with the right wing of the Crown Prince. 5th Dragoons at Pirmasens.

Thus 92 squadrons covered front and flank from Labach to beyond Pirmasens, a distance of 50 miles, giving 230 sabres to the mile.

Reconnaissances of the 5th & 6th Cavalry Divisions

During the night of the 5th, strong detachments of the 12th, 14th, and 15th Brigades pushed forward as far as the Saarguemund-Bitsche Railway, and destroyed the line in several places. They also discovered that the enemy had broken up his camp on the Bles River at Habkirchen, north-east of Saarguemund.

At the same time, a patrol of the 14th Brigade crossed the bridges between St. Johann and Saarbrucken, and drew the fire of the French outposts.

It was reported that troops had entrained at Forbach and at Morsbach.

At dawn on the 6th, the vedettes of the 17th Hussars, 13th Brigade, posted on the Lebach-St. Johann Road, observed that the Saarbrucken Ridge had been abandoned, and a squadron was sent forward through the town.

Reinforced by a troop of the 6th Cuirassiers, 14th Brigade, it crossed the ridge and descended to the valley by the Forbach Road, but between Drathzug Farm and the Spicheren Heights came into collision with hostile troops, and was driven back. The strength of the French was estimated at two battalions, a squadron, and a battery. No other troops nor camps were visible; and it was concluded somewhat hastily, for the country in advance was screened by woods and rising ground, that this detachment was merely a rear-guard covering the entraining of Frossard's corps at Forbach.

The 19th Dragoons, 11th Brigade, crossed the Saar by the Volklingen Budge at an early hour. Leaving a squadron to protect the left at Ludweiler, the officer in command pushed on with the remainder to Ham-sous-Varberg, 8 miles further south and 10½ miles from the river. East of this village his scouts observed a body of French cavalry, covering the eastward march of an infantry column upon Guerting, and a large camp was descried at St. Avold. The enemy deployed four battalions and two squadrons, but made no attempt to follow the dragoons as they fell back.

About 8 am, detachments of the 11th Hussars, 13th Brigade, also crossed, at Volklingen. A troop reached Gersweiler, and from this point the French forces were seen returning from the Saarbrucken Ridge (probably cavalry retiring from reconnaissance), and the existence of a camp near Stiring-Wendel was discovered. Another troop advanced through Schoneck towards the northern border of the Saarbrucken Forest, and between 10 and 11 o'clock were fired upon by hostile infantry. The commander of the regiment proceeded to Ludweiler, and from a hill in the neighbourhood caught sight of a camp near Forbach, and observed troops in motion on the Forbach-St. Avold Road. Patrols were sent forward to Carlsbronn and St. Nicholas, 4 miles to the front; and at 11.15 am, a squadron was despatched from the main body at Volklingen to Saarbrucken, 7 miles distant.

Lieut.-General von Rheinbaben, accompanied by two squadrons of the 14th Brigade, had, probably in consequence of the reports received from the 17th Hussars and 6th Cuirassiers, proceeded to the front at an early hour, and at 10.30 am his troopers surmounted the Drill-ground Hill under a brisk artillery fire from the Rotherberg. In addition to the guns, a few foot soldiers were seen upon the spur and small parties of infantry and cavalry were observed in the Forbach Valley. Patrols were at once sent forward, but were quickly driven in by the French guns. Towards 11 am the following telegram was sent to Prince Frederick Charles:

> The French occupy the Spicheren Heights with infantry and artillery: they are in the act of withdrawing.

But very shortly afterwards the French battalions began to take up positions for battle and a second telegram was despatched:

> Hostile lines are deploying on the heights this side of Forbach. Advanced guard of 14th Division has arrived at Saarbrucken to occupy the town.

These messages were received by the Prince at Homburg, about mid-day.

In addition to the reconnaissances of the cavalry, Lieut.-General von Goeben, commanding VIII Army Corps, had left his troops as they began their morning march, and riding forward to Saarbrucken, sixteen miles to the front, did not quit the ridge beyond until 10 o'clock.

Major-General von Doering, commanding 9th Brigade, 5th Division, who had also visited the heights whilst the day was young between 9 and 10, shortly after the first cavalry reconnaissance had been pushed back by the French outposts, observed columns of infantry advancing from Forbach, and disappearing from view behind the wooded heights which stand above that town.

Except in the case of the last-mentioned general, an impression that the French were retiring at all points appears to have taken strong hold on the minds of the German leaders. But, if we compare the evidence before them with the actual facts, we shall learn how difficult it is to escape erroneous deductions even when ample information is forthcoming.

The circumstances which seemed to point conclusively to a retreat of the whole French force may be thus recapitulated:

1. On the 2nd of August, the cavalry attached to the First Army, and the patrols sent out from the fortress of Saarlouis, had discovered that the number of the enemy in the neighbourhood of Thionville had decreased; and on the following days had reported that a general movement in a south-easterly direction was in progress.
2. On the 4th and 5th, patrols of Redern's brigade of the 5th Cavalry Division had crossed the Saar and penetrated to Emmersweiller, within 2 miles of Forbach. On both days troops and baggage were seen proceeding by road and rail in a southerly direction towards St. Avold.
3. Saarbrucken had been abandoned, and the ridge above, commanding the passage of the river and the roads issuing from the Kollerthaler Forest, was not even held by a line of outposts.
4. The hostile squadrons everywhere shunned contact with the German troopers, falling back whenever they were met with, and deliberately avoiding the risk of an engagement.
5. Only a small force of infantry and a few guns were visible from the Saarbrucken Ridge, having all the appearance of a rear-guard.
6. The situation of the hostile armies, if correctly appreciated, left but one course open to the French. Far superior forces were massing against either wing of their extended line; the sudden blow at Weissenburg, in French territory, must have revealed to them that the Germans were on the point of assuming the offensive; and the only means by which defeat in detail could be avoided, was by concentrating rapidly in some central position. Concentration can only be effected out of reach of the enemy, and retreat was therefore necessary.
7. The fact that the bridges across the Saar, the railways and the telegraph beyond, had been left intact, was, fairly enough, considered an indication of sudden change of purpose and hasty retreat consequent on the news of Weissenburg. This impression was heightened by the burning of the St. Johann railway station on the evening of the 5th.

Now, what was the truth?

1. The 4th Corps d'Armée had certainly quitted the Thionville district; but this movement had commenced before the action of Saarbrucken, and had been ordered by Napoleon with a view to the closer concentration of his forces on the frontier.
2. The troops seen in motion on the road and railway between Forbach and St. Avold formed part of Mountaudon's Division, which Bazaine had ordered to fall back to the latter town upon the 4th.

3. Frossard's intention, in abandoning Saarbrucken and its ridge, was merely to seek a stronger and less exposed position, and to draw his divisions together *in readiness* for retreat upon St. Avold, an operation which the instructions he had received on the 5th led him to anticipate.
4. The inaction of the French cavalry was the result of ignorance of the art of war, of indifferent training, and of a want of initiative on the part of their commanders.
5. Whether the peril of his army was realized by Napoleon we have no knowledge; but, as already recorded, he had no immediate intention of ordering a general retreat and rearward concentration.
6. The burning of the railway station had been purely accidental.
7. The evacuation of the Saarbrucken Ridge was a tactical error on Frossard's part, as was also the non-destruction of the bridges.

It will be observed that the discoveries made by the patrols who penetrated to the neighbourhood of St. Avold and scoured the woods on the left flank of the French positions on the morning of the 6th, have not been enumerated amongst the items of intelligence at the command of the German generals, for it is improbable that their reports as to the existence of large camps at various points had been received before the battle began. And it must be carefully noted that to the Spicheren Plateau, screened as it was by dense and lofty woods, or to the Forbach Valley, blocked by the Stiring Copse, no scouting party had penetrated. When Rheinbaben, therefore, telegraphed, to Prince Frederick Charles that the French were in the act of withdrawing, more than half the terrain which stretched before him had not yet been explored. It would have been well had he endeavoured to gain further information and had he couched his report in these terms: "The enemy has evacuated, the Saarbrucken Ridge. Only a small force is visible. They appear to be retiring, but neither the heights nor the woods beyond the valley have yet been examined."

THE BATTLE, 10–11 A.M.

ACTION OF THE 14TH INFANTRY DIVISION

Before the head of the 14th Division reached the village of Guichenbach, 7 miles from Saarbrucken, its commander, Lieut.-General von Kamecke, learnt, from the orderlies of the 17th Hussars, on their way to the Head-Quarters of the First Army, that the French had withdrawn from the ridge above the Saar.

Von Kamecke passed on this intelligence to General von Zastrow, commanding VII Army Corps, who was then approaching Dilsburg, 12 miles in rear, and, at the same time, asked permission to seize the ridge, in order to anticipate the French should they attempt to re-occupy the position, and thereby to secure the passage of the river. Von Zastrow replied that he might act on his own judgment, and at once reported his decision to von Steinmetz.

The advanced guard had meanwhile reached Guichenbach. The morning was still cool, and the march had scarcely exceeded 6 miles; von Kamecke, therefore, ordered his troops to push forward without delay to St. Johann, to cross the bridges, and to form a line of outposts on the ridge. 9/39 had been already sent to Neudorf, *via* Rockenhausen, in order to maintain communication with the 13th Division.

As the division neared the town, it was met by General von Goeben, riding northward. A short conference took place, and von Kamecke entered Saarbrucken, fortified by the assurance that, if the French turned back upon him, the 16th Division would come to his assistance. The advanced guard of this division had started from Schiffweiler, 16 miles distant from Saarbrucken, shortly after 5 o'clock, but, as the troops had already completed their day's march, and were distributed in cantonments, they could scarcely arrive before 3 o'clock. The Prussian system of quartering troops in farms and villages, often several miles apart, renders the process of forming up a long one. Further help was also secured. The commander of the 9th Brigade, von Doering, as already recorded, had visited Saarbrucken and had been made aware of the projected advance of the 14th Division to the ridge. Mistrusting the appearance of affairs at the front, he had already sent a message to his troops to march to the Saar; and had at the same time reported to the officer commanding the 5th Division the result of his reconnaissance and the orders he had given. It is improbable that he neglected to communicate with von Kamecke; and it may, therefore, be taken for granted that the latter counted also on the support of the 9th Brigade, the van-guard of which might be expected to reach Saarbrucken between 3 and 4 o'clock.

Of the independent action of these various officers it need only be said that it was in perfect accordance with the rules of war, showing a lively appreciation of the importance of mutual support, and a prudent apprehension of wasting time. "In war," said Napoleon, "time is counted by minutes, not by hours."

Occupation of the Saarbrucken Ridge by the Advanced Guard of the 14th Division

The van of the advanced guard reached St. Johann at 11 o'clock. The Saar was crossed by the lower bridge, and at 11.30, III/39 defiled upon the Drill-ground Hill, followed by von Kamecke and his staff.

Beneath them, bathed in glowing sunshine, lay the St. Arnual Valley, a few Prussian horsemen riding to and fro across the open fields.[3] Beyond were the hanging woods of the Spicheren Heights; directly in front the red escarpements of the Rotherberg; and further to the right the Forbach Valley, narrowed to a simple clearing by the Stiring Copse. Far over the Rotherberg rose the bare outline of a distant ridge, giving promise of more open ground, but to right, and left, and front, as far as the eye could range, except where the valleys and the red spur intervened, the face of the whole country was covered with a sea of foliage. On the crest of the Rotherberg, where the shadows of the trees lay dark and still, some companies of French infantry were visible. From the saddle in rear, a battery of guns played briskly on the Saarbrucken Ridge; and small bodies of troops were observed in the Forbach Valley.

Nothing betokened the presence of a considerable force; and, although nearly 28,000 men and 90 guns were in the immediate neighbourhood, they were so effectually concealed, that 7,000 infantry and 8 guns was the highest estimate of the Prussian scouts. But surely the scene before him was such as to impress upon a commander, viewing it as

3 See sketch of battlefield pages 126–127.

did von Kamecke, the necessity of thorough reconnaissance ere he threw his battalions into the recesses of those far-reaching woods.

The shells fell fast upon the drill-ground as the battery of the advanced guard clattered up the road, wheeled to the right past the Bellevue Tavern, and unlimbered west of the highway on the southern slope. The range was little over 2,000 yards; and although it was estimated that eight French guns were in action, neither man nor horse was injured.

The two remaining battalions of the 39th Fusiliers, losing men from the hostile fire as they attended the reverse slope of the ridge, had meanwhile taken post behind the northern crest of the Reppertsberg and whilst gun answered gun across the valley, the following orders were sent to the main-body of the advanced guard:

27th Brigader II/74 to cross the viaduct and to occupy the railway-cutting at German Mill.
I & F/74 to cross by the lower bridge, and to join the 39th.

The main-body of the division, together with the three batteries, was directed to halt on the slopes below the Kollerthaler Forest.

The security of the bridges was thus effectually provided for; and to dispose his advanced guard as a line of outposts would have doubtless been von Kamecke's next step, had not the presence of the French artillery on the Rotherberg, and the reports of the cavalry scouts, turned his thoughts in a new direction.

The commander of the cavalry divisions had been for some time present on the ground when von Kamecke arrived. The two squadrons which had accompanied him were posted in the Ehrenthal, the gully at the foot of the Drill-ground Hill, where those who fell at Spicheren now lie. Patrols had been pushed forward towards the Forbach Valley, and, although they had been driven back by the French picquets, von Rheinbaben was now able to report that besides the guns upon the Rotherberg, the presence of at least three regiments of infantry and some squadrons of cavalry had been detected. Still, the deployment of the Prussian battalions on the Drill-ground Hill and Reppertsberg had evoked no corresponding activity upon the French. In the woods beyond the St. Arnual Valley was no sign of life; and it seemed to the two Prussian generals, already convinced that the enemy were in retreat, that the slender force before them was but a rear-guard covering the entraining of the 2nd Corps at Forbach.

But so long as it held the Rotherberg, this hostile detachment commanded the length and breadth of the St. Arnual Valley and of the Saarbrucken Ridge; and, as the casualties of I and II/39 already proved, it had it in its power not only to inflict heavy loss upon the German troops as they ascended the road, but to make the occupation of the crest a somewhat costly proceeding. For this reason, von Kamecke at 12 o'clock, determined to attack.

The possession of the Rotherberg was certainly essential to the occupants of the Saabrucken Ridge; and, had it been the fact that but three regiments confronted his 10,750 bayonets, his decision would have been a sound one. But, as the event proved, it was too hastily conceived.

Von Rheinbaben could have told him that, in consequence of the natural difficulties, only a very partial reconnaissance had been effected. The Spicheren Plateau, a strong defensive position, and spacious enough to contain the whole French army, was effectually concealed by the woods which clothed its rugged slopes and lofty crest;

and the circumstance that only a small force of guns and infantry were visible on the Rotherberg, was no sure indication that the belt of forest and the rolling downs in rear were untenanted. The cavalry patrols had not been able to pass beyond the mouth of the St. Arnual Valley; and, although a narrow strip of the open ground which ascends gradually towards Forbach was under, observation, neither the Stiring Copse, the village of Stiring Wendel beyond, nor the great forest to the right had been examined. It was not impossible that the apparent weakness and inaction of the enemy was but a lure. Modern warfare, waged by skilful leaders, has its instances of snare and ambush. The situation assuredly demanded an extended and careful reconnaissance; and the secrets of the plateau and the forest should have been laid bare before the battalions of the 14th Division were ordered to advance.

If on the other hand, von Kamecke was not absolutely convinced that the French were retreating, but, counting on strong and speedy support, resolved, nevertheless, to accept the risk of an engagement, he took upon himself a perilous responsibility. A commander who commits his troops to action cannot withdraw without heavy loss in men and in *moral* from the deadly zone of fire which girds a modern battle-field. And, therefore, when the challenger and his adversary have grappled, the distant divisions hurry forward; and the knowledge that only a vigorous and combined effort can extricate their comrades, that when battle has been joined it must be fought out to the end, draws every leader within hearing of the cannon-thunder to the field. Thus, whole armies become involved in battle, which at the outset was but an isolated engagement of the advanced guards.

But battle is the end of the strategy of the Commander-in-Chief. For this he lays his plans; for this the marches and manœuvres of his Army Corps are directed; and the battle he proposes is one in which the advantage of position and of numbers shall lie with him, one which will perhaps lead to successes far more important than the mere overthrow of the hostile forces. If a subordinate leader, therefore, by a too precipitate attack, involve the mass of the army in a premature and unforeseen engagement, he may utterly destroy the combinations of his superior; compelling him to fight on ground where superiority of position and of numbers is with the enemy, and where the results of victory may be barren, of defeat disastrous. So, on the 9th September, 1882, the 1st Division of the English army repulsed the attack of the Egyptians on Kassassin, and followed them to within 5,000 yards of the camp they had so laboriously entrenched. Had the divisional commander ordered a resolute pursuit, "there is every possibility," says the Official History, "that it might have given us – though with considerable loss – possession of Tel-el-Kebir itself that day. But such a success would have been useless, only a fraction of the army would have been available to follow up the victory. The cavalry could not have advanced directly upon Cairo. Tel-el-Kebir, the desert fortification, might possibly have fallen and the troops therein dispersed; but the decisive battle of Tel-el-Kebir would not have been fought, the army would not have been placed upon the point of junction of the various detached portions of the Egyptian army. Cairo would not have fallen as a consequence of this premature blow, and it would have most probably been burnt before we could have reached it."

The commander of an advanced guard that cannot rapidly communicate with superior authority has often no easy part to play. He must be resolute and daring; a small rear-guard or detachment must not be permitted to delay his march; he must be ready to act on his own initiative and to accept weighty responsibility; and, if the situation demand it, as at Vionville, to attack an army without hesitation. But he must temper audacity with prudence; his reconnaissances must be thorough; he must be quick in his movements, but suspicious of ambush. Above all, he must never run the risk of involving the mass of the army in battle, unless it is exceedingly clear that a golden opportunity would be lost by holding back.

The direct approaches to the heights of Spicheren were blocked by the position of the French upon the Rotherberg, but the plateau was not inaccessible. A track led from St. Arnual through the climbing forest which overlooked the angle of the Saar; and further to the south, to the right rear of the French position, the Simbach Ravine opened a road to the higher ground.

At the same time, the cavalry were working in a strange country, of which their maps described only the general features, and it would have taken time to find a passage through the woods. Had the 7th Uhlans and the 1st Battalion of the 40th Fusiliers, the original garrison of Saarbrucken, been retained in the district they had so thoroughly patrolled, men who knew every path and clearing of the forest would have been at hand, and ample information as to the strength of the hostile force upon the plateau have been rapidly obtained. Unfortunately, a somewhat over-scrupulous regard for symmetry of organization had withdrawn these troops to the rear with their own, the 16th Division. Moreover, and this is a point worth close attention, a large force of cavalry had, since the early morning, been scouring the woods of the Saarbrucken Forest, endeavouring to obtain information of the movements and positions of the enemy between Forbach and St. Avold. Von Rheinbaben, to whom as commander of both cavalry divisions, all information would be brought, was at von Kamecke's side.

Of this force, the patrols of the 11th Hussars, which had left Volklingen about 8 o'clock, had observed hostile camps both at Forbach and Stiring Wendel. Had von Kamecke known that these camps were still standing at 9 or 10 o'clock, he would have doubtless modified his opinion that a general retreat was in progress, for a rear-guard must always remove its impedimenta if a withdrawal is imminent. But at 12 o'clock, this intelligence had not come to hand. A squadron of the Hussar Regiment, probably carrying the reports to von Rheinbaben, left Volklingen at 11.15. But Volklingen was 7 miles distant from Saarbrucken, and before the squadron arrived, the 14th Division was irretrievably committed to the attack.

As we are ignorant of the time when the French camps were first discovered by the Hussars, it is impossible to say whether the intelligence might have been more rapidly conveyed to General von Rheinbaben; but it may safely be asserted that von Kamecke was wrong in advancing before these reports came in; and we may also derive a lesson as to the absolute necessity of instantly transmitting the information obtained by the advanced scouts.

It is a curious circumstance that the Prussian cavalry, although they showed no hesitation in striking into the extensive forests on the left flank of the French position, should have altogether neglected the roads running on either bank of the Saar to Saarguemund. The road on the left bank, leading through St. Arnual, was undoubtedly a dangerous defile, with the river on one hand and heavily wooded heights upon the other; but, giving access as it did, by the paths which struck it, to the interior of the plateau, its exploration was well worth risking a patrol. It is not out of place to remark that a few mounted infantry, who could have left their horses and scouted through the thickest woods, would have rendered invaluable assistance. Their equipment would have made it exceedingly difficult for the cavalry troopers to work dismounted amongst the thick undergrowth of the steep hill-sides.

When von Kamecke decided to attack, the Spicheren Plateau, as already stated, had not yet been examined; little of the ground occupied by the enemy was under observation, and the country favoured the concealment of large bodies of troops.

If the French had not yet withdrawn from the district, a general engagement might possibly be brought about. But the 14th Division was far in advance, and it was only prudent to suppose that von Moltke, greatly superior in numbers, would prefer to deal with the French when he had concentrated his forces, examined their position and framed his own plan of battle.

If, again, as the Staff History relates, von Kamecke's idea in attacking was merely to clear the Rotherberg, he ran an unnecessary risk in committing his infantry to the operation. Were the French only present in small force, his four divisional batteries would have quickly rendered the spur untenable. In sending his infantry forward, before the reports as to the smallness of the enemy's numbers were confirmed, he acted with undue precipitation.

Supports were on the march, but still some hours distant, the head of the 5th Division 3¼ hours' march, of the 16th, 4 hours'; and, by hurling his isolated division on what might prove, not the rear-guard, but the outposts of a superior force – and, so long as the district had not been thoroughly reconnoitred, that possibility should have been held in view – there was every prospect of his battalions being crushed before a single bayonet came up to their assistance.

Little time would have been lost by delay. Whilst the guns assailed the Rotherberg, the infantry might have been placed in positions favourable for an immediate advance; and, in the mean time, further instructions might have been demanded from von Zastrow, who was at Dilsburg, only seven miles in rear. Lastly, the commander of the 14th Division might have had recourse to a reconnaissance in force. Whilst the artillery engaged the guns upon the Rotherberg a couple of battalions, sent out on either flank, into the Gifert Wood and the Stiring Copse, would have sufficed to develop the enemy's strength.

Students of the campaign may remember that the Staff History (page 252), speaks of "Prince Frederick Charles' orders (received by Rheinbaben), to keep the foe at the sword's point," and declares that "the independent offensive of the 14th Division was perfectly in accordance with the spirit of the German generalship, which directed every effort to hang closely on the adversary."

Now, in the first place, Prince Frederick Charles' orders were for the cavalry, and for the cavalry alone, to keep close touch of the retiring enemy. Not a word was said of an infantry advance. And secondly, whilst it is perfectly true that von Kamecke's independent offensive was in unison with the spirit of the German generalship, it is no less certain that his neglect to reconnoitre, and his precipitate attack, were by no means in unison with the spirit of sound tactics.

There were other circumstances, also, which must not pass unobserved. Although the Staff History states that his intention in attacking was to clear the Rotherberg, it is hinted in the concluding remarks that the idea of holding the enemy fast upon the Saar, or at least of keeping the touch, was uppermost in his mind. Now it was still possible, on the morning of the 6th, that the widely separated wings of the Army of the Rhine might effect a junction by retreating from Alsace and Lorraine on a central point in the interior of France. But the propriety of a single divisional leader taking upon himself the responsibility of deciding as to where and how this junction should be prevented, may be strongly questioned.

There can be no question, however, of the propriety of making every effort to keep the touch; and, in order to open the way to the cavalry, action was imperative. But no necessity, however pressing, absolves a general from neglecting ordinary precautions. And the first precaution taken should have been to ascertain whether the French were retiring or not.

At the same time the moral factors of the situation must not be forgotten. The urgency of a dashing offensive had been impressed upon the Prussian army; and secondly, on the very ridge whereon von Kamecke stood, 1,200 Prussian riflemen had held 50,000 French at bay for sixteen days. Was he to be imposed on in like manner?

One last excuse, and it is doubtless the true one, may be made for him, and it is that he trusted to the cavalry reports; and, that when he attacked, he did so in the belief that the French force before him was but a weak rear-guard. His conduct may be further criticised by the light of the orders given by Prince Frederick Charles, von Zastrow, and von Alvensleben. The Head-Quarters of the Second Army had been informed at an early hour of the evacuation of the Spicheren Ridge. As this seemed to point to the retreat of the French, "it was judged expedient to seize the passage of the Saar, and without inducing a premature offensive, to hang closely on the enemy. To this end the Prince ordered both cavalry divisions to keep the touch of the retreating foe; for the 5th Infantry Division to advance to Saarbrucken, and to move its advanced guard to Fosbach the next day."

Von Zastrow, also, when the news of Frossard's withdrawal reached him, resolved to push forward his whole corps to the Saar. But the 14th Division was ordered merely to occupy the Saarbrucken Ridge with a reinforced advanced guard, and to patrol towards Forbach.

Von Alvensleben, commanding III Army Corps, on ascertaining the enemy's retreat from Saarbrucken, ordered the 5th Division to occupy the place with a vanguard, and the main-body to advance within four miles of it.

Lastly, a clue as to what von Moltke would have advised under the circumstances may be gathered from his action on the days immediately following the twin victories of Spicheren and Woerth. The enemy's right wing, under Bazaine, was reported, on the 7th August, to be concentrated at Boulay and St. Avold; but no forward movement was allowed until the Second Army had reached the Saar, although three days elapsed before this operation was completed. The Chief of the Staff's purpose is evident throughout to meet the French army with superior numbers, to leave to the cavalry the task of keeping the touch, and to avoid premature collision.

General Konstantin von Alvensleben, commander of the German III Corps (Rousset/*Histoire*)

French dispositions

On the morning of the 6th, the three divisions of the 2nd Corps were encamped as follows:

1st Division	Jolivet's Brigade, N.E. of Stiring Wendel
	Valazé's Brigade, W. of Forbach
2nd Division	Oetingen, on the plateau, 3 miles south of Spicheren
3rd Division	Spicheren

No preparations for a further retreat had as yet been made, although Frossard had been warned on the previous day that such an operation might have to be carried out at any moment. Moreover, he had received sufficient information from spies or the country people to make him aware that he was threatened by a force far larger than his own; and, shortly after daybreak, the following telegram reached him from Le Boeuf:

> Be prepared for a serious attack, which may possibly take place to-day. Remain at your post, and do not come to meet the Emperor.

The last sentence referring to an order received during the night, summoning the general to take part in a Council of War at St. Avold.

In consequence of this warning, he immediately ordered intrenchments to be thrown up at certain commanding points. But his preparations went no further. Nothing was done in the way of surveying the position, or of arranging in what manner the troops were to be drawn up for its defence. Nor was any provision made for a further retreat, although instructions had been received on the preceding day that such an operation would eventually have to be carried out.[4] It is true that Le Boeuf's orders threw no light

4 See page 84.

whatever on the ulterior intentions of the Emperor, and that Frossard was quite in the dark as to the meaning of the proposed retrograde movement on St. Avold. But this ignorance by no means absolved him from holding his troops in readiness to fight a rear-guard action. He was aware that sooner or later he would be ordered back, and that he might be vigorously attacked before receiving instructions to do so. This knowledge should have been sufficient; and he should have kept in mind the possibility of his having to withdraw his troops in the face of the enemy.

Neither Frossard, Le Boeuf, nor Bazaine, appear to have given a single thought as to what was to be done if the Prussians, known to be in large force in the vicinity, and on the point of assuming the offensive, were suddenly to cross the river at Saarbrucken and attack the 2nd Corps; although it was obvious that the road and railway passing through that town were the most advantageous lines of invasion.

The command of the left wing had, it is true, been committed to Bazaine. But on the morning of the 6th, he had scarcely had sufficient time to take up the reins of command. He had no staff except that belonging to his own Army Corps, and little information as to the Emperor's plans.

And although the marshal was in close communication by telegraph with the commander of the 2nd Corps, the dangerous position of the latter demanded something more than merely waiting for orders. Events develop with such rapidity in war, and instructions so frequently miscarry, that every subordinate, when the enemy is near at hand, should act on Napoleon's maxim, and "ask himself several times a day, 'what shall I do if I am attacked in front, flank or rear?'" and frame his plans accordingly.

The dispositions of the French left wing were such that a speedy concentration in a central position was perfectly feasible. The disposition of the three divisions of the 2nd Corps permitted either an orderly retreat, or the occupation of a position for battle in front of Spicheren and Forbach. But the possibility of a sudden advance on the part of the enemy had not been considered, and the sequel shows how the difficulties and delays of communication in the field often make it impossible to put into quick execution plans which are improvised on the spur of the moment.

Bazaine, who appears to have appreciated the situation correctly on the morning of the 6th, suggested to Frossard that if the Prussians attacked him in force, he should retire on Calenbronn. That he did not insist on this measure or give an absolute order, probably arose from the instructions of the Emperor, limiting his command to "military operations only." As the Commander-in-Chief still dictated, as we shall hear, the disposition of the divisions belonging to Bazaine's own Corps d'Armée, it was but natural that the marshal should feel diffident about giving explicit orders to another corps.

It is on Napoleon and Le Boeuf that the blame must fall; and it is instructive to compare the directions issued by von Moltke to the First and Second Armies when it was still possible that the French might advance into the Palatinate. The combination of the two armies on the defensive was carefully provided for, a position selected, and nothing left to chance.

At 9.10 am, when the Prussian cavalry first crossed the Saarbrucken Ridge, and came into collision with his outposts, Frossard telegraphed to Bazaine at St. Avold:

I hear cannon firing at the front, and I am about to proceed thither. Would it not be well if Montaudon's Division were to send a brigade to Grossbliederstroff, and Decaen's Division to advance to Merlebach and Rossbruck.

About 10 am he again communicated with his chief:

The enemy has sent strong reconnoitring parties of cavalry and infantry[5] down from the Saarbrucken ridge, but as yet he has made no sign of attack.

And at 10.40 am:

I am advised that the enemy has shown himself at Rossbruck and Merlebach. You ought to have forces on that side.

At 11.15 came the reply to these despatches:

In accordance with the Emperor's order, I have posted Castagny's and Metman's Divisions at Puttelange and Marienthal. I have no one at Rossbruck or Merlebach. I am sending a Dragoon Brigade in that direction.

Although I have but a small force present to protect St. Avold, I have ordered Metman's Division to Marcheren and Bening, Castagny's to Farschwiller and Theding. It appears to me that your division at Oetingen can send a brigade to Morsbach to watch the Saarlouis Road. If the affair is really serious, you will do well to retire on Calenbronn.

Bazaine, it appears, had already received an intimation from Head-Quarters that the 2nd Corps was in jeopardy; but, besides Frossard's information, as to Rossbruck and Merlebach, reports had reached him from Saarguemund upon his right, and from Guerting on his left, of the presence of the enemy's cavalry; and, apprehensive of attack, he was for a long time undecided as to where the stroke would fall. Neither he, nor a single one of his divisional generals dreamt of endeavouring to clear up the situation by pushing a strong cavalry detachment through the cordon of the hostile scouts, in the supposed direction of the Prussian main-body. It would have been no difficult matter to ascertain the truth. In the neighbourhood of Saarguemund were a few squadrons of the 5th Prussian Cavalry Division; but the nearest infantry was the 10th Brigade, on the road to St. Ingbert, not less than 15 miles in rear; whilst the force which caused the alarm at Guerting, and induced the marshal to suggest that Frossard should send a brigade from Oetingen to Morsbach, was a troop or two of the 19th Hussars, scouting nearly twenty miles ahead of the 13th Infantry Division. The marshal himself, reconnoitring the Saarlouis Road, had fallen in with and had been fired upon by this detachment. The Prussians quickly fell back, but Bazaine took no measures to have them followed up, and contented himself with requesting Frossard to detach a large force to watch the road.

At the hour the above instructions reached Frossard (11.15 am) only a small force of German cavalry had as yet crossed the Saar. Half-an-hour later guns and infantry

5 No infantry had as yet crossed the Saar.

appeared upon the ridge, but in no great strength. Retreat on Calenbronn was perfectly feasible; and, perhaps had not Forbach held large stores of provisions and matériel, he would have executed such a movement.

But counting, on the strength of Bazaine's telegram, on the support of Metman's and Castagny's Divisions at least, and confident in the strength of his position, he resolved to stand his ground. It is difficult to blame him. A retreat would have lost the magazines at Forbach, and have affected the morale of his troops. Bazaine's despatch was vague; and he must be something more or less than a gallant soldier who retires, without a trial of strength, before an enemy who has not yet proved his superiority. "It would certainly have been better," he writes, "to have brought Vergé's Division on to the plateau, and to have left in the Forbach Valley merely posts of observation; but it was necessary to protect the railway station, the terminus of our railway communication, which held our supplies and stores."

He saw clearly enough, the disadvantage of the position he would be compelled to occupy in the event of battle, half on the height and half on the plain; but he was prevented from taking up a stronger defensive line by the faulty situation of the magazines. This location was doubtless favourable enough if the army had invaded Germany. But prudence dictates that the possibility of a retreat or of a defensive should never be lost sight of, and the supply depôt should have been established further to the rear. Had Frossard been untrammelled by the necessity of providing for the security of the magazine, he would, in any case, have occupied a far stronger and more concentrated position; or, had he had the wisdom to accept Bazaine's suggestion, have been able to withdraw to Calenbronn.

At the same time, had he left but a small force in Forbach, and occupied the plateau in greater strength, he would have been secure enough. But he was apprehensive of attack from Saarlouis, and had neglected to reconnoitre in this direction.

The evacuation of the Saarbrucken Ridge by the 2nd and 3rd Divisions of the 2nd Corps d'Armée was begun at 5 o'clock on the evening of the 5th.

It was carried out slowly, and with great precaution, under a heavy storm of rain. Some of the troops did not reach their new encampments until day-break; a circumstance which probably had its due effect on their conduct in the battle.[6]

It is impossible to defend Frossard's conduct in relinquishing a position which so effectually commanded the passage of the river, when he had every expectation of an attempt to force the passage being made. Had he occupied the Saarbrucken Ridge with a strong detachment, he would certainly have delayed the Prussian attack for many hours; have gained much needed time for the concentration of the French forces, for the removal of the stores at Forbach,; and, had a withdrawal to Calenbronn been ordered, have secured his own retreat from the position whereon he now found himself, and which, whatever may have been his intention in withdrawing to it, he was compelled to defend.

6 During this march, the 8th Regiment was joined at the Golden Bremm by 400 reservists from the depôt.

THE FRENCH POSITION

The Spicheren Plateau is a salient of the great table-land of Lorrain, rising squarely between the valley of the Saar upon the one hand and of Forbach on the other; separated from the Saarbrucken Ridge by the St. Arnual Valley, the breadth of which amounts on the east, near St Arnual Village, to 1,000; on the west between the Rotherberg and Reppertsberg, to quite 2,000 paces. The slopes of the plateau, save at the left-hand corner, where the Rotherberg juts out to the northward, are densely wooded, and on every side so steep and abrupt that even an unencumbered man finds it no light task to scale them. Beneath the oaks and beeches which clothe the cliffs from base to brow, the undergrowth flourishes in such luxuriance, as to present peculiar difficulties to the movements of a body of soldiers, heavily equipped, and bound to maintain formation. The crest of the heights is about 300 feet above the valley.

The Rotherberg, viewed from the Saarbrucken Ridge, appears an insignificant height, and easy of ascent. But from the valley at the foot, where the verge of the main plateau is no longer visible, the famous spur stands out a formidable hill, the crest about 150 feet above the level. East, west, and north the fall is steep, and where, at the date of the battle, the red rock cropped out from the scarped hill side, it was sheer and precipitous. The face of the acclivity was no smooth and uniform incline; and although little plots of cultivation, cut into narrow terraces, and holding often a clump of cherry trees, formed a rough and broken stairway, and, in no place, save where the cliff is quarried, did the gradient exceed 30 degrees, the surmounting of the salient was by no means less difficult than that of the wooded slopes on either hand. The surfaced of the spur, 250 yards in breadth, is bare and undulating, rising gently to the south, and joined to the plateau by a somewhat narrower saddle.

The Spicheren-Saarbrucken Road, which, after crossing the valley from the Nussberg, winds round the eastern shoulder of the spur, supported on a log embankment, was practicable for artillery.

East of the Rotherberg is the Gifert Wood, 1,300 yards in length and 600 broad. Divided from it by a clearing, with a thin belt of timber on the crest, is the Pfaffen Wood; and beyond again, overhanging the river and the village at its feet, the great Parish Wood of St. Arnual. South-west of the Rotherberg, nearly a mile back, and overhanging the Forbach Valley, is the Parish Wood of Spicheren.

The interior of the plateau

Standing on the Pfaffenberg, a long green ridge which formed the southern boundary of the battle-field, the surface of the plateau, hedgeless and unobstructed, chequered by the tiny plots and pastures of the peasants, furrowed by two parallel ravines, and framed by heavy timber, sinks gradually away towards the north. To the left front rises a treeless "berg" which takes its name from Forbach. Beyond and behind, a dark screen of foliage, the oaks and beeches of the Spicheren Wood, bound the view. Linked to the Forbacherberg by a narrow ridge, which forms the western part of the plateau and runs across the head of the two transverse ravines, a second hillock of inferior altitude, the Spicheren Knoll, fills the foreground to the north. Beyond, but hidden by the knoll, is the saddle and the gradual slope to the Rotherberg. Across the knoll, the vista opens out, for the spur below has broken a passage through the forest. In the middle distance is seen the western shoulder of the Saarbrucken Ridge; and, on the far horizon, the slopes beyond the river crowned by the dark outline of the Kollerthaler Forest.

Immediately at the foot of the Pfaffenberg, Spicheren, a compact and well-built village lies 150 feet below us, the tall church tower, and the red roofs of the substantial granaries peering through a screen of orchards. From the north and west of the village is well sheltered, for it stands at the head of a deep and narrow gully, the southernmost of the two transverse ravines, sinking sharply from the Forbacherberg to the Saar. Beyond, and parallel to the Pfaffenberg, is an open ridge, 400 paces wide. From the brow of this ridge the border of the forest, which crowns the northern crest of the plateau from the Rotherberg to the Saar, and which on the 6th of August hid the interior of the plateau and the camps of Laveaucoupet's Division from the observation of the Prussians on the Saarbrucken Ridge, is 1,000 paces distant; but between them, like a great dry ditch, is the Simbach Ravine, 500 paces broad and 200 feet in depth, the bottom thickly set with fruit trees. Besides the numerous paths and cart tracks which intersect the plateau in every direction, there are two excellent roads, firm and broad; one, running east and west, passes through Spicheren and its woods, and winds down the heights to Stiring Wendel and Schoneck in the Saarbrucken Forest; the other, already spoken of, leading northward from Spicheren descends the Rotherberg, and striking across the St. Arnual Valley climbs the Saarbrucken Ridge between the Reppertsberg and Nussberg.

West of the Forbacherberg, a long trough-like gully faces north, forming a wide and deep depression in the Spicheren Wood. The spur beyond, 250 yards in breadth, is free from timber, and forcing its way amongst the beeches, opens a view across the Forbach Valley to the Saarbrucken Forest.

Such were the principal features of the ground held by Laveaucoupet's soldiers, who, if they stood on the western crest, looked down from an altitude of 300 feet upon the left wing in the Forbach Valley, the rugged face of the plateau effectually preventing intercommunication and observation, and dividing the position into two distinct sections. The Rotherberg, jutting like a bastion from the northern face of the heights, commanded the length and breadth of the valley below, but the faces of the ascent were everywhere so steep and thickly wooded that they could not be swept by fire from the crest. An extensive view over the whole landscape, obstructed only by the Saarbrucken Ridge, is obtained from the spur. From the Pfaffenberg and the Forbacherberg, the Drill-ground Hill, and even the forest beyond the river, can be seen; and from the Forbacherberg and its northern underfeature the mouth of the Forbach Valley is effectively commanded. But, from the interior of the plateau, even from the Spicheren Knoll, the crest of the Rotherberg is nowhere visible.

THE VALLEY

The rolling pastures of the re-entrant which lie between the Spicheren Heights and the Saarbrucken Forest, ascend gradually toward Forbach. Here the boundaries converge, and the town stands at the very apex of the valley. Two miles north, the village of Stiring Wendel and the great spur covered by the Spicheren Wood form a barrier across the centre.

Between then creeps the Metz High-road, lined with lofty poplars; and on this road, where the valley opens out again, stood four buildings which played an important part in the battle to come. Nearest to Stiring Wendel, and fronting the long ravine which drops from the Forbacherberg, is the Banque Mouton, a substantial homestead, with granary and outbuildings. 400 yards north, to the east of the chausée, are the two houses which bore the sign of the Golden Bremm, surrounded by garden walls, eight feet in height, and shadowed by the foliage of the overhanging wood. Not many paces further north stood the French Toll House.

From the brow of the rising ground, north-west, the Toll House, and looking towards the Drill-ground Hill, two parallel undulations, across which the high-road passes, meet the eye. The first, and lower of the two, fills the foreground, from the railway to the Rotherberg, and closes the entrance of the Forbach Valley. This is the Folster Height – 270 feet below the crest of the Rotherberg, – and thereon was the German Custom House. 1,200 paces beyond rise the grassy knolls of the Galgenberg, midway between the Saarbrucken Ridge and the Spicheren Heights, and 240 feet below the crest of the Rotherberg.

Across the centre of the Forbach Valley runs the Spicheren-Schoneck Road, skirting the mound on which stands the Stiring Foundry.

Stiring Wendel is an industrial village of modern date; the streets straight and regular, the houses compact and strongly built. It is protected on the west by the deep cutting of the railroad. Beyond this cutting are a few houses; and the walls of a large garden form a bastion on this side, as does the foundry on the north.

The foundry, surrounded on two sides, north and east, by a railing made of iron uprights nearly six feet high, was capable, although the buildings were wooden, of protracted defence against riflemen unsupported by artillery. The western side was partially uncovered. Here the railway runs for 100 yards upon the level, but the foundry sheds stand back 50 or 60 yards from the line, and the yard in front was filled with trucks and heaps of slag. At the north-west and south-west corners, the ground sinks sharply. At the former angle, the railway crosses the Spicheren-Schoneck Road by a bridge, which is touched by the railing already mentioned; at the latter it runs through a cutting 40 feet in depth.

Beyond the railway, north-west of the foundry, are a few scattered cottages, which go by the name of Old Stirigen; and, further west, close to the encircling forest, crowning the gentle slope of a long, bare spur, is a group of buildings, tall and black, marking the site of a disused coal-pit.

In front of the foundry, across a little valley, and 600 paces distant to the north, is the Stiring Copse, a grove of lofty timber, concealing the village and foundry from the Drill-ground Hill. The trees are beeches, of good girth and tall; and, except near the border, there is no young growth or brush to hinder the passage of troops in extended order between their smooth and massive trunks.

The Saarbrucken Forest, extending from the banks of the river to the Kaninchenberg near Forbach, along the entire left flank of the position, is of a different character. Covering a broad tract of country, roads and clearings are not infrequent; but the trees stand close; the undergrowth is dense and tangled; and the task of moving through its dark recesses, except by the paths, is difficult and tedious.

North of the Stiring Copse, and below the slopes of the Folster Height, are the farm buildings of Drathzug, commanded at 1,800 paces from the western shoulder of the Drill-ground Hill.

The ponds along the railroad and at the foot of the Folster Height are shallow, marshy pools, but the first is so wide and treacherous as to form an effective obstacle.

Due west of Forbach and the railway, on the left rear of the position, the Kaninchenberg, a long and narrow ridge, forms a solid barrier across the *débouché* of the Saarlouis end, but is approached by woods on either flank.

It was reported by a newspaper correspondent that when the rumour that an attack on the Spicheren Heights was imminent spread through the French camps it was welcomed with stern satisfaction by the men. Without doubt, they had good cause for confidence.

The bold projection of the Rotherberg, lifting its red crest high above the open valleys and flanking every direct approach; the steep faces of the plateau, and the woods which hid the interior both from view and fire; the massive village of Stiring Wendel, perfectly protected from bombardment; the open ground which the enemy must traverse in his advance, and the absence of any commanding position for his artillery, rendered the position to all appearances exceedingly strong.

But natural difficulties do not of themselves make a good position. Ground which presents great obstacles to the passage of ordinary wayfarers, or to an army on the march, is often more favourable to the attack than the defence. This is especially true of positions of which high hills form a part. In 1863, a Confederate army, under General Bragg, drove the Northern army of the Tennessee into Chattanooga and taking post on the mountains which overlook the town, blockaded the defeated troops for several weeks. On the arrival of Grant, the heights on which the flanks of Bragg's line rested were attacked; Look-out Mountain (2,200 feet high) on the right was carried. On the left but little ground was gained. The Federal general then suddenly changed his plan, and hurled his reserve against the right centre of the enemy's position, a ridge from 500 to 800 feet high. The rifle-pits at the foot of the slope although covered by abattis, were carried at the first rush; and, with scarcely a pause, the troops dashed up the steep hill-side, swept over a line of trenches half-way up the ascent, and finally drove the Confederates in confusion from their earth-works on the crest.

The occupation of a position in a hilly or rugged country is then, a difficult business. As a Southern Staff Officer remarked, upon visiting Bragg's position above Chattanooga, "It may be a pretty view, but it is a d—d bad prospect;" and if we examine closely into Frossard's procedure at Spicheren, his use or neglect of natural difficulties, his choice of

View of the battlefield from the Winterberg

ground for his main line, and the advantages and disadvantages of his selection, we may learn a practical lesson of great value.

The position of the valley need not detain us long.

It may be said that here the homesteads, the Spicheren-Schoneck Road, the centre of the Stiring Copse, and the village of Old Stiringen, including the disused coal pit, was the main line, Stiring Wendel forming the second position or reduit. The position on the plateau is by far the more important, both as presenting greater difficulties to selection, and affording most useful tactical suggestions.

Bearing in mind the peculiar configuration of the heights, the densely wooded slopes, the steep and lofty crest, the broad space of open ground which divided the belt of forest from the commanding ridges north and south, of Spicheren it is obvious that there was much room for choice.

(1) The main line might be thrust forward so as to include the lower edge of the Pfaffen and Gifert Woods, and the crest of the Rotherberg, or (2) the crest within the Pfaffen and Gifert Woods, and the crest of the Rotherberg, or (3) might be withdrawn to the ridge north of Spicheren, and Forbacherberg, with the Rotherberg as an advanced post.

In his account of the battle, Frossard himself nowhere indicates on which of the three he decided, and it is exceedingly doubtful if he came to any decision whatever. There are critics, however, who hold that the crest of the plateau and the spur were held merely as an advanced post, but, as will be seen hereafter, the distribution of the French troops during the attack, the conduct of their generals, their strenuous efforts to maintain, and afterwards to retake, the Rotherberg and the woods, and to deny the Prussians a footing on the plateau, proves conclusively that the verge of the heights was the main line.

Deferring criticism for the moment, we will proceed to consider the advantages and disadvantages of this selection.

The advantages

1. From the Rotherberg, the whole of the ground, over which the enemy must advance after descending the Saarbrucken Ridge, was thoroughly commanded.
2. The approach to the woods on the right, and the entrance to the Forbach Valley on the left, were flanked from the spur.

3. Both flanks were fairly well protected; the right by the Saar, the left by the dense Saarbrucken Forest; and for the latter the foundry and Stiring Wendel Village formed a strong reduit, covered as they were from artillery fire by the Stiring Copse.
4. Lateral communications, the Spicheren-Schoneck and Etzling-Forbach roads, were good. Moreover, the surface of the plateau – except where the gullies intervened – and the unfenced pastures of the Forbach Valley, presented no impediment to the free movement of men and guns.
5. The St. Arnual Valley, severing the Spicheren Heights and the Saarbrucken Ridge, and extending along the whole front, was open and unobstructed, affording no cover to the assailant, and nowhere of less breadth than 1,000 paces.
6. The Folster Height, which, although far below the crest of the Spicheren Heights, was the only rising ground whence artillery fire could be brought to bear upon the centre of the Forbach Valley, was commanded and flanked at short range from the Rothenberg.
7. The ridge north of Spicheren, with a fair field of view and fire as far as the borders of the forest, 1,200 paces distant, together with the Forbacherberg, formed an exceedingly strong second line of defence – covered on the left by, the Spicheren Wood, and strengthened by the Simbach Ravine in front, and by the fact that, if the main line were carried, the assailant would be unable to find room, except above the Rotherberg, for his artillery.
8. The extent of front to be covered was not too great, for the numbers at Frossard's disposal. From the edge of the Pfaffen Wood, the extreme right, to the coal pit on the extreme left, is 4,700 yards in a straight line. Taking the strength of the 2nd Corps at 27,000, this gives 5½ men to the yard; according to our own drill-book, 5 men to the yard is sufficient.

The disadvantages

1. The position was a broken one, half on the heights, half in the valley; and the centre was ill-defined.
2. Artillery positions were few. Only from the Rotherberg could artillery play on the St. Arnual Valley, and it is faced by the long Saarbrucken Ridge at a distance of 2,000 yards. But there is also room for the deployment of two batteries on the spur of the Forbacherberg, commanding the Folster Height, and there was no obstacle to the deployment of a long line of batteries in the Forbach Valley.
3. The steep and thickly wooded faces of the plateau, and the unbroken area of forest enclosing the right front and flank, were distinct sources of weakness. The slopes were not under fire from the crest; and the lower edge of the timber, from the Rotherberg to the Saar, is 3,500 yards in length, an extent of woodland that would have required many hours of skilled labour to entangle. The whole border, as moreover, is within 2,000 paces of the Saarbrucken Heights; and, therefore, if occupied, would have been exposed to a bombardment to which no reply would have been possible. The obstacles to supervision and manœuvring in the great breadth of wood, which covered the right front, were insurmountable. On the steep hill-sides, if the lower edge were held, were no suitable positions for supports or reserves; and it may be pointed out that the Duke of Würtemberg has stated that an energetic defence of the border of the wood could not have been ensured, for the difficulties of retreat

up the almost perpendicular ascent would have had a bad effect on the *moral* of the defenders.

4. The main line of retreat, the road and railway Forbach-St. Avoid, was in rear of the flank, and not of the centre; and the secondary line, the Spicheren-Saarguemund Road, struck off at an obtuse angle to the front.
5. The position was somewhat unfavourable for counter-attack. The Saarbrucken Ridge offered a secure asylum to the enemy if repulsed; and artillery could only be brought to bear against him from the Folster Height and the Rotherberg. Nevertheless, as the action of the 2nd August had proved, the ridge might have been turned from the St. Arnual Forest; and, moreover, the enemy would have been compelled to fight with a river at his back.
6. The view from the height was blocked by the Saarbrucken Ridge. The road leading from the Kollerthaler Forest, but not those from the east, nor the viaduct across the Saar, can be seen from the plateau.

The ground then, although some of its characteristics undoubtedly favoured the defence, by no means fulfilled all the requirements of a formidable position. But Frossard had little choice; and, as is often the case in war, was called upon to show his skill in the occupation of the line rather than in its selection.

We have now to consider whether the selection of the crest of the plateau, the Stiring-Schoneck Road, and the centre of the Stiring Copse, as the main-line, was judicious or otherwise.

It has been laid down by Colonel Schaw, and it is a common-sense maxim, that where the slopes of a hill are commanded by fire from the crest, the crest is the most advantageous line, for the whole space over which the assailant must advance is swept by fire, and the fire is likely to be particularly efficacious during the last part of his movement, the ascent of the hill-side. But in the case we are considering, not only did the steepness of slopes everywhere preclude their being so commanded, but the existence of dense woods covering the hill-side, encroaching on the valley below, and hiding the crest above, made the selection of a position doubly difficult.

The French commanders chose to renounce the lower border of the woods and to station their men upon the crest, trusting perhaps to the flanking fire from the Rotherberg to prevent the Germans gaining easy access to the woods. As the sequel will show, in this they were unsuccessful.

Nor was the position on the crest a strong one. In wood fighting, when once the assailant has entered the covert, he is on equal terms with the defender, and the larger battalions will, *cæteris paribus*, prove victorious. The chief reliance of the occupant of a defensive position is on the difficulties of approach thereto. These neutralize the numbers of the assailant. But, by relinquishing the lower border, which commanded the broad and open valley, and deciding to meet the attack in the middle of the wood, the French lost all power of making the approach of the Germans a costly operation. The flanking fire from the Rotherberg could be easily kept in check by the German artillery; and the steepness of the slopes which led to the crest within the Gifert Wood, unswept as they were by fire, and concealed by timber, were a positive advantage to the assailants, permitting them to approach close to the main position with but trifling loss.

Again, as we have seen, Frossard might have made the Spicheren Ridge and the Forbacherberg his main line, maintaining the Rotherberg and the crest within the

Gifert as an advanced post; a post which might have made the advance of the Germans across the valley a costly operation, have delayed their attack on the main position, and exhausted the fighting powers of their men. When the post had fallen, or was abandoned before pressure of numbers, the assailants would have found themselves, as they lined the southern border of the Gifert Wood, with a broad open space and wide ravine, 200 feet in depth, between them and the enemy's main line, and without the means to assemble, or the room to deploy a strong force of artillery.

It is evident that Frossard's selection was the worst of the three; but which was the better of the other two, whether to hold the lower border of the woods as the main line, or to carry the main-line back to the Spicheren Ridge and the Forbacherberg, it is not so easy to decide. The lower edge of the woods was exposed, as has been said, to bombardment from the Saarbrucken Ridge; it was of great extent; there was no convenient cover on the steep hill-side for the supports; and the difficulties of retreat might, perhaps, as the Duke of Würtemburg has written, have had a bad effect on the *moral* of the defenders. Still, it was unnecessary to hold the border at every point; a few battalions, stationed at intervals, would have rendered the approach across the valley almost impossible by a frontal and cross-fire; and the bulk of the troops might have been detained behind the crest above until the advance of enemy's infantry masked the fire of his guns. As to the idea of the morale of the troops being affected by their position, this is more or less illusory. The slopes were so thickly timbered that the defenders, as they retreated, would have been well covered, nor could the fire of pursuers' artillery have followed them. In fact, retreat from the crest within the woods across the more open ground to the Spicheren Ridge, would be more likely to prove disastrous. Moreover, the position of the St. Arnual Parish Wood was favourable for a counter-attack on the Saarbrucken Ridge.

Had the main-line been withdrawn to the Spicheren Ridge and the Forbacherberg, the assailant, on gaining the Gifert and Pfaffen Woods, might have maintained them with a small force and have worked round the right flank of the main-line through the St. Arnual Wood, and by the Simbach Ravine. But he would have found it impracticable to bring up more than a few guns to the heights, and the front of his attack must have been greatly extended, thus giving an opening for a counterstroke. A position 1,200 paces in rear of a wood which guns cannot traverse, and which covers the whole front, is an exceedingly strong defensive line. It as probable then, that this would have been the best main line of the three; that which Frossard adopted being decidedly the worst.

In the other case, the right might have rested on the edge of the clearing between the Gifert and Pfaffen Woods, both borders of the clearing have been entangled, and a strong reserve retained on the crest to the right rear, in order to occupy the St. Arnual Wood in case of a flank attack, or to deliver a counterstroke against the Winterberg.

On the low ground, the selection of a main-line was an easier task; but here again we find the same disinclination to push forward. The northern outskirt of the Stiring Copse should have been occupied. Some 20 or 30 feet below the crest of the Folster Height, and divided from that undulation by a space of less than 300 yards, the field of view and fire was limited; but there was much advantage to be gained from such a forward disposition of the line of battle, and this will be clearly seen on a comprehensive survey of the position. The Rotherberg was salient to the French line; and, at the same time, it was something more than an advanced post. It was the key of the position. Once captured and strongly occupied, the main-line was broken; the enemy could cross the St. Arnual

Valley in security, and mass his troops at his leisure at the foot of the heights. Had the position been carefully examined with a view to the adequate co-operation of artillery and infantry for the defence of the main-line along the crest of the plateau, and also to bringing the two wings into adjustment, it would have been discovered, the left-wing being more retired than the right and the Stiring Copse left open to the hostile infantry, that the enemy's guns would be free to concentrate their efforts on the Rotherberg: the French batteries, owing to the lack of artillery positions on the plateau, and the impossibility of deploying in the Forbach Valley whilst the enemy's rifle-men occupied the Stiring Copse, being unable to oppose the enemy's guns, and thus support their own infantry upon the spur. Even had the lower edges of the Gifert Wood been occupied, the hostile guns, deploying on the Galgenberg and western knoll of the Folster height, would be able, as they actually did, to pour a heavy oblique fire on the defenders of the Rotherberg, and to open the way to its capture by their infantry. Salients in any line are weak unless they are well secured by flanking fire. The Rotherberg, was not so secured, and this neglect led to its ultimate loss.

Nor was any device attempted on either wing to strengthen the main line where it passed within the woods, or to obstruct the passage of the enemy. Not an axe was laid to the trees, though the timber both of the woods upon the plateau, and of the Stiring Copse, was suitable for abattis and entanglement. It may be that in the general dearth of matériel, felling implements were not forthcoming; but had the French taken to heart the lessons of the Secession War; or had they possessed the skill of the American volunteers in improvising breastworks, Frossard's position would have assuredly been greatly strengthened.

Had it been decided to hold the northern edge of Stiring Copse, the occupation of the Folster Height would have greatly strengthened the line of battle. It is commanded at 2,000 yards range from the Saarbrucken Ridge, but there is sufficient cover to be found behind it; and earthworks might have been rapidly constructed on the crest. There is a broad field of fire to the front; and the supports of the troops posted in the trenches would have found shelter in the rear, and it is protected on the left by the copse and pond. The batteries would then have been able to deploy in the valley.

The best excuse for Frossard's desire to refuse his left was his apprehension of an attack on Forbach from the Saarbrucken Forest; and the true explanation of his choice of a position on the heights, of his neglect to entangle the woods, and of his carelessness as to the adjustment of his wings, lies in the fact that, notwithstanding his knowledge that the enemy was approaching in great force, notwithstanding Le Boeuf's warning, he was completely surprised by von Kamecke's appearance, and had to frame his plan of battle on the spur of the moment.

DISTRIBUTION OF THE FRENCH TROOPS

On the night of the 5th, 5 companies of the 77th Line formed the outposts on the left and centre: one company in the Forbach Valley, three in the copse and Saarbrucken Forest, one near the Rotherberg. The regiment, with the 3rd Chasseurs, encamped between the copse and the foundry; the 76th behind Stiring Wendel.

Soon after day-break the cavalry of the various divisions was despatched to reconnoitre. A squadron of the 12th Dragoons was ordered by Vergé up the Metz High road , a second, at 9 o'clock, together with 10 companies of the 55th Regiment, through the Saarbrucken Forest on the road to Volklingen and Saarlouis; the remainder towards Saarguemund. The 5th Chasseurs, attached to Bataille's division, proceeded towards Grossbliederstroff; whilst Laveaucoupet watched the Simbach Ravine with two squadrons of the 7th Dragoons. The rest of the cavalry, the 4th Chasseurs and half of the 7th Dragoons, remained in bivouac at Forbach.

How the picquets were disposed on the heights is not known, but before 8 o'clock the Rotherberg was occupied; and under cover of a strong party of the 10th Chasseurs, posted at the foot of the hill, a company of sappers constructed a horse-shoe shelter-trench round the crest. Before the end of July, gunpits had been thrown up near the corner of the wood in rear.

Shortly before 12 o'clock, two companies of the 10th Chasseurs (260 rifles), took post in the trench, supported by two guns, 100 paces in rear. A third company formed a second line and an escort for the artillery, the remainder, still further back, the battalion reserve. 250 paces in rear of the left of the advanced section, was placed a second section of the 8th Light Battery.

The 40th Regiment of Micheler's Brigade was in immediate support of the Chasseurs, stationed behind the timber, with a battalion in the clearing between the Gifert and the Pfaffen Woods.

The 24th was held back for the present on the ridge north of Spicheren, where the brigade had bivouacked.

At 11.30 a.m., when the Prussian infantry first appeared upon the Saarbrucken Ridge, the 7th Light Battery was sent forward from its camp by Spicheren.

Two sections, to which was joined a section of the 8th Battery, were halted 200 yards north of the village, and a little east of the Spicheren Knoll, facing the clearing between the Gifert and the Pfaffen Woods. The remaining section of the 7th Battery proceeded to the Rotherberg, and took post on the right of the rear section of the 8th Battery, making 6 guns in all upon the spur.

Doen's Brigade, the 2nd and 63rd Regiments of the Line, stood, at 11.30, on the Pfaffenberg; but before 12 o'clock two companies of II/2 were dispatched to support the two squadrons of the 7th Dragoons in the Simbach Ravine, and it seems that a force of cavalry was stationed on the river road below.

In the Forbach Valley, I/76 occupied the French Toll House, the Golden Bremm, and Banque Mouton. The 77th Regiment had picquets in the Saarbrucken Forest; 4 guns were placed in epaulments, east of Stiring Wendel, 1,000 yards in front of the Iron Foundry; and the 3rd Chasseurs had entered the Stiring Copse, but the troops of Jolivet's Brigade were for the most part still in camp when the Prussian infantry ascended the Saarbrucken Ridge.

Valazé's Brigade watched the *débouché* of the Volklingen and Saarlouis Road, strongly posted on the Kaninchenberg and in Forbach Town.

Bataille's Division was in reserve at Oetingen, 3 miles in rear of Spicheren; of the Reserve Artillery 4 (9pr.) batteries were in Forbach, 2 (16pr.), near Morsbach.

Defensive works

The front was strengthened by the following field-works: The horse-shoe shelter trench encircling the crest of the Rotherberg; cover for the supports; and slight epaulments for artillery in rear. A line of shelter-trench along the Spicheren-Stiring road (constructed

Major-General von François, commander of the German 27th Infantry Brigade, 14th Infantry Division, VII Corps (Ruppersberg)

between 10 and 12 o'clock), and gun-pits for four pieces, 1000 yards north-east of the foundry. A shelter-trench, 1,100 yards in length, upon the Kaninchenberg.

These works were thrown up previous to the Prussian attack; but, during the course of the engagement, it appears that others were constructed both on the Forbacherberg and Spieheren Knoll. The foundry and some of the neighbouring buildings in Stiring Wendel were loop-holed.

Had the various roads leading to Volklingen and Saarlouis been properly reconnoitred, there would have been no necessity to retain the whole of Valazé's Brigade in Forbach. The reserve division was close by at Oetingen; and two battalions and a battery, thus supported, would have been sufficient to hold the Kaninchenberg; the remainder being brought forward to support the left wing in the Forbach Valley.

With this exception, little fault can be found with the dispositions of the French Commander and his divisional generals, expecting, as they did, to be attacked by a superior force; but, as before asserted, it was a gross and unpardonable neglect on the part of Frossard and his Cavalry Brigadier not to have taken steps to have the roads *beyond* the Saar constantly patrolled during the previous day, and also on the morning of the 6th, and thus obtain information of the enemy's strength and whereabouts.

This omission, more than all else, decided the battle against the French. So simple were the circumstances that it seems impossible that any soldier of standing, or even any man of ordinary common sense, should have neglected such a precautionary measure. But it is by omissions of this kind, by disregard of the primary and most familiar rules of war, that battles are lost and great disasters brought about; and hence the great strength of an army so thoroughly instructed as was the German. The judgment of the generals might err, but officers and men were so perfectly acquainted with their duty, that the traditional precautions which ensure the security of the troops from surprise, whether on the march, in the bivouac, in position, or during the attack, were very seldom overlooked. It is doubtless true, that a blind and absolute respect of rule is a frequent cause of military misadventure; but, nevertheless, there are certain elementary principles which cannot be neglected with impunity. Very necessary is it therefore, that every officer who has command of a body of troops in the field, however small, should be so thoroughly imbued with a knowledge of those principles as to apply them, as it were, instinctively. This knowledge the German officers possessed; it was acquired, in the first place, in the class-room; and, by constant practice in field manœuvres, the application of it had become a second nature. Throughout the war, therefore, we find that far fewer mistakes were committed by the Germans than the French; and in war, where the combatants are fairly equally matched, he wins who makes the least mistakes. These principles, moreover, are few and simple; and it would appear that any man of courage and common sense, without any previous training, would naturally apply them in battle. But, if there is one lesson more than another which history and experience impress upon us, it is that in war, common sense is a quality by no means to be relied on. Even the greatest generals, at the height of their fame, have committed errors so glaring as to excite the wonder of the youngest student; and it is absolutely certain that the knowledge which has solidified into instinct is more to be depended on when the lives of men, the honour of one's country, and personal reputation are at stake, than mere natural capacity.

ADVANCE OF THE 27TH BRIGADE

Shortly before 12 o'clock, General von François, commanding 27th Brigade, received orders from von Kamecke to drive the enemy's artillery from the Rotherberg. This, in all probability, was only preparatory to driving back the apparently weak force of French infantry from the heights which overlooked the Saarbrucken Ridge.

The 27th Brigade was at that moment disposed as follows:

39th Fusiliers, I and F/74, upon the Drill-ground Hill and Reppertsberg.

II/74, South of Drathzug Farm, with a section in the Stiring Copse.

French guns on the Rotherberg at Spicheren (Rousset/*Combattants*)

1/7 was already in action on the southern slopes of the Drill-ground Hill. The three remaining batteries I, II, 2/7 and the 28th Brigade were at Rachspfnhl – the rear of the column still involved in the Kollerthaler Forest – and nearly 3 miles distant from the ridge. The batteries were immediately summoned to the front, and von Woyna was directed to march the whole of the 28th Brigade across the viaduct, to attack the enemy's right flank, and to threaten his communications with Forbach.

Von François, sharing, in all likelihood, the conviction of his superior, that the Spicheren Heights and Forbach Valley held a force but little stronger than his own brigade, and relying on the speedy support of von Woyna's troops, determined to move against the Rotherberg on both flanks simultaneously. II/74, already at the Drathzug Farm, was to secure the right flank. III/39 was to attack the Spur from to west. I and II/39 were to advance against the enemy's right wing through the St. Arnual Wood. I and F/74 were to remain in reserve upon the Reppertsberg, and the 9th Company, 39th, was ordered up from Neudorf.

Now, from the Stiring Copse to the St. Arnual Forest is little short of 4,000 yards, a very great extent of front to be assaulted by 6 battalions and 4 batteries, the force at von François' disposal. The operation was to be supported, it is true by another brigade; but that brigade was still at some distance; it had been ordered to approach the field by the narrow defile of the viaduct and the ground beyond presented great impediments to rapid movement and deployment. The French position, as we know, had been by no means thoroughly reconnoitred, and it was possible that the rough estimate of 7,000 defenders, reported by the cavalry scouts, was very much below the total.

Nor did the situation demand an immediate advance. That von Kamecke should have allowed his leading brigade to assault a position which had not been thoroughly reconnoitred, in so weak a formation as that adopted by von François, has been stigmatized as foolhardy; and the risk he ran in engaging along an extended front, without waiting for his supports to close up, or preparing the attack by overwhelming the French guns upon the Rotherberg, can scarcely be justified.

As for von François, his numbers were inferior to those of the French, as reported by the patrols; and for an inferior force to attack a superior simultaneously on both flanks is a breach of tactical principles which can only be committed with impunity against an enemy weak in *moral*, armament, or discipline. Supports were certainly coming up, but they were still distant; and there was every chance, even did the French force consist only of 7,000 men, and was but a rear-guard, that one or other of his columns of attack would be crushed before assistance arrived.

Had a little more time been allowed, a more effective formation might have been adopted – the left attack have been committed to the 27th, the right to the 28th Brigade; and the evil of the troops under one command being dispersed over a front too extensive to be supervised by a single leader, have been avoided.

When instant action is necessary, the first line of attack must, as a rule, be entrusted to a single unit; but where there is time for preparation, the formation of the troops should be carefully considered. It is almost an impossibility to correct errors once a battle has been joined; and it is of the utmost importance that no single battalion, brigade, or division, should be asked to act upon too large a front. In such a case, as with the 27th Brigade at Spicheren, if a stout resistance be met with, the reserves will rapidly be drawn into the gaps of the long fighting line, and no force will be left in hand to resist counter-attack, to press the assault, or to cover a retreat. Success in battle turns, as a rule, upon the skilful employment of reserves. No commander, therefore, who has a definite task set to him, a particular point of the defence to carry, should be deprived of the use of his reserves at the critical moment, by having been compelled, at the outset, to occupy an abnormal front.

Although determined to lose no time, von Kamecke did not neglect to support von François with the portion of his force that was immediately available; nor did he leave the task of clearing the Rotherberg to the infantry alone. On the stroke of noon, the three batteries of the main-body deployed upon the southern slopes of Reppertsberg and in conjunction with 1/7 which, in order to bring an oblique fire to bear upon the hostile guns, now crossed the Ehrenthal and took post upon the Drathzug Knoll, concentrated their efforts on the spur. Covered by the fire of these twenty-four pieces, the infantry marched off on either flank. It may be noted that no escort was told off to the artillery.

THE RIGHT ATTACK – 12 NOON–2.30 PM

II/74 had occupied the Drathzug Farm with a company; two others were posted on either side the railroad; one was held in reserve, and the marksmen's section of the 6th Company had been despatched to search the north-east corner of the Stiring Copse.

The three companies of III/39, descending the Drill-ground Hill, and crossing the Folster Height in line of company columns, at deploying intervals, were assailed by hostile shells. The attention of the French infantry and artillery upon the Rotherberg appears to have diverted from this battalion, passing beneath the spur at short range, by the fire of the Prussian guns, or by the movements of the other attacking column, but the four guns in the Forbach Valley now first revealed their presence, and Chassepôts from the neighbourhood of the Toll House and the Golden Bremen, where the First Battalion of the French 76th was posted, opened fire at a range of 1,400 yards. Few casualties occurred in the Prussian ranks; but, in consequence of this fire, the 39th, instead of wheeling towards the Rothberg, entered the Stiring copse, moved forward on the left of the section of 6/74, and became at once engaged with the advancing skirmishers of the 3rd Chasseurs. At the same time, the marksman's section of the 12th Company, detached in order to cover the left flank, took up a position behind an undulation 1,000 paces from the German Custom House, bringing a brisk fire to bear upon the enemy's artillery and infantry in the neighbourhood of the homesteads.

Through the widely scattered trunks of the lofty beeches the Fusiliers pressed rapidly forward to the middle of the copse, the French riflemen giving way before them. At this point, however, the wood grows thicker; the enemy appeared in force, and the Fusiliers were soon hard put to it to hold their own. Support was not forthcoming, for II/74 had meanwhile crossed the railroad under a heavy fire from the foundry and Old Stiringen; and, with the 7th Company in advance, was moving forward through the Saarbrucken Forest, in the hope of outflanking the French left.

Reaching the northern limit of the clearing below the coal-pit, at 1.30 pm, the 7th Company 74th broke into a line of skirmishers along the border of the wood, two sections of the 6th being brought up to prolong the line to the right, whilst the 5th and 8th, in line of company columns at deploying intervals, formed the reserve in rear. The Coal-pit Ridge was occupied by three companies of the 77th of the French Line; these were speedily reinforced by another half-battalion, and the Prussians, although protected by

Général de Division Merle de Labrugière de Laveaucoupet, commander of the French 3rd Division, II Corps (Rousset/*Histoire*)

the timber, suffered heavily from the Chassepôt fire at a range of 700 yards. Nor was the position long maintained. The front of the whole right attack was far too weak. The French, so soon as it became evident that the operation was something more than a reconnaissance in force, gradually developed their strength. The mitrailleuse and the second field battery (6/5 and 7/17) of Verge's Division came into action near the Golden Bremm, on the right and left of the 5th Battery, which was now complete. The Second and Third Battalions of the 76th of the Line deployed 800 paces north-east of Stiring Wendel. I/77 was posted on the left of the railway, and furnished half a battalion for the defence of the Old Stiringen and the coal pits. II and III/77 held the village and formed the reserves. Within the copse the Chasseurs pressed hard upon the 39th, and a message was therefore sent to the brigadier for reinforcements. The commander of II/74, engaged himself with a powerful force, but attentive to the course of the action on his left, had become aware of the distress of the Fusiliers. Their line, it was apparent, was gradually receding. Should the French become masters of the copse, his own danger would be great; the 8th Company, therefore, was sent back to the railway crossing, south-west of Drathzug. The marksman's section deployed across the line, and checking detachments of French riflemen who were attempting to press forward along the permanent way, effectually secured the flank of the 39th; and by reserving its fire until the enemy approached within 100 paces, drove back a column that was advancing by the side of the pond.

The remainder of the battalion, without molestation, followed through the forest at short intervals. A position was taken up near Drathzug; and, at the same time, the much-needed support came up from the rear to the 39th.

3/74, it appears, had already, before the remainder of the battalion left the Reppertsberg, marched in rear of 1/7 by way of the German Mill, with instructions to approach unobserved the left flank of the enemy's artillery upon the Rotherberg.

1 and 2/74, led by General von François himself, proceeded towards the Stiring Copse across the Folster Height. Here they were met by 3/74, which, as it crossed the railway near Drathzug Farm, had lost many men from the fire of Verge's battery of mitrailleuses, posted parallel to the Metz High-road, between the Toll House and the Golden Bremm.

A portion of this company joined the brigadier; but the remainder, the larger portion, intent on carrying out the original order, moved eastward towards the Rotherberg, and halted under cover of an undulation, some hundred paces in rear of the marksmen of 12/39. The hostile fire from the slopes above the Golden Bremm prevented a further advance.

After advancing from the Folster Height into the Stiring Copse for about 300 paces, the 2nd Company (74th), joined the hard-pressed right flank of the 39th; whilst the 1st Company, further to the left, lent its support to the detachments as they fell back and again led them forward.

Von François, giving the conduct of this attack to Colonel von Pannwitz, commanding 74th Regiment, rode back to his reserves.

As the Prussian infantry advanced through the copse, the French guns (two field batteries and one of mitrailleuses) retired from their position near the Goden Bremm to the Spicheren-Stiring Road.

By 2.30 pm, the battle on the right was restored; the centre of the copse was regained; and II/74, once more crossing the railway, resumed its attack against the Coal-pit Ridge. The marksmen of the 6th Company had now rejoined their comrades.

The nine Prussian companies, more than 2,000 strong, engaged on this flank of the action, were now deployed along a front of 1,400 yards, an extension which permitted of no reserve and no manœuvring. Against them were arrayed six battalions (3,750 men), the 3rd Chasseurs, the 77th Regiment, and 2 battalions of the 76th, supported by the three divisional batteries, which, from their position on the road, swept the whole of the open space between Stiring Wendel and the woods.

THE LEFT ATTACK – 12 NOON TO 2.30 PM

In order to avoid the ground effectively commanded from the Rotherberg, I and III/39 made a long detour, marching along the crest of the Saarbrucken Ridge as far as the Winterberg, and descending to the level by the gully which falls to the St. Arnual Pond. During this movement, the Germans had their first experience of long-range fire. The column as it wound along the open heights offered a broad target; a hot fire arose from the Rotherberg, occupied by the 10th Chasseurs, and, at a distance exceeding 2000 yards, several men fell.

Leaving the gully, the battalion wheeled to the right, and passing round the pond, followed a track leading towards the saddle between the Gifert and Pfaffen Woods,

The French defend the Gifert Wood (Rousset/*Combattants*)

distinctly recognisable from the thinness of the trees. The formation adopted for the ascent of the wooded heights was as follows:

2/4 3/1 } 1st Battalion } In company column at deploying intervals
7 6/5 } 2nd Battalion }

The track passed through a hollow, but both shot and shell, we are told, fell from the Rotherberg amongst the Fusiliers before they reached the foot of the heights, and, covered by the salient angle of the Gifert Wood, gained shelter and concealment. Doffing their knapsacks before they entered the timber, the ascent was made without obstruction. The lower border was unoccupied and on the leafy slopes above them nothing stirred. But to advance directly up the cliff was almost an impossibility. The leading companies bore off to the right; in the dense thickets the ranks broke up into groups; connection between the successive lines was lost; the 1st and 4th Companies inclined too much to the left; whilst the 2nd Battalion, skirting the edge of the wood and assailed by musketry from the Rotherberg, commenced the ascent at a point further to the right, and nearer, therefore, to the spur.

Shortly after 1 o'clock the leading companies, 2 and 3, reached the crest, and here the Fusiliers again came under fire, for along an undulation within the Gifert Wood were posted the skirmishers of the 40th Regiment of the French Line. These, however, after a brief engagement, withdrew from the covert, and joined the main-body of their battalion, occupying a hollow road and some shallow ditches, a few hundred paces from the border of the wood. From this favourable position a heavy fire was poured upon the

2nd and 3rd Companies of the 39th as they lined the southern outskirts of the timber, and their further advance was stayed.

The companies of the second line came gradually into action in the thinner wood to the left, and the 4th Company, on the extreme flank, moved forward across the clearing between the woods in order to turn the enemy's right. But a company of the 40th had been posted in the thin wood on the saddle before the action began and a support of two companies occupied a ditch within the clearing. The Prussians advanced to the attack with the bayonet, but the advanced company of the French retiring to the corner of the Pfaffen Wood, repulsed the attempt with musketry. A second attempt to turn the enemy's flanks, by pushing through the wood still further to the left, met with no better success. French skirmishers appeared on every hand, contact with the battalion was lost, and the company again withdrew, without, however, drawing the enemy in pursuit.

Whilst the 1st Battalion was thus engaged, two companies of the 2nd came up upon the right. The 6th, which had suffered heavily from flanking fire as it attempted to enter the wood, was retained at the foot of the slopes, and, under cover of a swell of ground, engaged the enemy's riflemen on the Rotherberg at a range of 500 paces.

On the arrival of this reinforcement, the Prussians endeavoured to advance from the shelter of the wood, but the French were supported by the fire of the six guns below the Spicheren Knoll, and the attack was quickly beaten back. And, in truth, it should never have been made. From the border of the Gifert Wood the whole interior of the plateau was plainly visible. The battery below the knoll was little more than 1,300 yards distant, a column of three battalions was advancing across the ravine to the right front, for Laveaucoupet, as the attack developed, had ordered up the 24th to support the 40th. Down the green slopes of the Pfaffenberg, the back-ground of the picture, Doen's Brigade of six battalions was also moving forward, and it must have been evident to the Prussian leaders that, unless strong reinforcements speedily arrived, to hold the ground already won would be well-nigh impossible.

But at this critical moment (2.30 pm), the commander of the 14th Division could do nothing to extricate his troops from the trap into which he had so recklessly thrust them. The three squadrons of cavalry within the Ehrenthal had now increased to seven, but not a single company of infantry remained at his disposal. He could stir no hand to help the 39th, and in what manner his reserve had slipped from his hands must be next recounted.

The three batteries of the main-body, $\frac{\text{I, II, \& 2,}}{7}$ deployed at first upon the Reppertsberg, had failed from that situation to crush the fire of the French guns upon the Rotherberg. Before 1 o'clock, therefore, von Kamecke had ordered them to change position to the Winterberg, and very shortly afterwards the foremost section of the hostile battery upon the spur, exposed to the oblique fire of the battery on the Drathzug Knoll, was compelled to withdraw. Besides the lieutenant in command, several men and horses were wounded, and the two waggons were disabled. Retiring to the saddle, it again came into action on the left of the remaining section. About this time, the six guns upon the spur were reinforced by the divisional mitrailleuse battery, which, taking post to the left rear, engaged the Prussian guns upon the Drathzug Knoll at a range of 1,850 yards.

Général de Division Bataille, commander of the French 2nd Division, II Corps (Rousset/*Histoire*)

It would appear that the rearward movement of the two French guns on the Rotherberg, together with the withdrawal of the batteries in the Forbach Valley and the unobstructed passage of I and II/39 up the slopes of the Gifert Wood, had increased von Kamecke's conviction that the French were in small force. He believed, it appears, that one resolute effort only was required to master the plateau, for, shortly after 1 o'clock, he ordered the two battalions of the 74th, his sole reserve, to assault the Rotherberg in front.

To support this movement, the three batteries of the main body were brought from the Winterberg to the Galgenberg, and, although within long range (1,300 yards) of the enemy's musketry, and 200 feet below the horse-shoe trench, concentrated their fire upon the defenders of the spur. This attack, being distinct from, but linking together those in progress on either wing, may be termed:

THE CENTRAL ATTACK – 1.10 PM–2.30 PM

The Fusilier battalion of the 74th, accompanied by General von François and the colonel of the regiment, headed the advance from the Reppertsberg, formed in line of company columns at 80 paces interval, with the whole of its marksman's sections extended 150–200 paces to the front. As the First Battalion, following at short distance to the right rear, approached the Galgenberg, the brigadier received an appeal for help from the Stiring Copse, and led, as we have seen, the 1st and 2nd Companies in that direction.

It has already been recorded that the 3rd Company had before this been directed to the same quarter of the field. The 4th Company alone followed the Fusiliers.

As they crossed the open space between the opposing heights, these five companies suffered severely, for, disregarding the shells of the four hostile batteries, the garrison of the Rotherberg, riflemen and artillery, concentrated their fire on the advancing infantry.

More than fifteen hundred paces of absolutely open ground intervened between the Ehrenthal and the Spicheren Heights, nor was shelter to be obtained until the foot of the Rotherberg was reached. But despite the heavy fire which assailed them and the rapid thinning of their ranks, without breaking their formation or attempting to reply with the needle gun, the Fusiliers traversed this deadly zone at a steady pace. As they neared the heights, their losses became less frequent, and when they gained the shelter of the bank which runs round the foot of the Rotherberg, the hostile bullets passed harmlessly overhead. Here, his four companies hidden by the steepness of the slope from the trenches on the crest, and firing only when some adventurous Frenchman ventured on the face of the cliff, von François awaited the development of the flank attack of the 39th within the Gifert Wood. The men were with difficulty restrained from dashing forward up the height, but the attempt would have been useless. The defenders of the trenches were on the alert, and except 9/39, which had just arrived upon the drill-ground and had been already ordered to assist them, no support was at hand. The 4th Company had been directed to the east side of the Rotherberg, in order to protect the flank of the battalion against a possible counter-attack from the north west corner of the Gifert Wood. Without much loss, it had succeeded in joining 6/39, well covered from the spur by rising ground.

It appears at first sight almost incomprehensible, considering that a battalion of Chasseurs and a company of Sappers, 800 riflemen, besides 6 guns, were posted on the Rotherberg, and that the ground over which they advanced was perfectly open, that the five companies of the 74th were not absolutely annihilated before they reached the

The advance of the Fusilier Battalion of the German 74th Infantry Regiment against the Rotherberg (Ruppersberg)

spur. Their escape was, however, due more to the covering fire of the four batteries on the Galgenberg and Drathzug Knoll, than to the indifferent and uncontrolled musketry of the French. The regimental history of the 10th Chasseurs states that: "the German batteries concentrated all their efforts on the infantry, and their fire enabled the Prussian companies to gain ground." No less remarkable is the forward position taken by the German batteries on the Galgenberg, so close beneath the shelter-trench. It may be noticed that the four batteries of the 14th Division lost throughout the day but 2 officers,

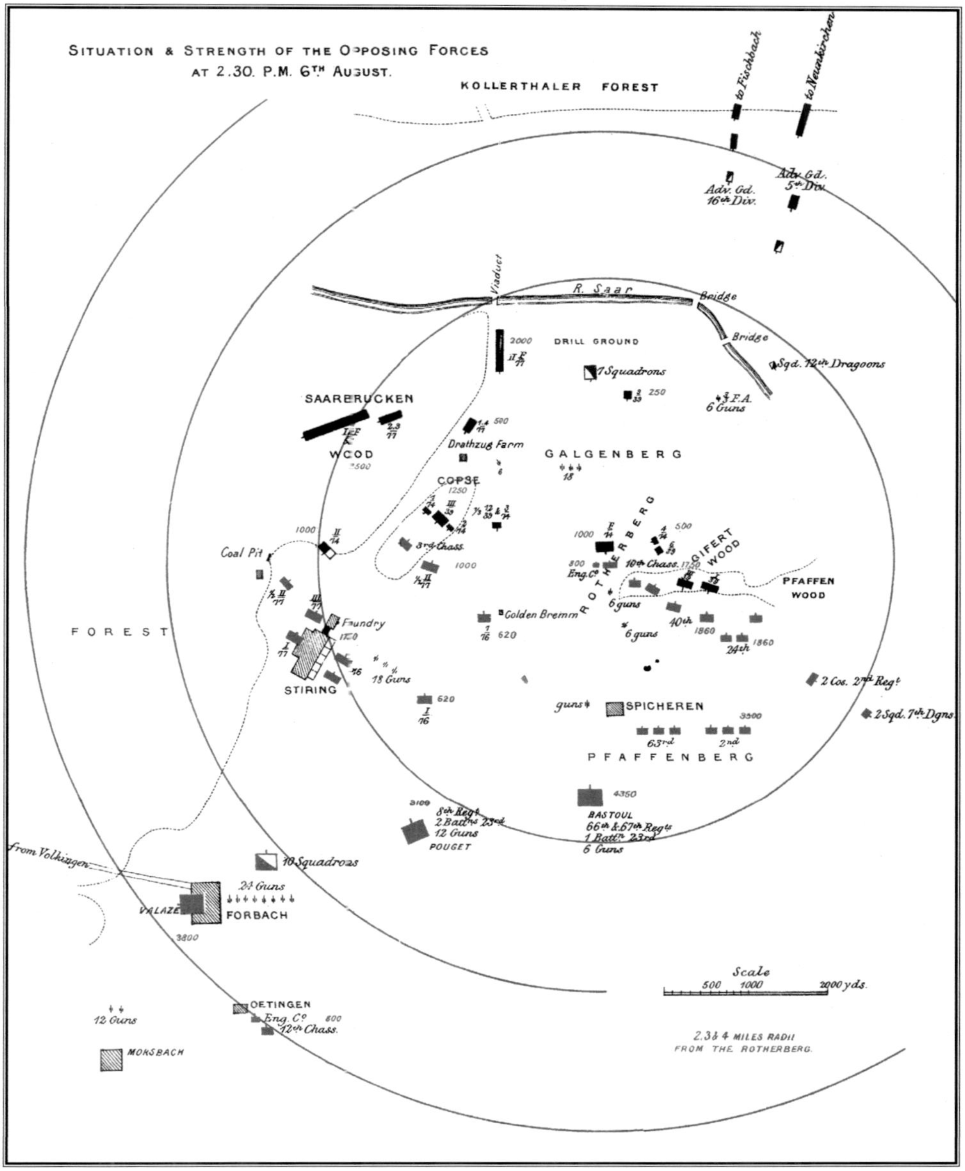

Situation and strength of the opposing forces, 2.30pm

24 men, and 45 horses, and that the very effective flanking position of the guns on the Drathzug Knoll – and later on the Folster Height – would have been untenable had the Stiring Copse been occupied.

THE STATE OF THE ENGAGEMENT AT 2.30 PM

At 2.30 pm, therefore, the Fusiliers of the 74th, already severely handled, could do no more than hold their position, to advance or retreat were alike impossible. On the left, the attempt of I and II/39 to move forward from the Gifert Wood had been crushed, and, on the right, within the Stiring Copse, the attack had gained but little ground. Along the whole line, the Prussians had lost heavily, and the troops were much exhausted. Every rifle of the 27th Brigade had been thrown into the fighting line, for 9/39 was already descending the Reppertsberg, and, although the advanced guards of the 5th and 16th Divisions were approaching St. Johann, they had still to pass through the towns, to cross the river, and to traverse the St. Arnual Valley, ere they could render effective aid.

The 28th Brigade, which, had von Kamecke's disposition been less hasty, would have been the natural support of the 27th, had passed the viaduct, but it had received instructions to attack the left rear of enemy, and the whole of the 53rd Regiment, together with a half-battalion of I/77, was already involved in the tangled thickets of the Saarbrucken Forest. 1 and 4/77 had just reached Drathzug, the remainder of the brigade was still some distance in rear.

A vigorous effort on the part of the French would, in all probability, have rolled up this attack. The German fighting line within the Stiring Copse, and along the northern edge of the Coal-pit Clearing, was composed of but nine companies of the 28th brigade. The 53rd Regiment, cut off by the dense wood, was in no condition to render effectual support, the column in rear was moving through a narrow defile, and the two companies at Drathzug could have scarcely done more than cover the retreat.

On the extreme left, the situation was still more critical. Save 9/39, 250 rifles, no support whatever was available. General von Doering, commanding the 9th Brigade, who had outstripped his advanced guard by some miles, was ascending the ridge with

3 L

3 (the escort squadron, 2nd of 12th Dragoons, he had sent up the left bank of the river to scout beyond St. Arnual), there were seven squadrons present in the Ehrenthal with Rheinbaben, and the cavalry of the advanced guards of the 5th and 16th Divisions was already entering Saarbrucken, but neither horsemen nor artillery could assist the two battalions within the Gifert Wood.

The left wing was at the mercy of the French. Had a good look-out been kept from the Rotherberg, the fact that the attacking force, including the troops at the foot of the spur, did not exceed 3000 men, and also that no infantry supports were at hand, must have been apparent. The moment was ripe for a vigorous counter-stroke. Already the reserve division, 7,000 strong, was approaching the front. Before noon, when the cannonade became audible at Oetingen, General Bataille, anticipating Frossard's instructions, had given orders for Bastoul's Brigade, accompanied by a battalion of the 23rd and a battery, to march on Spicheren, whilst he himself proceeded with the remainder to Stiring Wendel. Of Laveaucoupet's Division, three entire regiments, or nearly 6,000 men, had not yet been engaged.

Lieutenant-General von Barnekow, commander of the German 16th Infantry Division (Rousset/*Histoire*)

The accompanying sketch shows the strength and disposition of either side at 2.30 pm, and it appears probable that had the French leader ordered a general advance, von Kamecke's Division would have been driven back to the Saarbrucken Ridge, and perhaps across the Saar. His left was isolated, and confronted by overwhelming numbers, von Doering's battery alone occupied the Winterberg, nor were the supports of his right wing in a position to render assistance to the fighting line.

The Prussian leader, throwing precaution to the winds, and attacking a strong position without previous reconnaissance, had committed a flagrant error. Victories are won by taking advantage of such errors, and from the first moment of an engagement, a commander should be watching his adversary with eagle eye, ready to take instantaneous advantage of the first false move.

But to do so with effect, the presence and personal direction of the General-in-Chief is absolutely necessary. He alone can give the impulse which would combine the action of the widely separated wings, of the reserve and the artillery, and set the mass in motion to a common end. Unfortunately, however, for the French, Frossard was still at Forbach, in the centre indeed of his divisions, but unable to overlook the field. He does not appear, in truth, to have, thoroughly grasped the situation. He knew that three hostile army corps, 90,000 men, were converging on Saarbrucken, and that even if Bazaine were to come to his assistance, their united forces would number less than 70,000, Their best chance, therefore, was, if, possible, to deal with the enemy in detail. And in any case it was Frossard's bounden duty to dispose of the isolated portion that had so recklessly placed itself in his power, thus depriving the Germans of a considerable force, and invigorating his own people by a first success. He has given as his reason for not presenting himself on the field the necessity he was under of remaining near the telegraph, so as to be in constant communication with Bazaine, and that at Forbach he was conveniently situated for receiving and transmitting messages from and to his wings and his reserves. But his telegrams to the marshal proves that almost before a shot was fired he had become convinced that he was seriously threatened, that the engagement would be more than a reconnaissance in force, and under these circumstances his place was assuredly in the midst of his troops, on the commanding situation of the Forbacherberg, where he could overlook the field and make his influence felt.

Whether he was kept informed by the Chief of General Laveaucoupet's Staff of the state of affairs at the front is not known. The fact remains that he lost a golden opportunity. "Fortune," said Napoleon, "is a woman. Avail yourself of her favour while she is in the humour. Beware that she does not change, through resentment at your neglect."

And Frossard was doubly bound to get rid of his audacious antagonist. The strong reconnaissance which had been despatched at 9 o'clock in the direction of Volklingen, had returned at noon. An officer of the Staff was waiting to receive the information obtained, and this proved of the utmost importance. At Great and Little Rosseln, two villages about three miles from Forbach, Prussian troops had been encountered, infantry as well as cavalry, and had been driven back into the forest. The presence of the two arms combined would have been sufficient indication that this force was something more than a strong patrol, and full confirmation of the suspicion that it was more likely the advanced guard of a division was found in the villages. Every door had chalked on it by the Prussian billet-markers the number of men the house would hold, and the inhabitants had been warned to prepare for the reception of 12,000 men between 3 and 4 o'clock.[7] No doubt remained, therefore, but that the 2nd Corps might expect attack on its left rear before 5 o'clock. Forbach, the point threatened, was two miles in rear of the main-line, and the situation was, at first sight, decidedly embarrassing. But, on reflection, it seems that the French had no reason for apprehension. On the contrary, holding a central position, with 28,000 men, against 24,000, divided into two columns, and separated by several miles of forest, they had decidedly the best of it. The situation was one which Napoleon would have gloried in. Had Frossard been gifted with a spark of Napoleon's genius, he would have re-enacted Rivoli, and have destroyed one, if not both, of the hostile columns.

Detaching a regiment of infantry, part of his numerous cavalry and reserve artillery, he might have held the 13th Division in check for many hours in the Saarbrucken Forest. Bataille's Division, supporting that of Laveaucoupet, together, out-numbering von Kamecke's left wing by more than three to one, should have found little difficulty in clearing the plateau, in driving back the Prussian batteries, and in re-occupying the Saarbrucken Ridge. By such a stroke von Kamecke's right wing would have been cut off, and have been forced to retreat through the forest to Volklingen.

But at 2.30, Frossard, seemingly content so long as his divisional generals maintained their line unbroken, and careless of his adversary's mistakes, was still passively awaiting the arrival of reinforcements he expected from Bazaine. And, what is more, he did not report to the marshal the information that had been obtained at Great Rosseln.

7 This account of the reconnaissance made by the 55th Regiment is taken from the *Spectateur Militaire*, 1885, and was written by an officer present at the battle.

It will not be out of place if we now take note of the movements and position of the various bodies of troops which either general expected to assist him.

FRENCH TROOP MOVEMENTS

Shortly after 9 o'clock, Frossard had requested Bazaine by telegraph to order a brigade of Montaudon's Division from Saarguemund to Grossbliederstroff, and also that Decaen's Division might advance from St. Avold to Merlebach and Rossbruck. Grossbliederstroff is 4½ miles from Spicheren, Rossbruck 5 miles from Stiring Wendel.

At 11.30 he received a reply, to the following effect:

Metman's Division had been ordered to advance from Marienthal to Bening, 7 miles from Stiring Wendel.

Castagny's Division, from Puttelange to Theding, 6 miles from Spicheren.

At 2.25 came a second despatch, reporting that Montaudon's Division was about to proceed to Grossbliederstroll.

The roads were excellent and in good order, and it was even possible to march on a broad front across the open and unobstructed country. The morning camps were in no case more than 10 miles distant from the field of battle.

At 2.30, therefore, Frossard was under the impression that three divisions, numbering at least 25,000 men, were close at hand. He also appears to have believed that they were advancing to his assistance, although Bazaine had made no mention that such was the case, nor had he himself taken any steps to secure their aid.

What was the actual state of the case?

Metman, under instructions from Bazaine, had advanced on Bening at 10 am, but he did not arrive until 3 o'clock, having marched four miles in five hours. The cannonade at Spicheren was distinctly heard, but he made no attempt to communicate with Frossard. His troops went into bivouac and he stood waiting orders. Yet he was within reach of the telegraph, and two squadrons of cavalry were attached to his division.

Castagny, at Puttelange, heard the firing at 11 o'clock. Without waiting for instructions, and leaving his baggage behind and his camp standing, he moved at once on Spicheren. After marching three or four miles, in a direction too much to the right, he halted, for the sound of the battle was no longer audible, and before 3 o'clock, set out on his return to Puttelange. He appears to have been as indifferent as Metman to the state of affairs at the front, for not a single horseman was sent out to procure information.

Montaudon, at 2.30, had received no orders, and, although the continuous roar of cannon told him that the 2nd Corps was heavily engaged, he betrayed neither anxiety nor curiosity as to the progress of the fight.

Frossard, on his part, after receiving definite information from Marshal Bazaine that supports had been sent forward, can scarcely be excused for not having despatched couriers to take up communication with the advancing divisions. It is very necessary that every unit on the theatre of war should be linked by patrols with those on either hand. The task of establishing such connection is incumbent upon all.

Juniac's Dragoon Brigade reported to Frossard at 4 pm, but was sent back to Bening. There was no need for more cavalry, and it was necessary to keep the roads clear in case of retreat.

GERMAN TROOP MOVEMENTS – FIRST ARMY

It has already been noticed that General von Goeben Commanding the VIII Army Corps had promised his support to von Kamecke in the event of the French assuming the offensive. As he rode back through the forest, the sound of the cannonade was borne to his ears, increasing every moment in intensity. The 14th Division was already engaged. It was the advanced guard of the First Army, and must be supported by the main body, he therefore determined to move as rapidly as possible to the Saar.

The 16th Division led the march of VIII Army Corps, and its advanced guard had reached Fischbach at 12 o'clock. Here it had been ordered to halt, for the day's march assigned to it by the corps commander was completed. With this force was present Lieut.-General von Barnekow, commanding the division, and on reaching Fischbach, he too had heard the ominous sounds from the valley of the Saar. Without waiting for orders he had directed his advanced guard, consisting of the 9th Hussars, 40th Fusiliers, 6th Light and 6th Heavy Batteries, as it was in the act of establishing the outposts, to resume its march. The main body was also called to arms. When General von Goeben, arrived, therefore, he found that his intention had been partially anticipated. The 72nd Regiment, two batteries, and the 31st Brigade, of the main body, he ordered to follow the advanced guard. He considered it unnecessary to move the 15th Division, now standing with its head at Holz, and returned again to Saarbrucken.

At 1.30, the head of the van-guard debouched from the Kollerthaler Forest. Here an officer, who had been sent forward to communicate with von Kamecke, reported that there was apparently no immediate necessity for support, but that it would be desirable for the 16th Division to cross the river and occupy the ridge. The march on St. Johann was continued. At 2.30, the hussars and artillery were within Saarbrucken, the leading files of the 40th Regiment were entering St. Johann.

The 13th Division (VII Army Corps), had originally been ordered to take up a position at Puttlingen, but General von Zastrow, commanding VII Army Corps, when he empowered von Kamecke to act on his own judgement and, if necessary, to occupy the Saarbrucken Heights, had considered it advisable, at the same time, that the 13th Division should be pushed forward to the Saar, in order that, if necessary, it might be in a position to support the 14th.

To obtain the sanction of the Commander-in-Chief of the First Army, a Staff officer was sent to Eiweiler, where Head-Quarters had arrived about noon. General von Steinmetz replied, "The enemy must be punished for his negligence. In order to prevent him from re-occupying his position on the left bank of the Saar, that position must be seized in the interests of the Second Army. An attempt should also be made to interrupt the embarkation of French troops at Forbach, who are said to be weakly supported." This reached von Zastrow between 12 and 1 o'clock, and a despatch was immediately sent to the commander of the 13th Division instructing him to cross the Saar at Volklingen, to push forward his advance and proceed in the direction of Ludweiler and Forbach, sending put patrols to discover the strength and intentions of the enemy. At the same time, von Kamecke was ordered to occupy the Saarbrucken Heights with a strong advanced guard, to post his main body at Rockerhausen, to throw a bridge there, and to patrol towards Forbach. These instructions had, however, been already anticipated, not only by von Kamecke but by von Glümer, commanding the 13th Division.

The main body of the 13th Division had reached Puttlingen towards noon. The advanced guard had already crossed the river and taken post at Wehrden. Here the thunder of the guns was plainly heard, and intelligence was brought in by the cavalry patrols that the 14th Division was engaged near Stiring Wendel, and that hostile battalions were advancing from Rosseln. A squadron of hussars and the 7th Jägers were immediately sent in the direction of the latter village, and it was these troops whom the French reconnoitring detachment encountered.[8]

General von Glümer, taking with him a squadron of hussars and VI/7, rode on to Wehrden. On his arrival, he found that the commander of his advanced guard had already resolved to attack the left flank of the French. Approving the design, he sent orders for the main-body to follow. The advanced guard then moved on Forbach, 6½ miles distant, by way of Great Rosseln, a company of Jägers and a troop of hussars taking the road by Clarenthal to Schoneck, thus filling the interval between the 13th and 14th Divisions. At 2.30, the head of the advanced guard had reached Great Rosseln, 2½ miles from Forbach, without seeing anything of the French. As yet the divisions general had acted entirely upon his own responsibility. The orders issued by von Zastrow at Dilsburg had not reached him. The corps artillery was ordered to Puttlingen, north-west of Volklingen.

Von Zastrow and his Staff left Dilsburg for the Saar at 1 o'clock, the last reports from the front pointing, not to the retreat, but to the advance, of the French upon Saarbrucken.

General von Steinmetz, on receipt of the reports from the commander of VII and VIII Army Corps, sent his quartermaster general to Saarbrucken. This officer met on the road orderlies bringing intelligence of the state of the engagement from von Kamecke to his corps commander, von Zastrow. Their despatches, together with the increasing din of battle, left no doubt in his mind but that a severe action was in progress, and he sent, therefore, to his chief a message to this effect. General von Steinmetz at once rode forward to the battle field.

GERMAN TROOP MOVEMENTS – SECOND ARMY

The III Army Corps, forming the leading echelon of the right wing of the Second Army, had for its advanced-guard the 5th Division, of which the 9th Brigade was moving forward by the Neunkirchen-Saarbrucken, the 10th by the Neunkirchen-St. Ingbert Road, thus covering the approaches both from Forbach and from Saarguemund.

General von Doering, commanding the 9th Brigade, had, as we have already seen, taken the precaution to ride on to the line of foreposts early in the morning, and had witnessed the first reconnaissance of the cavalry squadrons towards Forbach between 9 and 10 o'clock. Soon after rejoining his brigade, the head of which was approaching Dudweiler, he received information that the 14th Division was marching through St. Johann with the intention of occupying the Saarrbrucken Heights. From what he had already observed, it appeared to him quite probable that the enemy had no thought of retreating, and that von Kamecke might find himself in a trap. He therefore resolved to continue his march beyond Dudweiler to the Saar. Reporting to this effect to his divisional commander, General von Stülpnagel, he rode to the front at 12 o'clock, taking

8 See page 146.

with him the 1st squadron of the 12th Dragoons and the 3rd Light Battery. When General von Doering's order to resume the march was issued, his brigade had already occupied quarters in the villages along the road, and the men were cooking their mid-day meal. The van-guard was at Dudweiler, the rear of the main-body at Bildstock, 4¾ miles distant. The sound of cannon had been already distinctly heard, and when the assembly sounded at 12.45, the companies were rapidly mustered, and marched off between 1 and 2: – the 48th Regiment from Dudweiler and Sulzbach forming the advanced guard, I/8th Regiment and 3rd Jägers from Freidrichsthal, II and F/8th from Bildstock. The morning march of five miles had lasted from 5.15 to 8.30 am. From Dudweiler, the Reppertsberg is five miles, from Bildstock, 10 miles distant.

The 3rd Company of the 8th Grenadiers was cantoned in a little village half-an-hour's march from Freidrichsthal, the place of assembly for the battalion. Intending to join his battalion on the march, the company commander struck the high-road in front of the 3rd Jägers, but in order to avoid the delay that might be caused were he to stand aside to allow them to pass and endeavour to pick up his proper place in the column, he pushed on at once, and found himself leading the main-body of the brigade.

As they passed through the road-side villages, the inhabitants thronged round the soldiers, pressing on them food and drink, and it was with some difficulty that order was preserved. At 2.30, the head of the 48th already was within St. Johann, the leading company of the main body had reached the southern border of the Kollerthaler Forest, and the divisional commander had arrived on the battle-field with the escort squadron and light battery, his brigade extending along the road as far as Sulzbach, distant eight miles or three hours' march from the Saarbrucken Ridge.

The 10th Brigade, with the exception of the 12th Regiment, still at Neunkirchen, had halted in or about St. Ingbert, 8½ miles from Saarbrucken. A communication had been received by General von Schwerin, the brigadier, from the 6th Cavalry Division, that hostile troops were advancing from Habkirchen, 6 miles north of Saarguemund on the Blies, in the direction of Annweiler. In consequence of this information, he had assembled the 52nd Regiment, 2 squadrons, the 4th Light and 4th Heavy Batteries at St. Ingbert, whilst the 6th Cavalry Division gathered together, between Ensheim and Ormesheim, in order to check the hostile movement. At 2.30, von Schwerin received orders from von Alvensleben to march all his available infantry and artillery to Saarbrucken.

The commander of the III Army Corps, General von Alvensleben, receiving at Neunkirchen General von Stulpnagel's (commanding 5th Division) report, ordered as many of his corps as possible to be brought up to Saarbrucken during the day. Two regiments, the 12th and the 20th, of the 6th Division, were to proceed by rail.

Thus, at 2.30 pm, the heads of the 16th Division and of the 9th Brigade had already reached St. Johann, the 12th and 20th regiments, and very shortly afterwards, the 10th Brigade, had been placed under orders to support the 14th Division. The 13th Division was pushing through the Saarbrucken Forest in the direction of Forbach, and 35,000 infantry, together with three regiments of cavalry and 66 guns, were in full march to the field of battle.

Although it is nowhere expressly stated, there is no doubt that as soon as these orders were issued, the commanders of the various corps and divisions immediately communicated with von Kamecke. At the time we are speaking of, the orderlies would not have yet arrived, but he was aware of General von Goeben's intention to support him,

View of the Rotherberg

and the roads converging on St. Johann were already covered with the leading battalions of the 16th Division and the 9th Brigade.

THE BATTLE ON THE PLATEAU – 2.30–3.30 PM

Although Frossard himself, too deeply enamoured of the passive defensive, was not minded to anticipate the arrival of hostile reinforcements by a counter-stroke, Laveaucoupet, commanding the right wing, had determined to do on a small scale what his superior should have done on a large, and to drive back the six companies of the 39th which immediately confronted him along the edge of the Gifert Wood. The whole of Micheler's Brigade, the 40th and 24th Regiments, was already in first line, and to support the counter-stroke, Doens' Brigade was now brought forward, the 63rd to the Spicheren Knoll, and II & IV/2 towards the Pfaffen Wood, in order to turn the Prussian left. I/2 was left behind upon the Pfaffenberg, and Frossard was requested to allow a brigade of Bataille's Division, now approaching, to occupy the position Doens had vacated.

Shortly after 2.30 the attack began. The Prussians held a strong position. The wood is densely timbered to the very edge. The bank of the road which skirts it gave good protection, and the slopes in front are smooth and easy, all supports had, however, been drawn into the fighting line, nor was there any reserve to meet the out-flanking movement of the 2nd Line.

Attacked fiercely in front, and its left threatened by superior numbers, the 39th gave way. Ammunition had begun to fail, the commander and several officers had fallen, neither supervision nor unity of action was possible in the wood, and the First Battalion, which had borne the brunt of the flank attack, was driven in disorder down the slopes, and across the valley to the Winterberg. The 2nd Line, led by General Doens, made, however, no attempt to pursue the Fusiliers across the open, but, lining the lower border of the wood, was content to ply their broken files with a devastating fire.

Further to the right, the three companies of II/39 yielded likewise to stress of numbers. A portion had already reached the valley in retreat, the 7th Company was still clinging stubbornly to the crest, in face of the superior force of the enemy, defeat seemed imminent, but all at once the hostile fire slackened, and the French, when another moment would have seen the Prussians plunging down the steep descent in flight, drew off to their left, and moved towards the Rotherberg. Relief had come to the little band of Fusiliers from an unexpected quarter, and it must now be related how this fortuitous result was brought about. At 2.30, the battle in the Stiring Copse had been restored in favour of the Prussians by the opportune arrival of two companies of the 74th. On the borders of the Gifert Wood, I and II/39 appeared to be still holding their own. The French batteries, both on the Rotherberg and near the Metz High-road, had fallen back. Strong reinforcements, the advanced guards of the 5th and 16th Divisions, were rapidly approaching St. Johann, and von Kamecke, therefore, believing that the French were yielding all along the line, or aware that his left wing (I and II/39) was confronted by a far superior force, and therefore desirous of diverting the attention of the enemy, had conceived the bold resolution of renewing the assault upon the Rotherberg.

The Fusilier Battalion of the 74th, with which was the brigadier, still crouched inactive beneath the bluff, but, 500 yards away to the left, the 4th Company, together with 6/39, was briskly engaging the defenders of the spur.

Enfiladed by this fire, harassed by the artillery, and never dreading a frontal attack upon their lofty stronghold, the French Chasseurs had withdrawn to the shelter of the trenches. None ventured to expose themselves above the parapet, none troubled to glance down the steep incline, and the musketry had died away.

With the order from von Kamecke to assault, came 9/39 across the valley, and, thus opportunely reinforced, the Fusiliers, von François leading, mounted the earthern bank, and faced the rugged cliff that towered to the height of near 200 feet above them. From terrace to terrace the toiling groups pushed slowly but persistently up the slope, from bush to boulder, throwing sword and needle gun before them, clambering up as best they might, each man for himself, careless of broken ranks or straggling files, making no halt where quarried bank or clump of cherry trees offered a tempting resting place, but pressing on with eager haste, intent only on reaching the crest which stood out untenanted overhead, on gaining an equal level with the enemy, and on going in with butt and bayonet. It was breathless work this desperate race, the climbers expecting every moment to hear the loud alarm, to see the height above them crowned with a serried line of hostile riflemen, to be caught red-handed in their audacious enterprise, and to be bourne backwards, helpless and defenceless, down the steep hill-side.

Fortunately, however, for these 1,000 Prussians no look-out was kept by the Chasseurs, the figure of no single sentinel cut the sky line, and in the din of musketry from the flank and of the shells screaming overhead, the rush of the stormers, the cries of the officers, and the noise of falling stones and cracking brushwood, were unheard. The crest was gained – the men with tired muscles and scant wind – but no warning shout had yet been raised, their approach was undiscovered. And then, whether the French suddenly awoke to their danger as the Prussians neared the earthwork, or whether the spiked helmets and bright bayonets bursting into view above the parapet were the first intimation of the presence of the enemy, there is none to tell us, be it as it may, the surprise was complete, and the Chasseurs gave way in panic. A few, more stubborn than their fellows, struggled bravely for a time, but the mass, flying upwards towards the saddle, took refuge behind an undulation of the higher ground.

In spite of the rolling fire at short range which now assailed them, the Fusiliers rallied quickly round their officers to follow up the first success, and make good their footing on the height beyond.

But the French had recovered from their surprise. Strong supports from the western quarter of the Gifert Wood were hurried to the front, and a sudden and heavy counter-stroke threatened the disordered ranks of the 74th.

But at this moment the 9th Company of the 39th arrived upon the crest.

The *pas de charge* of the drum was answered by a rolling cheer. Von François, sword in hand, with a shout of "Forward 39th!" sprang to the front, and, crowded together on the bare and narrow surface of the spur, the men dashed upwards from the trenches. The French advance was rudely checked, but at a terrible cost. Pierced with five bullets the brigadier fell, and the foremost files were swept away by the storm of musketry.

Further movement was impossible. But by the side of their dying general the five companies held fast, and sheltered by the earthwork so fortunately won, opposed strong front to the repeated attacks of the Chasseurs and 40th from the Gifert Wood, whilst the guns in the valley beat back more than one attempt of the 63rd to descend from the plateau to the saddle.

The surprise which gave the Prussians footing on the Rotherberg was due in part to the nature of the acclivity above which the horse-shoe shelter trench was placed. From the parapet there was command of view and fire over the valley below, but the hill fell away so steeply that the face of this slope could not be seen by men standing within the earthwork. Such a position, as was afterwards demonstrated at Majuba Hill, though apparently strong, is exceedingly unfavourable for defence. Its seeming inaccessibility gives a false sense of security, and, as we have seen, no sentries were maintained within the entrenchments by the French. Had this precaution been adopted, and the stormers been met as they neared the summit by a charge of the whole line, the attack in all probability would have failed disastrously. "*How often in military history has success been achieved by a movement over ground deemed impassable, and therefore left unwatched?*"

The flank movement of the 40th Regiment towards the Rotherberg, on the capture of the trench, was as injudicious as useless. The 63rd was already in support of the Chasseurs, and in many cases, where the flank of a body of troops committed to a resolute attack as was the 40th is threatened, it is wiser to meet the counter-stroke by a detachment from the reserve, and at the same time to prosecute the frontal attack with even more vigour than before. The object of such a flanking movement is to relieve the front by checking the advance against it. This is what the enemy desires, and this is precisely what he must not be permitted to effect. At the same time, the sudden check to the forward movement may be noted as an instance of the extraordinary influence the mere threat of a flank attack has upon troops operating in thick woods or in country

The 9th Company of the Prussian 39th Infantry assault the Rotherberg, led by General von François (Scheibert)

where the view is limited, and neither the extent of the danger nor the means of meeting it (*i.e.*, the supporting forces on the threatened flank), can be seen by the men in front.

Meanwhile, on the withdrawal of the French battalions immediately opposed to them, the 5th and 7th companies of II/39, together with two sections of the 3rd Company, which had escaped the discomfiture of the First Battalion, re-occupied the ridge within the Gifert. Nor, although a much larger force was in their neighbourhood, was any vigorous effort made by the French to thrust them from their point of vantage.

When the left of the Prussian line broke and fled, the two battalions of the 2nd Line had descended as far as the lower border of the wood. If they had then entered the valley, and, wheeling sharply to the left, whilst the 24th attacked the little force within the Gifert Wood, had swept along towards the Rotherberg, the remnants of the 39th (including the 6th company and 4/74 which lay in the open) must have been driven back, the stormers of the spur, assailed in front and flank have been compelled to withdraw, and the line of guns from the Galgenberg, notwithstanding the presence of the cavalry in the Ehrenthal, have been exposed to imminent risk.

But at this juncture the promptitude of the German generals bore good fruit. At the first alarm of battle, without waiting orders, they had hurried their batteries and battalions to the front, and, as General Doens, in pursuit of the broken 39th, reached the lower outskirts of the wood, a dark line of infantry (the 48th Regiment, van of the 9th Brigade, 5th Division) was in the act of deploying upon the Saarbrucken Ridge. The sight held back the French. Leaving a thin line of skirmishers to occupy the depression between the Gifert and the Pfaffen Wood, Doens drew back his two battalions to the plateau, and the attack, which should have been pressed with the utmost vigour, was suffered to lapse into a desultory skirmish.

Laveaucoupet's troops were now disposed in the following order: On the right, II and III/2; prolonging the line in a north-westerly direction, through the Gifert Wood, I, II, and III/40; on the Rotherberg the 10th Chasseurs; the 63rd north of Spicheren, in second line upon the left; the 24th upon the right, outside the wood. The battery, together with, the mitrailleuses had already withdrawn to the Spicheren Ridge, but the remaining six pieces of the divisional artillery were still posted 200 yards north of Spicheren Village, and below the eastern slope of the Spicheren Knoll.

On the Prussian side, the 48th Regiment, of which the 2nd Battalion had not yet reached the ridge, arriving in time to witness the disaster of their comrades of the 39th, was immediately disposed as a defensive line. The 3rd and 4th Companies occupied the ravine between the Nussberg and the Winterberg; the 1st Company, the Reppertsberg; the 4th Company, the height above St. Arnual. In the rear was the Fusilier Battalion, formed in two lines. A squadron of the 12th Dragoons watched the river road. The 3rd Light Battery had taken post on the Winterberg, and the 1st Battalion of the 39th was gradually assembling, after its flight across the valley, at the foot of the slopes. Thus, two battalions and six guns (for the First 39th could scarcely be considered as effective), were all the troops at hand to hold the Saarbrucken Heights and the bridges against a counter-attack from the Gifert and St. Arnual Forest.

Fortunately, however, for the Prussians, both circumstances and ground were in their favour. Before the French could advance across the valley, the Rotherberg must be re-won. It was impossible to prepare the attack on the position held by the 48th with artillery. Time would have been lost in bringing down a large force of infantry rough the Gifert, and in moving a flank detachment through the St. Arnual Forest, and long before such an operation could have been completed, strong reinforcements would have arrived upon the ridge.

It is worth while remarking the many obstacles to the counter-attack in a rough wooded country.

Not the least of these is the impossibility of the General-in-Chief obtaining a clear view of the situation.

THE BATTLE IN THE VALLEY – 2.30–3.30 PM

At 2.30, the Prussians in the Stiring Copse began once more to press back the enemy's first line. As the advance progressed, the two and a half companies of I/74 took post upon the right, leaving the left to three companies of I/39.

II/74 had, meanwhile, resumed its attack upon the Coalpit Ridge. Three companies, with their marksman's sections extended, forming the fighting line; the fourth was near the railroad, in reserve.

Towards, 3 o'clock, a portion of the 53rd Regiment, of the 28th, von Woyna's Brigade, came up in the rear, and working along the edge of the clearing, drove back a hostile detachment and menaced the left flank of the defence. The skirmishers of the 74th then charged across the open and carried the ridge and the adjacent buildings, the battalion of the French 77th retiring to Old Stiringen. A company the 74th occupied the coal-pit and the houses, extending its skirmishers as far as the forest on the right, two companies held the cutting on the road, whilst the fourth moved up to the foot of the slope. At the same time 1 and 4/77, of von Woyna's Brigade, approached the right of the 39th within the copse.

Although the Prussians were in reality rather inferior in strength to the garrison of Stiring Wendel, General Vergé commanding the French left wing was so impressed by the vigour of their attack that he had already called upon Frossard for support, and very shortly afterwards the 3rd Chasseurs, influenced probably by the capture of the coal-pit, abandoned the copse, the southern border of which was immediately occupied by III/39.

The two and a half companies of I/74, which had hitherto been fighting alongside the Fusiliers, issuing from the western edge of the wood, attempted to prolong the line to the right across the railroad, but were severely handled in doing so by the French guns, east of Stiring Wedel, and by heavy musketry from behind the heaps of slag and refuse in front of the foundry. To oppose the latter, the captain of the 1st Company led half his command forward through the swamp, the men sinking to the hips in the miry ooze, and in spite of the enemy's fire, seized a house upon the railway close to Old Stiringen. From both storeys a flanking fire was brought to bear upon the French before the forges, and the remainder of the two 74th Companies were enabled to gain shelter in the wood at the foot of the Coal-pit clearing.

The fire of the 39th from the southern border of the copse soon compelled the four batteries posted on the Spicheren-Stiring Wood to limber up and retire.[9] An ammunition waggon blew up, five guns had to be abandoned owing to casualties amongst the teams, and two batteries were rendered useless. The German Staff History attributes this achievement to I/7 which had advanced to its third position, the centre

9 A 12 pounder battery from the Reserve had shortly before arrived.

knoll of the Folster Height, about 3 o'clock, after the withdrawal of the hostile guns from the Rotherberg, but Frossard distinctly states that as the Prussian infantry progressed through the copse they took the guns in flank, and killed a great number of both men and horses. He further fixes the time when this took place by adding that a caisson exploded, and increased the confusion. The south-west corner of the Stiring Copse is little more than 500 yards from the road, and the range was, therefore, all against the artillery. The remaining pieces, nineteen in number, withdrew to a safer distance, and were joined by General Valabrègue, commanding the cavalry division, whom Frossard had sent forward to fill the gap between Stiring Wendel and the Spicheren Heights with a battery of horse artillery, and four squadrons, two of the 4th Chasseurs, and two of the 7th Dragoons. The cavalry were posted behind Stiring Wendel.

At the same time, in answer to Vergé's request for reinforcements, the 32nd Regiment arrived from Forbach. Two battalions were brought up to the foundry, the third remained in reserve within the village.

The battalions of the extreme French left wing now numbered nine, or nearly 6,000 infantry. Opposed to them, in the fighting line, were 11½ companies. Part of the 28th Brigade had now come up, and formed the support; II/77 in the centre of the copse; on the northern border, F/77; and working through the forest beyond the coal-pit, I/53, making a total of some 5,000 bayonets.

The other half of the 28th Brigade, F/53 and 2 and 3/77, cut off by the thickets of the Saarbrucken Forest, was still some distance from the scene of action, and it will be well if we now follow the movements of von Woyna's regiments.

The 53rd (two battalions) leading the march of the 28th Brigade, had reached Rachspfuhl at 12.15. Here the brigadier received instructions from von Kamecke to cross the viaduct, and attack the enemy's left. By 1 pm, the foremost regiment had completed the passage of the river. The 1st and 4th Companies were in front, the 2nd and 3rd, and the 10th and 11th as half-battalions, both commanded by lieutenants, in second line, the 9th and 12th as reserve, under the regimental commander. Advancing along the road beside the railway, the edge of the clearing below the coal-pit was found in possession of II/74, for the ridge had not yet been carried. General von Woyna, who accompanied the leading half-battalion, resolved to wheel half right, and, passing in rear of the 74th, to seek out the extreme left of the French line.

Sweeping round the clearing, the left leaning on the western border, I/53, as has been already related, drove back some hostile skirmishers, apparently a picquet or detached post of the 3rd Chasseurs, and by threatening the flank of the defence, assisted the capture of the ridge by the 74th. As the enemy fell back, von Woyna led his troops still further forward through the wood. But, through the tangled undergrowth, the half-battalions in second line and in reserve found it exceedingly difficult to keep the general direction. Files were sent out to maintain connection with the leading companies, but much ground was lost, and the Fusilier Battalion, which had sent the marksman's section of the 11th Company left of the railway, to cover the flank, inclined too far to the right, and, after driving back a strong party of the enemy and losing its commander, found itself isolated in the centre of the wood. The leading half of the brigade was thus completely split in two, and we shall now learn not only how a still more decided severance occurred between the leading half and the rear half, but how the latter became completely lost to the control of the brigadier.

The original order to the 77th Regiment had been to follow the 53rd. The 2nd and 3rd Companies had consequently ascended the Schanzenberg at the German Mill and forced their way through the thick and pathless forest in a south-westerly direction. But the 1st and 4th Companies, attracted, probably, by the heavy firing, had proceeded along the railway directly to the front, joining, as told above, the 39th and 74th shortly after 3 o'clock, and thus occurred the first break in the order of march.

When the 2nd and Fusilier Battalions of the 77th, following in the rear of these two companies, arrived at the German Mill they were met by the adjutant of I/74, who, as his battalion neared the Rotherberg, had been despatched by General von François to tell the two battalions of the 77th, visible from the rising ground between the Rotherberg and Drathzug, to attack the western face of the Spicheren Heights. The Second Battalion, therefore, entered the copse shortly before 3 o'clock, and, in half-battalion columns held the centre of the wood. The Fusiliers, who in the first instance had followed the 2nd Battalion, quitted the road at Drathzug, and occupied the north-east corner of the copse, supporting the sections of 3/74 and 12/39, who were confronting the homesteads on the Metz High-road.

The 28th Brigade had now drifted into four distinct portions, with a total absence of all intercommunication or unity of command, and a reference to the sketch which shows the distribution of the German troops at 3.30 reveals a curious state of affairs along the whole line. Although only one division, 10,750 men, was engaged, regiments had already become separated from their brigades, battalions from their regiments, companies from their battalions, and sections, and even half sections, from their companies. It will be well to devote some consideration to the causes and effects of such an extraordinary dispersion, and, also, to the questions of battle formations and brigade leading.

The 27th Brigade, when it advanced to the attack, occupied a front of nearly 3,500 yards. A strong resistance was met with, every rifle was drawn into the fighting line, and the supports had to be furnished on the right by the 28th Brigade, on the left and centre, as will be seen hereafter, by battalions which belonged to different divisions, different Army Corps, and even different Armies.

Now, unity of command throughout the depth of an attack is generally essential to success. The commander, the staff, the regimental officers and men, should be acquainted with each other, so that there may be no doubt or hesitation in the mind of any individual as to whom he is to look to for, or from whom he is to take, orders. Again, it is of the utmost importance that the second line and reserve, on whom the general in charge of the operation relies for his ultimate victory, should be under his own control, and not under that of an independent leader. In the case of the 14th Division, the fighting line was composed of a single brigade, the right under von Pannwitz, the centre under von François, the left under the senior officer present with the 39th, each unable, owing to the great extent of the front of battle, to communicate with the other, and as the supporting troops were under independent leadership, unity of command was manifestly impossible.

At 1.30, when the 14th Division had not been engaged for more than an hour and a half, no general reserve of infantry remained. Every single company had been sent to the front upon the left and centre, and the 28th Brigade, part of which was already committed to the turning movement, could only have been made use of on the right. But a line of troops without support or reserve, which has made little impression on the enemy, is in a very perilous position, and if the enemy is in greater strength and acts with determination, will be easily defeated, as was proved by the expulsion of the 39th from the Gifert Wood.

Von Kamecke erred in allowing von François to attack on too broad a front.

The engagement at Spicheren, even before a shot was fired, promised to be something more than the mere brushing away of a trifling detachment, or the driving back of a small rear-guard, for, besides cavalry and guns the presence of at least three regiments of hostile infantry, a force superior to the 27th Brigade, to which the assault was entrusted, had been reported.

Under such circumstances, even if a rapid attack was deemed essential, time would not have been wasted had the 53rd Regiment been first brought up to the Drathzug, and the battle on that flank committed to von Woyna, the left attack to von François, and the 77th Regiment brought up to the Saarbrucken Ridge as a general reserve. If the French had fallen back at once, the pursuit, with each brigade concentrated and in hand, would have been so vigorous as to compensate for time lost in adopting a suitable formation. If they retained their ground, the suggested disposition would have secured a unity of command throughout the length and depth of the attacking force. Each brigadier would have an objective proportional to the number of men that he commanded, have been enabled to retain his own reserve, and much of the subsequent confusion, loss of tactical order, and impossibility of manœuvering, would have been avoided.

When the 28th Brigade arrived upon the Prussian right, there were two brigadiers upon the scene, von Woyna and von Pannwitz, the latter in command of the two-and-a-half battalions of the 27th Brigade engaged in a frontal attack on Stiring Wendel.

Von Pannwitz had already deployed his whole force. Von Woyna, bound on an independent enterprise, that of threatening the enemy's left, ordered his whole brigade to follow him through the Saarbrucken Forest, a movement which, had it been carried out, would have left von Pannwitz absolutely without support. Again, owing to von François' action in calling on the 77th Regiment, (von Woyna's command), to attack the Spicheren Heights, the greater portion of the 28th Brigade slipped away from the control of their own commander in a fashion, which, as will be seen hereafter, brought his efforts to naught, and reduced the battle of the right wing to a series of independent and isolated attacks, not wanting in resolution, but lacking the strength and energy of united action under a single head. In fact, the projected turning movement of the French left by the whole of the 28th Brigade, luckily, frustrated by von François' summons to the 77th, was injudicious. It is true that the appearance of the leading battalion on their flank brought about the evacuation of the Coal-pit Ridge, but five battalions, the number von Woyna intended should be employed, was far too large a detachment, and one which, had he himself been placed in sole control of the right attack, would, in all probability never have been permitted. It was dangerous in the extreme, had the French force been even smaller than it actually was, to leave von Pannwitz without support.

Flank attacks are most certainly the surest means of bringing about the evacuation of a position and the enemy's defeat. But the principle, if its adoption absorbs too many troops in the firing line, as proved by the somewhat critical situation of the 14th Division between 2 and 3.30 o'clock, involves the greatest risk. Such attacks are dangerous unless the assailant has a superior force; that is, it is dangerous to enclose the adversary's position with a thin weak line. A flank attack necessitates, as a rule, an extended front, but that front must be strong in all its parts, or, before the turning movement can take effect, the centre or elsewhere may be pierced by a counter-stroke. Against commanders of inferior capacity, even when there is little disparity of numbers, such manœuvres may be successful, against troops whose leader posses a practised tactical *coup d'œil* they will but renew the disasters of Austerlitz and Rivoli, of Rossbach and Salamanca.

As to a question of brigade-leading, von Woyna's advance of the 28th brigade is a remarkable instance of the difficulty of holding a brigade in hand in a wooded country, when troops are engaged in front, and, also, of the embarrassments which may arise from the independent action of subordinate leaders. Von Woyna directed his five battalions after crossing the viaduct to enter the Saarbrucken Forest, and to seek out the enemy's flank. The First 53rd, which he himself accompanied, followed his instructions, and struck the clearing north of the Coal-pit Ridge. Finding that the French left extended further than anticipated, he sent back orders to the 77th to bear more to the south-west. The two leading companies obeyed, but the remainder of the First Battalion moved along the railway, and joined the direct attack on Stiring Wendel. The two other battalions, presumably as they were about to wheel to the right and enter the Saarbrucken Forest, received at 1.45 von François' request for support, moved directly to the front, and reached the copse shortly before 3 o'clock. But at 4.30, nearly three hours after they parted company with their own brigade, General von Woyna, as we shall learn, was not only ignorant of the fact that two-and-a-half of his five battalions had thus disposed of themselves, but had to retire from a forward position he had taken up on the enemy's flank, because he had no available reserve.

It has been said that the projected turning movement with an entire brigade was injudicious, and von Woyna's subordinates, better informed as to the situation than their brigadier, acted wisely enough in bringing aid to the troops within the copse on their own responsibility. But that their commander should have been left without intelligence of this diversion, which withdrew half his force from his disposal, is a circumstance scarcely capable of satisfactory explanation. At the same time, the paucity of staff officers in the German Brigade, viz. one brigade-major and one aide-de-camp for a force of six battalions, and of mounted officers, other than captains of companies, in the German battalion, may be held accountable, in some degree, for the absence of all communication between the brigades when once engaged, and between the various portions into which each became dissolved. The lack of messengers might, however, have easily been met, had a few troopers from the large force of cavalry been placed at the disposal of the regimental commanders.

The difficulty of maintaining connection between the five battalions of the 28th Brigade was, of course, greatly enhanced by the sudden divergence of the two leading companies of the 77th from the general direction. But even between the half-battalions which followed the brigadier, connection was ultimately lost, although the expedient of linking the columns by a chain of men was adopted by the 53rd. The incident is worthy of notice, and it may be remarked that, for the passage of troops through a thick and extensive wood, the same precautions appear necessary as for a night march, and also, that in battle, a large staff is by no means an encumbrance.

It has been lately suggested by an Austrian officer that a certain number of mounted men should be trained and employed by each infantry regiment (3 battalions). They are preferable, he states, to orderlies taken from the cavalry, for they look at things with the eye of the foot-soldier, they would be acquainted with officers and men, trained with the regiment, and accustomed to the work, there would be no difficulty about their rations and quarters, and their presence would relieve the cavalry commanders from the hardship of losing some of their best men when they are most wanted. The author illustrates his ideas by the advance of the 77th Regiment into Stiring Copse.

"Let us suppose," he says, "that the colonel of the 77th had had twelve mounted infantry soldiers at his disposal. It is probable that one would have been with each battalion commander, one with the massed ammunition column of the regiment, one with the transport. After crossing the viaduct, three men might well have been sent off to maintain connection with the 53rd, the leading regiment of the brigade, now rapidly advancing, two to the drill-ground and to the west side of the Galgenberg. By means of such an arrangement it is probable that the two regiments of the 28th Brigade would not have become totally separated from each other. The splitting up and dislocation of the leading battalion of the 77th would have been still more difficult, to say nothing of the total disappearance of these two portions for something like two hours."

Let us, however, leave matters as they occurred, until the period when the wounded adjutant of the 74th, in accordance with the instructions from his brigadier, requested II and F/77 to eject the enemy from the copse, and afterwards move towards the Spicheren Heights. At this period the 77th had lost touch with the 53rd Regiment, with the General commanding its own, the 28th Brigade, and even with its own First Battalion.

In deciding to comply with the request of the wounded adjutant, the colonel broke the order of march of the brigade, and the 77th no longer formed its rearmost regiment. His next duty was a careful preparation for the entry of his regiment into the action. This consisted in:

1. Calling together the separated portions of his regiment.
2. Reconnoitring to the front in the direction of the copse.
3. Reconnoitring to the left in the direction of the Folster Heights and Galgenberg.

The last was necessary in order to obtain information from the neighbouring troops as to the state of affairs.

Intelligence as to the position of the batteries and the object of their fire was also necessary, for some idea of the ground available for the advance of his regiment would thereby be obtained.

Of less pressing importance, but still necessary, were:

4. Orders to the ammunition waggons and the transport.
5. A report to the brigadier.

To recall the First Battalion two, or better still, three mounted men would be sent, as the thick forest was likely to enhance the difficulty of finding it.

Through Drathzug towards the copse it would be necessary to send at least two, if not three, of the sharpest men. This was the most important direction, for it was there that the fighting was going on, and the copse was the immediate objective.

Two mounted men would also be sent to the Folster Height to obtain information from the troops there about the fight, and to examine the ground with a view to the regiment approaching the copse under cover. One to return with the report, the other to remain out in front.

It would also be desirable to send a mounted man with orders to the ammunition waggons to close up and follow the regiment, and to direct the regimental transport to halt north of the viaduct, and also to despatch another orderly with either a verbal or written report to the brigadier acquainting him with the contemplated action of the regiment.

It is possible that had the mounted orderlies been employed in this manner the 77th would have come up into action some minutes later, but it would have come in a more compact body, and with more knowledge of what was going forward, and with consequently greater effect. At any rate, the colonel would have remained in command of his regiment for a longer period. The Staff History is silent as to the action of the colonel. He and his adjutant probably watched helplessly the gradual splitting up of the regiment.

It may be added that these mounted men would facilitate the transmission of intelligence from the fighting line to the General Commanding, a matter of the utmost importance but generally overlooked. For intance, when I and II/39 gained the southern border of the Gifert, and the French camps and masses of hostile infantry were revealed, the information should at once have been sent back to von Kamecke.

In the Wilderness campaign of 1864, General Grant, in command of the Federal Army, was well served by a civilian who volunteered to visit certain points in rear of the line of battle and to make rough sketches of the progress of the action. These sketches, sent back at short intervals to head-quarters, proved of the utmost value in enlightening the commander as to the strength and intentions of the enemy.

It cannot, indeed, be said that the attack of the 14th Division was carried out with the precaution, the method, and the judicious arrangements which the incessant practice and sound training of the Prussian army would have led us to expect. But it was the initial mistakes of the general in command, the failure to push reconnaissance, the precipitate rush forward, and the neglect of careful dispositions for battle that were the true cause of the derangement of tactical order which ensued, and, "he who has never made mistakes has never made war."

We may take warning, therefore, from von Kamecke's errors, grasping the truth that simple go-ahead is a very different thing from initiative, but it will be more to the purpose if we mark and take to heart the determination of the attack in every quarter of the field, the resolute leading of the subordinate commanders, the readiness with which each grasped the spirit of the enterprise and the end to be achieved, and, when left to their own resources, and unable to communicate with their immediate leader, went about that achievement without hesitation or delay, the skilful co-operation of the artillery, the strong support that infantry afforded infantry, the rapidity with which the weak points of the defence were marked and seized, and the errors of the commencement redeemed by the tactical adroitness of the regimental officers and the stubborn hardihood of their men.

CHAPTER VII
THE BATTLE OF SPICHEREN – CONTINUED

AFTER 3.30 PM

THE BATTLE ON THE PLATEAU – 3.30–5 PM

General von Goeben, commanding VIII Army Corps, had arrived upon the Reppertsberg about 3 o'clock, and, as the senior officer present, had assumed direction of the fight.

At this time the dense columns of the French reserve division could be seen from the drill-ground descending the Pfaffenberg towards Spicheren, and the day was not many minutes older when the, Gifert Wood disgorged the broken companies of the 39th.

On the right wing the battle was going well, and the French were in the act of falling back on Stiring Wendel. But on the left and centre, despite the fact that the Fusiliers of the 74th had won the crest of the Rotherberg, and that II/39 still clung to the ridge within the wood, it was evident that, without strong speedy help, the position on the heights, held by not more than 1,800 rifles, could not be long maintained. Von Goeben, therefore, determined to use every rifle of the fast-arriving reinforcements to restore the fight upon the plateau.

At 3.15 came the 9th Hussars and two batteries of the 16th Division. The cavalry was sent to the Ehrenthal, the guns to the Galgenberg, where they took post on either side the high road, and concentrated their fire on the mitrailleuse battery, which, after the rout of the 39th, had advanced to the south-west corner of the Gifert Wood.

Ten minutes later, two battalions of the 48th Regiment, the van of the 9th Brigade, deployed along the ridge. The divisional commander, von Stulpnagel, as well as the Brigadier, von Doering, were both present, and the former, so soon as it was clear that the French had no intention of pressing the pursuit of the 39th across the valley, led the First and Fusiliers of the 48th towards the saddle which connects the Gifert with the Pfaffen Wood. It was evidently considered that a flank attack was the surest means of diverting the attention of the enemy from the slender force upon the Rotherberg.

The 48th advanced in a deeper and more compact formation than was generally the case with the Prussians at Spicheren or elsewhere.

The 9th and 12th Companies, in line of company columns at 80 paces interval, with marksmen advanced, led the way.

The 10th and 11th Companies followed as a half-battalion in second line.

In rear of all came the First Battalion, also in half-battalions.

To this distribution may be attributed the fact that the 48th preserved its tactical cohesion during the heavy fighting which followed its advance up the heights, that the companies, well in hand – for the front was small – showed no disposition to drift

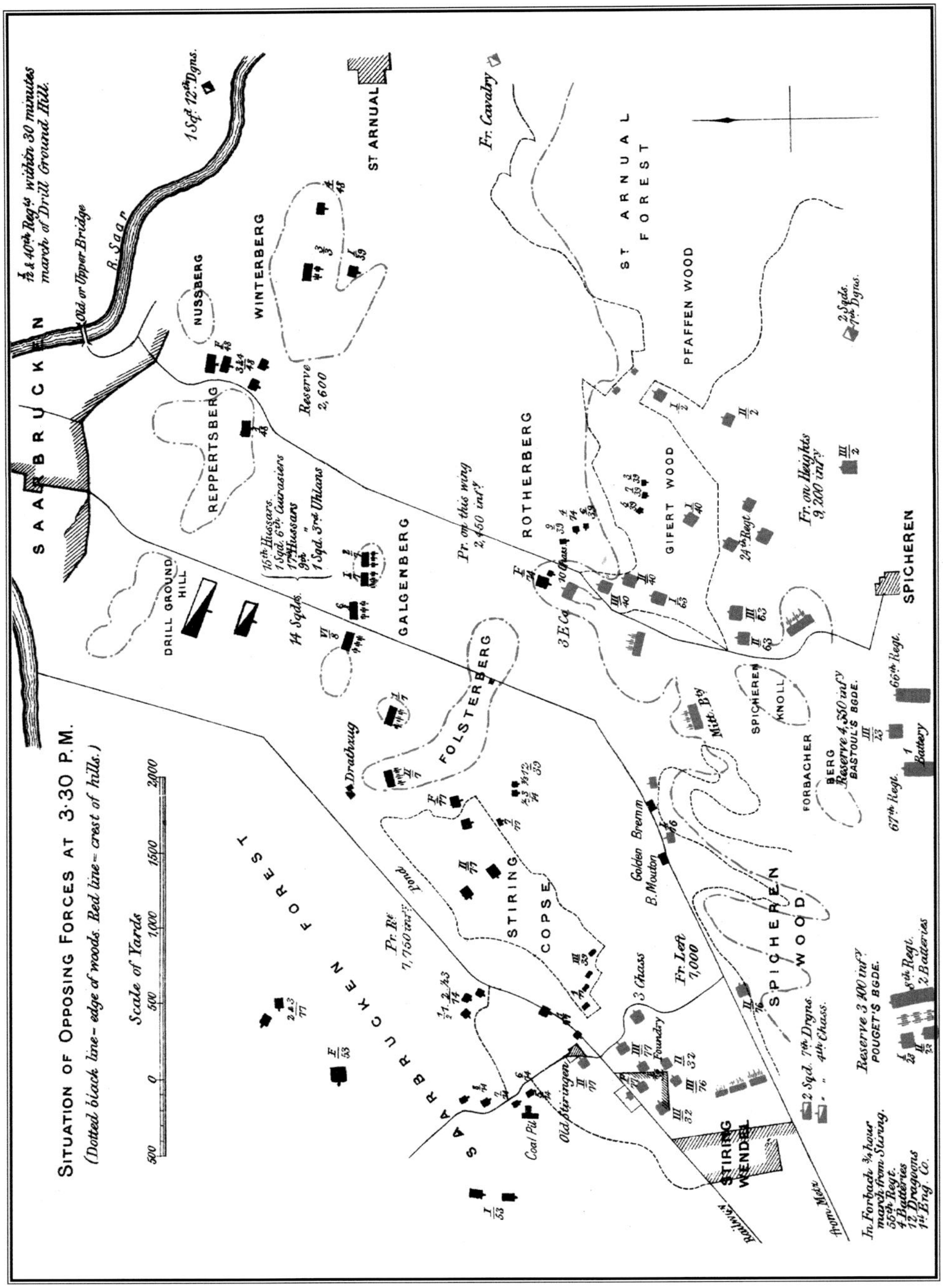

Situation of the opposing forces, 3.30pm

asunder, and that reserves were forthcoming when they were required. The old rule of a formation in three distinct lines once more proved its efficacy.

Even before the two battalions left the ridge the fire of the French skirmishers in the opposite woods was felt, and men were wounded at a range of 2000 yards, and as two leading companies of the Fusiliers (the 9th on the right, 12th on the left) neared the foot of the thinly-wooded slope the enemy's musketry became so lively that the men broke into a double, and the 12th Company diverged to the left in order to gain the shelter of the timber. The French skirmishers, covering the withdrawal of Doens' battalions to the crest, retreated upwards to the saddle between the woods, and, although they fired heavily on the disordered line, as, using their hands to assist them, the Prussians scaled the hill, the steepness of the slopes, bare as they were beneath the gap, eventually protected the assailant, for the 9th Company, which faced this portion of the ascent, lost but few men until they reached the plateau. Here, the supporting section was sent forward to turn the enemy's left, and the French skirmishers fell slowly back towards the Pfaffen Wood. The 12th Company followed through the thickets, but the French held fast to the southern quarter of the wood, and, at 5 o'clock, were still opposing a strong front.

The companies in second line, 10 and 11, losing their commander before they left the valley, were ordered to incline to the right, and to ascend the hill along the eastern edge of the Gifert Wood. A section of the 11th Company, which had been sent out to cover the left flank of the first line, did not hear the order for the change of direction, and, moving straight to the front, followed the 12th Company through the Pfaffen Wood. Within the covert, the subaltern in command sub-divided his little force into two sections of 30 men each. Giving charge of the second section to another officer, he himself joined the firing line of the 12th Company, and remained with it to the close. It is significant that the leader of the half-battalion in second line was very soon able to form the stragglers

The Prussian 40th and 48th Infantry Regiments assault the heights at Spicheren (Hiltl)

Major-General von Doering, commander of the German 9th Brigade, 5th Infantry Division, III Corps (Rousset/*Histoire*)

into a section, which he seems to have retained in rear with the section that formed the escort to the colour. The latter section he divided into two, and it is worthwhile noticing the care the Prussian officers invariably took to form even the smallest units into a firing line and support.

At 4 o'clock the greater part of the 40th Regiment, the heroes of August the 2nd, and the foremost infantry of the 16th Division, ascended the Reppertsberg. The first six companies were immediately set in motion towards the Rotherberg, the remainder to the Gifert Wood, in order to fill the wide gap which existed between the 48th upon the extreme left and the 74th upon the spur – an interval hitherto occupied only by two companies outside the wood, 6/39 and 4/47, and by the three companies of the 39th on the crest above. The regiment, before it was ordered to march on Saarbrucken, had been already distributed in the villages it was to occupy for the night, and, on being directed to the front, had pushed on without concentrating, by half-battalions. Thus, about an hour after the arrival of the first half of the Third Battalion, the 10th and 11th companies came up and were ordered to support the other two.

The railway had already brought from Neunkirchen General von Alvensleben, commanding III Army Corps of the Second Army, and I/12th Grenadiers of the 10th Brigade, 5th Division. The general galloped forward to the Reppertsberg, and the battalion, on its arrival shortly after 4, was sent forward to the right rear of the 40th, in the direction of the Rotherberg. At 4.30, nearly half-an-hour later, II/12 which had been also conveyed by train, reached Saarbrucken. And now, as the rest of the 9th Brigade was approaching through St. Johann, II/48, which had reached the ridge before 4 o'clock, and had been hitherto retained as general reserve, was ordered to advance from the Winterberg, and to occupy the space which intervened between I and F/48 and the troops proceeding from the Reppertsberg. II/12 was ordered to take the same direction.

The Prussian 12th Grenadiers storm the left side of the Rotherberg (Pflug-Harttung)

Thus, eight battalions, less one company,[1] a strength of 7,750 rifles, moved out at different intervals between 3.30 and 5 o'clock, to support the 1,800 Prussians who had won a footing on the Spicheren Heights; but the French opposed to them, Laveaucoupet's entire division and Bastoul's powerful brigade of the reserve division, numbered 12,000 men, of whom twelve battalions, over 7,000 rifles, the 24th, 40th, 63rd, 10th Chasseurs, and II and III/2nd, were either in front line or in close support, and the advantages of position lay with the defence.

During the advance of the German reinforcements, the contest on the plateau was confined to the Rotherberg, where the five companies of the 74th and 39th held the shelter-trench under a heavy fire of musketry, and against repeated counter-strokes of the French 40th, Chasseurs, and 63rd from the Gifert Wood.

The reverse slope of the earthwork gave the Prussians shelter, and, before them, looking up the spur, stretched the bare and gently rising surface of the saddle, less broad than the front they held, and converging to a narrow neck with steeply sloping sides. Here was a fine field for the needle-gun, here rush after rush of the hostile infantry was driven back. Still the French were in overwhelming force, supports came thronging up, and it seemed likely that, by mere stress of numbers, they would drive the Prussians down the hill.

But, throughout this stubborn struggle, this give and take of staggering blows, the slender line of infantry was not left unaided. The six-and-thirty guns upon the Galgenberg and Folster Height, having driven back the hostile batteries, gave stout support. Two of the batteries, those on the left flank, searched out the main plateau, and swept the Forbach Road. The three in the centre played upon the Toll House and the

1 7/40 as escort to headquarters.

Golden Bremm, at a range of 2,000–2500 yards, whilst II/7, which had taken post on the Folster Height after 3 o'clock, thus flanking the approach to the Rotherberg by the saddle, appears to have made most effective practice. Hostile guns which attempted to come into action on the western crest of the plateau were speedily overpowered,[2] of the mitrailleuses, which had sought a new position on the spur above the Golden Bremm, two were dismounted, and the battery was forced to withdraw towards Spicheren. And, more than all, a keen lookout was kept upon the French infantry. Several times Laveaucoupet's second line attempted to cross the saddle and rush down upon the 74th, but immediately his masses showed upon the crest, front and flank were rent by shells, and the shattered columns, for the very nature of the ground forced the troops into a compact formation, dissolved and disappeared.[3]

A little later, Captain Seton, who was still accompanying VII Army Corps, reached the Galgenberg. "While the fresh infantry," he writes, "passed by the left of the batteries and entered the forest, I stayed with the artillery and watched their practice, which was now directed principally against unseen batteries on the plateau, the trenches at the head of the ravine (the Spicheren Knoll), between the salient and the Spicheren Wood, the reserves in rear, and against visible batteries in the Forbach Valley."

"It was not safe to shell the wood in front and half-left, for any time after the troops had entered it, for the distances which they from time to time penetrated were not definitely marked by the musketry smoke rising above the trees. It was a beautiful sight to watch the working of these guns – I mean the morale of the service in particular. What I admired was, in the presence of so much temptation to fire rapidly, the care and deliberation with which the distances were estimated, and with which each gun was laid, then the trouble taken, and the time allowed, to watch the effect of a shot before another was fired. The practice struck me as very accurate. For instance, a French general with his staff showed for a few minutes on the plateau, as soon as they were observed a shell was sent, which burst amongst, or so close to them, that as the smoke cleared away, the different officers were to be seen galloping off."

The chief command of the German troops changed hands, for the third and last time, when General von Zastrow, commanding VII Army Corps, arrived at 4.30 upon the field. The dispositions for the future conduct of the fight were, for the most part, mutually agreed upon by the various commanders. Generally speaking, von Alvensleben, von Stulpnagel, and von Doering directed the operations on the left, von Goeben, von Kamecke, and von Barnekow, those by the Reppertsberg and Galgenberg in the centre. The right attack appears to have remained in the hands of von Woyna and von Pannwitz.

The dispositions made by these generals, the formations adopted by the reinforcing infantry, the places occupied by the battalions in the fresh line of attack, and the position of the batteries, are indicated in the accompanying sketch.

We have now, for the next half-hour (4.30 to 5 pm) to deal with eight battalions, advancing along a front extending from the Winterberg to the Drill-ground Hill, at short intervals of time, and, as there are many points of interest in the doings of each, it will be more instructive to take them singly. It must first be noted that the French now deemed it advisable to occupy some portion of the lower border of the wood, and

2 There is no mention of this in French records, though those of the Artillery are sufficiently full.

3 III/3 had come up before 5 o'clock, and moved to the Galgenberg with 3/3 but did not come into action, space being limited.

to bring the valley under fire, for the thickets which encircle the rim of the deep ravine lying immediately east of the Rotherberg, gradually filled with skirmishers, and, as the Prussians approached, amongst the bushes and broken ground at the head of the winding road which climbs the spur, red *képis* and burnished Chassepôt barrels were plainly visible. Moreover, the fight upon the salient showed no signs of failing, every bullet which flew over the heads of the defenders of the shelter-trench fell within the valley, accompanied by shells both from the batteries far back on the plateau and those south-east of Stiring Wendel. The zone of fire to be crossed by the Prussians was a broad one, and there was no shelter from the storm.

At 4.30 the leading echelon, F/48, upon the extreme left, had, as already stated, reached the foot of the slopes below the saddle between the Gifert and Pfaffen Woods, and, scaling the hill under a brisk fire, had gained ground on the heights above.

The First Battalion was halted behind an earthen bank below, and the Fusiliers, although suffering heavy losses, had, up to 5 o'clock, no need of help. The French skirmishers, probably few in number, and with orders to fall back as the attack developed, assailed in front by the 12th Company, and threatened in flank by the right wing of the 9th, withdrew slowly through the wood.

This phase of the engagement had scarcely opened, when the first half of the Third Battalion of the 40th Hohenzollerns, the van-guard of that regiment, approached the heights, but on the other side of the salient of the Gifert Wood. During its progress across the valley, it received an urgent request from the troops on the Rotherberg for assistance, as they were hard-pressed and running short of ammunition.

For more than an hour the five companies on the spur had been left without infantry support. The French, in superior force, occupied two positions, the first an undulation, some 80 or 100 yards above the horse-shoe trench, the second the gun-pits on the most elevated part of the saddle, close to the corner of the Gifert Wood, and the wood itself was swarming with their infantry. Here were no less than six battalions – the Chasseurs, I and II/40, and the 63rd Regiment – for General Laveaucoupet had brought the whole of the latter to the front, replacing it on the entrenched Spicheren Knoll by III/2, withdrawn from the right. The French position, was, however, somewhat awkward, for they could not venture on the open saddle without drawing the concentrated fire of the enemy's guns. Moreover, at this moment, a strong line, namely, the 9th and 12th Companies of the 40th, followed by I/12, I and II/40, II/48, and II/12, were fast approaching the ravine to the east of the Rotherberg, diverting the attention of the enemy from the troops upon the spur.

9/40, scaling the northern face, now joined the five companies upon the crest. A sudden rush drove the French from the cover of the undulation, and, on the appearance of 12/40, which had made a wide circuit to the eastward, upon his right flank, the enemy again fell back, after a short but vigorous musketry action, and sought shelter in the gun-pits and the nearest part of the Gifert Wood.[4]

The First Battalion of the 12th was the next to arrive upon the scene. Advancing from the Reppertsberg, along the Metz Road, it had wheeled to the left behind the

4 When 10 and 11/40 arrived about half-an-hour later they were at first directed by the major in command to remain at the foot of the Rotherberg as reserve, but were presently ordered by General von Barnekow, commanding 16th Division (with whom was Colonel von Rex, commanding 32nd Brigade, to which the 40th belonged), to join the troops upon the height.

Galgenberg, and fronted towards the Rotherberg on the Saarbrucken-Spicheren Road. Here the hostile fire was first felt, and the 1st and 2nd Companies, extending their marksman's sections and loading rifles, advanced on either side of the road, the remaining companies forming a half-battalion to the left rear.

At 1,200—1,300 paces from the enemy's position, within the zone of unaimed fire, men began to fall, not only amongst the extended sections, but also amongst the supports. The regimental commander was struck by a shot, and his charger, and that of the captain of the 1st Company, were both wounded.

The flat shelf of the Rotherberg, and the belt of timber behind, were shrouded in smoke. A dark line of figures lying on the verge of the crest, and a few small groups pushed forward to the right front, showed the position of the 74th. The two companies of the 40th had not yet reached the spur, and men were observed waving handkerchiefs on the height as if calling for support. It was evident that the Prussians were hard pressed. The 1st Company, therefore, pushed rapidly forward towards the salient, but the remainder of the battalion inclined too much to the left, facing the mouth of the ravine. The officer commanding sent his adjutant to bring them nearer to the Rotherberg, but the messenger fell mortally wounded, and the order did not reach them. Under the north face of the spur, the 1st Company found cover. Knapsacks were taken off, and the men ascended, but not without loss, for the French riflemen, posted on the border of the wood across the ravine, found means to bring fire to bear upon them.

The top was reached at a critical moment. The 10th Chasseurs and 63rd were issuing from the Gifert Wood in a vigorous effort to drive the Prussians down the hill, but the 1/12, breathless as they were, throwing themselves into the trench upon the crest, assisted the 74th (who had by this time come to their last round), and the two companies of the 40th and 9/39 in beating back the counterstroke by rapid independent firing.

The charge was pressed with much determination, and it is said that in some cases French soldiers fell within 20 paces of the Prussian linen, But the ceaseless drift of lead, which swept the open surface of the spur, shattered the strength of the attack, and, leaving many dead and wounded to mark his course, the enemy withdrew in confusion to the wood and to the gun-pits.

The Second Company, on the left, had moved off in the direction of the ravine, but the captain falling wounded, the lieutenant who had taken up the command drew off to the right and attempted to ascend the spur by the road. So heavy was the hostile fire that connection between the extended section and the support was lost, the marksmen inclining to the left, and occupying with a rush a hollow within the ravine, 300 paces from the edge of the wood, the supports diverging to the right. The leading section of the latter, however, exposed to a concentrated fire from hostile skirmishers lurking in the bushes at the head of the winding track, was quickly made to seek cover beneath the log embankment. Here the whole once more extended, and facing the ascent, gradually worked their way towards the crest. But they were without support, cut off from the rest of the battalion, and a sudden volley from the Gifert Wood upon their left sent them plunging down the hill. At the same time they were fired into by Prussian troops approaching from the Reppertsberg, and a private soldier won his Iron Cross by crossing the shot-swept zone and stopping the fire of the advancing troops.

The 3rd and 4th Companies, moving directly on the ravine, extended their marksmen's sections at 800 paces distant. So fierce was the fire they encountered, so great the excitement of the men, that the supports were quickly drawn into the intervals of the fighting line, and the whole, despite the efforts of their officers and the presence of Prussian troops in front, opened fire upon the woods. The Third Company was now sent half-left, but the Fourth on the right conformed without orders to the movement, and the intended divergence of a portion of the force against the enemy's flank was frustrated. Manœuvering was thus found impossible, but to the left front, two hundred paces from the edge of the wood, lay a small detachment of Prussian troops, well sheltered in a hollow. These were 4/74 and 6/39, who signalled, by waving handkerchiefs, that the random fire of 3 and 4/12 was passing in perilous proximity. The two companies rushed forward to share this cover, the officers regaining control over their men during the rapid and disorderly advance.

When they reached the hollow, the 3rd Company received orders to remove their packs, but whilst they were in the act of so doing, a murderous fire from the north-west corner of the Gifert struck the 4th Company in flank.

Movement had become imperative. So, leaving their packs behind, the little force, in size a battalion, and in crowded formation, rushed pell-mell upon the border of the wood.

The French did not await the onset, but, yielding the edge without a struggle, withdrew rapidly up the cliff. The Prussians followed, but the cohesion of the units, already broken by the scrambling charge, was completely lost on the densely-wooded slope, and the four companies, belonging to three different regiments, became mingled in inextricable confusion.

In this advance against the Gifert Wood, which occupied about fifteen minutes from the time the marksmen's sections first extended, the two companies of the 12th lost 5 officers and 150 men.

The extreme edge of the ravine had now been carried, and, almost simultaneously, the north-western quarter of the Gifert Wood was wrested from the French. II/48 had formed line of company columns at deploying intervals as it neared the heights, and, in this formation, severely handled as it swept forward up the ravine, inserted itself into the interval between the troops upon the Rotherberg and the mixed force whose adventures have just been narrated. Here, as elsewhere, a swift and resolute rush brought about success. The defenders of the wood fell back, and the battalion entered the thickets, the right wing pushing upwards along the western edge, the left, with drums beating and loud cheers, scaling the wooded steep above them, and driving the enemy back to the south-western corner of the wood.

The First Battalion 40th had advanced in half-battalion columns, the right being directed on the Rotherberg, the left on the centre of the Gifert Wood. The former, consisting of the 1st and 4th Companies, reinforced the troops on the eastern crest of the spur and within the western quarter of the wood, the latter, entering the covert far away to the left, came up to the assistance of the 39th still holding the ridge within the wood. Breaking into a line of skirmishers, they endeavoured to push forward through the timber, but the French 24th, together with I/40, held the southern quarter of the Gifert Wood at this point, and against this superior force the Prussians were unable to make headway.

The Second Battalion, 5th, 6th and 8th companies, broke into the forest still further to the left.

II/12, which had only disembarked at St. Johann at 4 o'clock, had, in its advance from the Reppertsberg, taken a direction midway between the Rotherberg and the eastern part of the Gifert, with a view of maintaining the communication between the separated wings of the 5th Division, a duty which had been originally assigned to II/48.

The 5th Company moved on the right of the Spicheren-Saarbrucken Road, the 6th on the left, the 7th and 8th in half-battalion column as reserve. As they neared the ravine the divisional commander, von Stulpnagel, ordered the reserve to move up on the left of the first line. The northern border of the Gifert had by this time (5 o'clock), fallen into Prussian hands, but the battalion suffered some loss from stray bullets as it advanced across the valley. Before entering the wood, knapsacks were taken off, and when the men, exhausted by their rapid march and the steep ascent, reached the summit of the hill, they found the French still offering a fierce resistance

Still, at 5 o'clock, the edge of the Rotherberg, the long ravine, and the north-western corner of the Gifert, were in possession of the assailant, whilst to the left, a force composed of II/39, I and II/40, and 11/12 had won the ridge within the wood. Nevertheless, the French line, extending across the spur, and bending back at an angle through the timber, was still strongly held.

Of Bastoul's Brigade, one battalion of the 66th had been posted in the Spicheren Wood, but a second, with that of the 23rd detached from Pouget's Brigade, had moved up in support of the troops within the Gifert. The third, with 1/2, remained at Spicheren in reserve. The battery with the brigade was deployed on the spur of the Forbacherberg, and the 67th Regiment, at 5 o'clock, was posted behind the same hill. Thus, allowing for losses, a force of 12,000 French infantry[5], and 4 batteries, faced the 10 battalions[6] of the Prussians on the heights. The latter had done little more than gain a footing on the crest, the advanced line of the enemy was still intact, on the left, the village of Stiring Wendel still resisted all attack, but in the very centre of the field the Prussians had won a distinct success, a success which appeared trifling at the time, but had, nevertheless, much influence on the immediate issue of the struggle.

THE BATTLE IN THE VALLEY – 3.30–5 PM

The centre

From the beginning of the engagement, the French Custom House, the Golden Bremm, and the Baraque Mouton, the two latter 1,900 and 2,300 yards respectively south of the German artillery position on the Galgenberg, had been held by the First Battalion of the French 76th, and a battalion of the 66th had been placed in support within the Spicheren Wood. Moreover, east of Stiring Wendel, less than 1,600 yards from the Baraque Mouton, and 2,000 from the Golden Bremm, three batteries[7] were in action, and not far in rear of the guns General Valarbrègue was present with four squadrons.

The open undulating arable and pasture to the north and east, as well as the wooded slopes behind the buildings was covered with skirmishers. The range was but 1,200 yards to the corner of the Rotherberg, and the western face of the heights was thus effectually flanked. However, from their post upon the Galgenberg, two of the six German batteries

5 40th, 24th, 2nd, 63rd, 10th Chasseurs, I and II/66, I/23, 67th.

6 48th, 40th, F/74, I and II/12, 6, 7, 8, 9, 3/39.

7 The two batteries which had lost guns had been withdrawn, and also the mitrailleuses.

The German 77th Infantry capture the Golden Bremm (Ruppersberg)

had for some time directed their fire upon the homesteads, and prevented the French from occupying them in strength.

At 3 o'clock, 5 Prussian , companies, viz. half of 12/39, a, section of 3/74, and F/74, were facing this advanced post, and 7/77, detached from the Second Battalion in the centre of the Stiring Copse, was soon afterwards ordered to join them.

With the advent of this force, the leading sections, 12/39 and 3/74, whether under superior orders, or on their own initiative, began to move forward in the direction of the Custom House. Colonel von Pannwitz, commanding 74th Regiment, and, after von François' death, senior officer of the 27th Brigade, now ordered F/74 to advance in support, and himself took charge of the attack. The Stiring Copse had already been evacuated by the enemy. The 28th Brigade had come up on the extreme right, and the defenders of Stiring Wendel showed no disposition to attempt a counter-stroke. It appeared, therefore, to the brigadier, that the time had come to carry out the original order issued by von François, *i.e.*, to attack the western face of the Spicheren Heights.

The progress of the attacking line was slow, 7/77 losing all its officers, but the French were much harassed by the fire of the Prussian artillery, and ground was slowly gained. Ascending the first slope of the rise which culminates in a round open ridge 400 paces from the Golden Bremm, von Pannwitz formed F/74 into two half-battalion columns, directing the left against the tavern, the right against the farm.

As they topped the brow they were received by a murderous fire of musketry and artillery. Of the right half-battalion the commander and a hundred men fell in a few minutes, but the battalion leader placed himself at the head, and, with drums beating, the whole force dashed down the grassy slope. The French skirmishers fell back to the buildings, but the 74th pressed so closely upon their track, that the outer walls were scarcely manned before the enemy had reached them. The fight was stubborn, but the French tactics were weak, supports were wanting, no counter-stroke was made, and, before 4 o'clock, after a fierce struggle, both the Golden Bremm and Baraque Mouton had fallen to the Fusiliers, the enemy taking refuge in the Spicheren Wood, whence he assailed the homesteads with a bitter fire. The Custom House had already been seized by the mixed detachment which had originally formed the first line of attack.

Accounts of this daring, but somewhat fortunate, exploit are nowhere to be found in detail, but it is very evident that the flanking fire of the German batteries greatly weakened the resistance of the defence. At the same time, the efforts of the French were by no means commensurate with the importance of the post. The buildings, massive and substantial, were not prepared for defence, and, when stormed by the 74th, no attempt was made to retake them by an instantaneous counter-stroke.

Exposed as they were to a heavy shellfire, their continued occupation was only harmful, the defenders were therefore rightly placed well to the front. But, when the advance of the German infantry masked the fire of their batteries, a body of men should have been at once thrown into the houses, and from the very commencement of the action, a reserve should have been drawn up beneath the wooded slopes in rear, ready, either to manœuvre against the flanks of the attack or, if the post fell, to deliver a counter-stroke before the intruders had recovered from the confusion of their successful onslaught.

The Fusiliers, on seizing the buildings, in spite of the heavy fire poured upon them at short range from the over-hanging heights, immediately began to prepare them for defence. The battalion lost during this attack 7 officers, 17 non-commissioned officers and 215 men, one-fourth of its strength.

By this time, the greater part of Bataille's Division had arrived upon the field, and it appears that whilst Bastoul's Brigade, together with a battalion of the 23rd and a battery, were directed to the plateau, Pouget's Brigade, accompanied by the two remaining divisional batteries, had joined General Vergé in Stiring Wendel, the two battalions of the 23rd taking post in the southern quarter of the village, the 8th Regiment, outside, to the south-east, in reserve.

A large force was thus present in the immediate neighbourhood, but neither infantry nor artillery were employed in resolute combination to oust the enemy from the homesteads.

It may be noted, at the same time, that but two batteries of Frossard's large artillery reserve (six batteries) had as yet been brought into action.

The French are ejected from Old Stiringen (Ruppersberg)

A glance at the contoured map shows that a long ridge rises between the homesteads and the Stiring Copse. It was by taking advantage of this cover, and probably by advancing up the re-entrant, the crest of which is little more than 400 paces, from the homesteads, that the Fusilier Battalion of the 77th was enabled to make its decisive charge.

It will also be noticed that the exposed flank was nearly 1,500 paces distant from Stiring Wendel, and was protected in that direction by rising ground. It may be questioned, also, whether the French Cavalry, if a lookout had been kept, had not here an opportunity.

The right wing

From 3:30 to 4, no material change took place in the state of the fight round Stiring Wendel.

That portion of the 28th Brigade which had followed von Woyna, leaving the Coal-pit Ridge and the nearest houses of Old Stiringen in possession of II/74, had advanced still further into the forest in a south-easterly direction, still driving before it small hostile detachments. This wide turning movement appears to have alarmed General Vergé. Fearing for his communications with Forbach, he had demanded further support from Frossard. Towards 4 o'clock, in compliance with his request, the 55th Regiment came up from the Kaninchenberg and two of the reserve batteries from Forbach.

About the same hour, Old Stiringen fell into the hands of the Prussians, the attack being carried out by II/74, 4/77, two companies of I/74, and a detachment of F/53, this last being probably the marksmen's section of the 11th Company, which had been detached in order to secure the left flank during the progress of the battalion through the forest.

4/77 now occupied the nearest houses on the other side of the railway.

Meanwhile, along the southern borders of the Stiring Copse the tide of battle ebbed and flowed.

At 3.30, the three companies of the 39th, together with 1/77, held the outskirts, but General Vergé, the 32nd having come to his assistance, had already initiated a counter-stroke.

A heavy fire of artillery and musketry was poured upon the timber, and then Jolivet's Brigade, leaving the 32nd and 55th in Stiring Wendel, broke forward from the foundry. More than once the steady fire of the Prussians drove them back, but at length the defence yielded, and by 4 o'clock the French had rewon the outer edge, and were pressing forward through the beeches. But their progress was not long continued. The three companies of II/77, hitherto stationed in the centre of the copse, brought strong support to the broken and receding line. Deploying rapidly and filling the gaps between the scattered groups of the 39th, this powerful reinforcement of 750 rifles bore back the French, and at 5 o'clock, Jolivet's troops withdrew once more to Stiring Wendel. On both sides the loss was great, and beneath the spreading foliage of the beeches, the dead and dying lay in scores.

The 39th and 77th re-occupied the border of the copse, 6/77 taking post behind an undulation outside the eastern edge, thus securing the left flank. An effort was made by 5/77 to reach the five guns which had been abandoned by the French, but the assailants were compelled to re-seek the copse without carrying off the prize.

Old Stiringen does not appear to have been menaced by the counter-attack of Jolivet's battalions. After the capture of the Golden Bremm, the garrison which had been driven from it, was placed in reserve between the artillery and Stiring Wendel. Guns were also introduced into the village, one piece into a house facing the copse.

During the period of the engagement, General Vergé had at his disposal the whole of his own division, thirteen battalions, in close support were 3 battalions under Pouget, and no less than seven batteries. Opposed to him were but 2 battalions of the 27th, and 4 of the 28th Brigade, and we must now advert to von Woyna's turning movement, which, menacing his communications, had hindered his employing his overwhelming force in a general counter-stroke.

Turning movement of the 28th Brigade

At 4 o'clock, whilst the fight was raging fiercely on the borders of the Stiring Copse and round about the foundry, General von Woyna, accompanied by I/53, was forcing his way through the forest and inclining gradually towards the railway and the Stiring-Forbach Road.

About 4.30, the branch tramway from the coalpit was struck at the edge of the wood, where it bends abruptly to the south. Here the 53rd, as it formed up for attack, was received by a very heavy fire from the church tower and the village buildings, and several officers fell.

Connection with the Fusiliers had been lost, and their whereabouts was unknown. There was no support at hand, and the enemy was in far greater strength. Von Woyna, therefore, fearful that his isolated battalion would be crushed before help could be attained, and desirous of regaining touch with the rest of his brigade – which he knew not was otherwise employed – decided to retire from his exposed position.

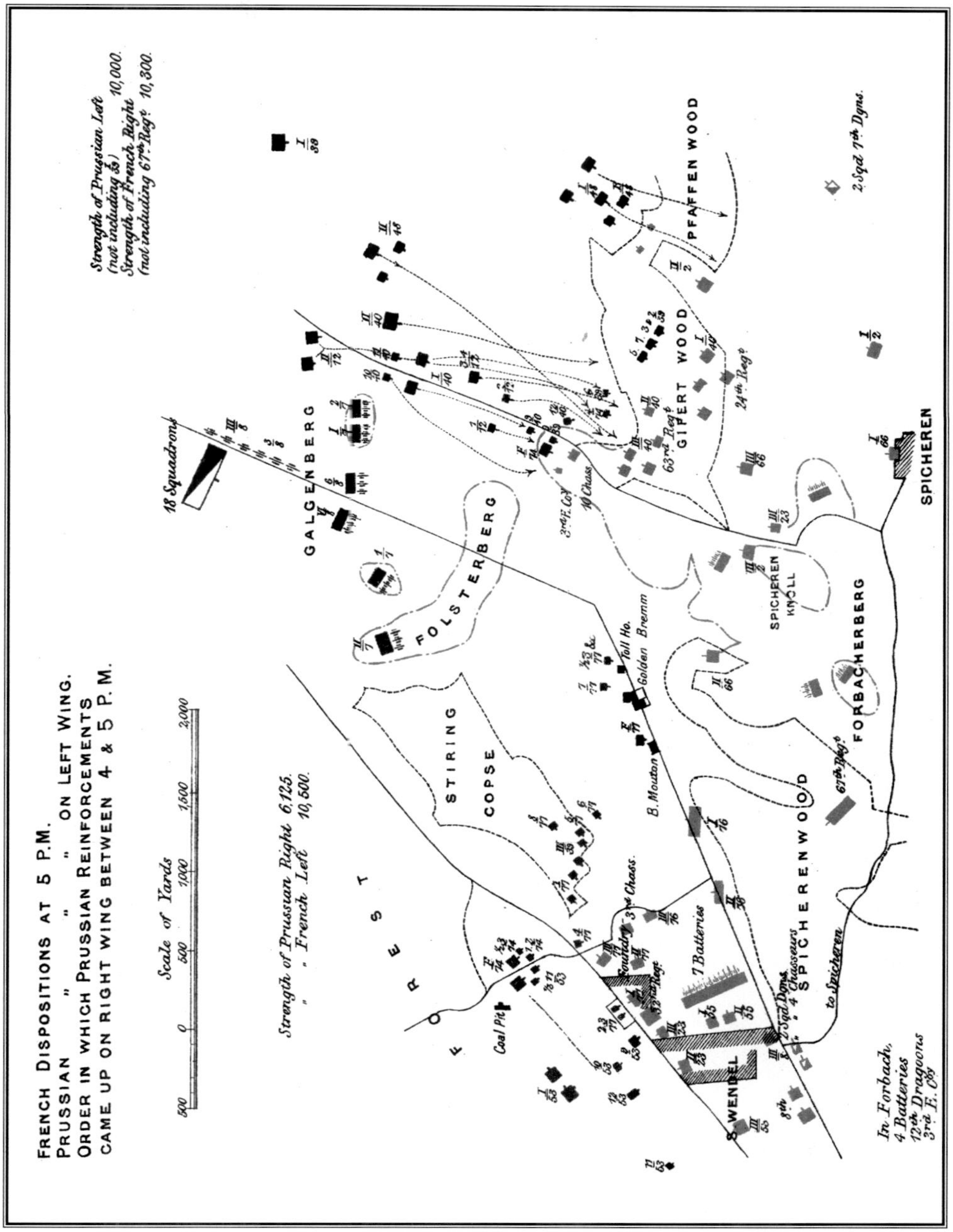

Situa:ion of the opposing forces, 5pm

Withdrawing to the wood, under cover of the 4th Company posted on the tramway, the battalion took ground to the left in the direction of the coal-pit. The covering detachment then fell back in the same manner, leaving the marksman's section to protect the retreat.

This small rear-guard was hotly engaged and losing heavily, when F/53, ignorant that the First Battalion had fallen back, emerged into the open between Old Stiringen and the railway station, and prepared to join the attack which 4/77 and the six companies of the 74th were pushing from Old Stiringen. The 9th Company, the whole extended, was ordered to storm the houses and garden on the near side of the railway, whilst the 12th, posted on the skirt of the wood, secured the outer flank, the 10th and 11th forming the reserve.

The assault was successful. The French were compelled to abandon the north-west corner of Stiring Wendel, and to fall back over the railway to the foundry. Between the houses and the foundry yard, the railway cutting was 40 feet in depth, crossed by a narrow bridge. Some men of the 9th Company had already crossed, and the gate of the yard had just been broken in, when the order was received to retire at once. The scouts of the 12th Company, sent out to explore the forest on the right, had reported the approach of hostile troops on that flank.

The houses already occupied were, therefore, hastily abandoned, but not for long. The alarm came to nothing. The 11th Company was ordered to move into the forest to the

The Prussian 48th Regiment and French troops exchange fire in the Gifert Wood (Ruppersberg)

right, 2/ and 3/77 having joined the Fusiliers from the left rear, thus regaining touch with their brigade, the senior officer of the 53rd then present combined them with the 9th and 10th Companies of his own battalion, and after a sharp musketry fight once more took possession of the building on the railway. 11/53, driving before it French detachments through the wood, moved on to the glass works, and occupied the ridge in front.

The struggle for Stiring Wendel now resolved itself into a stationary musketry action. About 5 o'clock a mixed detachment of Prussians endeavoured to turn the left flank of the foundry buildings from the railway cutting. But a strong force of French was posted behind the slag-heaps and the railway plant in the yard, and, although the skirmishers came within 70 paces of each other, the assailants were unable to make the slightest progress. Moreover, Old Stiringen and the railway embankment were heavily shelled by the French batteries, and, at 5 o'clock, although the 39th and 77th had re-won the copse, and the outlying portion of the village had been captured, the situation of the Prussian right wing was exceedingly precarious. The French force was more than twice its strength, assisted by seven batteries of artillery, and closely concentrated in Stiring Wendel.

The Prussian companies, on the other hand, so intermingled and spread out as to make unity of command impossible, enveloped the north and west sides of this strong position, and even threatened it in rear, but so long and attenuated was their line, and there were so few officers remaining, that there was little hope of resisting even the semblance of a counter-stroke at any point whatever. Not a single battalion was available for their support, nor could the artillery render help. Guns could not move in the dense woods upon the right, and the batteries were unable to advance from the Galgenberg up the Forbach Valley so long as the French infantry still held the north-western crest of the Spicheren Heights. If, therefore, at 5 o'clock, the left attack had made some progress on the Rotherberg, and within the woods, the general situation was anything but promising. On both wings the Prussians were fighting in disorder, confronted by superior numbers supported by artillery, and it was impossible for their own batteries to render effective aid. Nevertheless, the resolution with which the attack on Stiring Wendel had been pressed, and the appearance of von Woyna's troops at a point which threatened the communications with Forbach, had not only held back the French in Stiring Wendel from employing their superior numbers in a vigorous attempt to roll up the slender line opposed to them, but had induced them, just as the Prussians left wing made good its footing on the crest within the Gifert, to send the 67th Regiment, hitherto held in reserve on the Forbacherberg, to reinforce the troops in the valley below. The force on the heights was thus reduced at a critical moment by 1,860 bayonets, the numbers on that flank were now well nigh equal, and the French reserve on the Spicheren Ridge consisted of but two battalions.

On the other hand, the French in Stiring Wendel, when joined by the 67th Regiment, outnumbered the Prussians opposed to them by more than two to one, and whilst the latter had no reserve whatever, at least six of the French battalions had not yet been engaged. At 5 o'clock, therefore, Frossard's prospects of success were still favourable. It is true that the seven remaining battalions of the 5th Prussian Division were close at hand, still, this reinforcement would by no means have equalized numbers, and the French had the advantage of position. But their foe had hope of assistance from another source. Between 3 and 4 o'clock, on his way to the field, General von Zastrow, receiving a report from von Kamecke, had sent word to the commander of the 13th Division, whom he had already instructed to push forward an advance guard from Wehrden towards Forbach, that the 14th Division was heavily engaged, and requested at the same time, that he would co-operate in the action. If this officer realized the situation, and threw a portion of his force against the enemy's line of retreat before he could crush the weak right wing round Stiring Wendel, all might yet be well. The issue of the battle, therefore, depended on the energy and judgment of a single man, and we may note, as a proof of the confidence with which each German officer relied on his comrades and subordinates, that when the seven battalions of the 5th Division arrived, not a single bayonet was sent to the right wing, although a portion had already given way. No one appeared to doubt that the commander of the 13th Division would come up at the right time and in the right place.

THE BATTLE ON THE PLATEAU 5–6 PM

Shortly after 5 o'clock, the Fusilier Battalion of the 48th, on the extreme Prussian left, had reached the road which crosses the clearing between the Gifert and Pfaffen Woods.

The French battalion confronting them, the second of the 2nd Line, had withdrawn to the ditches further south, with the design of crushing an advance across the open, and, at the same time, had left a detachment in the Pfaffen Wood, the flanking fire of which caused the Fusiliers some loss. At 5.30, therefore, the First Battalion of the 48th, hitherto held in reserve, was ordered by the divisional commander, General von Stulpnagel, then present, to clear the Pfaffen Wood and to threaten the enemy's right.

The left-half battalion, with two sections extended, struck through the wood well to the left, and without encountering any decided resistance, reached the southern border, the skirmishers taking post in a salient angle of the timber. The right-half battalion came into line with the Fusiliers, just in time to assist in repulsing a strong counter-attack of the French. In this position, each company with two sections in the firing line and support, the two battalions, notwithstanding, the heavy shell and rifle fire that assailed them, held fast until the battle ceased.

In the meantime, to the right, within the dark interior of the Gifert Wood, the fight raged fiercely.

Independently of the more isolated action of the 48th, here were 32 2/3 Prussian companies employed between 5 and 6 pm in the Gifert Wood and on the Rotherberg. Of these, the Fusiliers of the 74th were alone collected as a battalion. On the ridge within the wood, were 18 2/3 companies of the 39th, 40th, 48th and 12th, much mixed up, and dissolved into a long line of skirmishers, with here and there a group of stragglers, which the strenuous efforts of the company officers had assembled as supports. On the French side, the 67th Regiment of Bastoul's Brigade had been withdrawn from the Forbacherberg to the valley, and a battalion both of the 2nd and 66th still remained in reserve, but with these exceptions, the whole of Laveaucoupet's Division, as well as I/23 and I/66 – 14 battalions, or nearly 9,000 rifles – joined by degrees the struggle on the crest, and endeavoured to drive the Prussians but little superior in numbers from the heights.

The front of battle swayed backwards and forwards, ground being won or lost as fresh troops came up on either side. That portion of the wood which crowns the height nowhere exceeds 500 yards in breadth, no wide interval, therefore, lay between the hostile lines, and, although at times the combatants, it is said, approached so closely that the officers were driven to use their revolvers, so heavy was the smoke, so dense the timber, so loud the din, and so universal the confusion, that no formed body of troops could be mustered in order by a concentrated effort breach the hostile ranks. Many of the battalion and company leaders were already down, and those who still stood amidst the storm of bullets commanded merely handfuls of men, and men not of their own companies, nor even of their own battalions, but of every regiment engaged.

But the Prussian infantry was true to its discipline and training, and when, in the turmoil and excitement of the fight, the soldiers found that they were parted from their own immediate commander, or that their own leader had fallen, they sought out the nearest officer, irrespective of the number on his shoulder straps, and looked to him for orders. And so the Prussian line, although deprived of the strength and cohesion which tactical order and familiar association gives, was still in hand, and where the skill of a leader found an opening he had men wherewith to seize it. Still in the thickness of the wood, and the stunning roar of battle, no officer, however high his rank, could influence more than the nearest files on either side, and, therefore, on the commanders of small groups, whatever their grade might be depended the handling of the men and the ultimate issue of the struggle.

Nor, although on both sides there was equality in courage and in numbers, was there much doubt as to the result. Here, swarming up from the hollow and across the leafy ridge, with their faces set towards Spicheren, were men with deep instincts of obedience, trusting their leaders and following the slightest sign, here were officers trained in battle exercises, seeing, in the deadly strife which raged in the thickets, but a livelier picture of their accustomed work, and recalling without effort the shifts and expedients learnt in more peaceful autumns, gathering, as it were by mere force of habit, the scattered files together, cheering and directing, thrusting ceaselessly at the flank of hostile groups, recognising clearly the purpose of the fight, and accepting as readily as composedly the responsibilities that the situation forced upon them, and to which their training had inured them.

Opposed to them were men, staunch and impetuous, but ill-disciplined, each fighting for his own hand, relying more on the rapidity than the accuracy of their fire, vigorous in individual effort, but regardless of their leaders, and ignorant of the power of united action. Nor were the officers better fitted than the men to cope with their more skilled antagonists. That they were in no wise wanting in warlike spirit the number that fell at Spicheren attests. In dash, in resolution, they were not inferior to their foes. But the majority knew little of the handling of troops, of the tricks of fence, the tactical devices, which every Prussian officer had at his fingers' ends, and those who possessed such knowledge could seldom find men to follow them. Careless of discipline in time of peace, without the taste or opportunity for earnest work, they had lost the confidence of their men, and the latter no longer looked to them instinctively under every circumstance of difficulty and danger.

And so, by six o'clock, superior training, skill, and discipline prevailed against mere courage. The successive battalions that Laveaucoupet threw into the fight failed to drive the enemy from the crest, and whether by order of the divisional commander, of Frossard himself, or by the pressure of the attack, the wood was yielded, and the Prussians lined the southern border. Laveaucoupet's battalions retired in good order, notwithstanding the fall of General Doens during the withdrawal, in echelon from the left towards Spicheren.

In face of the heavy fire which the mitrailleuses and artillery now poured upon the forest, it was impossible for the disordered throng of Prussians to pursue, nor could the south-west corner of the Gifert be maintained. III/2, reinforced probably by portions of the 66th and 63rd, still occupied the Spicheren Knoll, and, by a vigorous counter-stroke, re-won this important angle for the French.

Such was the confusion in the Prussian ranks during the struggle within the Gifert Wood, that it is impossible to follow the progress of each battalion, but a description of the advance of II/12, and of a portion of II/40, will give some idea of the difficulty of wood fighting, and of the manner in which the extraordinary loss of unity came about.

The 5th and 6th Companies of the former battalion, forming the right wing, and the first to reach the crest, gradually moved off to the left as the French began to give ground. The 7th Company, forming, with the 8th, the left wing, extended its marksmen when half way up the height, and during the ascent extended the supports also. On surmounting the crest, the left wing companies sought to regain connection with the right, but, the latter having gone forward, the endeavour failed. The left wing crossed diagonally in rear of the right in a south-westerly direction and, in the thick covert, the battalion became divided into two distinct bodies. During the subsequent advance, men of I/39, 40th, 74th and II/48, were drawn into the ranks, and whilst, near the *south-eastern* corner of the wood, far to the left of their original direction, 70 men of the 6th Company carried a little wedge-shaped copse, separated from the forest by the road, men of the 7th Company, reaching the *western* edge of the wood, were able to pour a flanking fire into the French as they finally retired from the Rotherberg. Along the entire southern border the battalion was scattered without tactical formation, the officers accompanied, perhaps, by only a single section of their own companies, and by men of various battalions, and, in many cases, the combat was carried on by small bodies fighting on their own account.

8/40 entered the wood with one section extended, but had soon to extend the remainder also. On getting through to the open it was stopped by a heavy crossfire. Here, on the southern edge, were found two of the regimental colours, of which each battalion has one, escorted by half a section only. 7/40,[8] on reaching the border, formed itself opposite an outlying copse, which appeared to give good shelter. The company leader, therefore, with the help of about a section of the 48th, accompanied by one of its majors, an adjutant, and another officer, rushed towards it, across an open space of some 400 paces in breadth, and held on there till dark.

During the struggle in the forest, the Prussian troops upon the Rotherberg, still exposed to the fire of Laveaucoupet's batteries and of a strong force of infantry, were unable to make way. The First Company of the 12th attempted to capture the gun-pits to which the enemy had been driven, but the attack was beaten off, as also were two counter-strokes on the part of the French, and when Laveaucoupet withdrew his troops, and the gun-pits were abandoned, the fire of the infantry holding the Spicheren Knoll, and the south-west corner of the wood, effectually hindered all endeavours to gain ground beyond the saddle.

8 This company had been detained as escort to headquarters, and did not arrive till 7 pm.

But although General von Goeben had already telegraphed to the King that the success of the day was to all appearance assured, it was soon found that further progress was impracticable. The French were in superior numbers and their second position was much stronger than the first. Not only was the ground which intervened between Laveaucoupet's new line and the woods held by the Prussians clear and unobstructed, but there was ample room on the downs behind Spicheren for the deployment of the whole artillery of the Second Corps. As General Laveaucoupet gave the order to retire, his artillery fell back, the 7th Battery taking post upon the Forbacherberg slopes. Here, where Bastoul's battery was already in action, it was joined by the 8th (which had exhausted all ammunition but case shot and had now to borrow from the 7th), with the exception of one section, which came into action on the Spicheren Ridge and did not rejoin the battery until night had fallen and its ammunition was exhausted.

The mitrailleuses appear to have already retired to the Forbacherberg, and from this commanding position a heavy fire was poured on the border of the woods.

It was impossible for the Prussians to establish on the plateau sufficient artillery to prepare the way for a second attack, or even to draw off the attention of the hostile batteries from the infantry, and the French right was secured by the ravine.

All idea of a frontal attack, or attempt to turn the right flank was abandoned, and it was determined to employ the reinforcements which had arrived after 5 o'clock, in ejecting the enemy from his advanced post on the Spicheren Knoll, and, when that was effected, in striking the *left* flank of his position on the plateau.

The exact position of the French battalions on the new line cannot be ascertained, but there is reason to believe that the 40th Regiment, which had been engaged throughout the day, was now withdrawn to the Pfaffenberg, and that two battalions of the 8th Regiment were sent up about this time by Bataille from the Forbach Valley to reinforce the battalion of the 66th in the Spicheren Wood.

The losses of the French artillery, which for nearly six hours had been established on the Rotherberg and the north-west crest of the plateau (although 36 guns had been in action against it at no great range,) were curiously small. The 7th Battery (one section engaged upon the spur), lost one man and two horses killed, one man and two horses wounded. The 11th (mitrailleuse) Battery had five men wounded, some horses killed, and two pieces temporarily put out of action. The 8th Battery (2nd section engaged on spur) had lost one officer and three men killed, two officers and five men wounded, nineteen horses killed or wounded, and three caissons disabled.

Further reinforcements, F/12[9] and the main-body of the 9th Brigade, 5th Division, consisting of two battalions of the 8th Grenadiers and the 3rd Jägers, in all 4,000 men, had by this time reached the Saarbrucken Ridge. The 3rd Company of the 8th, which, owing to circumstances already recorded, headed the column, was accompanied by the regimental commander, and as the troops neared St. Johann, this officer had received an order from a galloper on von Doering's staff, to move through the St. Arnual Wood, and to turn the enemy's right. Accordingly, on reaching the Reppertsberg he bore off to the left with the leading company, but, when the three remaining companies, following the Jägers, arrived upon the ridge, fresh instructions were received, directing the First

9 4 and IV/3, preceded by the 3rd and 4th squadrons of 12th Dragoons had already arrived, and had moved on to the Galgenberg.

Battalion of the Grenadiers to advance towards the western slopes of the Spicheren Heights, for the purpose of attacking in flank the saddle south of the Rotherberg and the Spicheren Knoll. Two battalions, the Jägers and II/8 were sent to the Drill-ground Hill, F/12 was retained for the present on the Winterberg. The men of the First Grenadier Battalion had already taken off their packs, coats and cooking utensils, and had loaded their rifles. Across the valley, the Rotherberg was veiled in dense clouds of smoke, and above the dark crown of the Gifert Wood the white wreaths rose slowly in the still evening air. The line of guns upon the Galgenberg was dimly seen, with Rheinbaben's squadrons, ready to support or pursue, a little to the rear. Wounded men, singly or in groups, staggered out from the shadows of the forest and across the fields. Under the long shadows of the poplars the field hospitals were busily employed, and the endless rattle of musketry and crash of bursting shells told that the battle was at height. At 5.30, the word was given "Stand to your Arms!" The colour was unfurled, and the march began, the 1st and 4th Companies, in company column at open interval, leading on either side the *chaussée*, accompanied by the brigadier, von Doering, who gave the high steeple of Forbach Church as the point of direction. The captain of the 4th Company, von Blumenhagen, had assumed command of the battalion, for the major, with the 3rd Company, was far away upon the left and ignorant of the change of orders.

The guns were passed upon the right, and the three companies moved along the foot of the Rotherberg, the battle raging fiercely overhead. Von Doering pointed to the formidable heights that the 48th Regiment of the same brigade had done its share in storming, and bade the Grenadiers emulate their comrades. His words were answered by loud hurrahs. 500 paces from the Toll House the order was given to wheel sharply to the left, in order to gain a ravine which gives easier access to the plateau. A section of the 4th Company was sent off to the right in order to reach the ground in the direction of the Golden Bremm, but received by a heavy fire from the wooded slopes above the tavern, was forced to halt and take cover, and in spite of efforts to regain it, connection with the battalion was lost.[10]

The main-body halted for a few minutes before commencing the ascent. Skirmishers were sent out in front, and then the 1st and 4th Companies pressed up the rugged slopes, scrambling from rock to rock, clutching the tree-roots and bushes, each assisting his comrade as he could. Frequent halts were made, partly to give the men time to recover their breath, partly to restore order in the broken ranks. Close to the brow a last halt was made, each man rallied to his place, and with loud shouts of "Forward!" the plateau was gained. 600 paces south-east was the entrenched Spicheren Knoll. The south-west corner of the Gifert Wood, directly facing them, not more than 200 paces distant, was also occupied, and, on the extreme right flank, the outskirt of the Spicheren Wood. A withering fire struck the Grenadiers in front and flank. To remain halted on the exposed crest was impossible. 300 paces to the right front was a small ravine, and thither the leading companies were directed, but, during their rush across the open, officers and men fell fast. Little shelter was found when the cover was attained, and, after halting there for ten minutes, and in vain endeavouring to crush the fire of the well-covered enemy, Captain von Blumenhagen led his two companies across the saddle, leaving a section behind to cover the advance. The losses, of the 1st Company especially, were

10 What eventually became of this section is not recorded.

very heavy, but such was the resolution of the attack that the French within the corner of the Gifert Wood gave way and withdrew to the Spicheren Knoll. The 2nd Company, reaching the height about fifteen minutes later, came under a heavy fire from the knoll. The captain was wounded. The lieutenant ordered the sections to reform, but in carrying out this order the three section leaders were badly hit, and many men fell. When order was restored, the commander was enabled to make an effective distribution of fire. Two sections faced the Spicheren Knoll, whilst a third swept the long ravine descending to the Golden Bremm, and drove back hostile columns that were attempting to attack the tavern.

The Gifert which had been since 1 o'clock the scene of such fierce and bloody fighting, was now entirely in the hands of the Prussians. By the capture of the south-west angle the French were deprived of all opportunity of making a sudden counterstroke, and the flank of the defenders of Rotherberg was secured.

The direction of the charge of the Grenadiers was such that the flank of the assaulting line was enfiladed at a range of 400 paces of the French shelter trenches on the knoll, but the sudden rush, the short distance, 200 paces, to be traversed, and the effective fire of the covering section were probably the reasons that the battalion escaped annihilation.

This successful advance, it may be noted, was the first advantage which the Prussians owed to the capture of the Golden Bremm and Baraque Mouton. If Frossard had divided his portions into three distinct sections, assigning to each divisional leader a definite portion of the front commensurate with the numbers of his troops, the fall of the homesteads would probably have been prevented. As it was, the centre of his line, (that is, the western face of the plateau, the homesteads, and the Spicheren Wood) was occupied first, partly by Laveaucoupet, partly by Vergé, afterwards by Bataille and Vergé; the latter was chiefly concerned for his left at Stiring Wendel, and when Bataille reached that village with Pouget's Brigade to support his colleague, he appears to have considered the threat of the enemy against the principal communication of the Army Corps, the Forbach Road, so strong as to cause him to neglect the centre. Only one battalion was sent to the Spicheren Wood, afterwards reinforced by two of the 8th Line.

Here we see clearly the disadvantages of a broken position, such as Frossard's. The attention of all the divisional leaders, fighting on an extended front, was drawn to the outer flanks, and the central battle was left to take care of itself, without proper supervision or unity of command.

At the same time, as Frossard was placed, it was no easy matter to distribute his force in such a fashion that the central section of the position would come under the immediate supervision of a single leader. Still, when the reserve division appeared on the scene, Bataille might well have been entrusted with the charge of this important point, and his three divisional batteries have remained at his disposal.

This division was directed to the field in two distinct portions: Bastoul's Brigade with one battery making for Spicheren, Pouget with two proceeding by Forbach to Stiring Wendel.

Bataille, it appears, accompanied the latter. About 5 o'clock, owing to the vigour of the Prussian attack, the situation of the defenders of Stiring Wendel appeared critical; part of the garrison, it is said, had already fled in panic towards Forbach; he therefore called down the 67th Regiment from the Forbacherberg and led them across the valley in the direction of the Stiring Copse. At this point was General Vergé, and the presence of another officer of equal rank was scarcely necessary. Had Bataille, after sending Bastoul to the assistance of Laveaucoupet and Pouget to that of Vergé, taken charge of the central battle, each of the three lieutenant-generals would have had a definite command, and every point of the line have come under supervision.

As will be hereafter seen, the homesteads were of the utmost importance, even after 6 o'clock, when the main position upon the plateau was definitely abandoned, for their possession gave the Prussians a *point d'appui* opposite the very centre, the weakest quarter of the second line. Between 5 and 6, several attempts were made by the French to recapture the Golden Bremm and Banque Mouton, the attacks proceeding from the long ravine and up the Forbach Road, but with the help of the artillery on the Galgenberg, the Fusiliers of the 77th held fast. We may notice at the same time that the buildings were not subjected to a heavy fire, which, had the French batteries been judiciously employed, might have been brought to bear from the position east of Stiring Wendel.

CHAPTER VIII
THE BATTLE OF SPICHEREN – CONTINUED

THE BATTLE IN THE VALLEY – 5–7.30 PM

The Prussian attacks on Stiring Wendel had come to a standstill by 5 o'clock. 6,000 men, extended over a front of 3,000 yards, with few officers remaining, and with brigades, regiments, and companies shuffled in a strange medley, and unsupported by either artillery or infantry, encompassed the French stronghold. The men were worn out by the protracted struggle. Their losses had been heavy, their power of resistance was strained to the utmost, the little ground that had been won had been purchased at a heavy price. It has often been observed that in fiercely-contested battles a moment comes when the physical and moral vigour of the soldiery relaxes and the bare aspect of a reinforcement turns the scale. Such a crisis had now arrived. From the Coal-pit Ridge, through the white clouds of smoke that rolled between the tall black chimneys of the foundry, a strong column of French infantry was seen approaching along the slopes of Spicheren Wood to the south of Stiring Wendel, and the very sight of its serried ranks and gleaming bayonets brought about the retreat of the exhausted Prussians.

The senior officer present with the 74th, without sending for instructions to the brigadier, gave the order to retire, and partly by way of the railroad, partly by Schoneck, his six and a half companies fell back on Drathzug. The fusiliers of the 53rd followed, joined by the 2nd, 3rd, and 4th companies of the 77th. Old Stiringen, and the Coal-pit Ridge, together with the whole of the field to westward of the railroad were evacuated. Withdrawing in great confusion, the men made no halt until the Drathzug Farm, one-and-a-quarter miles in the rear, was reached. Here the greater part of five battalions was assembled, but so shattered and disorganised that it was long before order was restored.

Notwithstanding the retreat of their comrades, the three companies of the 39th and four of the 77th, though much reduced in officers and men, still held fast along the border of the copse. It was the 39th that fired the first shot of the battle. From 1 o'clock, without stay or respite, they had been engaged within the wood, attacking and attacked at times, driven back by the heavy pressure of the more numerous French infantry, but retiring slowly, and with their faces to the enemy, rallying quickly on the reinforcements appearing, and pushing forward again with unabated courage and persistence. The 77th had also shared the fluctuations of the fight for the copse since 3 o'clock, and with the loss of three company leaders and their adjutant, had materially assisted to repulse two strong attacks on the border of the wood.

The general rearward movement that now swept past their right, and left these two attenuated battalions exposed to the full brunt of the enemy's attack, strengthened as it must shortly be by the column that was bearing down across the valley, in no degree infected these men of Hanover and the Rhineland. Spent with fighting and reduced to a few hundred rifles, but resolute to cover the retreat of von Woyna and his broken troops, they steadfastly awaited the imminent attack of the hostile masses.

But their numbers were few, and an hour of triumph had come for the French. Not only had the throng of assailants which had so long beset the village melted away at the sight of the approaching reinforcement, but a leader, quick to realize and grasp his opportunity, was present on the field.

Of Pouget's Brigade, the two battalions of the 23rd had been placed in Stiring Wendel, in order to meet the outflanking movement which was constantly threatening from the Stiring Forest, but a battalion of the 8th had remained south-east the village in reserve, and the divisional commander as already recorded, had called down the 67th Regiment from the Spicheren Heights.

This last was the force which the Prussians had descried. On its arrival at the village the 1st Battalion was thrown into the foundry, the 2nd and 3rd, with which, backed by the battalion of the 8th in second line, Bataille purposed to drive the enemy from the copse, deployed behind a steep undulation to the east. Vergé, at the same time, as soon as the Prussians began to give way, had brought up two battalions of the 55th, and drawn them up for attack in the hollow across which runs the Spicheren-Schoneck Road, behind the same undulation which covered the 67th, and 700 yards from the south-east corner of the Stiring Copse.

Two companies of the 55th deployed as skirmishers, 200 yards to the front. The remainder of the battalion was massed in column, the two battalions of the 67th in close column of sections on the left. The second battalion 55th was held back in third line. Covered by the advance of these troops, some of the French batteries again advanced, and opened a vigorous fire on the borders of the copse. Vergé then ordered an advance, and the skirmishers of the 5th, the columns in rear being still sheltered in the hollow, moved on to a point within 300 paces of the border of the wood.

Although confronted by an overwhelming force, and assailed by an artillery fire to which they could make no reply, the seven Prussian companies still held fast. A detachment occupied the embankment of the railway, but mounds of slag and refuse protected the French left from this cross fire, the effect of which was confined to the narrow space of 200 yards that intervened between the slag-heaps and the copse. The fight was protracted for nearly thirty minutes, at length the fire of the defence began to slacken, the French skirmishers rushed forward and the columns followed. "It was necessary," writes a participant in the charge, "to cross a space of more than two hundred yards in width exposed to a heavy flanking fire. The earth was covered in a couple of minutes with dead and wounded."

In this attack the 55th did not even fix bayonets, and such was the excitement of the men that the column broke up, those superior in wind and strength far outstripping their comrades. But the border of the copse was carried, and the Prussians, still fighting desperately, were pushed back into the interior with heavy losses.

The First Company 77th was almost entirely dispersed, the weak remnant was collected and led back to Drathzug by the sole remaining officer, leaving but six companies, (and these reduced to the strength of a section each), to withstand the advance of Vergé's and Bataille's battalions.

The French batteries, which had followed the infantry, now re-entered the five pieces that had been earlier abandoned, moved up the valley, and, in concert with the artillery on the Forbacherberg, engaged the enemy's batteries upon the Galgenberg. In fact the counter stroke was a vigorous one, supported by the whole of the artillery at the general's disposal.

Despite the resistance of the 39th and 74th, the attack in the copse was progressing favourably, and some of Bataille's troops were pressing down the valley. On the plateau too the south-west corner of the Gifert Wood had been re-taken, and all the efforts of the enemy to advance across the open towards Spicheren had been crushed, whilst from the ravine above the Golden Bremm, strong detachments of the 8th were now descending to the assault of the Baraque Mouton.

At this hour, shortly after 6 o'clock, fortune appeared to have declared against the Prussians, but, within a short space of time, the Fusiliers of the 77th, drawing reinforcements from the Golden Bremm, and effectively supported by the artillery, had beaten back the attempt upon the farm, the flank attack of the 8th Grenadiers had re-won the south-west corner of the Gifert Wood, and a skilful stroke of tactics checked the advance of the French infantry and guns down the Forbach Valley.

Since 1 o'clock, the Prussian batteries had remained upon the Galgenbexg, II/7 alone assuming, shortly after 3, a more advanced position. So long as the Toll House and the Golden Bremm were in possession of the French, the remainder were unable to follow, and when these posts were taken, although shortly after 5 o'clock the guns had ceased fire for the want of a target, still the presence of hostile infantry on the north-west slope of the plateau, distant not more than 700–1000 yards, was a sufficient hindrance to an advance to the Folster Height.

But the advent of the 2nd Company, 8th Grenadiers, on the western crest of the heights cleared the way, and when shortly before 6.30, a report reached General von Zastrow that the right wing within the copse was sorely pressed, and he saw the enemy's shells bursting on the Galgenberg, he rode forward to the Folster Height, directing the guns to limber up and follow.

Eight batteries obeyed, but so cramped was the space that two (6/8 and 4/1) were unable to come into action, and were held back under cover.[1]

This strong artillery counterstroke not only brought the French infantry who were moving down the Forbach Valley to a standstill, but proved more than a match for the hostile guns. Nevertheless, within the copse, the débris of the 39th and 77th was step by step forced back, and by 7 o'clock the wood was evacuated by all save the shattered remnant of the Fusiliers.

Riding forward to the copse, von Zastrow bade this handful of riflemen, at all hazards, to hold the northern outskirt. If they yielded their position, and permitted the French to break out across the Folster Height, the line of batteries would be placed in the greatest jeopardy. Then, galloping to the Drathzug, he ordered von Woyna to bring forward the battalions there assembled, although some of them had not yet reformed, to the assistance of their comrades.

For more than six long hours the 39th had been at close quarters with the enemy, and by far the greater number lay stretched beneath the giant beeches. But the stubborn

1 West of the high-road, facing the French guns, four batteries of the 14th Division, 1, 2, I, II/7. East of high-road, facing the long ravine two batteries attached to 10th Brigade, 5th Division, 4 & IV/3. 6/8 & 4/1, at first employed east of road, but soon withdrawn. VI/8 remained on the Galgenberg. 4/1 had arrived upon the field at 6.15.

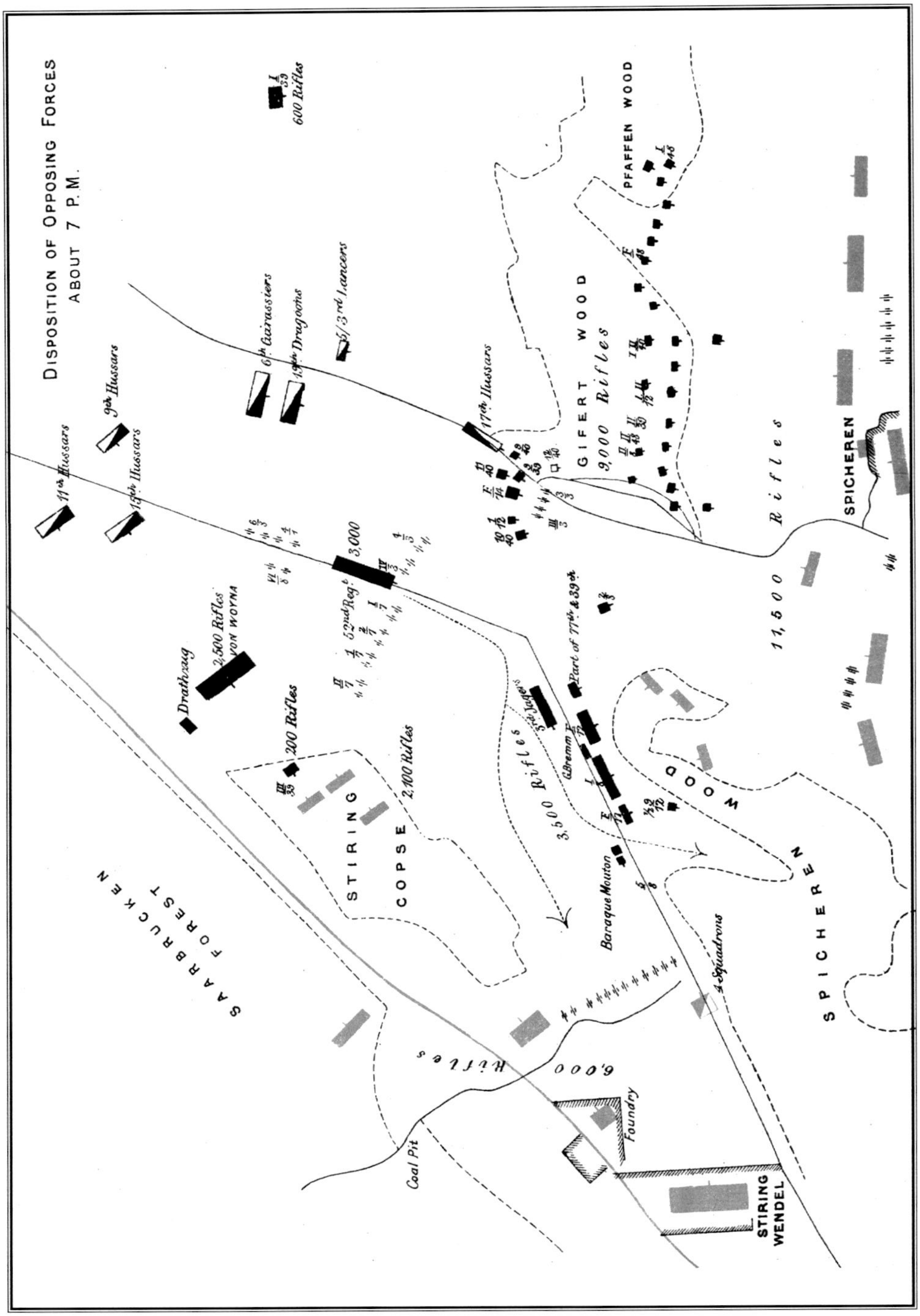

Situation of the opposing forces, 7pm

courage of the whole appears to have been concentrated in the few survivors, and when von Woyna's men, reduced by losses and by stragglers to 2,500 bayonets, came at once more into line, the northern border of the copse was still in the hands of the Fusiliers.

Notwithstanding this gallant stand against overwhelming odds, it is, nevertheless, exceedingly improbable that the Prussian right could have long resisted the attack so energetically pushed by Generals Bataille and Vergé. Besides the troops that had stormed the copse, 6,000 infantry, at least, the whole garrison of Stiring Wendel, were close at hand, and it is not too much to assert that one vigorous effort would have given the French the battle.

But that effort was never made. Scarcely had the 28th Brigade taken post alongside the 39th, when the pressure of the attack began to slacken, and, under cover of a heavy fire, the enemy rapidly fell back. The Prussians followed cautiously, but the French did not await the encounter, "and, after a short distance," says the Staff History, "no serious opposition was met with." By 7.30, every French soldier, save the dead and dying, had vanished from the wood, and von Woyna was suffered to re-establish his line before the Stiring Foundry. The explanation of this startling change in the aspect of the battle is not far to seek. Von Zastrow's confidence was justified. The 13th Division had come up.

At 22 minutes past 7, the following telegram was patched by Frossard to Bazaine:

"We are turned from Wehrden, I am bringing my whole force to the heights."

Half-an-hour before, the advance of hostile troops along the Volklingen-Forbach Road, which led to the rear of his position, and was unguarded, save by the two squadrons of dragoons and the company of sappers that garrisoned the Kaninchenberg, had been reported. Every one of his battalions had become involved in the fight in front, he had expended his last reserves, his line of retreat was seriously menaced, and he therefore ordered Bataille and Vergé to withdraw their divisions from the valley to the plateau.

When von Woyna re-entered the Stiring Copse, this order had been communicated to those battalions who pressed so heavily on the 39th, the attack had been suddenly arrested, and the French skirmishers were already disappearing in the shadows of the wood.

Frossard has given us his reasons for retreat:

"The events," he writes, "which were taking place at the *débouché* of the Saarlouis Road, were reported at Stiring just as the First Division, supported by the Second, was making a supreme effort to check the Prussian advance. That endeavour was successful, and there, as on the plateau, the enemy gained no more ground. But under the circumstances, the General-in-Chief, abandoned to his own resources, in face of the fresh reinforcements which the Prussians continually received, recognised that left to himself he could not maintain the whole of his position. The Army Corps, exhausted by a long struggle, seriously menaced on the right – though there the enemy was still held back – was taken in reverse on the extreme left, and the troops engaged at Stiring would probably, on hearing the cannonade at Forbach, have become apprehensive that they were cut off. As for assistance, not one of the promised divisions of the 3rd Corps had marched to the sound of the guns."

The artillery was first drawn off, taking post when it reached the heights, upon the slopes of the Pfaffenberg, the cavalry, and then the infantry followed, leaving a detachment in the village to cover the retreat.

The troops filed on to the plateau in rear of Laveaucoupet's Division, which was still in occupation of the Spicheren Ridge and the Forbacherberg.

There are several points worth notice in this battle round Stiring Wendel. In the first place, the French were always superior in numbers, but it was not until Bataille's arrival that they attempted a general counter-stroke. Their offensive sallies, although numerous enough, at no time took the form of a vigorous attack made both on the front and flank, but were local and isolated, designed merely to repel for the moment the pressure of the enemy's advance. It must be remembered, however, that the movements and numbers of the Prussians were concealed by the thick woods, and that General Vergé, who was in command of this wing, shared, in all probability, the apprehensions of the army that the enemy was in greatly superior strength. Even the most resolute of men, guarding the line of retreat as he was, might have hesitated to commit a large portion of his force to an attack on a large scale. The Prussians showed no indication of weakness until shortly before Bataille came up. Their line of battle, so far from contracting, extended further and further round the flank, the audacity and persistence with which they pushed from house to house was sufficient in itself to induce the belief that they were strongly supported, and it was impossible to detect their real inferiority. But, after 5 o'clock, there were signs that the strength of the attack was well-nigh exhausted. A battalion of the 53rd had fallen back from the right flank without a serious engagement, and troops on the same flank that had entered Stiring Wendel, suddenly evacuated it. From this evident uneasiness of the Prussians from their right, it might have been fairly inferred that the necessary supports were *not* forthcoming, and that this flank was the point where they most dreaded attack.

Secondly, if these symptoms were either unobserved or misinterpreted, and such might easily have been the case, they still suggest very forcibly the method in which the village might have been best defended. The French tactics consisted in constantly reinforcing the garrison, and in making frontal counter-strokes against the Stiring Copse. Secured by the railway cutting, they allowed the Prussians to envelop the west side of the village without making a single offensive effort. The village, protected from bombardment, served all the purposes of a strong fortification. But instead of utilising its advantages, to make one man do the work of three, the French actually maintained a garrison within it that was superior in numbers to the attacking force. So long as the foundry was held, Stiring Wendel was safe, and the greater part of the garrison might have been set free, without the slightest risk, to strike the outer flank of the Prussians from the direction of the glass works, Such tactics would have been far more decisive than merely keeping the troops under cover, and firing at the enemy across the cutting. When the assailant exposes a flank so rashly as did the Prussians, it is flouting fortune to let him go unpunished.

It may be argued that, surprised as the French were, deceived by the energy of the attack, and unable to estimate the numbers concealed in the surrounding forest, they could not have acted otherwise than they did. But this is not to the point. With the difficulties of the situation we are not now concerned. The teaching to be drawn from the fight round Stiring Wendel is this: had the general principle been regarded, that a fortified point enables the defender, leaving there a sufficient garrison and no more, to employ a portion of his force for other purposes, several battalions of Vergés division might have been more effectively used than as the superfluous defenders of bricks and mortar. The French looked upon Stiring Wendel as a point to be held at all risks, not as a pivot for, and an aid to, offensive action. We may also notice that the garrison of the village showed a decided want of initiative in not supporting Bataille's attack by an advance west of the railroad.

THE BATTLE ON THE PLATEAU – AFTER 6 O'CLOCK

The disposition of the French force, after the final capture of the south-west angle of the Gifert Wood by the 8th Grenadiers, was as follows:

In advance of the left were eight companies of the 2nd posted on the entrenched Spicheren Knoll. Two battalions of the 8th, which Bataille soon after withdrawing the 67th had sent up from the valley to the heights, and one of the 66th, held the head of the ravine above the Golden Bremm, and the adjacent Spicheren Wood.

On the Spicheren Ridge, and the Forbacherberg, were ranged the 63rd, 24th, 2nd, and 10th Chasseurs III/23 and I and III/66; the 40th occupied the Pfaffenberg. Thus, nineteen battalions, or allowing for losses, 11,500 rifles, backed by guns and mitrailleuses, confronted 44 companies, which at their full strength, had not numbered more than 11,000 men.

The Prussians had won the northern crest of the plateau, the Gifert Wood, the Rotherberg,,and the homesteads, but the enemy had withdrawn to a still stronger line, and the desperate fighting had by no means tamed his power of resistance. Several disjointed efforts were made about this time to advance on Spicheren from the Gifert Wood. That made by a portion of the 12th will serve as an instance. Joined on the left by a portion of the 48th, two companies rushed into the ravine in front, but cover was wanting, the leaden hail beat fiercely on the slopes, support was not forthcoming, and the attack dissolved, the sections losing all cohesion and connection during the retreat. Not only was a direct forward movement quite impracticable, but there was some reason to fear, in face of the repeated, though isolated, counter-strokes of the enemy's battalions, that if the infantry were left without strong support, the ground already won would have to be relinquished.

"We did not consider," says von Hohenlohe, "that the Rotherberg had been definitely occupied by us until batteries had established themselves upon it and had repulsed several efforts of the enemy to retake it."

So even before the 8th Grenadiers arrived upon the heights the generals in council on the Saarbrucken Road had determined to bring up cavalry and artillery.

Von Alvensleben, commanding III Army Corps, and in charge of the left attack, immediately issued the necessary orders. General von Rheinbaben, who by this time had seventeen[2] squadrons of his own divisions assembled round him in the Erenthal, was requested, if possible, to send a force of horsemen to the plateau, and to General von Bülow, chief of the artillery of III Army Corps, was entrusted the direction of the batteries.

The 17th Hussars, a regiment of Brunswickers, who wear the motto, *Death or Glory*, breaking into column of troops, trotted forward into the open ground west of the heights, over which the Grenadiers had lately passed. The officers sent to the front could

2 17th Hussars, 4 squadrons; 11th Hussars, 4 squadrons; 3rd Lancers, 1 squadron; 19th Dragoons, 4 squadrons; 6th Cuirassiers, 4 squadrons.

The first German gun ascends the Rotherberg to support the hard-pressed infantry (Ruppersberg)

find no path, the troopers in vain essayed to scale the cliffs, and, assailed in flank by musketry from the slopes above the Golden Bremm, were quickly compelled to retrace their steps. In compliance with the request of von Alvensleben, the road which winds round the eastern face of the Rotherberg was next attempted, and though steep and narrow, flanked on one side by a sheer descent, and on the other by a lofty sandstone cliff, was surmounted with little difficulty.

But, on reaching the crest, the leading squadron was prevented from deploying, as much by the rugged nature of the ground, covered with boulders and loose stones, and broken by shelter pits and quarry holes, as by the Chassepôt fire from the Spicheren Knoll.

The enterprise had to be abandoned, and a retreat was made to the road, where the regiment remained for some time, huddled in half sections on the narrow track.

The artillery was more successful. The two batteries detached to follow the hussars, 3 and III/3, from the Galgenberg, became involved in the vain endeavour to scale the western slopes, and when the Spicheren-Saarbrucken Road was reached, it was found so contracted by the presence of the horsemen, and so deeply scored by shells, that, at the first trial, one gun only of the 3rd Light Battery was able to reach the crest, the second capsized over the bank to the left. Nevertheless, a single piece of ordnance represented much to the hard-pressed infantry. Subjected to a long-range fire, under which their numbers were steadily wasting, and unable to make reprisal, they saw, in the solitary 9-pounder, a weapon which promised to restore the balance of the fight.

On the narrow level of the spur every yard of front was already tenanted by a rifleman, and even a powerful reinforcement of infantry would have been less welcome than an auxiliary which had the power to cope with the hostile batteries, and to divert the pitiless stream of musketry.

And so it was amid loud huzzas from the groups of officers and men which crowded behind bank and boulder, that the panting team, urged on by whip and voice and spur, dashed up the broken slope and drove the swaying fieldpiece forward through the smoke.

At the edge of the forest, beyond the foremost line of skirmishers, and not 700 yards from the French trenches, the gun came rapidly into action. But its appearance provoked a concentrated fire, the men fell fast, and, after a few rounds, it was withdrawn to the shelter of a bank 100 paces to the rear.

Here the remainder of the battery came into line, followed by two 12-pounders of III/3, which, diverging to the right, took post upon the western crest.

Guns in the open were now opposed to a line of infantry (eight companies of the 2nd Line) entrenched, and the interval which separated them did not exceed 800 yards. But the heavier projectiles, bursting in quick succession and with mechanical accuracy on the hillock, shook the nerve and disturbed the aim of the French riflemen. Under the ceaseless hail of bullets nearly half the gunners and many of their officers fell, but still, with the same relentless precision, shell after shell searched out the hostile trenches. The earthen parapets crumbled fast, and at length, after a duel which had lasted, according to the history of the French regiment engaged, for half an hour, the batteries triumphed, and the trenches were abandoned. The four remaining pieces of III/3 were now enabled to come into action between the left of the light battery and the wood, and the engagement on the western part of the plateau was for the present confined to the artillery.

The intervention of the guns had somewhat relieved the strain upon the infantry, but at 6.45, the battle had come to a standstill, the French still presenting an unbroken front, and overwhelming with fierce bursts of musketry every effort made by the Prussians to break forward from the wood, and maintaining a constant and heavy shell fire on the border.

During the movements which took place in the last phase of the battle on the heights, from 6 o'clock to the close of the engagement, although attempts were made to push forward towards Spicheren, the heterogeneous chain of infantry which formed the Prussian line from the Pfaffen wood to the western verge of the Rotherberg could do no more than hold its ground.

In face of the still vigorous foe, and under fire of his numerous guns, it was impossible to attempt the restoration of tactical order. It was even with the greatest difficulty, and only by their personal influence and fearless exposure, that the leaders were able to maintain a hedge of rifles along the border, and to restrain the men from seeking safety from the crashing shells in the centre of the wood. Not a few who had slipped away were found by officers who were seeking to collect supports for the fighting line, and, by the employment of energetic language, were assembled in scattered groups in the rear.

The following extract from the Regimental History of the 12th Grenadiers, gives us a striking picture of the situation:

"At the south-west corner of the Gifert Wood were collected the 7th company, men of the 40th and 48th Regiments, of the 2nd and 4th Companies of the 12th, and Grenadiers of the 8th Regiment. The hostile fire on this angle was very heavy, and it was repeatedly attacked by the French 63rd, 24th, 40th, and 66th."

"The loss along the border was so great, that the only remaining officer with the 2nd Company led his men forward into the ravine in front, from which the enemy had retired to the higher ground near Spicheren. Some of the 6th Company followed, but so many officers and men had fallen, that the detachment dissolved, part going to the right and joining the 5th Company, part to the left to the 48th, a section only remaining with their leader."

"The men of the 5th Company had meanwhile advanced into the ravine on the right of the 6th, and, although reinforced by some of the 48th, the casualties became so numerous that retreat became necessary, and it was with difficulty that the troops were retained even on the border of the wood under the fire of the artillery and the Chassepôts."

As an instance of the little influence superior officers can exert when once their men have been absorbed into the firing line, Captain Seton relates that ascending the Rotherberg in the wake of the guns, he found there General von Barnekow, commanding the 16th Division, and Colonel von Rex, commanding 32nd Brigade. There were also present the officer commanding the 40th Regiment, and the leader of one of his battalions; the latter, with a few of his men, under shelter of an earthern bank. It is almost needless to say that not one of these officers was in a position to communicate with more than a very small portion of his command, their men were scattered at intervals over the whole front of the left wing, and they were powerless to support, to rally, or direct.

On the arrival of the first reinforcements at 3.30, the German leaders, constant to the tactical principle that a flank attack is the surest means both of warding off attack, and of reaping success from the offensive, had struck at the enemy's right through the Gifert and the Pfaffen Woods. But, when the southern border of the forest was gained, it was found that further progress was impossible. The open slopes in front were commanded by the Spicheren Ridge, and the orderly withdrawal of the French infantry gave the outflanking battalions no opportunity of involving Laveaucoupet's right in a struggle at close quarters, and of so holding it fast in an advanced position. Neither did the successful charge of the Grenadiers, nor the support of the two batteries, bring about any decisive change. When once the crest of the Rotherberg was lost, the French had been powerless to regain it, but the Prussians were equally powerless to advance, and the narrow saddle, inviting concentration of fire, and contracting all formations into deep column, was left untrodden by either side.

And so, as the sun neared his setting, both antagonists found that they held positions exceedingly favourable for defence. But the French possessed a resource which their enemy lacked, and that was the line of batteries on the Forbacherberg and Spicheren Ridge. Not only were the Prussian guns upon the Rotherberg few in number, but those upon the Galgenberg, and, after 6.30, on the Folster Height, were hindered from directing their fire on the plateau by the presence of their own infantry, 2/8, on the western crest. It was possible then, for the French commanders to subject the hostile front upon the heights to a vigorous and accurate cannonade, and, having shattered the enemy's power of resistance, to put the finishing stroke to the battle by a general advance upon his disheartened line. This was the course on which, in effect, the Imperial generals decided.

The French infantry, although it had withdrawn to the Spicheren Ridge, was by no means disheartened. Not only was a constant fire maintained upon the whole line won by the Prussians, but repeated, if isolated, counter-strokes tried the fortitude of the Prussians to the utmost. It was felt by the Prussian generals that the ground already won could only be maintained by a strenuous effort, and it is noteworthy that this effort took

The Prussian 3rd Jäger Battalion, commanded by Major von Jena, assault the Spicheren heights (Hiltl)

the shape, not of a strengthening, by sending in reinforcements, of the disordered and unsupported line along the border of the Gifert Wood and on the Rotherberg, but of a flank attack. More judgment appears here than in the defence of Stiring Wendel.

But the French position, formidable as it was, was not without its weak point. The capture of the Golden Bremen and the Baraque Mouton had driven a wedge into the centre, and it was possible for the Prussians, by a vigorous attack from this foothold, if not to breach the line, at least to seriously threaten the left flank of the force upon the plateau, and to thus avert the counter-stroke presaged by the continuous cannonade.

About 6.15, the Fusilier battalion of the 12th was on the Winterberg, the 3rd Jägers and II/8 on the Drill-ground Hill and Reppertsberg, and three battalions of the 52nd in process of concentrating on the Saarbrucken Ridge. The general commanding III Army Corps, after communicating with the other generals of the corps who were present, resolved to employ these six battalions in a flanking movement against the *western* slopes of the Spicheren Heights, following the path already taken by the I/8th Grenadiers. As the line of batteries advanced to the Folster Heights, the three leading battalions, the Fusiliers of the 12th, 3rd Jägers, and II/8, under Colonel L'Estocq, moved forward to the battle, followed to the right rear by the 52nd, directed by Major-General von Schwerin, and by the two batteries attached to the 10th brigade.

In company columns, the 9th, with skirmishers extended in front, the Fusiliers from the Winterberg led the way diagonally across the valley. As they passed the Rotherberg they were met by many wounded men of their own First Battalion, and officers and privates beheld brothers and near kinsmen carried dying from the fight. 700 paces east of the Toll House, the foremost company struck the road, and, under the fierce fire of the mitrailleuse battery on the Forbacherberg, and of musketry from the Spicheren Wood, brought up their right shoulders, and ascended the ravine that faced them. But on the slopes all symmetry was lost. A quarry blocked the way, and the men diverged to either flank, splitting into two half-companies, which did not again resume cohesion. The remaining companies, before they reached the shelter of the ravine, suffered many casualties, and their leaders were compelled to dismount.

So heavy was the hostile fire that the 9th Company was withdrawn, and ordered to cover the advance of the battalions by an attack on the spur of the Forbacherberg from the direction of the Toll House. But, as has been related, this company had become divided by a wide interval, only the right half followed the captain, and, assailed in flank as they dashed down the incline, the men broke in disorder, and were not rallied till they reached the Golden Bremm.

Meanwhile, the main body of the Fusiliers had reached the crest. Here they found themselves confronted by a line of hostile infantry half-right (probably behind the crest of the Spicheren Knoll). The skirmishers extended, but made no progress, except on the right, where, after a hard fight, a detachment of French riflemen was routed by a sergeant and a few of the marksman's section with the bayonet. In the position they now held along the western brow of the plateau, the front of the Fusiliers extended north and south, their line almost at right angles to the main position of the French, which ran from east to west along the Forbach mamelon. The riflemen half-right were but advanced skirmishers, and to attack the enemy in front it would be necessary to swung round to the right under a heavy flanking fire, and to advance across the open. The impracticability and uselessness of such an operation was quickly gauged by the battalion commander, and he determined to bear off to the right beneath the brow of the hill so as to gain the enemy's flank. Two sections were left to cover the movement, but, so steep was the descent, and so great the difficulty of working under fire on the broken slopes, that all order was lost, and, as the 9th Company had done already, the men broke loose from control and rushed in confusion on the Golden Bremm.

To the left of the Fusiliers, the Jägers had also surmounted the height, and had there taken up connection with the right of 2/8, which, though the remainder of its battalion had entered the Gifert, still clung to the western crest. To the left rear followed the 2nd Battalion of the Grenadiers.

During the ascent the losses of both battalions were by no means inconsiderable, and on the skirmishers of the Jägers taking post upon the exposed crest under the flank fire from the Forbacherberg and Spicheren Wood, casualties rapidly increased. A vigorous counterstroke was repulsed, but Colonel L'Estocq, who had joined this battalion, recognising, when he reached the brow and found the French posted several hundred paces away to his right, that from his present position he could not deliver a flank attack, immediately ordered the two battalions to descend the ravine, and move upon the homesteads, determining from that base to strike the left wing of the hostile force upon the plateau. The two batteries, finding it impossible to act, had already been withdrawn.

The Fusiliers had reformed behind the Golden Bremm, and, with the four companies in line of company columns, marksmen extended, prepared to assault the spur of the Forbacherberg.

L'Estocq's remaining battalions were now advancing along the highroad under a heavy fire from the Spicheren Wood, and it will be well to observe the precautions adopted by commanders of various grades to protect the exposed flank during the subsequent attack.

Baroque Mouton, 400 yards southwest of the Golden Bremm, had been hitherto held by the Fusilier Battalion of the 77th, and formed a strong outwork, as it were, against any hostile movement from Forbach, or Stiring Wendel, or from the long ravine which cleaves the Spicheren Wood, but it appears that on the Fusiliers of the 12th arriving on the scene, this battalion abandoned both the tavern and the farm in order to join in the assault.

The commander of II/8, who had instructions to prolong von L'Estocq's line of attack to the right, directed his 5th Company to occupy the tavern. It will be remembered that a half company of the Fusiliers of the 12th had been ordered from the first to protect the flank of its battalion. With this object it had entered the tavern garden, probably after its evacuation by its former garrison. Lining the high eastern wall, and finding foothold in the vine espaliers, it had kept up a fire on the borders of the opposite wood, and then, on the approach of 5/8, jumped down from the wall, and, not without loss, gained shelter under the slope beyond the road. 50 men were here collected, of whom half were at once extended, half held back in support, and patrols under non-commissioned officers were sent out right and left. The French skirmishers retired, but still intent on his mission of covering the right flank, the subaltern in command bore off to his right along the thickly wooded slopes of the long ravine, driving the French riflemen up the hill.

5/8, on relieving this detachment of the 12th, occupied the yard, and in order to cover the advance of the battalion along the high road, opened a brisk fire on the opposite wood.

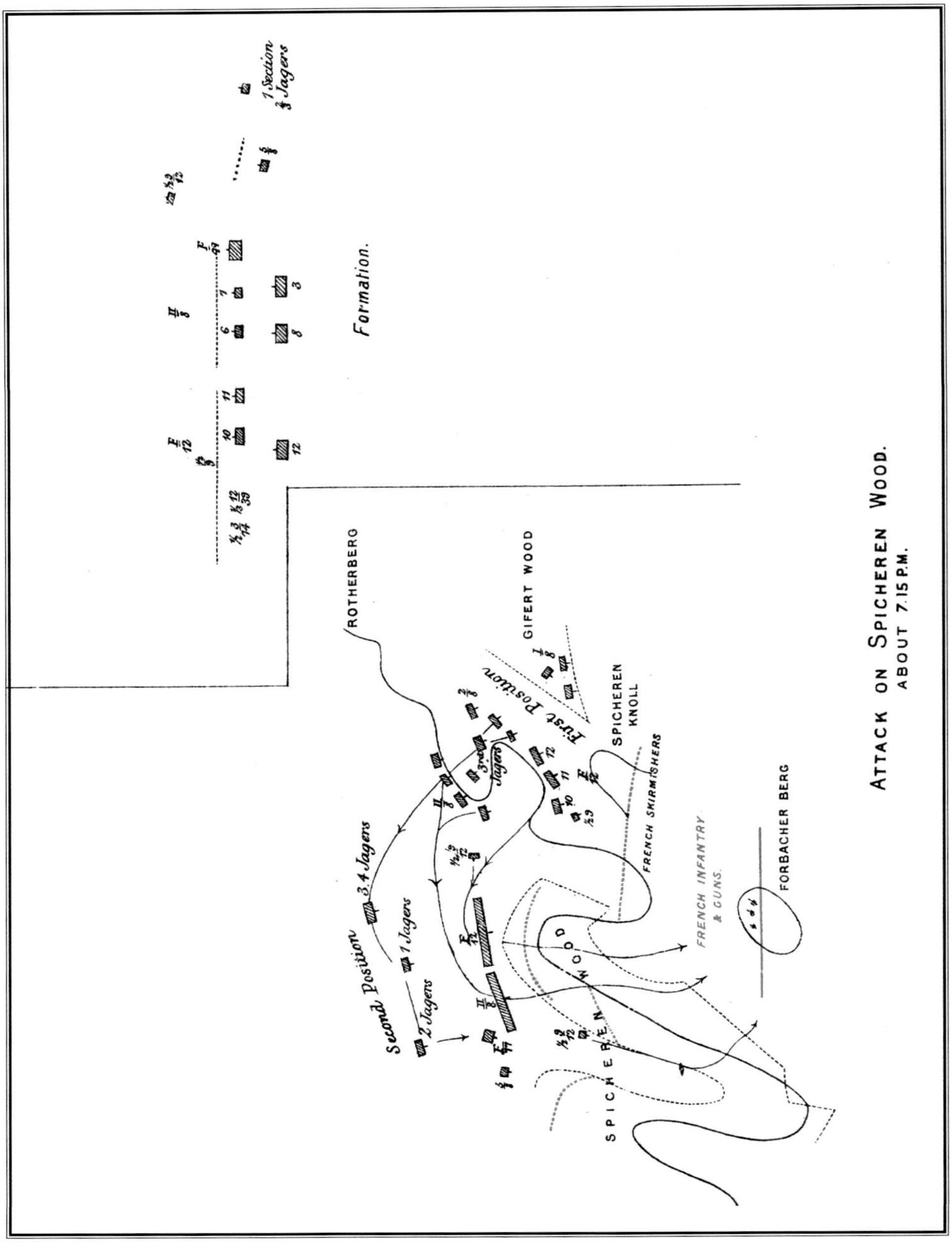

Attack on Spicheren Wood

Colonel von L'Estocq, committing the first line of attack to the two battalions of the 12th and 8th, ordered the Jägers to take post in the Golden Bremm and Baraque Mouton. The 1st Company occupied the tavern, making a banquette of furniture along the garden wall, the 2nd established itself in the farm, the 3rd and 4th were placed behind the Toll House.

5/8, being in its turn relieved, went forward to the Baraque Mouton. Hostile detachments were observed in the ravine beyond the wood. The lieutenant in command took post along the wood with two sections extended north of the *chaussée* and one in support behind the farm, drove back the French, and sought connection with his battalion by patrols.

About this time II/8 was reinforced by the 3rd Company, which, as has been related, had been withdrawn from the extreme Prussian left, and had thus traversed, before it joined the 2nd battalion, the whole length of the attack upon the Spicheren Heights. The battalion was ordered to advance against the wood in the formation indicated in the accompanying sketch, and the sketch shows, also, the general disposition of von L'Estocq's troops when the assault commenced.

As to the formation or position of the French troops, nothing can be definitely ascertained, but it may be inferred that, in the Spicheren Wood and on the spur of the Forbacherberg, they were present in considerable force, for the Prussian battalions had suffered heavy loss during their advance to the Golden Bream.

The Fusiliers of the 12th had just reached the wooded slope of the Forbacherberg spur, driving the French skirmishers before them; the Grenadiers on their right were prepared to assault the apex of the salient, and the Jägers were advancing towards the Golden Bremm along the high road, when, from the ravine half left, a fierce counter-stroke broke forth. The foliage of the lofty poplars which lined the broad *chaussée* was cut to shreds by a storm of bullets, and the Jägers dropped fast on the dusty track beneath. A swarm of infantry thronged down the ravine. The tirailleurs in the Spicheren Wood were reinforced and turned upon their pursuers, driving the marksmen of the 12th and Grenadiers before them. The edge of the wood was yielded. The Fusiliers, attacked in flank and front, were pressed back, skirmishers and supports together, but were rallied by their officers on the road. II/8th, closing quickly, sought cover to the right. But the Prussian artillerymen on the Folster Height, keeping vigilant watch on every quarter of the field, sent a storm of shell into the descending column. The French wavered, Colonel von L'Estocq ordered an immediate advance, and with drums beating, under a murderous fire which fell with especial fierceness on the supports, the troops once more, at charging pace, rushed over the open ground. The French fell back, and the counter-stroke was checked. But the wood beyond was not won without a struggle, behind every bush and tree stood a hostile marksman, and the precipitous ascent was soon covered with dead and wounded. Still, through the dense mist of smoke that shrouded the thickets and the lofty beeches, the enemy slowly though surely gave ground, and at length, after many a halt and with heavy loss the Prussians reached the crest.

To cover the flank of the Grenadiers, a section of the 2nd Company of the Jägers had mounted the ravine that faces Baraque Mouton, and now, along the upper border of the Spicheren Wood, were assembled, at 7.30, in front line, 3 companies of the Fusiliers upon the left, 3 of the Grenadiers in the centre, a section of Jägers on the right, and scattered along the entire front, men of the 74th, 77th, and 39th. Both the 12th and Grenadiers still retained a company in reserve, whilst far away to the right, almost in rear of the Forbacherberg, the half-company of 9/12 was on the point of debouching from the wood. This detachment had been followed by a small portion of 5/8, which, observing a hostile movement against the right of von L'Estocq's line, had advanced up the long ravine, and, by drawing the enemy's attention to itself, had effectually arrested his attack.

In front of the main line of the 9th Brigade, the open ground rose at a gentle gradient to the crest of the Forbacherberg, 50 feet above them, and 600 or 700 paces distant. Shelter trenches, filled with infantry, girdled the grassy knoll, and the appearance of the Prussians on the left front and flank, was the signal for a rapid and unrestrained fire. Further advance up the smooth glacis-like slope was impossible, so Colonel von L'Estocq sent down an order for the Jägers to advance to his support, and, when his right was strengthened by the approach of this battalion, gave the word to renew the attack.

The 12th, one company in reserve, faced the open slope, but the Grenadiers, in the same formation, brought up their left shoulders so as to profit by the wood which curved round towards the rear of the Forbacherberg. Small parties of the enemy barred their passage through the thickets, and the desultory wood fighting was renewed, prisoners being taken on either side. However, the battalions were making progress, and away on the right the truant half company of the Fusiliers had actually penetrated unperceived to the rear of the French position, and had arrived within a hundred paces of the flank of the artillery. This venturesome detachment had dwindled to two officers and a dozen men. The rest of the original fifty had succumbed either to the enemy, or to exhaustion, or had straggled in the wood, and the unexpected appearance of this handful of riflemen although it had surprised, had not disconcerted the enemy. A rush was made upon the guns, but a strong force of infantry charged down on front and flank, and drove back the little band to the cover of the wood. Here, on the border, it faced about, for 5/8 together with men of the 74th and 77th, came up most opportunely on the left, and a hot independent fire quickly put an end to the pursuit.

The time was now about 7.45, and in every quarter of the field fortune appeared declaring for the Prussians. Von Woyna's Brigade had re-won the copse, and was pressing forward towards Stiring Wendel; the left wing in the Gifert Wood and on the Rotherberg, although fiercely assailed by the French batteries, still held its ground; and the position gained by von L'Estocq's battalions threatened to pierce the very heart of the defence.

Frossard's troops had been engaged since 12 o'clock. The heat had been oppressive, the battle fierce, and the men had not eaten since the early morning. The last reserves had been exhausted shortly after 5 o'clock, and whilst a steady stream of reinforcements was still supplying fresh strength and energy to the enemy, no tidings had been received of the approach of Bazaine's divisions, and it must have become apparent to the French soldiery that the Second Army Corps d'Armée was abandoned to its own resources.

It has been the fashion to praise the offensive dash of the French soldier at the expense of his powers of resistance, it is almost traditional to exalt the one and to depreciate the other, and there is no doubt that the attack is more congenial to the national temperament. Nevertheless, we find Frossard's men at Spicheren, after a defensive battle of seven hours duration, during which the right wing on the plateau had executed one of those retrograde movements which are generally supposed to weaken the morale, still opposing an unbroken front to the constant pressure of the enemy. But, although the second line was still intact, the main position had been lost, and if, realising the quality of the men, we might believe that they were capable of further resistance, still after the work they had done and the heavy stress of the battle, we should certainly expect to find them too disheartened and exhausted to venture once more upon the counter-stroke.

But there was one French general on the field who knew the temper of those he commanded, who felt that despite their weariness, their losses, and their repeated failures to recover their lost ground, the spirit of his infantry was still untamed. Whether the movement was intended to cover the withdrawal of the troops from the valley, or whether it was a vigorous effort to drive the Prussians from the heights and dash them back upon the Saar, must remain unsolved, but it is a matter of fact, that between 7 and 8 o'clock, General Laveaucoupet gave orders for a general advance of his whole line, covered by the fire of the reserve batteries, which had by this time taken post upon the Pfaffenberg. As the twilight began to settle on the field, the grassy slopes of the Forbacherberg and the Spicheren Ridge became alive with men. Leaving their trenches and dissolving into swarms of skirmishers, supported by battalion columns, the French with loud cries and a fierce storm of musketry swept down the surface of the plateau.

And now was seen the value of the position von L'Estocq, ascending from the homesteads, had won upon the flank. The men of the 12th fell back before the rush, but the Grenadiers, favoured by the shelter of the wood, held fast upon their right. Each battalion, fortunately, had retained a company in reserve and this accession of strength at a critical moment gave fresh vigour to the hard-pressed Prussian line. After a brief, but bloody combat, the enemy was driven back to the Forbacherberg.

But, whilst a portion was left to clear the flank, the main-body of the French had pressed on rapidly towards the Rotherberg and Gifert. The reserve company of the 12th, held back on the slope to the left rear of the battalion, was roused by the shouts of the French and the heavy fire. To the left was a little clearing, where the thin outskirt of the Spicheren Wood gave a view of the open ground beyond the deep ravine. The left section rapidly deployed, and lining the border of the clearing, assailed at a range of 500 yards the flank of the attacking column. In the fast gathering darkness, the effect of the first two volleys could not be seen, but, at the third, large numbers were observed in confusion and falling back, and a rapid independent fire scattered them in flight. The Rotherberg was saved; against the guns and worn-out infantry that held the spur, only unsupported groups advanced, to be easily repulsed.

But on the southern border of the Gifert the storm broke fiercely. The throng of skirmishers, dashing quickly forward, and firing as they came, covered the advance of the solid lines in rear with a veil of smoke, and this and the failing light combined to render the aim of Prussian riflemen uncertain. Already the line, under the tempest of shells that preceded the infantry attack, had begun to waver, the trees were cut to pieces by the iron splinters, and the countless echoes crashed through the darkening thickets with a stupendous din. Only the entreaties of their officers, and their gallant example, had hitherto held the men fast under the cannonade, but when the hail of bullets mingled with the heavier missiles, and the line of fire pressed rapidly up the slopes of the great ravine, when the detachments in the open rushed back in confusion to the wood, for a moment it seemed as if the border must be yielded. But, dating from the extraordinary victories of 1866, the Prussian soldiers had come to have a supreme reliance on the needle-gun, and when the attacking swarms, led by their officers, mounted and on foot, with a gallantry which, even at that moment, extorted admiration from their foes, rose from the ravine and came within effective range of the trusted weapon, the wavering line grew strong as a bar of steel. Discipline and training once more asserted themselves, the independent fire was steadily delivered, and, at a distance of 200 yards from the position, the attack was checked. The French battalions, unable to push on further, held for some time the ground they had re-won, but, as darkness fell, drew slowly back on Spicheren, whilst from the commanding slopes of the Pfaffenberg, Frossard's massed artillery swept the field.

No attempt was made by the Prussians to follow the retiring foe towards Spicheren, although some small detachments, composed of officers and men of various battalions, once more moved into the open, but, on the extreme right, a desperate onslaught was made by von L'Estocq's battalions on the Forbacherberg. During their advance upon the shelter trenches, the companies lost all semblance of tactical order, and systematic prosecution of the attack became impossible. Groups of men of different regiments rushed forward under the guidance of individual officers, sergeants, or even energetic privates, at one time beaten back, at another swept on by the accession of small supports collected by some one in authority and thrust into the fighting line. The fight raged hotly at short range, and a few brave men, in isolated clusters, dashed up the slope against the trenches and came to close quarters with the foe. Bayonets were even crossed, but the French stood firm, covering the retreat of their comrades to the Pfaffenberg, and the Prussians were beaten back to the shelter of the wood.

Von L'Estocq's attack had been so effectually checked, that F/8 together with two battalions of the same Army Corps having arrived, the commander of the 9th Brigade wished to employ these fresh troops against the Forbacherberg, and subsequently to advance on Forbach with a mixed detachment of various regiments. Both enterprises were, however, countermanded by General von Stülpnagel, commanding 5th Division, in consequence of the darkness, and the apparently general retreat of the French.

The fight for the Forbacherberg died away, the hostile fire ceased, and the round hill, so lately girdled by a ring of rifles, stood out lonely and silent in the darkness. The defenders had withdrawn in good order, leaving neither guns nor wounded behind them, and when the assailants gained the crest the hostile columns were seen vanishing across the dusky ridge. Six full ammunition waggons, whose teams lay dead or disabled, fell into the hands of the Fusiliers, together with a quantity of entrenching tools, and behind the hill were found the knapsacks which their opponents had thrown off before they joined the fight.

Away to the left Spicheren was burning, and on the slope of the dark upland beyond were seen the incessant flashes of Frossard's guns, blots of flame on the heavy cloud of slowly rising smoke. The roar of musketry and the harsh rattle of the mitrailleuse, which for seven long hours had pealed across the plateau without a moment's respite, had ceased at last, though deep in the valley, round the blazing roofs of the Stiring Foundry and far away at Forbach, still rose the tumult of the battle.

Shortly after 7 o'clock, General von Steinmetz reached the field, but refrained from interfering with the conduct of the engagement.

THE BATTLE IN THE VALLEY AFTER 7 O'CLOCK

At the time when the French were pressing rapidly through the copse and down the Forbach Valley, and General von Zastrow was directing the Prussian artillery to advance to the Folster Heights, the three battalions of the 52nd, Regiment, accompanied by their brigadier, von Schwerin, were approaching the Galgenberg.

These troops comprised the whole of the infantry available as reserve, and it is certainly remarkable that when von Zastrow, the senior officer present on the field, ordered the artillery to move forward, he did not at the same time call upon the 52nd to assist in checking the French advance against the Prussian right.

Why he did not ask for support must remain unexplained. Be this as it may, about 7.15 pm, when von Woyna was bringing up his broken brigade to the support of the small force still within the copse, the 52nd approached the line of guns upon the Folster Height to assist von L'Estocq's attack on the Spicheren Wood.

But, just as L'Estocq's battalions deployed before the Spicheren Wood, the French artillery opened a heavy fire from Stiring Wendel, in order, probably, to cover the retreat of their infantry from the copse, and General von Schwerin thereupon sent six companies of the 52nd against Stiring Wendel; five, the 11th and those of the 2nd battalion, continuing the wheeling movement which had already commenced against the Spicheren Heights. It may be mentioned, before relating the result of the last attack upon the village of Stiring Wendel, that the latter battalion advanced with the 5th and 8th companies in front, the remainder following in second line. After passing the Baraque Mouton, and driving back some parties of the enemy who still hung about the woods, the five companies, preserving the same order, advanced up the ravine, (the leading companies on either edge, the others in close column along the trough), gained the upper edge of the Spicheren Wood, and moved on to the deserted Forbacherberg.

Meanwhile, over the open and undulating ground which stretched before the right wing in the valley, the 4th and 10th Companies, with marksmen extended, led the attack on Stiring Wendel and the French artillery. The 9th and 12th, in company columns, furnished a second line, the 2nd and 3rd, in half-battalion column, the reserve. Within

The Prussian 52nd Infantry advance on Stiring Wendel (Ruppersberg)

the copse, upon the right of the 52nd, the mixed battalions of the 27th and 28th Brigades, under General von Woyna, were rapidly pressing forward, but the progress of General von Schwerin's six companies, exposed as they were to the heavy fire of the hostile guns, was slow and difficult, and after a short time came to a stand.

The officer commanding the artillery on the Folster Height was, however, keenly observant of the fight, and as von Schwerin ordered up the 5th Company of the 2nd Battalion 8th Grenadiers, which had hitherto been stationed at the mouth of the Baraque Mouton ravine, to reinforce, more powerful assistance was sent forward in the form of a light battery.

Taking post on the level near the Golden Bremm the six 9-pounders engaged the enemy's guns at a range of 1,400 paces. Von Woyna's skirmishers had meanwhile reached the southern outskirt of the copse, and the French batteries fell back, but the check they administered to the attack of the 52nd had enabled Bataille's battalions and part of Vergé's Division to withdraw unmolested to the heights. The village, however, was not left untenanted. A strong rear-guard remained to cover the retreat of the left wing and with these troops von Woyna's and von Schwerin's men became briskly engaged.

It has been remarked by one who has studied the Franco-German War very thoroughly indeed, that the French, inferior as in many essential respects their tactics were, possessed extraordinary skill in the art of conducting retreats. Of this capacity Spicheren is almost as remarkable an instance as Beaumont itself, and the manner in which the garrison of Stiring Wendel was drawn off to the Spicheren Heights deserves particular and detailed mention.

When the French artillery withdrew, the troops left in position were the 32nd in the foundry, the 55th between the foundry and the high road, and the remnant of the 3rd Chasseurs in the wood to the right. There were also many stragglers and stray detachments in Old Stiringen and in Stiring Wendel. The 55th Regiment (two battalions), in execution of the order to fall back from the northern quarter of the Stiring Copse, whither they had pursued the 39th and 77th, had re-formed on the southern edge. The officer in command then gave the edge of the Spicheren Wood, on the other side of the valley, near the cross-roads, as the point of assembly, and the battalions dashed across the open at the double. The Prussian 52nd was then advancing from the Folster Height, and the 55th, passing straight across its front, was assailed in flank by a heavy fire. In the twilight, at a range of 600–800 yards, the needle-gun proved very ineffective, and when three of von Schwerin's companies advanced at the charge, the 55th had already reached the wood.

The Prussians appear to have hesitated to move forward whilst it was uncertain whether the foundry was still strongly held, and the commander of the 55th, calling up his reserve battalion, prepared to defend the village until the troops ascending the heights had got well away.

Moving into the open ground in rear of the Spicheren-Schoneck Road, he first of all, with whatever materials came to hand, made a barricade from the edge of the foundry mound to the high road, and then, behind this shelter, deployed two battalions in a thick chain of skirmishers without supports. Two companies of the reserve battalion were extended 300 yards in the rear as second line, and 200 yards further back on the right and left flanks were posted two small columns of two companies each.

Lieutenant-General von Stulpnägel, commander of the German 5th Infantry Division, III Corps (Rousset/*Histoire*)

According to the French account from which these details are taken, these dispositions had all been made before the Prussian attack was renewed. The movement began from the copse; a thin line of skirmishers, backed by reserves, which every moment increased in strength, advanced by rushes of 50 paces towards the barricade. The French fired slowly, for even when the attack came to a stand along the road, 200 paces distant, so dark was the night, and so dense the clouds of smoke that rolled across from the blazing foundry and the village, that the flames of the conflagration served to show no more than a thick black line, indistinctly seen against the dark background of the slopes in rear.

The fire of this line was irregular but heavy, and it was observed that the skirmishers were being gradually reinforced.

At the end of twenty minutes, the fire ceased. A loud hurrah rose in the enemy's ranks. The French, rifles at the "ready," awaited the assault. A second hurrah, and then – silence! Was it doubt, or hesitation? A third hurrah! This time the silence was rudely broken. Through the night, from beyond the barricade, rang out a cry of 'Vive L'Empereur,' and taken up by a thousand voices, it was the signal for a crashing volley, followed for two or three minutes by rapid independent fire. When the smoke cleared away, the Prussians had disappeared, and the flash of their rifles on the border showed they had once more retreated to the copse.

The Staff History mentions nothing of this phase of the engagement, but the account is so circumstantial, and explains so satisfactorily the fact that the French retreat from Stiring Wendel was unmolested, that despite the silence of the Prussians, it bears the stamp of truth. After the repulse of the 52nd, General Vergé withdrew the 32nd

Regiment from the foundry and with it all the stragglers that he could find, but it seems that many were left behind, for an obstinate fight broke out in Old Stiringen and about the slag heaps near the foundry, and the French continued to offer resistance to von Woyna's men until after 11 o'clock.

The 55th had been ordered by their brigadier to hold the barricade until the 32nd had made good its retreat. About 9 o'clock, the regimental commander, finding the Prussians disinclined to advance, withdrew the two battalions of his first line, and reformed them 200 yards behind the reserve. An hour afterwards, the enemy's patrols appeared. The French retired slowly, halting and fronting whenever the Prussian scouts fired on the extended line that covered the retreat. This was repeated ten times, and it was long past midnight before the battalions, by the light of the rising moon, found themselves on the Schoneck Road within the Spicheren Wood.

The Prussians, in the meantime, according to the Staff History, although they had penetrated to the foundry, showed little inclination to push forward towards Stiring Wendel. "The fighting became more languid, General von Schwerin, however, did not deem it advisable to remain for the night immediately in front of a place not entirely abandoned by the enemy, therefore, with the concurrence of the commander of the division, he withdrew the troops (52nd), who had meanwhile reformed, from Stiring Wendel at 8.45 pm. Some isolated detachments still offered stubborn resistance at this point." This paragraph fits in well enough with the French account of the defence of the barricade, and the events described in the succeeding sentences may have easily occurred after the withdrawal of the 55th. "In order to prevent our own men firing into one another in the dark, the General sounded the 'cease fire,' and ordered the whole of the troops to advance with loud hurrahs against the west side of the village, whereupon the enemy gradually ceased to offer any further resistance. While the 52nd thus captured the greater part of the south of Stiring Wendel, and in searching it made 300 prisoners, the 3rd Battalion, 39th Regiment, (reduced to 6 officers and 150 men), scoured the northern farm-buildings and slag heaps. 1,200 to 1,500 unwounded prisoners," adds the Staff History, "fell into the hands of the victors," the majority of whom, it appears, were taken in Stiring Wendel. It must be allowed, notwithstanding, that the French retreat, considering the darkness, the dispersion of the troops in the houses, the difficulties of extricating masses of men from a maze of narrow streets, the long train of artillery, and the confusion incident on hard fighting, was an exceedingly well-executed movement.

This phase of the battle, we may notice, offers further instances of the difficulties of leading the larger units.

General von Schwerin, commanding the 10th Brigade, led the 52nd from the Reppertsberg in person. The 12th Regiment, forming the other half of his command, had been already disposed of; the 1st and 2nd Battalions taking part in the holding of the Rotherberg and the attack on the Gifert Wood, the Fusilier Battalion in von L'Estocq's flank movement from the Golden Bremen, and the two squadrons of cavalry patrolling the left flank on either bank of the Saar. When the 52nd reached the homesteads the regiment broke into two, the general accompanying the right wing and calling to his support a company of the 8th Grenadiers, belonging to the 9th Brigade.

Moreover, at the close of the engagement, the infantry of the 5th Division, of which the commander, General von Stulpnagel, was present after 8 o'clock at Stiring Wendel, was distributed piecemeal over the whole front of the line of battle, from Stiring Wendel to the Pfaffen Wood, the right wing of the 52nd on the extreme right, I & II/48 on the extreme left.

THE TURNING MOVEMENT OF THE 13TH DIVISION

The general direction of the advanced guard of von Glümer's Division was the road leading from Wehrden through Great Rosseln to Forbach. A company of Jägers and a troop of hussars were pushed forward by Clarenthal towards Schoneck on the left flank, whilst the remainder moved in the following order:

Van {1st and 3rd Squadron 3rd Hussars
{2nd Company 7th Jägers
Reserve { 5/7 F. A.
{ I & F/55
{1 Company 7th Jägers

At 4 o'clock the column approached Great Rosseln, and the orders dispatched by the corps commander from Dilsburg at 1 o'clock, directing the divisional commander to throw out outposts towards Forbach and Ludweiler, to retain his main-body at Wehrden and Volklingen, and to discover by means of patrols the strength and intentions of the enemy at Forbach, were now received.

These orders had already been anticipated.

A communication had also been received from the headquarters, First Army, from which von Glümer gathered that the Commander-in-Chief had no intention of entering upon a serious engagement beyond the Saar. Nor had the enemy been met with. The hostile advance reported at noon had come to nothing, and the din of battle, lost in the leafy forest, was no longer heard. The troops since 5 am had marched 23 miles without halting to cook; the divisional commander, therefore, ordered, the advanced guard to halt north of Great Rosseln and to establish outposts. The main body went into bivouac at Volklingen, whilst the cavalry patrolled towards Forbach, where a considerable camp was visible. At 6 o'clock the cannonade again became audible, at the same time the hussar patrols brought back intelligence that the battle was still proceeding, and a galloper who had been sent off by the corps commander at 4 pm arrived with a despatch giving information of the position of affairs, and demanding the intervention of the division.

Without delay, the troops were set in motion to the assistance of their comrades marching along both sides of the brook which takes its name from the villages of Rosseln, F/55 and 5/7 on Emmersweiler, the Jägers on the Tan Mill, I and II/55 directly up the highway. The 6th Light Battery was ordered up, and the main-body ordered to follow as rapidly as possible. The 1st Squadron of Hussars, reconnoitring to the front, reported that the heights west of Forbach were entrenched and strongly occupied.

I and II/55 thereupon formed half-battalion columns in the forest, preparatory to an advance on either side the road. About seven o'clock 6/7, coming into action in an open field between the chaussée and the brook, brought a steady fire to bear upon the left flank of the enemy's position on the Kaninchenberg, at a range of 2,100 yards, F/55 occupied Emmersweiler and the wood in the rear.

On the 1st Battalion 55th attempting to debauch from the forest north of the road, it was received with so hot a fire that it could make no progress. The advance of the 2nd Battalion was, on the other hand, unchecked, a portion of the shelter trenches was

The church in Spicheren after the battle, when being used as a field hospital (Pflug-Harttung)

carried, and the Jägers, ascending the southwest slope of the ridge from the Tan Mill, took the position in flank.

The French were very weak. 1 company of Engineers (100 men), 200 reservists of the 2nd Line, under a sub lieutenant, who had arrived during the afternoon by railway, two squadrons of the 7th Dragoons, besides two batteries of the reserve artillery, were the only troops available for the defence of Forbach. The guns remained within the town. The dragoons dismounted and helped to man the trenches, but when the Prussians began to envelope the left flank of the position, Colonel Dulac ordered his two squadrons to mount and cover the withdrawal of the infantry by a charge.

Though boldly executed in the failing light, the attack was repulsed, the 5th Company of the 55th and the 3rd of the Jägers reserving their fire until the horsemen came within point blank range.

4 officers, 25 men, and as many horses were killed or wounded.

But the infantry was enabled to pursue its retreat unmolested. The Prussian commander was unwilling to risk a night attack upon the town, and only a few small parties followed the French. From a point where the railway crosses the high road a brisk fire was opened on them, and the advanced detachments retired to the Kaninchenberg.

The restaurant at St Johann railway station after the battle (Hiltl)

The right wing column had meanwhile reached Emmersweiler, and 5/7 took up a position on the heights west of Forbach. 6/7 also moved to the front, and the two batteries brought an effective fire to bear upon the outskirts of the town and on the railway. A train which was starting south was compelled to put back, another, bringing the first and only infantry reinforcement sent by Bazaine from St. Avold, retired without entering Forbach. The main-body of the division assembled about 9 o'clock at Little Rosseln. A report from the battlefield, probably from the detachment on the left flank, had caused the 15th Regiment to turn in the direction of the Stiring Wendel, but the darkness prevented it taking up connection with the 14th Division, and the movement was not long continued.

The small French force had done its duty well; of the 13th Division, 5 officers and 92 men fell, of whom 80 belonged to the 55th.

As we have already seen, both on the heights and in the valley, the detachments left by the French to cover the retreat had repulsed every attempt of the enemy to interfere with the operation.

The stand made on the Forbacherberg and before Stiring Wendel had enabled the Second Corps to get clear away. So exhausted were the Prussians, and in such extreme confusion at every point, that a further advance would have been no less difficult to initiate than to carry out. By nine o'clock, when, although the French rear-guard was still holding out, it was certain that Frossard had definitely abandoned the field, five fresh battalions had reached the Spicheren Heights, and the remainder of the 16th Division, nine battalions, was assembling at St. Johann. These reinforcements were not, however, brought to the front until the action ceased, nor, save by patrols, was any effort made to push beyond the ground that had been won with so much difficulty. The French battalions were still intact, their retreat, so far from being a rout, was made in so leisurely a fashion that the bivouac fires of their rear-guard were to be seen upon the Pfaffenberg.

At the same time, the Prussians had been careful, even before the outposts were established, to secure themselves from attack and to discover what they could of the enemy's movements. Sentries were posted by each battalion immediately the battle ceased, and frequent patrols reconnoitred far to the front. Some men of the French rearguard in search of water were taken by a sergeant's patrol of the 48th Regiment, and the information extracted from them confirmed the impression that the Second Corps d'Armée was actually retreating and had not retired merely to take up another position.

PRUSSIAN OUTPOSTS AFTER THE BATTLE

In the valley, picquets were established on either side of the Forbach high road, between the town and Stiring Wendel, the right wing resting on the glass works, the left on the wooded crags of the Kreutzberg.

III A.C., drawing forward its two last arriving battalions, F/8 and F/20, furnished the outposts on the plateau, south of the Gifert Wood, as far as the Spicheren Knoll the ground was occupied by F/8. Next in order, on the right, came II/8, extending as far as the northern slope of the Forbacherberg, the further slopes were held by F/12. A wide gap intervened between the latter battalion and the left wing of the 52nd Regiment beneath the Kreutzberg, but all the roads were guarded, and the woods patrolled.

The 3rd and 4th squadrons of the 12th Dragoons were also brought up to the heights, and two troops, sent forward beyond Spicheren, found a camp still occupied near Etzling. In the course of the night, moreover, two squadrons of the 17th Hussars advanced by St. Arnual and Grossbliederstroff, and captured prisoners.

No attempt, however, was made by the cavalry to maintain touch with the retreating foe, of the cavalry division (the 12th Dragoons were attached to the 5th Infantry Division), not a single squadron ascended the plateau.

The infantry of the 5th Division which was not employed on outpost duty, concentrated on the Reppertsberg, viz., I and II/48th, I/8, 3rd Jägers, I and II/12. I and II/20, which had reached St. Johann by rail late in the evening, followed their Fusilier Battalion, and took post near Baraque Mouton. The Fusiliers of the 48th, who received no orders where to assemble, retired to Saarbrucken, and bivouacked in the square of the Town Church.

The 14th Division assembled generally in the low ground about Stiring, round the copse. Some battalions, amongst them those of the 39th Regiment, remained for the night where they had been last engaged. The second battalion 53rd had arrived shortly after seven o'clock, having marched 27½ miles from Wadern, viâ Neunkirchen and Lebach, in thirteen hours.

The main body of the 16th Division did not come up until the struggle was over, it bivouacked between St. Johann and Malstatt, where it is joined by the 40th Regiment.

The artillery bivouacked generally in their final positions, on the Rotherberg, the Folster Height, and Galgenberg.

In addition to those which had taken part in the fight, the whole of the horse artillery of III and VII Army Corps (4 batteries), and two F.A. batteries of the 6th Division (III Army Corps) came up during the evening, a second battery of I Army Corps, making 18 batteries in all, also arrived by rail from Neunkirchen.

Besides the 1,200 to 1,500 unwounded prisoners, many wounded officers and men fell into the hands of the victor; camp equipment abandoned by the 1st and 3rd divisions, and, on the day after the battle, the great magazine at Forbach, and a pontoon train, were also seized.

THE PERFORMANCE OF THE FRENCH HIGH COMMAND

We have now followed, hour by hour, the fortunes of the battle, from the appearance of the Prussian scouts upon the Saarbrucken Ridge, to the retreat of the French from Spicheren and Stiring Wendel. We have seen the 14th Division hurled against a formidable position which had not been reconnoitred, we have seen it from 1 to 3 o'clock struggling unsupported on a wide-extended front – 11,000 infantry against 25,000. And whilst von Kamecke's slender line bent round the flanks of the enemy's position, and, dashing again and again at his heavier masses, staved off defeat by the vigour of its attack, we know that, within 15 miles of Spicheren, stood 40,000 French and 36,000 Prussians.

Had the whole of these assembled on the field, the French would have outnumbered the Prussians by 18,000 men.

Between 3 and 6 o'clock, 12,000 Prussian infantry reached Saarbrucken, well-nigh equalizing the numbers of the opposing forces, and rescuing the 14th Division from imminent defeat. On the other hand, except Juniac's Dragoon Brigade, Frossard had received no reinforcements whatever.

But even at 6 o'clock the French were not inferior in strength, and, although pushed back upon the plateau and deprived of the Golden Bremm, the heavy counter-strokes which they dealt on either flank before retreat was ordered proved that the Second Corps d'Armée was still an effective instrument for battle, and that the veterans of France were not surpassed in gallantry and endurance by their younger enemies.

If, then, Frossard's battalions, at the close of the day, when the numbers on both sides were practically equal, came within an ace of regaining their lost ground, is it possible to doubt, had even half of Bazaine's 40,000 men appeared at any period of the battle, that the Prussians would have been driven back upon the Saar?

We may well ask, therefore, how it was that, although four divisions of French infantry were encamped on the morning of the 6th within 12 miles of Spicheren, not a single bayonet came to the assistance of the Second Corps.

These four divisions composed the 3rd Corps, commanded by Bazaine. The 2nd Corps was also under the order of the marshal, forming his advanced guard. How far was Napoleon's favourite general responsible, not only for the defeat of a portion of his force, but for the loss of a victory?

On the evening of the 5th he had been placed in command of the French left wing, but, in consequence of the failure of the cavalry to procure information, he was without knowledge of the enemy's dispositions, and unable to conjecture where the attack that was believed imminent would fall.

Moreover, for the past 48 hours, the movements of von Steinmetz's troops along the Saar had rivetted the attention of the Imperial Staff, and had induced them to suspect that the Prussians would cross the frontier near Saarlouis. This impression had been communicated to Bazaine, and the whole of the information that came to hand, on the night of the 5th and the morning of the 6th, assisted to confirm it. A despatch from Metz advised him of an approaching attack on his left flank by way of Carling. Spies had reported that the villages from Conz to Saarlouis were full of troops, and that on the heights above the latter fortress a large force of artillery and infantry had been observed. Hostile scouts were also seen near St. Avold, and from the 4th Corps d'Armée on his left came news of the presence of the enemy's patrols near Ham-sous-Varberg.

What intelligence he received from the Second Corps, covering the centre of his line, we do not know. General Frossard says that the marshal asked for information on the night of the 5th, but he does not state how far he himself was able to comply with the demand. In fact, his account of his relations with his superior is unsatisfactory in the extreme, some telegrams, and those not the more important, are given *verbatim*, others in general terms, some he omits to mention, and, as to the hour of despatch, a matter of the greatest moment, in one instance at least he has made a grave error. Thus, he tells us that, between 10 and 11 o'clock, he informed the marshal that he was engaged in a battle. Now, at that hour, only three Prussian squadrons and no infantry whatever had crossed the Saar. The attack of the 14th Division did not begin till after 12.

A great mass of evidence as to the proceedings of the French generals on the 6th of August was elicted at the court-martial held on Bazaine in 1871, but the statements are so conflicting that the whole must be rejected, and with it Frossard's narrative, except where it is confirmed by outside or hostile testimony. This will not, however, preclude us from examining the circumstances. There are facts which cannot be disputed, and telegrams, the authenticity and receipt of which have never been questioned. On these we may base our conclusions.

At 9 o'clock, Frossard telegraphed that he heard cannon firing at the front, and suggested that Montaudon should send a brigade from Saarguemund to Grossbliederstroff and that Decaen should advance to Merlebach and Rossbruck.

At 10.40 he reported that the enemy had shown himself at Merlebach and Rossbruck.

At 11.15 Bazaine replied that he had sent Metman's Division to Bening, and Castagny's to Theding, and asked Frossard to send a brigade to watch Rossbruck, adding that if the Prussian attack was really serious it would be well for the French to concentrate on Calenbronn.

About this time, the marshal himself proceeded with a reconnaissance towards Carling and was fired at by Prussian scouts.

At 2.25 he telegraphed that he had ordered Montaudon (by telegraph) to Grossbliederstroff. Now, a reference to the map will show that these various movements would have brought the three divisions of the 3rd Corps into line on the Calenbronn position, with Montaudon at Grossbliederstroff in advance of the right, and Decaen at St. Avold in rear of the left, maintaining connection with the 4th Corps. The marshal had also advised Frossard, if the Prussian movement from Saarbrucken was really serious, to retire on Calenbronn. In fact, the dispositions adopted were equally well-adapted to meet attack from Saarbrucken or Saarlouis. So far so good, but Bazaine, having issued his orders, appears to have awaited the development of events instead of using every effort to discover what the enemy was about. He sent no strong reconnaissance in the direction of Saarlouis, nor did he attempt to ascertain through one of his own staff officers the importance of the attack on the Second Corps, or whether Frossard was about to fall back on Calenbronn. St. Avold, be it remembered, is but twelve miles from Forbach, and connected with it by a line of railway.

The reason he himself did not proceed to the scene of action was, he explains, the necessity of remaining in close communication with the Imperial Head-Quarters. We may profitably compare with this the conduct of the Commander-in-Chief of the First Prussian Army, when he first received news that a serious engagement was in progress. Except in this respect, Bazaine was not to blame. Immediately Frossard reported an attack probable, Metman's and Castagny's Divisions were ordered to advance, and Frossard informed of their destinations. On receipt of a further report, at 2 o'clock or thereabouts, to the effect that the actions had already attained the dimensions of a battle, the marshal telegraphed to Montaudon to march to Grossbliederstroff, without impedimenta, in order to support Frossard's right, despatched Juniac's Brigade to Forbach, and at the same time sent a staff-officer with orders for Castagny to join the Second Corps. In effect, what he did was this. 1st. At the first alarm, 20,000 men were advanced in support to within six miles of the advanced guard, and the advanced guard advised to fall back into line with the support. 2nd. When the engagement was announced as serious, 10,000 men were ordered to support the advanced guard, and 10,000, with the Dragoon Brigade, to march directly to its assistance.

From 2 to 5 o'clock, he appears to have received no further communication from Frossard, for at the latter hour we find him telegraphing – "*Donnez-moi des nouvelles pour me tranquilliser.*"

Between 5.30 and 6 o'clock he hears that Frossard's right has been obliged to fall back, and in response to an urgent demand for succour, recapitulates the position of the divisions he had sent forward in support.

A few minutes afterwards another telegram comes in, announcing that "The battle, which has been very heavy, is dying away, but will doubtless recommence," and adding, "send a regiment."

The 6th Line Regiment of Decaen's Division proceeds in two trains to Forbach.

Towards 8 o'clock, comes the last despatch, "We are turned from Wehrden, I have retired to the heights."

To this the reply is, "I have sent all I can. I have only three regiments to guard the St. Avold position. Explain exactly the positions that you consider should be occupied."

With the marshal's conduct, no fault, save that already alluded to, can be found. It was not his fault that Frossard refused to fall back on Calenbronn, nor that, after 2 o'clock, when withdrawal was no longer possible, that he should have neglected to call up or communicate with the three divisions that had been sent up to support him. It was not his fault that the telegram sent to Montaudon should not have been delivered to that general, who was conducting a reconnaissance beyond Saarguemund, until after 4 o'clock, nor that the messenger sent to Castagny should have been nearly three hours finding a division, which was wandering vaguely about the country.

Frossard, when he made up his mind to hold his ground, would have been perfectly justified in calling up the divisions that had been sent to support him on the Calenbronn position, Bazaine evidently expected him to do so, and very properly left it to him, as it was impossible with the very meagre information forwarded by Frossard, not knowing whether the attack was being delivered in front or flank, to decide, at a distance from the field, to what point the divisions ought to march – whether they would be required for an offensive movement, or merely to cover a retreat on Calenbronn. It probably seemed superfluous when indicating their positions, to add, "they are at your disposal." In fact, Bazaine acted more like an officer trained under the German system and relying on the judgment and initiative of his subordinates, than one accustomed to the red-tape routine of France.

The marshal did all he could, and it is important to notice that when he learnt, for the first time, that a battle was in progress, the various mischances which occurred would have made it impossible, had all his subordinates merely waited for orders, to have brought up his three divisions to Frossard's help before a very late hour. Montaudon did not reach Grossbliederstroff till 7 o'clock. The messenger did not find Castagny until 6. Metman, at 3, was still seven miles from Stiring Wendel.

We shall see, if we compare the proceedings of the French and Prussian subordinate commanders, that when bodies of troops are located at a distance of several miles from Head-Quarters, their timely intervention in an unforeseen battle must depend on the initiative of their immediate commanders. Had Bazaine's generals been capable of acting with the same promptness and decision, and kept themselves as well informed of the state of affairs at the front, as the commanders of VIII and III Army Corps, and of the 16th and 5th Divisions, at least 30,000 of his troops would have reached the field in time.

Observing then, first of all, that Frossard, when he ultimately fell back on Saarguemund, made no attempt either by messenger or telegraph to inform the marshal of the direction of his retreat, or indeed, that he had retreated at all, thus rendering it impossible for Bazaine to come to any decision as to future movements, the following account of the proceedings of the three divisional generals, makes it evident that the French General Staff was as incompetent as that of the Germans was efficient. And to show that disregard of the value of time was a vice not confined to the 3rd Army Corps, it may be added that at the battle of Woerth, the twin disaster to Spicheren, it deprived Marshal McMahon of the support of the 5th Corps, numbering 28,000 men:

(1) At midday the cannonade at Spicheren was heard at Saarguemund, but General Montaudon, although he had sent out reconnaissances in the direction of Neunkirchen to his front, took no steps whatever to ascertain the meaning of the action on his left. At 3 o'clock the order was received to move to Grossbliederstroff to support Frossard's right. The troops were not set in motion, as the general was on reconnaissance, until 5 o'clock, and did not arrive in position until 7. No staff officer was sent either to communicate with Frossard, or to obtain information of the progress of the fight. During the night, the division retired on Puttelange.

(2) Castagny's division heard the cannonade at Puttelange towards 11 o'clock. At 11.30, without waiting for orders, the general marched on Spicheren. After marching four or five miles, in a direction too much to the right, the sound of the guns was no longer heard, and the division halted. A staff officer sent out to reconnoitre met some peasants, who assured him that the French were victorious in the battle, and both he and his general were satisfied with the intelligence so obtained. The division returned to Puttelange. At about 5 o'clock, the guns were heard once more, and the troops again took the road. At 6, Castagny received an order from Bazaine to join the Second Corps. At 9, Folkling, three miles from Spicheren, was reached, and the leading brigade, being pushed

on to Forbach, learnt that the Second Corps was retreating towards Saarguemund. The division fell back on Puttelange.

(3) At midday, Metman's division received orders from Bazaine to move on Bening, where it arrived at 3.30. The cannonade was heard distinctly, but, no attempt was made to discover its meaning, and a third French general appears to have forgotten that the chargers of even infantry adjutants have legs.

At 7.30, on receipt of a telegram from Forbach, which Frossard declares was despatched at 4, it advanced on Forbach, and about 9 o'clock passed through the town. Learning that the Second Corps had fallen back, it ascended to the plateau and withdrew to Puttelange.

(4) Of the 4th Division, one regiment was sent at 6 o'clock to Forbach by Bazaine. The first train was arrested at 8 o'clock by the fire of the Prussians from the Kaninchenberg, and put back without entering the station. The remainder did not pass Bening, the troops, according to Bazaine, being ordered to disembark by the railway officials.

For the non-appearance of Montaudon's and Castagny's Divisions, Bazaine, as we have seen, was not responsible. To both he sent orders to join Frossard, but in the one case the troops did not start until two hours after the order had been received, in the other, they had already left their camp, and the staff-officer had many miles to ride before he met them.[3]

It may be remarked, however, that the Germans did not consider it sufficient, where time is all important, for a superior officer merely to issue orders. In such cases the representative of the commander who brought the orders remained, as a rule, to see that they were obeyed, or to notify immediately impediment or delay.

To say that the marshal should have proceeded to the battlefield in person, or have sent his Chief of the Staff with power to act in his name, is not the slightest excuse for the indifference of his divisional generals to the sound of the cannonade and their neglect to communicate with Frossard.

Throughout the day, so fateful to France, Bazaine's generals had behaved like mere machines, incapable of supplying themselves with information or of looking beyond their immediate commands. Their conduct was equally wanting in energy, in initiative, and in discipline, for the neglect of ordinary precaution, the lack of interest in the fate of the neighbouring divisions, the carelessness as to the issue of the day, point to an enfeebled sense of duty and indiscipline of the most harmful kind.

They have, however, found apologists, and, in order to point a moral, it may be well to discuss briefly the whole situation, both as regards themselves and their adversaries.

It has already been recorded how the Prussian divisions, brigades, and even smaller units, obeyed the mandate of the cannon thunder, and marched without halt or stay to the assistance of their comrades, and each division and brigade, by the system of patrols, which brought every separate body of troops into close connection, and, at the same time, disseminated the intelligence procured by the scouts over the large area occupied by the invading armies with extraordinary rapidity, being made aware of the point where the enemy's main force was assembled.

3 As a detail of staff work, we may note that the orders to Metman and Castagny are carried by the same officer.

The leaders, fortified by this knowledge, were relieved of all doubt as to the security of their flanks, and could calculate to a nicety the locality of the field of action.

The French, on the other hand, had neither patrols nor scouts. They were ignorant of the whereabouts of the hostile masses, unable to forecast, with any degree of precision, the point where the enemy would strive to break their line – Saarbrucken, Saarlouis, or Saarguemund – and absolutely without an inkling of Napoleon's design; whether to assume the offensive, to defend the line of the Saar, to march by the flank on Bitsche, or to retreat into the interior of France.

When the cannon was heard from the direction of Spicheren, and even when reports came in that Frossard was heavily engaged, doubts must have arisen whether this was not a feigned attack, and apprehensions have been excited that the real blow was about to fall elsewhere.

To the uncertainty, which, as a general rule, is the chief disadvantage of the defence, and almost invariably follows the loss of the initiative, the irresolution of the French generals must be attributed.

Nor was it possible to determine exactly the locality of the real attack. The advantages offered by the road and railway passing through Saarbrucken were great, and could scarcely be neglected by invading army, but the fact of the advantages being unmistakeable, would doubtless lead to the belief that the Prussians would avoid direct attack on that point, for there they would be expected, and would endeavour to secure the possession of the highways by skilful strategy.

Neither must the moral factors of the question be overlooked.

It was easy enough for the Prussians, with their ample information, with the knowledge of their superior numbers and of von Moltke's intention to attack, to march to the cannon. Such a forward movement was strictly in accordance with the general idea. And it was clear enough, also, that the point of collision, should such take place, would be found on the Saarbrucken-Metz High-road.

There was no hesitation, therefore, when the reports of battle were received, in moving in the same direction. But it was far otherwise with the French. The vague information as to the numbers, dispositions, and designs of the Germans, served only to confuse. Moreover, all the subordinate leaders were utterly in the dark as to the intentions of Napoleon.

The movements he had ordered during the past few days appeared to point to a concentration eastward, for there had been a gradual drawing together in that direction, but all was indefinite and uncertain. The impulse which the haughty challenge and the rapid advance to the frontier had communicated to the army had died away. The indecision which prevailed in the Imperial councils had become apparent, and the subordinate leaders, without any tangible purpose to lay hold of and follow out, had become infected with this worst of military vices.

But, even if we admit that the initiative which resolves on a march to the cannon is far more difficult when holding a frontier than when attacking it, the French generals cannot be in the least degree absolved from blame. When an officer in command of a body of troops in the vicinity of the enemy has been ordered by superior authority to occupy a specific position, and the sound of distant battle strikes upon his ear, then, unless he has discovered by reconnaissance the position of the enemy's main force, and has thus obtained a clue to his designs, he will, in all probability, as were Bazaine and his divisional leaders, be embarrassed by the enemy's feints, by the presence of the enemy's scouting parties, and will become a prey to apprehension and vacillation. Even if he has specific orders, he should prepare himself for the unexpected. He should so study the situation, looking to front and flanks and rear, that in case any emergency not covered by his instructions demands his intervention, he may be able to act resolutely and wisely. More than all, he should be careful to establish and maintain constant communication with all bodies of troops within a days march.

It was in their neglect to use this simple means of extricating themselves from their embarrassments, that the French generals were so terribly to blame.

CHAPTER IX
THE TACTICS OF THE BATTLE

Under cover of a mixed detachment assembled and placed iu Spicheren by his chief of engineers, Laveaucoupet's Division began its retirement on Saarguemund at 9 o'clock. The reserve artillery and Vergé's battalions followed, but by various routes, neither Frossard nor his Staff officers having done more than indicate the general direction of the retreat. Bataille, ordered to form the rearguard, fell slowly back on Oetingen, and thence at daybreak upon Puttelange.

The rearward movement of the 2nd Corps d'Armée, considering the severity of the fighting, the heat of the weather, and that the troops were fasting, was conducted at first in fairly good order. But it soon became apparent that the *moral* of the soldiery had suffered. The men felt instinctively that more than once victory had been within their grasp, that not they but their leaders had been defeated, and that, owing to the blunders of those in authority, their dash and endurance had been wasted. During the long night march the ranks became thinned by stragglers, many abandoned their arms, insubordinate cries were heard along the toiling column, and the name of the commander was made the burden of a ribald song.

Short halt was made at Saarguemund, and not until Puttelange was reached after midday upon the 7th, were Vergé's and Laveaucoupet's wearied troops, who had not eaten for more than six-and-thirty hours, allowed to rest. Bataille's Division had already arrived.

Such was the general dislocation that it was found impossible to make any distribution of rations, and the men had left their knapsacks on the field. The troops were supplied on the following day, but much distress and privation resulted from the fact that the cooking utensils had been lost with the packs, nor was it until the 12th and 13th, after the arrival of the Corps d'Armée at Metz, that these indispensable articles were replaced and the men enabled to prepare their meals.

Such was the French retreat. It was not a rout, the troops were not followed, and the greater part of the Prussian out-posts were not even advanced so far as the second line of the defence. Not till the whole force had vanished in the darkness did the enemy set foot on the position. Almost the last blows that were struck beat back the foremost bodies of the assailants, and, at the end of the fight, in two places alone, against the Forbacherberg and Stiring Wendel village, was the attack being pressed, elsewhere it had come to a standstill.

Was it necessary to have retreated? Metman's and Castagny's Divisions were almost on the field, Montaudon within 4½ miles. The battle might have been re-commenced on the following morning with 30,000 fresh troops. It is true that Frossard was unaware that reinforcements were so close at hand, but we can imagine a man of more energetic and stubborn character holding on in the hope that during the night he would be able to bring his colleagues to his aid. Those familiar with the history of the Secession War will remember how, on the 1st of July, 1863, the Federal advanced guard, consisting of two

Army Corps, was roughly handled at Gettysburg, but, although confronted by superior numbers, driven from its first position, and its right flank and rear threatened, held fast to its ground throughout the night. It had suffered far more severely, and had been driven further back, than the second corps at Spicheren, the remaining corps were at a much greater distance from the field than were Bazaine's divisions, but it was held by General Hancock in command, that "to have withdrawn would have been a retreat, and might have discouraged the Federal, as it would certainly have elated the Confederate troops. It would have been to acknowledge a defeat where there was no defeat." The ground was, therefore, held, and the battle of the next two days ended in a decisive victory for the Federals. But mark the difference between the French and American generals. Immediately after posting his troops in their new position and handing over the command to General Slocum, Hancock rode back thirteen miles to the head quarters of the Commander-in-Chief, Meade, and the latter, who had already sent orders for the remaining Army Corps to move forward by forced marches, started for Gettysburg shortly before midnight. And to make the parallel closer between the actions, Meade, before his advanced guard became committed to an engagement, had half decided to concentrate on a position many miles in rear of Gettysburg.

The Prussian Staff History prefers to attribute Frossard's resolution to retreat to the attack on the Forbacherberg from the Golden Bremm. Frossard himself distinctly states that it was the appearance of the 13th Division before Forbach Town that chiefly influenced him, and, looking on the battle as a whole, it is difficult to disagree with him. At the same time, it is possible that the fact of finding a hostile force in such close proximity to his centre may have had much to do with his final decision. When he reported to Bazaine that his left was turned, he merely said that he had withdrawn his whole force to the heights, and it may be the truth, notwithstanding his statement, that von L'Estocq's attack ultimately induced him to abandon his position. We must remember that the Prussians would be naturally more inclined to attribute this retreat to their more skilful tactics and superior courage, than to the somewhat fortuitous appearance of a large body of troops on an unprotected flank, and we may be allowed, therefore, to hold the opinion that moral effect, rather than sheer hard fighting, was the true cause of the Prussian victory.

That Frossard was not merely unlucky there can be but little doubt. He had many difficulties to contend with, it is true, yet fortune was not unkind and his soldiers fought on with unflagging spirit. But throughout the operations, from the hour he abandoned the Saarbrucken Ridge, to that when he departed for Saarguemund without informing Bazaine of his destination, his errors were very numerous. From many of these he would probably have been saved had his staff been more experienced. It does not appear that he assured himself by personal inspection that the arrangements for the defence were adequate, nor, especially important in the case of a broken position, that the different sections were so marked out and allotted as to render mutual support, and he himself has recorded that, up to the time the first gun was fired, he was engaged in settling questions of administration with the Mayor of Forbach. Throughout the day, his influence on the action was confined to sending up supports as they were asked for. Thus, each individual commander was left to make his own arrangements for attack or defence without reference to his neighbour, and the whole lacked the superintendence of the single authority who could ensure the adjustment of the several parts. It is possible, however, owing to the general want of organization and method, that Frossard was compelled to give his personal attention to numerous details, which, in an army fully mobilized and well ordered, would never have come before him. It must also be remembered that he was surprised by the attack, and that the field, wooded, broken, and extensive as it was, was a difficult one to supervise or to arrange for battle off-hand. At the same time, we cannot fail to appreciate the advantage that would have been gained had the ground been surveyed, and a line of defence selected, whilst the troops were falling back from the Saar. But, even if it could be shown that of this and other defaults paucity of staff-officers or some other equally good reason was the cause, it is impossible to avoid the impression that the French commander lacked energy, and this impression becomes the stronger when we consider the promptitude and activity of his opponents. And this is especially true of his conduct of the battle. Until a late hour, he had hope of reinforcement, and intended, it seems, merely to hold his ground until the arrival of Bazaine. But, up to 3 o'clock, his 27,000 men were opposed by less than 12,000. Surely it was his bounden duty to have crushed, by a strong return, the inferior force which had placed itself so completely in his power?

The leader who elects or is compelled to act on the defensive from first to last should have but one idea, and that is the offensive. Even if fighting a rear-guard action or merely holding his ground until reinforcements arrive, he must be ready to attack. Unless he has explicit orders to entice the enemy's whole force into a trap, he should watch for an opening, and if possible, deal with the attacking force in detail. War is too full of risk and mischance to admit of opportunity being allowed to pass.

The change from the defensive to the offensive is undoubtedly the most difficult operation of war, seldom carried out even by the greatest captains, and it is this fact that renders the success of a defensive battle less decisive than the victorious offensive. It is no easy matter to gauge the right moment for the counter-stroke, but it must be remembered that from the Spicheren Heights the approach of von Kamecke's troops was clearly seen, and that their inferior strength must have been known soon after the battle opened. Never had a general a fairer opportunity for a decisive counter-stroke than Frossard.

The question arises, how should this have been executed, at what time, on which flank, and with what troops?

As to the time, the counter-stroke made by Laveaucoupet with Doens' Brigade, was well chosen. There were then no troops whatever to be seen on the Saarbrucken Ridge. As to the place, the right flank seems in all respects to have been the most favourable. In the first place, an attack from that quarter, threatened directly the enemy's line of retreat, and it was possible to turn the ridge from the St. Arnual Wood, repeating the manœuvre of the 2nd, and passing over ground with which the staff, if not the troops, was already familiar. Had the 24th Regiment of Micheler's Brigade, together with the 40th, been ordered to clear the Gifert and hold the lower edge, Doens' Brigade sent down through the St. Arnual Forest to attack the Winterberg, and Bastoul brought up, as he was, to support the main-line, it is difficult to conjecture how the Prussians could have maintained their hold upon the ridge. Moreover, ten battalions, half of Micheler's and the whole of Bastoult's Brigades, still available, would have been an unnecessarily large force to have retained on the heights in order to support the troops holding the Rotherberg; a regiment, at least, might have been set free to reinforce the flank attack.

From the position of Doen's Brigade at 2.45, the time of Laveaucoupet's counter-attack, to the foot of the Winterberg by St. Arnual, is about two-and-a-half miles. The troops ought to have been in readiness to commence the attack at 3.45, and at that hour the Prussian force on the heights consisted only of two battalions of the 48th and a single battery; other troops were approaching, but the ridge was difficult of access, except by the two roads, and exceedingly inconvenient for manœuvre.

The other alternative was a direct frontal attack on the Winterberg, avoiding the great extension of front necessitated by a turning movement on the far side of the St. Arnual Pond, and this, if undertaken by the twelve battalions available, would have been equally promising of result, although the immediate loss might have been greater. The chief dangers to be guarded against were the cavalry in the Ehrenthal (7 squadrons), and the guns upon the Galgenberg. But the latter is only 2,500 paces from the Spicheren Knoll, and, had the battery posted at the foot of the knoll, facing the clearing between the Gifert and Pfaffen Woods, been brought up to the crest, it would have enfiladed the Prussian guns, had they faced eastward to strike the flank of the attack against the Winterberg. It would itself have been exposed to oblique fire from the battery above Drathzug, but the guns which had already been driven from the Rotherberg, and those which accompanied Bastoul's Brigade, might have been well used on the western edge of the heights to draw on themselves, or at least to distract, the fire of the Prussian battery. Either operation would have been facilitated had the whole of Bataille's guns and a portion of the reserve artillery been ordered to the heights. Whilst we can quite understand that Frossard's preoccupation for his line of retreat, threatened as it was from Volklingen, induced him to take careful measures for the security of his left, it is not so easy to see why more artillery was not sent to the right wing. There was scarcely room in the main-line for more guns than were already present, but that artillery could descend the slopes and act in the St. Arnual Valley had been shown on August 2nd.

The counter-strokes of the French were frequent throughout the battle. That which drove the First Battalion of the 39th from the Gifert Wood, that by Jolivet's Brigade at 4 o'clock which re-won the Stiring Copse, and that carried out by the battalions of the 55th, 67th, and 8th, at 6 o'clock, were more or less successful. The first and third, which were the more decisive, were made by fresh troops, as all strong counter-strokes should be, and the two last were prepared and followed up by the artillery.

But on the other hand, there were many, on a somewhat smaller scale, which, although well-timed as, for instance, the attack of the part of the 40th and 63rd on the stormers of the horse-shoe trench directly after its capture, and the re-taking of the south-west corner of the Gifert Wood after 6 o'clock, in the majority of cases were useless, sapping the vigour that should have been used for a more general offensive.

Of this sort were the many isolated efforts to retake the Gifert and Pfaffen Woods. It is true that the enemy was thereby harassed, and prevented from reforming his disordered line, but the work might well have been left to the artillery.

If well-timed, the counter-stroke delivered by a small body may be of the utmost value. When a portion of the assailing force advances without securing its flanks, when artillery exposes itself without support, or when an integral part of the defence is surprised, as was the Rotherberg, an immediate counter-stroke is perfectly justifiable, and should be undertaken by any body of troops that is favourably placed to do so. But a blind isolated frontal attack on a far stronger force holding a formidable position, is but a waste of life and strength.

Of the counter-stroke which was directed against the homesteads from Stiring Wendel, simultaneously with the advance of the 55th and 67th on the Stiring Copse, we have no details. It appears to have been accompanied by cavalry, uselessly enough, but not to have been prepared by artillery. The presence of the latter, in an attack upon substantial buildings, was most essential, and there were several batteries in close proximity. Here, again, there was no adequate arrangement, no combination of the different arms.

Analysing these various operations, we find that those alone were decisive, although only in their immediate effect, which were made in strength. As for any other attack, troops must be massed, and provided with a second line and reserve, if any permanent result is to be hoped for.

It is also noticeable that the French stood artillery fire badly. The columns which attempted to advance over the Rotherberg saddle to re-take the trench, and those which descended the ravine to the westward against the homesteads, were several times driven back in confusion by the guns alone. This may be explained, first, by the fact that the formations of the attacking troops offered an excellent target, and secondly, to want of discipline. German writers, in comparing the different conduct of their own infantry and of the French when exposed to shell fire, are unanimous in attributing the steadiness of the former under such circumstances to their superior discipline. It was apparently more than the French were capable, either of standing their ground or advancing when men were falling fast around them, without replying in the one case, or, in the other, breaking to seek cover.

That such is a characteristic of troops who have no deep instinct of subordination and obedience may be inferred from the earlier battles of the Secession War, where the same phenomena were the general rule. The American soldiers, until the time came when the ranks were filled with the veterans of many battles, lacked those qualities which carried the Fusiliers of the 74th from the Ehrenthal to the Rotherberg, without a shot being fired and with unwavering ranks, under a storm of shell and bullets from the summit of the spur. In this, as in other respects, the presence of the reserve-men, some of whom had forgotten military habit, whilst others had never acquired them, had doubtless a prejudicial effect on the bearing of the French battalions. The effect of artillery fire on troops, who although ill-disciplined cannot be set down as wanting in pluck or stubbornness, is well worth notice.

Von Kamecke's mistake in attacking without reconnaissance, and its harmful consequences, have already been discussed. His precipitate attack on an extended front prevented those who afterwards assumed the command from using the reinforcements which came up in any other manner than that of "dribbling" them into the fight, and made a strong and sustained assault on a single point impossible. It was only, moreover, the tactical capacity and initiative of the battalion leaders that provided the support which saved the troops in the Stiring Copse from defeat at 2.30. Von Kamecke had ordered von Woyna's whole brigade to pass through the front and strike the French rear. Had his instructions been implicitly obeyed, III/39 would have been overwhelmed, and the centre broken. Otherwise his tactics were commendable. It is true that the front of the 14th Division was too much extended, but believing as he did that only 7,000 French infantry and a few guns were opposed to him, and these only a rear-guard, his idea of throwing the weight of his attack on the French line of retreat was sound enough.

But it is no justification of his conduct in attacking at 12 o'clock to say that it led to victory. Nor can the Battle of Spicheren be held out otherwise than as a warning to the leaders of advanced guards and of detached bodies of troops. Within three hours after the attack began, the 14th Division was only saved by Frossard's incapacity from suffering defeat, and moreover, although that opportunity was allowed to slip, had the leaders of Bazaine's Divisions acted in accordance with the first principles of war, the troops who hurried to von Kamecke's assistance would in all probability have been heavily repulsed.

It is idle to speculate on the results of such a contingency but they could scarcely have been favourable for Germany. Von Kamecke's rashness gave the French an opportunity of balancing the defeats of Weissenburg and Woerth, of strengthening the morale of their men, of creating amongst them confidence in their leaders and themselves, and in checking the extraordinary boldness which characterised both the strategy and tactics of their adversaries.

At the end of the battle, 29 squadrons of cavalry were on the ground, but as the night was dark and the country unfavourable, it was thought unadvisable to send large bodies of horsemen in pursuit of an enemy retiring in good order.

No attempt was made by the cavalry division to hang on the skirts of the enemy and to ascertain the direction of his retreat. The eccentric movement on Saarguemund doubtless made it difficult to pick up the traces, and it was probably believed in the German camp that Bataille's force, which remained during the night at Etzling, was the rear-guard of the whole army.

Nor was the infantry, had light permitted, in any condition to pursue. Tactical order had been lost in almost every quarter, and it would have been impossible to transmit orders, to rally the battalions, to distribute ammunition, or to exercise definite command, under several hours.

In an infantry attack which meets with stubborn resistance, confusion is inevitable. This experience is no new one. At the Alma and at Gettysburg, in the days of close order, units became intermingled as they did at Woerth and Spicheren. No matter what the formation or the nature of the ground may be, an advance under fire is destructive, to a greater or less degree, of unity and organization.

But an attack often divides itself into more than one phase. The battle does not always end in the capture of the position immediately in front. When, at 6 o'clock, the Prussians left wing had won the crest of the Spicheren Heights, the French fell back to the Forbacherberg and the adjoining ridges, and a stronger second line, and a still more difficult enterprise, confronted the stormers of the Gifert Forest and the Rotherberg.

Seven battalions were available at that hour as second line and reserve, and these were immediately employed against the enemy's left flank upon the plateau.

Two hours later, the French infantry and artillery, having covered the retreat of Bataille's and Vergé's Divisions from the valley to the heights, abandoned the Forbacherberg.

The withdrawal, although perhaps accelerated by the loss of the Spicheren Wood, was made in obedience to Frossard's order for a general retreat, and not in consequence of the flank attack. This movement then, was but partially successful; and for this reason, because it was an isolated attack, unsupported by even a demonstration from the border of the Gifert.

Again, when a first position has been carried, it is always possible that the assailant's second line and reserve may already be employed elsewhere. If, under such circumstances, it is necessary to oust the enemy from his new stronghold, and a turning movement be the most effectual means of so doing, the detachment for this purpose will have to be furnished by the first line, and the force remaining in front will have to support the movement by at least a feigned attack.

But with a confused mob of men, such as were the Prussians on the Spicheren Heights, an immediate attempt either to carry a second position, to pursue a retreating foe, or even to demonstrate against his front, is absolutely impossible. In the first place, orders can not be readily communicated to troops in such a state of disorganization. Secondly, each new phase of the attack must be carefully prepared and systematically carried out, and to do this, tactical unity must be first restored. But to evolve order out of such wild disorder as existed from the Rotherberg to the Pfaffen Wood is the work of hours, and the army that finds its ranks in the same state of confusion must perforce acknowledge that it can do no more.

The necessity for a series of attacks on a series of positions will often arise in war, and we may fairly ask whether an army after a first success is to tamely relinquish the contest, and to leave the enemy the hours of the night in which to bring up reinforcements and ammunition, to construct entrenchments, and to relieve his exhausted troops?

Is it to allow him to withdraw unmolested, and to confess that the troops, who have captured his main position, are incapable of even a demonstration against his second line? To do so is to despair of bringing a battle to a decisive conclusion. To reap the fruits of victory, the enemy must be driven from position to position, the attack must be pressed with such energy as to allow him no breathing space in which to rally his battalions, to man his entrenchments, or to recover his *moral*. No matter how great the exhaustion of the victorious troops, the defeated will be in a far worse plight, and on this action must be based.

The preservation then of tactical unity throughout an attack, in such measure that within a few minutes of successful assault, every battalion shall have assembled its remaining files, and have resumed a condition of mobility, is necessary for decisive victory. The fighting line must be capable, immediately after storming a position, of reforming its second line and reserve, and of reestablishing that unity which alone enables a general to make his orders known with rapidity, or have them executed with precision.

Now, although bound to recognise that confusion is inevitable, we are by no means bound to admit that it is so to the same degree as in the great battles of 1870. It is impossible to prevent it altogether, but it does not follow that it may not be minimised so far as to enable order to be readily restored, and by examining the conditions under which the Prussian infantry attacked, we may get some idea how this may best be done.

1. Generally speaking, so soon as the enemy's fire began to be felt, in some cases even earlier, the whole battalion deployed into line of company columns, each captain assuming control of his own supports and reserves, and whether in close or open country, the battalion commander very soon found that, owing to the difficulty of transmitting orders, the companies had slipped from his hands, and that his supervision was limited

to that portion of his force which he accompanied. The company commanders, therefore, at an early stage of the attack, found themselves absolutely independent, with nothing more to hope for from their own battalion. No central body remained to draw the companies together, and it was therefore but natural that each leader should pursue his own course in advance or retreat, and thus lose touch of the remainder.

We may notice that those battalions which postponed their deployment until they came to closer quarters, as did F/74 in the first advance against the Rotherberg, those of L'Estocq's brigade when they attacked the Spicheren Wood, and I and F/48 on the extreme left, were able to preserve their cohesion throughout. We may therefore conclude that deployment should be delayed as long as possible, and when in brigade, even if he has to thrust the whole of his second line into the combat, that the battalion commander should take care to retain a small portion in rear of the centre as a rallying point, serving the same purpose as did the colours in the days of close order, linking the whole together, and forming a nucleus from which the company commanders will hesitate to cut themselves adrift.

2. The Prussian formation in line of company columns provided for the full development of fire, and in 1866 had had the most extraordinary success against an infantry which could make no effective reply to the needle-gun, but in 1870, against an enemy armed with a superior weapon, its results were very far from being so decisive. The company columns managed to push back the French lines, but they did no more; they persuaded the enemy to give ground, but they did not annihilate him, and annihilation is the end at which the attack should aim.

There were two causes which prevented the Prussian attack being pressed with decisive vigour. The first – that the importance of tactical order and the maintenance of cohesion had been somewhat overlooked since the comparatively easy victories of 1866, the second – that the remarkable effect of fire in the Austrian war had led men to forget that of a bayonet charge, *made by troops whose tactical unity is still intact, and, bringing about the insertion of an ordered body of rifles into the midst of the enemy's line*, is essential to decisive success. The same two causes the neglect of the principle of unity, and the secondary importance attached to the advance of a second line in compact order contributed very largely to the confusion which invariably existed after an assault.

Fascinating as it may be from a captain's point of view, it may be doubted whether the size of the Prussian company was not in itself a strong temptation to independent action, and it may, moreover, be questioned whether the fact that the captain's command was strong enough to supply a firing line, a support, and a reserve, did not tend very greatly to dislocation and dispersion. We may be permitted also to believe that the extensive authority allowed to the company chiefs in quarters, despite its numerous advantages, was not altogether an unmixed blessing, and that our own system of smaller companies, of the more limited independence, and, at the same time, almost equal responsibility of the company commanders, is better calculated to preserve unity and cohesion. And, as regards the strength of the company, it is open to question whether 100 rifles are not more easily handled by one man than 240, whether they are not, as a body, more flexible, more readily reformed, more easily covered, and more adaptable to detached duties, such as covering the flanks, outposts and the like.

Captain Seton, it may be added, considered that the mode of advance by columns in first line, rendered the companies "more liable to disorder when passing over high ground or through thick cover, than an English battalion advancing by fours from the flanks of companies." We may also note that he recognised in the majors of an English battalion a means whereby the commanding officer is free to "use his discretion whether to lead the battalion as an entire unit, or to divide it according to the number of field officers available."

To sacrifice initiative to cohesion and to trammel the independence of the leaders of the firing line, as will be hereafter shown, would be to forego victory; still, whilst prepared to act on his own judgment, there must be none the less a determination on the part of every officer to maintain the touch with his battalion as long as possible, and to restore it at every available opportunity.

Where all ranks have been taught the importance of cohesion, understand that it must never be abandoned except for some very strong reason, and make every effort to regain it when the necessity for dislocation has passed away; where the men are accustomed, when their own immediate leader has fallen, to seek out and to attach themselves to another, much will have been done to check straggling and disorder, for the men will find themselves, however often they may change their commanders, still forming part of groups which are all, through their leaders, actuated by the same impulse of gravitation towards a common centre.

It will sometimes happen, as already observed, that both the second and third line may have been employed elsewhere, or *that battalion may have been piled upon battalion in order to carry or to hold against counterattack the enemy's first position*, and that nevertheless further efforts, either by way of demonstration, of a flank, or even of a direct attack, may be demanded from the firing line. Only the most strenuous efforts on the part of the officers and group leaders to keep their men in hand and in touch with their comrades, and constant practice in rallying speedily under such conditions, will enable the battalions to reform readily. The greater the familiarity of all ranks with such situations – and such familiarity may be easily acquired where the battle exercises of the troops are made the close representation of war – the more rapidly will order be restored.

Again: if after the assault has been prepared by the first line, *the position is carried by a body of troops in compact order*, there will be little difficulty or delay in assuming a new formation, either to beat back a counter-stroke or to prosecute a fresh attack.

As to the question of the charge of a second line, it is true that von Boguslawski, perhaps the best representative of the general current of Prussian opinion after 1870, tells us that "as the absolute impossibility of bringing troops in close order into the front line, so much practised on the parade-ground, was apparent to our generals, it was never attempted on the offensive." But the storming of the Golden Bremm and Baraque Mouton by the two half-battalion columns of F/77 is a remarkable instance of a successful charge in close order made by the second line, the advance of F/74 from the Drill-ground Hill to the foot of the Rotherberg was made for the most part in close order, under heavy fire, and over open ground, and yet the battalion was able to scale the heights and carry the horseshoe trench, nor were the columns of the 55th and 67th checked in their rush upon the border of the Stiring Copse.

It is doubtless true, as a rule, that troops in close order cannot be brought up to the front without many casualties, but if troops are thoroughly disciplined, if they know what is expected of them, if they believe that no matter how great the slaughter, to give ground or to break the ranks is to incur dishonour, if they are imbued with the idea that annihilation is preferable to retreat, and are skilfully commanded, the bayonets of the second line will yet decide many a field.

Those who argue that, when they have lost one-third of their number, troops will give way to their own volition, and who base their theories on this, are bad teachers. If such is the fact, then there is something wanting in the discipline or mettle of the men. How many instances may be gathered from our own history and from that of our kindred beyond the Atlantic, of soldiers that bore a far heavier loss than this and never flinched? What was the strength of the Fusilier brigade when the great French column at length went reeling down the hill of Albuera? How many of Pickett's men had fallen when his division reached the crest at Gettysburg? We should train our troops for battle not by complacently telling them that there are limits to their endurance, but by impressing on them that human virtue is equal to the human calamity, that what men of the same race have done they can do also; and, whilst weighing the experience of others, by recalling our own traditions. Then, amidst the slaughter of a modern battle-field, the endurance of Waterloo and Inkerman, the reckless valour of Badajos and Balaclava will again assert themselves.

The startling effect of the appearance of a body of troops with ordered ranks was proved over and over again in the war of 1870, and Spicheren is not without an instance. The sight of Bataille's fresh battalions, while they were yet far distant, brought about the retreat of the Prussian 74th from Stiring Wendel, and if, when the enemy has been exposed to a heavy fire, a closed body can be brought up to the front, the very aspect of the line of bayonets and the advance of a force, strong with the strength of unity and order, will often bring about his retreat.

At the same time something more than courage and discipline is demanded for such an operation. Unnecessary loss is to be avoided, and as many men as possible must be present at the decisive moment. Only the most constant practice over broken country, and the most careful instruction will give officers the necessary skill in turning the accidents of ground to the best account. Formations cannot be stereotyped. Ground has an all-important influence on tactical procedure, and formations must vary with the natural accidents of the field of battle, as well as with the morale and armament of the enemy.

If the ground be open, and cover wanting, it may be necessary to make the advance of the second line with the companies or even half-companies at deploying intervals, to relinquish the direction of such detachments to their own leaders, leaving them free to change formation as the ground varies, demanding from them only absolute subordination as to the end in view, *i.e.*, the simultaneous arrival of their commands in rear of the skirmishers and the simultaneous advance of a number of unbroken units in one strong, solid line. In a close country, or where the ground affords much shelter, it will be possible for the leader to keep the units in his own hand, and to avoid the mischances which will inevitably attend the independent advance of several small bodies at wide intervals.

The experience of the Soudan campaigns, moreover, enlightens us as to the extraordinary strength of a force that is determined to push the charge home. And this strength will be felt more especially in a close-wooded country, where troops are able to approach their enemy unobserved. In such a country, men who are sufficiently disciplined to abandon the rifle for the bayonet at the word of their officers will possess a very great advantage. Had the defenders of the woods round Spicheren and Stiring Wendel been the resolute warriors of Tofrek, what would have been the fate of the long, straggling, and confused lines of the Prussian infantry?

It is perhaps a fault of the present day that it is sometimes forgotten that close order is as important a part of the mechanism of the attack as skirmishing, that the second line is often the deciding factor of the fight, and that the advance of this line depends on the expertness of the officer in handling his men, and on the ability of the men to exchange one formation for another. Extended order produces straggling and the intermixture of units. Close order obviates these evils. The first, then, necessary as it is to avoid heavy loss during the first stage of an attack, to render possible a rapid advance from cover to cover, and to give each man latitude for the use of his rifle, should never be resorted to except under compulsion, the second should be maintained as long as possible without incurring useless loss, and restored at every available opportunity. Straggling was the curse of the Prussian Army in 1870. Many a time when we read that a force on reaching a position found itself wanting a number of bayonets, which neither the struggle it had passed through nor the death-roll of the battalions by no means accounts for, we are tempted to ask, where were the rest? And officers, who served in the great war, have not hesitated to confess that so innumerable were the opportunities for escape offered by the skirmishing fight, that it was only the braver spirits that disdained to profit by them. This was more especially the case when the fighting took place as at Spicheren, in wooded country. "A wood" says a recent German pamphlet, "resembles a filter, a great deal goes in, but very little trickles out." Allowing therefore that the advance of the second line will be attended by heavy losses, the latter will be more than balanced by the absence of stragglers and the maintenance of tactical cohesion.

3. The Prussian battalions and even companies, at Spicheren, owing to the attack of the 14th division on too wide a front, were thrown haphazard into the fight and were often called upon to fill a gap which demanded the presence of every available rifle in the firing line, thus leaving it to other organizations to furnish the second line. We gather then that attacks made without very careful preliminary dispositions, without giving each division, brigade, and battalion a front adequate to its strength and no more, are greatly conducive to disorder.

Our own offensive tactics are based on the principle that every attacking force should be disposed in not less than three lines. This was the normal formation of the Peninsula battles; its employment at the Alma, rather because it was traditional than for any other reason, snatched victory out of the confusion on the heights; and in the Secession War more than one famous charge owed its success to the inherent strength of this system of attack. One of the chief advantages of this principle being embodied in official regulations, is that it becomes so firmly established as the first step in offensive action, that, as happened at the Alma, it is carried out almost instinctively. As the battle comes into view, during the excitement that reigns during the first rush of shells and bullets, habit asserts itself and acts, and so, when the commander comes to take stock of the situation and to improvise his plan, or even when, as at the Alma, he simply orders the whole to advance, he finds his troops drawn up in a formation suitable to every emergency, minimising confusion, susceptible of modification, and promising sustained energy. Whatever happens, the framework of his battle, as von Moltke has called it, is the best that can be devised. The first step has been already taken in the right direction, and in war, as elsewhere, it is this that tells. Not only at Spicheren, but throughout the campaign, the Prussians seem to have set this principle aside. In the peace manœuvres, over-prominence had been given to the use of extended lines, attacks were seldom made in mass, the formation in three lines was not demanded as an essential, its advantages were not drilled into them, and, as a general rule, they were disregarded. To this fact we may fairly attribute the precipitate rush into action, the confusion that followed, and, more than all, the almost invariable failure of the frontal attack. It may be remembered that the general who commanded one of the Guard Brigades in the disastrous attempt to storm St. Privat, stated, in his official report of the battle, that when the assault came to a stand within 400–600 yards of the enemy's line, the French already showed a disposition to retreat, and that he then felt that had support been forthcoming, the position might have been stormed without waiting for the turning movement to develop.

This incident, brought into special prominence by the terrible losses of the assailants, is still one of the strongest of stock arguments against the frontal attack. But the Guard advanced in line of columns and in two lines only, it was outnumbered by at least two to one, and the village of St. Privat, the key of the position, was as yet untouched by a single shell. Give these circumstances their full weight, add the abnormal difficulties of approach, and it will at least be open to doubt whether they, rather than the intrinsic strength of the defence as compared with the attack, were not the true causes of the failure. So far as history goes, some exceedingly good reason is invariably to be found for the non-success of frontal attacks in line. Either they were not made in sufficient strength, the lines were too far apart, there was no third line, or the preparation by fire was omitted. There are very few instances, on the other hand, where these conditions were fulfilled, that victory did not follow.

We may be permitted, then, to hold the opinion that too much stress has been laid on the impossibility of the frontal attack against a position defended with breech-loaders. Nor is it a wholesome doctrine, for, as the tendency of modern tactics is to envelope, we may be sure that in the warfare of the future the defender will devote far more attention to securing his flanks than did the French in 1870, and, if the assailant wishes to win the battle out of hand, he will be compelled to make his main effort directly in face of the hostile line. The same rule will hold good of the counter-stroke.

There can be no question that the frontal and flank attack combined is the most effective form of offensive tactics. But where such a proceeding is impracticable, there is no need to abandon all hopes of success. By skilful manœuvering the adversary may be induced to weaken one point in order to reinforce another, a defensive position can seldom be everywhere strong, and, if successful, the frontal attack effects a saving of time and is more likely to be decisive.

Gravelotte would have been a more complete victory had the Guard carried St. Privat at 6 o'clock. At 7.30, darkness was fast settling on the field, and want of light, as much as the confusion that existed in the village, prevented any vigorous attempt to sweep down the ridge from left to right and roll the enemy back on the Moselle.

It may be remarked that late improvements in artillery, in accuracy, projectiles, and killing power, are all on the side of the offensive, and also, that the introduction of rifled howitzers, from which no bomb-proof is secure, and which need not be withdrawn from action until the assailant has approached within point-black rifle range of the parapet, will, by facilitating the frontal attack, and thus making it more frequent, render the question of how it is to be carried out one of the utmost importance. Fortunately, there is no need to refer further than to the drill book of 1889, to learn not only the principles to be observed and the appropriate distribution of the infantry, but also the manner in which the three arms may be most effectually combined both to achieve and to improve success.

4. The rôle of the first line is to shatter the enemy's power of resistance, and this is done either by obtaining a superiority of fire, not necessarily along the whole front, but at some particular point, and not necessarily by opposing him with a larger number of rifles, but by striking him in flank or obliquely, or by surprising him by a sudden fire at short range. When the zone of heavy loss is reached the command of the firing line must be surrendered to the company and section leaders, and the task of obtaining superiority of fire is imposed on them. To accomplish this, their leaders must be self-reliant, accustomed to act on their own initiative, carefully trained to make use of ground, and quick to recognise the weak points of the enemy's line. Moreover, if the discipline of the men is such that when their immediate leaders have fallen they at once attach themselves to the nearest officer, officers who find a favourable opportunity will have the men wherewith to seize it, and all the rifles available will be employed to the best advantage.

"A skirmishing line," says Lord Wolseley, "formed here and there by a few files only, at other points where a dip in the ground affords shelter, by several companies, taking advantage of every little inequality of surface in front to push on nearer and nearer to the enemy's position, will soon find some chink in the enemy's armour, some weak point from which he will recede, and thus enable you, by working in there, to take the stronger points in flank."

Such are the principles that should guide the action of the firing line, whether it is employed but to prepare the way for the bayonets of the second line, or whether, as with the Prussians in 1870, it is regarded as the decisive factor in the infantry fight. It was on these principles that the Prussian battalions acted, it was to them that they owed their success. The officers were trained to responsibility, skilful in detecting and using opportunity, and the men were sufficiently disciplined, generally speaking, to follow without hesitation.

The presence and initiative of a large number of well-trained leaders along the whole front, together with the habit which had been instilled into the men of obeying strange officers as they would their own, gave extraordinary energy, strength, and elasticity to their attack. The company and section leaders, abandoned, when the heavy firing made the transmission of the battalion leader's orders impossible, to their own resources, knew that the successful issue of the fight depended on their skill and resolution. When some new phase of battle opened, or unforeseen obstacle intervened, they never looked behind or hesitated, but lent all their energies to overcoming the unexpected difficulties. When an opening appeared, a company, a section, or even a handful of men, led perhaps by a subaltern or sergeant, dashed in without hesitation, no time was lost in asking for permission or waiting for orders, and even the cohesion of the command, was, in case of necessity, for the time being neglected. Thus the strength of the adversary's line was tested at every point, and although the tactical units, that is the companies, were weak, so thoroughly was the system of mutual support applied, that where a point was seized sufficient strength was generally forthcoming to retain it.

In the French attack, on the other hand, the influence of the subordinate leaders was not apparent, and the action of the firing line was rather a dead pressure against the adversary's front than a resolute search for his weak points. Either the effect of small bodies acting against the adversary's flanks was not appreciated, or a want of energy, owing to the repression of individual initiative on the part of the officers prevented such tactics being employed.

But at the same time it must be observed that owing to the retention of the battalion as the tactical unit, the French appear to have preserved their cohesion better than did the Prussians. Had the disorder in Frossard's ranks been as great as that which existed on the crest of the plateau or in the woods round Stiring Wendel, it would have been impossible either to have drawn back Laveaucoupet's Division to the Forbacherberg and Spicheren Ridge in the "fairly good order" with which the Staff History admits the movement was carried out, or to have transferred the whole of Vergé's and Bataille's troops, artillery, infantry, and cavalry, from the narrow streets of Stiring Wendel to the heights above, within three hours of darkness.

Both systems, therefore, had their strong and weak points, and it is evident that a continuation of the elasticity of the Prussians with the cohesion of the French attack, would give better results than either. How these two conflicting elements, individual initiative and the unity of the mass, are to be reconciled, is a question well worth the serious consideration of every soldier.

The subdivision of the section into groups multiplies the number of trained leaders along the front, and whilst it ensures the most energetic search for the enemy's weak points, keeps the men better in hand, giving them a larger number of rallying points, and providing a constant gravitation towards the centre of the tactical unit. These leaders must gain their experience in battle exercises, and it is by this method of practical instruction that they will learn to exercise independent judgment and at the same time in what manner cohesion may be best maintained. It is necessary also that every officer should understand the conditions of battle, and recognise that when once the firing line has reached the zone of heavy fire the further guidance of the men who compose it must be left entirely to the company commanders, and when their influence is unable to make itself felt, to the officers and noncommissioned officers in charge of sections or groups. *The devolution of responsibility*, at each successive stage of the advance, is one of the first requirements of modern fighting.

In bringing up the second line in good order, in selecting the most favourable point for assault, in initiating or beating back a flank attack, and in the judicious occupation of a captured position, the officer in command of the force, whether it be a battalion or a brigade, has enough upon his hands. If his second and third lines are unavoidably drawn into the firing line, in such case his functions are for the time being in abeyance, and only by example can he influence his troops.

Lastly, both officers and men must be so trained that obedience to orders becomes absolutely mechanical, for only the obedience that has crystallized into deep-rooted instinct is to be relied upon in the stress of modern battle. But when orders are not forthcoming, or when affairs have developed in such an unexpected manner as to make them so inapplicable, then individual initiative must be called upon to play its part. It is doubtless difficult to combine two such opposite characteristics, but it is not impossible. Did not the soldiers of Wellington's Light Division unite with that steadiness in line which has never been surpassed, the intelligence, and the self-reliance, which made them skirmishers as skilful as the famous Voltigeurs of France?

The Battle of Spicheren is a notable example of wood-fighting, and it will be worth while devoting some attention to the manner in which the existence of the woods in front and on either flank of the French position affected the progress and issue of the action.

Both flanks of the French rested on woods dense enough to make the combined action and effective co-operation of several battalions a matter of great difficulty, but by no means impenetrable, and affording the assailant an opportunity of approaching close to the flanks of the position unobserved. The possibility that the Germans would take advantage of this opportunity was not without effect on the minds of the French commander and his divisional generals. The great Saarbrucken Forest, extending round Stiring Wendel, and bordering the line of retreat to Forbach and beyond, was an incubus from which they could not free themselves. This absolute ignorance of what was going on within its coverts, the apprehension that the force, which the imagination of the spies had conjured up at Saarlouis, might be there concealed – an apprehension confirmed by the resolute attack of the Prussian battalions that lined the border of the wood – appears to have held back the far superior force which garrisoned Stiring Wendel from a general counter-stroke. Moreover, reading between the lines of Frossard's report, there is reason to suspect that, on the opposite flank, the movement of the two battalions of the 48th through the Pfaffen Wood had a share in bringing about the withdrawal of Laveaucoupet's Division from the Gifert.

We have here, then, an instance of the moral effect produced on the attitude of the defenders when the ground on the flanks cannot be observed, and when they have no knowledge whether the enemy is in occupation of such ground or not.

That neither Frossard nor his subordinates took any precautions to secure this knowledge we have already observed, and it is needless to make further comment, but it is worth while noting the very valuable assistance that a force of mounted infantry would have rendered in reconnoitring the forest-tracks, and readers who are interested in the duties of this arm of the service are recommended to study the methods of the American generals and the American horsemen in the Virginian Wilderness. Neither Lee nor Grant, although the country in which their campaigns were carried on was far more extensively wooded than the borders of France and Germany, were troubled by the apprehensions which beset the French commanders, but they were both careful to secure early information of the enemy's movements, and were both well served by the officers who led their cavalry.

Far and wide, to front and flanks, rode Stuart's and Sheridan's mounted marksmen, obstructing the path of the enemy's patrols, laying ambushes for his advanced guards, contesting every inch of ground, and penetrating his lines, for in such a country it was impossible to watch every path. More skilled as foot than cavalry they did not hesitate to engage the infantry, and even when in inferior force, their superior mobility rendered them capable of taking up position after position, and by a series of rear-guard actions, of delaying the advance of the enemy's main body or the approach of his flank attacks.

A single battalion of such troops, had it been pushed forward on the French left towards Volklingen and Gersweiler, would probably have checked the advanced guard of the 13th Prussian Division long enough to have prevented the decisive movement on the Kaninchenberg. Throughout the war, the helplessness of the Prussian cavalry screen against even a small force of infantry was remarkable, and it has already been recorded that the 5th Dragoons from Pirmasens, at a time when it was of the utmost importance to obtain information of the French movements on the Saarguemund-Bitsche Road, was accompanied by riflemen in carts.

We may therefore, from these considerations, draw deductions; first, that if possible the flanks of a position should embrace an extensive view; secondly, that where this is impossible, the ground beyond should be thoroughly reconnoitred; thirdly, that the force entrusted with this duty should be capable of offering effective resistance.

But both fighting and movement in a thickly wooded country are difficult, and troops should be carefully trained in these operations whenever such country is available. And it is not sufficient that such training should be applied to small bodies alone. To ensure the combination and cooperation of several tactical units is the chief difficulty, and without practical experience in the means of overcoming it, the disjointed advance of the 28th Brigade through the Saarbrucken Forest, and the isolated and ineffective attacks of the various battalions which composed it, will find its counterpart.

It may be added that since the war of 1870–1, the Germans have incessantly practised their troops in fighting in and advancing, in battle order, through dense woods, and it is interesting to notice the tactical details which have been accepted as generally essential to such operations. Deployment is postponed as long as possible, and all supporting bodies are retained in close order on the roads or paths, every opportunity of a clearing or otherwise is used to reform the ranks, and, when the further end of the wood is reached, the first thing to be done is to restore tactical order, until this has been effected, no further advance is permitted.

German writers have not hesitated to attribute the successes of the army during this campaign in part to the superior shooting, accurate and careful, of their infantry. That this had much to do with the result of their battles would not be discovered from the relation of the incidents thereof, but we must accept the evidence of men who were eyewitnesses of the engagements and were able to judge from personal experience.

It must be remembered that at Spicheren the greater part of the fighting took place in thick woods, and here the struggle unavoidably developed into a series of trials of skill between more or less isolated groups of riflemen, and in these circumstances, good shooting, the tactical abilities of subordinate leaders, and the training of the individual soldier in working in combination with his comrades, had their full effect. There is little wonder that the German infantryman, trained to accurate and careful aiming at short ranges, and accustomed, when on the defensive, never to open fire except by word of command, should prove the better marksman. Habit is everything in battle.

As now understood, there was little fire discipline on either side, no idea of concentrating the fire of groups or sections on carefully selected objectives. The fire once opened, the men shot at will, and amongst the French it appears to have been considered that the duty of the infantry soldier when skirmishing, or on the defensive, was to shoot and to shoot always, covering the ground with a hail of bullets, regardless of where they fell so long as they fell in the direction of the enemy. The advance of F/74 across the open valley to the foot of the Rotherberg was a splendid opportunity for demonstrating the power of the Chassepôt, but the fire of the 10th Chasseur battalion and 3rd Company of Engineers failed to arrest the movement. There was no other opportunity of bringing long-range fire to bear, and we may take away this lesson from Spicheren that, in a wooded and close country, the infantry fighting will be at close ranges, and, also, that long range fire at a moving target, unless, as at St. Privat, it is delivered by such a crowd of rifles as to cover the whole of the terrain with bullets, is of doubtful efficiency. The German system of allowing the attack to arrive within effective range before opening fire is far preferable.

We may note that the author of *The Nation in Arms* states that the French regulars shot well at long ranges, and this is borne out by the histories of the German regiments engaged at St. Private

Fire was often opened at a range of 1,500 metres and more, despite both the official regulations and the efforts of the officers, and it is explained that the presence in the ranks of each battalion of 150–250 reserve men, unused to discipline, as well as untrained in the proper tactical use of the rifle, exerted the worst influence, and that their example, their uncontrollable desire to employ the extreme range of the Chassepôt, ruined the discipline of the rest, took the whole direction of fire out of the officers' hands, and led to want of ammunition when it was most required.

Too much praise cannot be given to the Prussian artillery, and it may be confidently asserted that, more than once, disaster was averted by the bold and adroit disposition of the guns.

The action of artillery may be divided into four episodes.

1. The driving back of the French guns under the Rotherberg.
2. The massing of 18 guns upon the Galgenberg, only 1,300 yards distant from the French trenches.
3. The counter-stroke on Bataille's attack, made by the advance of 36 guns to the Folster Height.
4. The surmounting of the Rotherberg by two batteries.

It will be interesting to note in detail the services rendered by this arm during each of these episodes.

1. The French guns upon the Rotherberg were driven back by oblique fire to a position where they could no longer command the St. Arnual Valley below the Gifert and the Pfaffen Woods. A mitrailleuse battery was compelled to withdraw from the heights above the Golden Bremm.
2. The fire from the Rotherberg was silenced, the defenders of the horseshoe trench demoralized, and the way prepared for the attack of F/74. Hostile columns advancing over the crest of the plateau to the recapture of the spur were several times driven back. The Golden Bremm and the Baraque Mouton were rendered untenable, and the attack of F/77 on this important post materially facilitated. Counter-attacks on

these buildings, down the ravine from the south-west, appear more than once to have dissolved under fire of the guns.

3. The advance of Bataille's infantry and artillery down the Forbach Valley was checked, and the attack of the 52nd vigorously supported.
4. The hold of the infantry on the Rotherberg was confirmed, and the French driven from the Spicheren Knoll.

Massed batteries, concentration of fire, great boldness in advancing to the most favourable positions, incessant attention to the support of the infantry, accurate shooting, and much readiness in identifying the relative importance of objectives, were the characteristics of the Prussian artillery tactics at Spicheren. Nor were guns retained in reserve so long as there was room for their deployment and a target for their fire.

The French artillery, on the other hand, was by no means skilfully employed. It was useless to have left two batteries in Forbach. One, it is true, fired a dozen rounds to cover the retreat of the defenders of the Kaninchenberg, but the other never came into action at all, and it is manifest that, had it been brought up to the Forbacherberg, it would have done good service.

Again, in the Forbach Valley, the batteries came into action by detachments, not *en masse*. They were placed at first within too short a range of the Stiring Copse, and it was a mistake to have sent the whole of the available reserve as well as two of Bataille's batteries to the valley. Until the retreat was decided on, the right wing on the plateau was supported by only four batteries out of a total of fifteen, the left wing in Stiring Wendel by nine. Two of the latter were certainly disabled at an early hour, but it would have been well to have reinforced Laveaucoupet by a battery from Forbach and a second of Bataille's division. Posted on the Spicheren Ridge they would have made it very difficult for the Prussians, on capturing the Gifert and Pfaffen Woods, to have held the outskirts, and would have done much to assist the last great counter-stroke at 7.45. At the same time it must not be forgotten that the French position was unfavourable to the employment of artillery, and the guns could do little to support the infantry defending the Rotherberg and the Gifert. The mitrailleuses were used as field guns, and consequently without effect. Stiring Wendel and the Spicheren Ridge, where they could not be assailed by hostile artillery, were their proper place.

The advance of the German cavalry up the Rotherberg was a desperate and useless measure, and Rheinbaben's squadrons were prevented by the nature of the ground from taking part in the fight. It may be questioned, however, whether they were sufficiently utilized. Several squadrons were on the ground when the battle began, and although it was impossible to break through the French picquets, it is surprising that no attempt was made to penetrate to the plateau by the track through the St. Arnual Wood, or by the Simbach Ravine. Again, not until 2.30 was a single patrol sent out to explore the road which runs from St. Arnual Wood to Grossbliederstroff up the valley of the Saar. After that hour, the omission was rectified by General von Doering, who despatched in this direction a squadron attached to his own, the 9th Infantry Brigade. Outside St. Arnual this force was confronted by a more numerous body of French horsemen, and its further progress checked. Nor was any attempt made to communicate with the 13th Division

Lieutenant-General von Glümer, commander of the German 13th Infantry Division, VII Corps (Rousset/*Histoire*)

and to hurry von Glümer to the field. The Staff History states that an officer's patrol reconnoitred during the battle towards St. Avold, but by what road we are not told. Near Carling it was met by a body of French cavalry and retired by way of Lauterbach.

The difficulty of concentrating cavalry on the field of battle, when an engagement takes place unexpectedly and the front of observation is a wide one, is well illustrated by the fact that, by 5 o'clock, but 10 of the 56 squadrons which composed the 5th and 6th Cavalry Divisions had joined Rheinbaben. By 7, 17 squadrons had assembled, and there were three regiments (12 squadrons) of divisional cavalry also present.

At the same time, it must be remembered that a false alarm from Saarguemund had caused a portion of the 6th Division to concentrate at a point 14 miles distant from Saarbrucken. The 15th Brigade of this division was also employed in observing Saarguemund on the left flank, the 12th Brigade of the 5th Division moved still further to the west, met French infantry at Rohrbach, and was able to report that the hostile camp in Bitsche was gradually increasing. During the day, the 3rd Cavalry Division advanced on Saarlouis, and by means of its patrols, discovered large bodies of French troops in the neighbourhood of St. Avold and Tromborn.

The practice of route-marching had received due attention in the Prussian Army, moreover, the distances covered by the troops in their annual manœuvres generally corresponded with the tasks demanded from them on a campaign. During the forward movement of the First and Second Armies to the Saar this training bore good fruit. Part of the 14th Division on the 2nd of August traversed 27 miles under a burning sun. The 33rd Regiment of the 15th Division accomplished a march of 69 miles over mountainous country in three days, and the 5th Division, over unfavourable ground, made marches of over 14 miles on four consecutive days. The advanced guard of the 13th Division, when it came into action against the Kaninchenberg, was more than 20 miles from its bivouac near Lebach, and had not halted to cook; the 2nd Battalion 53rd Regiment took only 13 hours to cover the 27½ miles from Wadern to the Rotherberg. The 4th Light Battery of the 1st Army Corps had come direct from Konigsberg, in Prussia, in the same train, and was to have disembarked at Neunkirchen. In consequence of a report of an action raging to the south of Saarbrucken, the commander at once resolved to continue his journey to St. Johann, and arrived in time to take part in the battle.

It will be well to add the criticism of the German Staff History, that is, of Field Marshal von Moltke, on the earlier engagements of the campaign:

"Changes in the appliances of war, which in these August battles were for the first time manifested in the field on both sides, led also, in a tactical point of view, to many unwonted phenomena."

"Conspicuous, in the first place in contrast to former times, is a great change in the employment of the German artillery. Placed at the head of the marching columns, it appeared with the foremost on the battle-field preparing the great offensive blows. Fearlessly holding to the position it once took up, it may be said to have formed a solid framework to the order of the battle, whilst the French batteries in general only appeared as an easily transferable force. Favoured by its better matériel the German artillery was able to afford the infantry that support of which it was in need against the superior small arm of the French."

"In the German leading, the effort was conspicuous in all these battles to employ the artillery at the outset in masses, and afterwards in most intimate connection with the task of the infantry. The increased losses of artillery through musketry fire, however, demand more and more that that arm should be afforded ample protection by throwing forward detachments of infantry."

"But from the nature of things it was not always practicable to push the German infantry so far forward as to afford complete protection to its artillery against an enemy equipped with a long ranging rifle. The advantage to the infantry of being able to shoot at very long distances was therefore proved on many occasions, but on the other hand it was also apparent, especially in the defensive struggles, in which the infantry were later engaged, that the true effect of the rifle lies at close ranges and that only a well-grounded training confers the degree of certainty of aim, which can foil every frontal attack over open ground."

"The less they were in position to answer the volleys from the Chassepôt at the longest ranges, the more was the attention of German infantry directed, as a matter of course, to a specially careful use of the ground, and the employment of company columns."

"*The self-dependence of the subordinate commanders, so thoroughly inculcated by the peace manœuvres, in conjunction with the well-grounded training of the individual, have asserted themselves with all their advantages.* The novelty of the phenomena which were met with certainly caused surprise at first, but the officers and men very soon knew how to accommodate themselves to the changed requirements, and to understand that it is above all necessary, on the one part, to keep the action under control even under antagonistic circumstances – on the other to use every effort in their power to rejoin with the least possible delay the controlling authority, and their own particular unit. *The maxim 'aus der Tiefe zu fechten,' in consequence of the general instinct to close rapidly with the enemy, was but seldom properly carried out, and degenerated mostly to an impatient rush without waiting the arrival and deployment of the supporting troops.* So at Spicheren, and Metz, cases were frequently seen of isolated struggles without connexion, and oft-repeated intermingling and dispersion of tactical units."

CHAPTER X
THE TRAINING OF THE TROOPS, AND THEIR TACTICAL LEADING

In addition to the initial error which marred the Prussian generalship, minor tactical mistakes can be pointed out, as for instance, Major Werner's withdrawal of his six companies from Stiring Wendel without first communicating with superior authority; the attempt of I & II/39 to advance against Spicheren from the Gifert Wood before 3 o'clock, and of several mixed detachments to do the same after the final capture of the southern edge; the evacuation of the Golden Bremm and Baraque Mouton by F/77, in order to join the assault of F/12 on the Spicheren Wood; the futile attempt of the 17th Hussars to act upon the plateau; the attempt to place the whole of the 28th Brigade on the French left flank and rear at 3 o'clock, thus leaving the hotly-engaged troops in the copse without support; the failure of the regimental commanders of this brigade, when, in obedience to the demands of the situation, its dissolution came about, to communicate with the brigadier; and lastly, the impulse of both companies and sections to drift apart and to act as perfectly independent units. Opportunities of escaping from control were eagerly seized, perhaps as promising individual distinction, and officers who had been temporarily detached, as flank guards or otherwise, displayed no impatience to resume connection with their battalion. Alongside great energy, a deep appreciation of the principle that the attack cannot be too strongly pressed, and much initiative, appeared a certain want of caution, a tendency to regard the action immediately in front as a whole, and not as only a part, and to subordinate unity of action to isolated enterprise and local success. But on the whole, the Prussian officers of every rank displayed great tactical ability.

The nature of the country, the position of the enemy, the circumstances under which the battle had to be conducted, were all unfavourable to the assailant. Nevertheless, even before the advent of the 13th Division, he had achieved a measure of success, and the question must needs force itself on the most careless reader, to what was this result due? It was not to personal courage, for in this quality the combatants were well matched. It was not to greater natural aptitude for war, for what nation can boast of more victories than France? Nor was it to the bad use made by the French of a strong position, for the commander of the 14th German Division replied with an error of even greater magnitude. To none of these, then, was the Prussian success due, but to the superior tactical skill of the officers, and the stronger discipline of the troops. In the employment of the battalions that reinforced the fighting line, in the recognition of important tactical points, and of the weak places in the adversary's line, the Prussians displayed a readiness which the French did not possess. Von Goeben's determination, when the left attack had already been partially defeated, to throw every rifle into the fighting line, and to maintain, at all risks, the grip upon the Rotherberg; the complete change of plan in the assault upon the plateau, and the flank attacks on the *western* slopes of the Spicheren Heights; the rapid shift of L'Estocq's brigade to the Golden Bremm and the Spicheren Wood; the support of the defenders of the Rotherberg by the two batteries; von Pannwitz's storm of the homesteads; von François' capture of the horse-shoe trench, and von Zastrow's brilliant counter-stroke with six and thirty guns to meet the last attack of the French down the Forbach Valley; the self-sacrificing support given to the infantry by the artillery; the self-reliance and cool judgment, which, when the sound of battle was heard, anticipated orders, and brought divisions, brigades, and batteries far on the right road before instructions for their march had been issued by the superior authorities; the readiness with which the principal requirement of the situation, *i.e.*, the energetic prosecution of the attack, was seized by officers and men; the unity of purpose which animated the whole mass, although that purpose had in few instances been communicated by the generals; against these there were few bright instances of tactical capacity on the part of the French to be set off and they are the more conspicuous in being interwoven with so many errors, and accompanied by a general want of energy and combination. It is true that Laveaucoupet's flank attack on the 39th at 3 o'clock, Bataille's counter-stroke on the copse, and Dulac's defence of the Kaninchenberg, were each one of them ably executed, but, as regards the regimental officers, the Prussians showed greater power of initiative and of meeting the needs of the situation than did the French.

There was little reckless and wasteful long range fire, great care was invariably taken to secure the flanks, to collect supports, whenever the inevitable intermingling of battalions took place – indispensable precautions in all fighting. There was no blind obedience of orders given before the situation had fully developed, no waiting for further instructions when matters were critical. On the part of the French, on the other hand, except those already quoted, there were no instances of effective independent action, although there were many opportunities for its exercise.

And in an army whose training was limited to the barrack yard, in which every action was regulated by routine, and where all independence even of thought was stifled and discouraged, where the habit of waiting for orders or unreasoning obedience had been fostered at the expense of individual judgment and resolution, it is little wonder that they never occurred. A military life, passed in a mere routine of acting in accordance with minute regulations, and in drill and manœuvre exercises, the precise execution of which as officially laid down was the only aim, tended very powerfully to destroy initiative, and to stunt the capacity for independent resolution.

"If in an army," says the author of *The Nation in Arms*, "the habit prevails of only doing what is ordered, its movements are by fits and starts. It experiences an interruption whenever unforeseen circumstances intervene, because all concerned await the dispositions of the superior commanders. The disconnected nature of many of the operations executed by the French Army in 1870, can only be explained by the lack of independence in the lower grades."

"Clausewitz declares it a sign of mediocrity to do what one is officially ordered. We call it an insufficient conception of duty."

Now the truth of this theory of the necessity of initiative, long before the era of the breech-loader, so early as 1814, had been recognised by one of the greatest of Prussian leaders, General Gneisenau, and the divergent views which existed then, as they in some degree do still, are well expressed by his colleague von Muffling, the Prussian Commissioner with the English Army at Waterloo. Both parties appear to have recognised the value in war of not losing time in asking questions, but Gneisenau's opponents, appealing to the precepts of Wellington, declared that the risks of such a mode of action were too great.

Now, in the first place, there was misconception of the views of Wellington. It is true that he had established a rule, "that a general placed in a fixed, pre-arranged position, has unlimited power to act within it, according to his judgment; for instance, he may choose to defend his first line, or to meet the enemy with a counter-attack from a position in the rear, and in both cases he may pursue him, but never further than the obstacle which defines the line assigned to him; in one word, such obstacle until fresh orders, is the limit of his action."

The wisdom of this rule, a most excellent tactical precept, none could deny, but, be it noted, it refers only to the defensive, and at the same time, gives as much latitude to a subordinate commander when on the defensive, as the most strenuous advocate of the theory would be disposed to allow. To decide what the Duke's precepts were as to the initiative of his subordinates when on the offensive, we must look to his practice, and it will be discovered from the history of his battles, that when once his divisions had had their special tasks assigned to them, their leaders were free, so long as they furthered the general plan, to execute them as they thought best. Nor does it appear that his subordinate generals were expected to lose opportunity rather than act without orders. One of his chief complaints against them was their inability to act upon their own responsibility. This does not imply, however, that the duke would have approved of the precipitate action of some of the German leaders of advanced guards in 1866 and 1870. Far from it. Rash independent action he always censured with special severity.

Gneisenau's ideas, then, and those of the advocates of this theory, have been misunderstood by their opponents. What he enjoined was that when a subordinate commander had an opportunity of furthering the general plan of attack, and when, were time to be lost in waiting or sending for orders, the opportunity might escape, he was to act without delay. Such, too, were the views of Wellington. But when the rifle and the breech-loader came to be employed, it was not at first understood that a deeper zone of fire and a wider front had so increased the difficulties of command, and occasioned so much delay in transmitting orders, that the same latitude which had hitherto been allowed to the leaders of advanced guards and other detachments, must now be granted to the leaders of the fighting line.

In the fighting line, when contact with the enemy is close, and the fire of both sides is fully developed, an officer's command, no matter what his rank, covers only the few files on either side. His orders can reach only a very small number. It follows, then, that as orders cannot be passed, the leaders of the smaller bodies, of companies and sections, must be given a free hand, and be expected to act on their own initiative. If the initiative is in accordance with the general design, the battle will be fought out as the commander designs, and no danger nor loss of opportunity will result from the lack of orders. But the difficulty is the same that was felt by Gneisenau's opponents, how is this intelligent initiative to be secured? Now we have seen in the preceding pages that the Prussians in 1870 had done much in this direction, and if we turn to *The Nation in Arms*, we shall see how they had solved the problem.

Speaking of the German Army, and the self-same system obtained in 1870, von der Goltz writes as follows: – "We rigidly adhere to the principle that in the case of an officer who has been guilty of neglect, an excuse to the effect that he has received no orders, is of no avail. Passive obedience is not enough for us, not even the mere fulfilment of what is enjoined, when the occasion has demanded that more should be done."

"It cannot be denied, that independent action may be sometimes inconvenient, by crossing and running counter to the higher views of the commander-in-chief, and by '*faits accomplis*' which cannot be undone, robbing him of his liberty of action. Especially in the higher ranks, therefore, careful consideration must precede such action, because here a part is staked, the fate of which influences the whole; this is not the case when the initiative is taken by leaders of subordinate rank. But nothing would be more erroneous than if, because inconveniences may occur, one were to attempt to curb the general initiative of the army. In order to avoid a mistake being made, a hundred promoting impulses would be blotted out, and an enormous amount of strength lost."

"There is," he continues, "only one means of preventing the ill consequences of the initiative, and that is a uniform training of the intelligence and judgment."

It was this uniform training, then, that enabled the Prussians to add to their armoury this powerful weapon, a general initiative.

Now how was this training given? Assuredly not in the barrack, nor on the drill-ground, nor by the incessant practice of precise manœuvres. These, on the contrary, tend rather to destroy initiative.

Nevertheless, barrack-life and the drill-ground were as much a part of the German officer's life as they were of the French. But they were not the whole. They were but the foundations of his military efficiency; they did not form the whole structure.

Yet even in the barrack and on the drill-ground much was done to foster initiative and independent judgment. Every action of the officer was not regulated by authority. Routine was not universal, but large demands were made on individual intelligence. To the officers, down to the company and section leaders, the instruction to their men was entirely given over. They were hampered by no exact instructions.

They were allowed to employ their own methods, zeal and the efficiency of the command being the only matters looked to by their superiors, and all interference with their methods, so long as they tended to the desired end, was contrary to the traditions of the service. Under this system, therefore, every officer acquired habits of independent judgment and self-reliance, for he was daily compelled to exercise these qualities.

But it was not to their regimental system alone that the Prussian officers owed their initiative and self-reliance. It was beyond the precincts of the barrack and the parade-ground that they were principally trained to exercise these qualities. Battle-exercises, as we have already noted, both on a large and small scale, were the constant practice of the German troops.

Here the Prussian company and section leaders, especially in the greater manœuvres of large bodies of troops, which assuming many of the characteristics of modern battle, and conducted over close and broken country, rendered independent action and resolve on the part of the leaders inevitable and constant; already thoroughly instructed theoretically, they learnt to exercise initiative and self-reliance, and to apply the lessons they had imbibed from the experience of others, that is, from the study of tactical operations. Here they received a uniform training, and, at the same time, acquired skill in leading troops in action.

Here the lack of acquaintance with actual war was, as far as possible, made good, and officers, whose commanders had grasped the changed conditions of tactics, were taught, while using their own judgment when circumstances required it, to bring their action into adjustment with the general design.

In these exercises, too, the men acquired that battle discipline in which they were so much superior to the French. They became accustomed, in some degree at least, to the confusion and loss of tactical order consequent on the attack of large bodies over broken ground. They learnt, without waiting for orders, to obey strange officers, to work with other commands, and to feel at home under such circumstances. They became expert in making the best use of cover, and in the duties of outpost and patrol. To reserve their fire, to husband their ammunition, became second nature. From the pictures of war so often presented to them, they derived a useful familiarity with the conditions of battle, and with the liberty of action it accords to all, freedom almost bewildering after the mechanical movements of the drill-ground. They, too, (for much attention was given to their individual instruction), became skilled fighting-men, capable, when needful, of using their reason and intelligence, and not merely a well-drilled and courageous mass.

Moreover, by this uniform training, under the supervision of von Moltke and the staff, unity of action was guaranteed. To paraphrase von der Goltz: – "There was a certain harmony in the manner of performing the tasks that battle set forth. Sound principles had been engrafted into the flesh and blood of the officers by teaching and training, for only thus was it possible that a certain task should be performed by all on whom it might be imposed, not indeed after one single fashion, but on similar principles." The value of this unity of action cannot be denied. In ill-trained armies, as these of the French in 1870, and of both the Federal and Confederate States in the earlier campaigns of the War of Secession, its absence was conspicuous, and marred, over and over again, the best-laid schemes of their commanders. "Experience taught me," says von Muffling a veteran of many wars, "that the habit of acting according to the circumstances and not on fixed principles, makes characters otherwise the most confident, mistrustful, and that one soldier will not trust another, if he never knows beforehand how the latter will resolve to act in this or that position."

It is not surprising that in the French army, already ill-disciplined, when the soldier saw his leaders acting on divergent principles, and failing to render each other loyal support, the cry of treachery should have arisen, or the old vigour in attack and tenacity of defence have become relaxed.

And I ask the reader to note with particular attention that this acting on similar principles, and the consequent confidence of the Prussian officers in one another, was in a large degree due to the influence of the General Staff. Trained and instructed for more than ten years by von Moltke himself, the generals and subordinate officers who had passed through his hands had all been educated on the same lines; the same important principles had been impressed upon the minds of all; those who could not be trusted, from some deficiency of character, to apply those principles, were not placed in positions of responsibility; the influence of the remainder permeated the whole army and brought about the harmonious co-operation, the daring and the mutual confidence, which was so well exemplified at Spicheren. Had this not been the case, should we have seen that resolute pushing of the attack on the part of every leader, which contrasted in so great a degree with the wide differences in resolution that were seen amongst the French, and which contributed more largely than all else to the ultimate success of the Prussian armies in the campaign of 1870?

"Of all the elements of superiority which Prussia would possess, the greatest and most undeniable," wrote Baron Stoffel, the French military attaché at Berlin, in 1868, "will be that she will obtain from the composition of her Corps of Staff Officers ..." "My conviction on this point is so strong," he adds, "that I would once more express it, *Let us distrust the Prussian Staff*."

It is perhaps the brightest, as it has been the least recognised, of von Moltke's laurels, that he taught the Prussian generals the way to victory, and it is impossible not to realize, when we look at the extraordinary results of his teaching, that this was a work worthy of the greatest soldier, and it is impossible to overlook the fact that the permanent chief of the staff, whose duty was the instruction of the leaders of the army in the art of war, and the selection of those best fitted for such grave responsibility, was perhaps the most important factor in the military system of the Prussian kingdom.

Regarding tactical leading: – To those have never seen war, it may seem that the tactical strokes of the battle which have been characterized as skilful and even brilliant, were exceedingly obvious means of meeting the difficulties that presented themselves, and that any man of common sense, with a cool head and a stout heart, would, under similar circumstances, have acted in like manner. But what says von Clausewitz, first of military writers? "In war all is simple, but the simple is difficult." The weakness of our common humanity renders tactical leading no easy task. Without practical experience, the most complicated problems can be readily solved upon the map. To handle troops in battle exercises or on manœuvres, where an officer's military character is in some degree at stake, and quick decision is demanded, is a harder task, but its difficulties decrease with practice. But before the enemy, where the honour of the nation and the judgment of the present and of future generations are at stake, where history is making and the lives of thousands may be the cost of a mistake, there, under such a weight of responsibility, common sense, and even practised military judgment find it no simple matter to assert themselves. "Very frequently," says von der Goltz, "the time will be wanting for careful consideration. Sometimes the excitement does not permit it. Resolve, and this is a truth which those who have not seen war will do well to ponder over, is then something instinctive." And if this is true of the general, who is at least undisturbed by heavy fire, though borne down by a heavier responsibility, it is doubly true of those who lead the fighting line. Amid the infernal din of musketry and the crash of bursting shells, when death is rife, and the will struggles for the mastery with the body, when the excitement is intense, and events succeed one another with bewildering rapidity, when the whole attention is irresistibly attracted to the enemy in front, to the spot whence comes the hottest fire, and when at the same time the men must be held in hand and their every action supervised, is such the moment for calm and deliberate calculation? Can the man of common sense now be trusted, inexperienced and untrained, first, to discover the principle on which he should act, and that done, to conceive a resolve which promises success, and is yet in harmony with the operations of those about him?

There are few with experience of actual service who have not to acknowledge mistakes committed in the tumult of battle, which on the map or on the field of manœuvre would have been avoided. In the *Krieg Spiel*, or in peace exercises, human nature does not interpose, there is time for thought and consideration, the glance is calm and comprehensive, embracing front and flanks as far as the eye can range, the mind is undisturbed, and can deliberately weigh the merits of various modes of action. But in battle the officers and men of the fighting line can act only as it were by impulse, on the instinct of habit, and this instinct should be founded on true principles, created by constant practice, and confirmed by discipline.

A strong spirit of initiative, correct and deep-rooted instinct, and unity of action, are the qualities which are essential for the successful leading of the fighting line, and these are created by sound general principles being engrafted into the flesh and blood, thereby securing intelligent decision, by a careful training of the capacity for independent action, by the uniform tactical education of the officers, and by the constant practice of battle exercises.

These in conjunction, and these only, produce tactical skill. And without tactical skill, an army, however brave the individuals who compose it, will, like the French in 1870, lose every opportunity, and, as they did at Spicheren, will fail to profit by the enemy's mistakes.

We need not go further than Spicheren to understand the extraordinary influence of individual character in war.

When we compare the conduct of the Prussian leaders, anticipating orders and marching to the sound of the cannon with the indifference of Bazaine and the generals on whose dull ears the same sound fell, we cannot fail to realize what an important part is played by resolution allied to knowledge and by ignorance combined with negligence. An absolute want of energy was perhaps the most conspicuous failing of the French generals in 1870, whilst on the German side its existence was almost superabundant. It is instructive to note that in the campaign of 1805, the parts played in 1870 were reversed. On the one side was an army, practically acquainted with war and acting on sound general principles, on the other, an army without experience, and generals striving to apply, without considering the surrounding circumstances, the identical tactics and manœuvres successfully employed in a bygone era. On the one side was energy and initiative, tempered by prudence, on the other, rashness, and vacillation.

The courage of both was equal, the tactics of the Prussians were obsolete.

But the systems under which the armies were trained were also reversed. Napoleon inspired his soldiers with his own resolute and daring spirit: despising over-caution, he encouraged initiative, and officers and men were eager to reap the laurels which his example showed them might be won by skill and daring. The Prussians, on the other hand, relying on tradition, knew war as it had been, but not as it was; ardour and ambition were crushed, for high rank was the reward only of seniority or birth; the generals, unable to apply the tactics of Frederick, were without resources, nor had they learnt from recent history that the lightning stroke of the conqueror of Montenotte and Marengo was very different from the deliberate movements of the Austrian Marshals of the Seven Years' War.

The unflagging and calculated energy which distinguished the armies of Napoleon, which, personified in Blucher and Gneisenau, brought the Prussians up in time to Waterloo; in Lee and Jackson, held the hosts of the North at bay for four long years; in Grant and Sherman, carried Richmond at last; and in Moltke and his soldiers, defeated Austria in seven weeks, Imperial France in ninety days, is not the gift of nature, but the fruit of an abiding sense of duty, however inspired, whether by the influence of the commander, or by discipline, the outcome of familiarity with war and of the moral courage which fears not responsibility.

Energy unaccompanied by knowledge is of little worth. A man ignorant of the channels into which he should direct it, expends it uselessly, its effects are not apparent except for evil, and without the aid of discipline neither native resolution nor patriotic: enthusiasm will outlive the hardships and fatigues of a campaign. *To create a fruitful and abiding energy in both officers and men the Prussian system of command, of training, and of decentralization, was devised*, and the deeper our study of military history, the surer grows our conviction that in so doing they acted in accordance with the greatest of the fundamental principles of war, and that to this quality, not to superior numbers or courage, their extraordinary success was due. "The world has seen before," says Hamley, "war-like people and victorious armies, but never before a people or an army who have sought the secret of success with study so thorough, and with zeal and self-denial so stern as those which serve the German Emperor."

In the science of war there are certain invariable principles, and history proves for us that the most important is this: – The army which employs the tactics best adapted to the weapons in use, unless grave errors of generalship, like von Kamecke's at Spicheren, intervene, will prevail in battle. The French, in both the revolutionary and Napoleonic wars, defeated the heavy columns or rigid lines of other nations by means of clouds of skirmishers and small flexible columns. But in the Peninsula matters were reversed, the English made the battalions the tactical units, and these, on the offensive, advancing rapidly in quarter-distance columns and as rapidly deploying, or, on the defensive, forming independent fractions of the front of resistance, and charging independently for a short distance in line, were invariably successful against the heavy columns which their enemy had now resorted to. At Waterloo, again, Napoleon himself, although commanding an army of thoroughly well-trained veterans, unaccountably abandoned the battalion columns which had proved so effective in his campaign of the preceding year, and his massed divisions were everywhere defeated. It is a curious fact that the French, although recognising the superior efficacy of fire and flexibility, and generally developing them to the utmost against the continental nations, should, with a fatal persistency, have adopted the unwieldy formations and inferior "shock" tactics which had so invariably failed themselves, whenever they met the English. At the Alma and at Inkerman, shock and fire formations were again pitted against each other, and again the best tactics won. The same was the case in 1866. Before 1870, the Germans had foreseen, in some degree, the tactics best adapted to the breech-loader. They had recognised the efficacy and necessity of flank attacks, the strength of the offensive, the vigour and elasticity of a flexible line of small tactical units, and the ascendency of accurate individual fire.

By a system of careful individual training, theoretical and practical, applied both to officers and men, they provided for the prosecution of these correct tactics, and in an unbroken series of victories over a brave and warlike enemy, they found their due reward. Once again the best tacticians conquered, for the French, although wanting both in discipline and organization, were still perfectly capable, as we have seen at Spicheren, of rapid manœuvres, tenacious defence and vigorous attack, but the unskilful tactics of their leaders utterly wasted the martial qualities of the men.

It was not the commanders alone who were at fault. We have few details of the battalion and company fighting of the French regular army, but nevertheless, from the somewhat meagre records of Frossard's troops, we can gather sufficient evidence to prove the general incapacity of the subordinate leaders, confirmed as it is by the history of the remaining battles of the campaign.

We may instance the failure of the cavalry officers to procure information; the unskilful defence of the homesteads; the sudden and injudicious suspension of the counter-attack on the 39th Fusiliers in the Gifert Wood; the absence of any look-out from the trenches on the Rotherberg, prior to their capture by the 74th; the failure to engage or even to threaten strongly the right flank of the assailants of Stiring Wendel; the isolated counter-strokes, delivered by successive battalions, and unsupported by the artillery; together with the general reckless and uncontrolled fire of both the infantry and artillery.

The Emperor and his councillors relied on the experience of the army, although gained under obsolete conditions, on its courage and warlike aptitude, but they taught it nothing. The nation, blindly believing in the invincibility of its arms, and ignorant of the causes of success and defeat in war, acquiesced in this neglect, and in the hour of trial, the army, although conspicuous as ever for gallantry and devotion on the field of battle, proved unable to arrest the victorious march of a well-trained enemy. I do not for a moment intend to assert that the French, inferior in numbers, in organization, and in generalship, could possibly have succeeded in driving the Germans back across the frontier. But what I do affirm is this: – If the French officers had been educated on sound tactical principles, if they had recognised the power of the offensive, the necessity of information, the importance of united action, and the value of controlled fire, and had learnt by constant practice – the only possible method – to act upon these principles; if, again, the most ordinary duties of the staff and regimental officers, those pertaining to reconnaissance, to the outpost line, to the maintenance of communications and to the defence of posts, had been properly carried out, not only would the mistakes of the generals have often been prevented and their consequences always mitigated, but the losses and the difficulties of the Germans have been greatly increased, the unparalleled catastrophes of Sedan and Metz avoided, and the nation, under cover of the protracted resistance of the regular army, have gained time to develop its immense resources, and have at least obtained more favourable terms.

France was betrayed by her Government, which had cried "We are ready!" when all was in confusion, and had neglected to instruct her soldiers. Ninety days after the declaration of war the Imperial army had ceased to exist. It had been engaged in eight great battles. More than once was victory within its grasp, but the incapacity of the leaders let it slip. More than once was it surprised, and almost on every battle-field the lack of tactical skill and of that ready initiative which practice alone gives, prevented its officers from recognising and using favourable opportunities. In 1870, for the first time, an army trained upon the old system encountered with equal armament, an army trained upon the new, and even when numbers and position were against it the triumph of the latter was so complete, that all question as to the value of tactical knowledge and the practical and individual training of both officers and men, was at once and for ever set at rest.

Spicheren is a remarkable instance of the good results of the Prussian system. It has often been cited as an instance of the superior fighting qualities of their army. For this opinion there is no warrant. The position on the heights was formidable. But the very indifferent tactics of the French surrendered all its advantages. The assailant gained the crest of the plateau without loss or difficulty, and the real battle was fought out on equal terms as regards the ground. The storm of the Rotherberg was a daring feat of arms, but it was a surprise, and, as a defensive post, the spur had all the disadvantage of steep hill-sides which were not commanded from the crest. This achievement, as well as the capture of the Golden Bremm, the two most brilliant incidents of the engagement, were, moreover, made possible by the very effective aid of the artillery. It is true, also, that the Prussians drove an equal number of French infantry from the Gifert Wood, but against the latter was the moral effect of the capture of the Rotherberg, and the out-flanking position of the 48th Regiment along the Pfaffen border. The Spicheren Wood was also carried, but here again the French had a very strong second line, from which their reserves never moved. On the left, in the copse, the Prussians were really heavily defeated. Only the opportune intervention of the 13th Division saved the battle.

The true causes of success were the celerity with which every body of troops within hearing marched to the sound of the cannon; the combination of the artillery and infantry; the energy of the attack; the moral advantages of the latter in a close country, where the defender is always uncertain of the numbers opposed to him; the constant turning movements; and, lastly, the errors of the French generals. At no single point did the Prussians show themselves superior in courage or hardihood to their opponents. But they did not, like their opponents, rely on natural attributes or martial spirit alone. Officers and men had received the highest training, both of mind and body, that was possible in peace. It was this training which turned the scale.

APPENDIX I

I.1 STRENGTH OF THE PRUSSIAN FORCES AT THE BATTLE OF SPICHEREN[1]

			Total Battalions	Squadrons	Batteries
First Army					
I Army Corps	4 H/I, 4 L/I		-	-	2
VII Army Corps	13th Division	55th Regiment	3	-	-
		7th Jägers	1	-	-
		8th Hussars	-	4	
		5, 6, II, III/7	-	-	4
	14th Division	The whole except 8/39	11¾	4	4
VIII Army Corps	16th Division	40th Regiment	3	-	-
		9th Hussars	-	4	-
		VI, 6L/8	-	-	2
Second Army					
III Army Corps	5th Division	The whole except 1/52	12¾	4	4
	6th Division	20th Regiment	3	-	-
		3 batteries	-	-	3
5th Cavalry Division	19th Dragoons		-	4	-
	11th Hussars		-	4	-
	17th Hussars		-	4	-
6th Cavalry Division	6th Cuirassiers		-	4	-
	3rd Uhlans		-	1	-
			34½	37	18

The average strength of 13th Division – 930 rifles per battalion
The average strength of 14th Division – 925 rifles per battalion
The average strength of 16th Division – 900 rifles per battalion
The average strength of 5th Division – 940 rifles per battalion
The average strength of 6th Division – 920 rifles per battalion
The average strength of Squadrons – 140 sabres

Totals	**Infantry**	**Cavalry**	**Artillery**
VII Army Corps	14,589	1,120	48
VIII Army Corps	2,700	460	12
III Army Corps	12,905	560	36
5th Cavalry Division		1,680	12
6th Cavalry Division		700	
	30,194	4,520	108

1 From the *Militär Wochenblatt.*

I.2 STRENGTH OF THE FRENCH FORCES AT THE BATTLE OF SPICHEREN

	Battalions	Squadrons	Batteries	Engineer Companies
2nd Corps d'Armée	39	16	15	2

Average strength of battalion, 620
Average strength of squadrons, 130
Average strength of engineer company, 119

Totals:
24,419 infantry (including sappers)
3,200 cavalry
90 guns

I.3 PRUSSIAN LOSSES

III Army Corps

	Officers	Men	Horses
48th Regiment	25	548	–
8th Grenadiers	12	380	–
12th Grenadiers	35	771	–
52nd Regiment	4	116	–
3rd Jagers	3	56	–
12th Dragoons	–	1	2
3rd F. A. Regiment	4	39	42
Sanitary Detachment	–	1	–

VII Army Corps
13th Division

	Officers	Men	Horses
55th Regiment	3	85	–
7th Jägers	1	7	–
7th F.A. Regiment	1	–	1
8th Hussars	–	–	4

14th Division

	Officers	Men	Horses
Staff	1	–	–
39th Fusiliers	27	628	–
74th Regiment	36	661	–
53rd Regiment	14	209	–
77th Regiment	26	602	–
15th Hussars	–	1	–
7th F.A. Regiment	2	24	–
Sanitary Detachment	1	–	43

VIII Army Corps

	Officers	Men	Horses
40th Fusiliers	25	468	-
9th Hussars	–	5	18
8th F.A. Regiment	–	10	17

5th Cavalry Division

	Officers	Men	Horses
19th Hussars	1	7	11
11th Hussars	–	9	5
17th Hussars	2	19	32

6th Cavalry Division

6th Cuirassiers – 1 man, 4 horses wounded

Total Casualties

	Officers	Men	Total
Killed	49	794	843
Wounded	174	3482	3656
Missing	–	372	372
	223	4648	4871

In the 12th Grenadiers, the regiment which incurred the heaviest loss, the casualties were thus distributed:

	Officers	Men	
First Battalion	13	356 }	
Second Battalion	13	210 }	8 officers & 132 men killed
Fusilier Battalion	9	206 }	
	35	772	

	Officers	Men
The First Company	5	76
The Second Company	3	128
The Fourth Company	4	86
The Ninth Company	5	62

Out of a total of 62 officers the regiment lost 36.

In the next battle in which it was engaged (Vionville), it suffered a further diminution of 13 officers and 424 men; at Gravelotte, two days afterwards, it mustered but 11 officers and 1,800 men, and there were but two company officers, and these second lieutenants, to each battalion.

The three companies of the 8th Grenadiers, which captured the south-west angle of the Gifert Wood by a charge across the saddle of the Rotherberg, lost 8 officers and 289 men; the five companies engaged in the Spicheren Wood, 5 officers and 68 men.

The 77th Regiment also suffered heavily:

	Officers	Men
First Battalion	7	147
Second Battalion	11	221
Fusilier Battalion (captured Golden Bremm and Baraque Mouton)	7	234

I.4 FRENCH LOSSES[2]

	Officers	Men	Total
Staff	4	-	4
First Division			
3rd Chasseurs	6	225	231
32nd Regiment	20	310	330
55th Regiment	5	200	205
76th Regiment	18	217	235
77th Regiment	8	280	288
Sub-total	57	1232	1289
Second Division			
8th Regiment	15	295	310
23rd Regiment	7	?	?
66th Regiment	12	201	213
67th Regiment	4	?	?
Sub-total	38	?	?
Third Division			
10th Chasseurs	10	215	235
2nd Regiment	24	357	381
63rd Regiment	14	158	172
24th Regiment	25	462	487
40th Regiment	33	531	564
Sub-total	106	1723	1829
Cavalry			
5th Chasseurs	1	9	10
7th Dragoons	2	8	10
12th Dragoons	5	21	26
Artillery			
Artillery	3	57	60
Engineers			
13th Company	3	29	32
Total casualties	219	?	?

The French battalions mustered about 20 officers each, and the missing, who included both the wounded left in the woods and those captured, amounted to 44 officers and 2,052 men. Many of the former doubtless died of their wounds, and it is

2 The breakdown of losses are taken from individual regimental histories. Frossard's Report gives the following figures: First Division 1185, Second Division 731, Third Division 1784, Cavalry 46, Artillery 60, Engineers 23. His overall total (although it does not compute from these sub-totals) is 4078.

useless, therefore, to attempt a detailed list of the killed and wounded. The losses of some of the batteries have been alluded to in the body of the work.[3] It may be mentioned that the casualty lists of the German officers contain the names of the non-commissioned officers holding rank of vice-sergeant major and ensign, whilst those of the French have only the names of those who held commissions. Were the former eliminated, the loss of the 12th Grenadiers, in officers, would sink to 29, of the 74th to 30, of the 39th to 22.

Both battalions of Chasseurs and also the 2nd Regiment suffered very heavily. The former lost each a third of their strength, and the latter, of which four companies remained in reserve the whole day, and the total effective strength did not exceed 1,700 bayonets, lost 24 officers out of 52 engaged, and 357 men out of 1,140, of whom, according to the Regimental History, 109 were killed or died of wounds.

I.5 NUMBERS ENGAGED

The numbers actually engaged on either side were:
French, 23,679 infantry, 72 guns, and 18 mitrailleuses
Prussian, 26,494 infantry, and 66 guns.

I.6 PERCENTAGE OF LOSS

French 17:36
Prussian 17:21

I.7 NOTE

It has been suggested to me that I should make some reference to the effect smokeless powder, a more powerful artillery, and a longer-ranging and more accurate rifle would have had upon the course and issue of the battle. I can only say that, in my own opinion, although the losses would probably have been greater, the tactics would not have been materially affected. Smokeless powder would have made no difference whatever. The Prussian battalions attacked certain parts of the position regardless whether they were held or not. The fact that no enemy was to be seen in the Gifert Wood or Stiring Copse was not taken into consideration. The attack was pressed on until the losses became too heavy or the fire ceased. As regards the rifle, the chassepôt was little inferior to those now in use, and it is noteworthy that the Prussians on the offensive were able to approach within 600 yards, that is, within effective range, with very little difficulty. The decisive fighting took place inside 300 yards, a distance at which even the needle-gun was almost as effective as the rifle of to-day. Magazine fire would possibly have saved the Golden Bremm, and made the recapture of the Copse a more costly operation, but it is a weapon as useful to the attack as the defence.

3 See page 183.

APPENDIX II
GERMAN ORDER OF BATTLE

FIRST ARMY. GENERAL VON STEINMETZ

VII Army Corps – General von Zastrow	13th Infantry Division Lieutenant-General von Glumer	25th Brigade	13th Regiment 73rd Fusiliers
		26th Brigade Major-General von de Goltz	14th Regiment 55th Regiment
		Divisional troops	7th Jägers 8th Hussars 4 Batteries, 7th F.A. Regiment
	14th Infantry Division Lieutenant-General von Kamecke	27th Brigade Major-General von François	39th Fusiliers 74th Regiment
		28th Brigade Major-General von Woyna	53rd Regiment 77th Regiment
		Divisional troops	15th Hussars 4 Batteries, 7th F.A. Regiment
	Corps Artillery	6 Batteries, 7th F.A. Regiment	
	Corps Troops	7th Pioneer Battalion 7th Train Battalion	

VIII Army Corps – General von Goeben			
	15th Infantry Division	29th Brigade	33rd Fusiliers 60th Regiment
		30th Brigade	28th Regiment 67th Regiment
		Divisional troops	8th Jägers 7th Hussars 4 Batteries, 8th F.A. Regiment
	16th Infantry Division Lieutenant-General von Barnekow	31st Brigade	29th Regiment 69th Regiment
		32nd Brigade Colonel von Rex	40th Fusiliers 72nd Regiment
		Divisional troops	9th Hussars 4 Batteries, 8th F.A. Regiment
	Corps Artillery	7 Batteries, 8th F.A. Regiment	
	Corps Troops	8th Pioneer Battalion 8th Train Battalion	

3rd Cavalry Division		
	6th Cavalry Brigade	8th Cuirassiers 7th Uhlans
	7th Cavalry Brigade	5th Uhlans 13th Uhlans
	Divisional troops	1 H.A. Battery, 7th Regiment

SECOND ARMY. HRH PRINCE FREDERICK CHARLES

III Army Corps – General von Alvensleben			
	5th Infantry Division, Lieutenant-General von Stulpnagel	9th Brigade, Major-General von Doring	8th Body Guard Grenadiers 48th Regiment
		10th Brigade, Major-General von Schwerin	12th Grenadiers 52nd Regiment
		Divisional troops	3rd Jägers 12th Dragoons 4 Batteries, 3rd F.A. Regiment
	6th Infantry Division, Lieutenant-General von Buddenbrock	11th Brigade	20th Regiment 35th Fusiliers
		12th Brigade	24th Regiment 64th Regiment
		Divisional troops	2nd Dragoons 4 Batteries, 3rd F.A. Regiment
	Corps Artillery	6 Batteries, 3rd F.A. Regiment	
	Corps Troops	3rd Pioneer Battalion 3rd Train Battalion	

SECOND ARMY. HRH PRINCE FREDERICK CHARLES

5th Cavalry Division – General von Rheinbaben	11th Cavalry Brigade	4th Cuirassiers 13th Uhlans 19th Dragoons
	12th Cavalry Brigade	7th Cuirassiers 16th Uhlans 13th Dragoons
	13th Cavalry Brigade	10th Hussars 11th Hussars 17th Hussars
	Divisional Troops	1 H.A. Battery, 4th Regiment 1 H.A. Battery, 10th Regiment
6th Cavalry Division – General von Rheinbaben (temporary)	14th Cavalry Brigade	6th Cuirassers 3rd Uhlans 15th Uhlans
	15th Cavalry Brigade	3rd Hussars 16th Hussars
	Divisional troops	1 H.A. Battery, 3rd F.A. Regiment

FRENCH ORDER OF BATTLE

Second Corps D'Armée – General Frossard	1st Division – Vergé	1st Brigade – Valazé	3rd Chasseurs 22nd Line 55th Line
		2nd Brigade – Jolivet	76th Line 77th Line
		Divisional Troops	3 Batteries, 5th Regiment (1 Mitrailleuse) 1 Sapper Company, 2nd Regiment
	2nd Division – Bataille	1st Brigade – Pouget	12th Chasseurs 8th Line 23rd Line
		2nd Brigade – Bastoul	66th Line 67th Line
		Divisional Troops	3 Batteries, 5th Regiment (1 Mitrailleuse) 1 Sapper Company, 2nd Regiment
	3rd Division – Laveaucoupet	1st Brigade – Doens	10th Chasseurs 2nd Line 63rd Line
		2nd Brigade – Micheler	24th Line 40th Line
		Divisional Troops	3 Batteries, 15th Regiment (1 Mitrailleuse) 1 Sapper company, 3rd Regiment
	Reserve Artillery	8 Batteries, 5th, 15th and 17th Regiments	
Cavalry Division Valabrègue	1st Brigade Valabrègue		4th Chasseurs 5th Chasseurs
	2nd Brigade Bachelier		7th Dragoons 12th Dragoons
Third Corps d'Armée – Marshall Bazaine	1st Division. Montaudon 2nd Division. Castagny 3rd Division. Metman 4th Division. Decæn Cavalry Division		

Fourth Corps d'Armée General L'Admirault — 3 Infantry and 1 Cavalry Division

Lapassets' Brigade of Fifth (De Failly's) Corps d'Armée

APPENDIX III
QUESTIONS TO BE WORKED OUT BY THE READER

(GUIDES TO THE ANSWERS WILL BE FOUND ON THE PAGES REFERRED TO.)

1. How would you dispose the outposts of 1 battalion of 500 men and 3 squadrons on the Saarbrucken Ridge? What orders would you give as to patrolling? Pages 68–69.
2. How would you dispose the outposts of 3 battalions, 40th, 1 Company, 69th, and 3 squadrons, and 1 battery? Pages 72–73
3. How would you occupy the Saarbrucken Ridge in case of attack, and how would you conduct the action? Pages 74–79
4. Draw up orders for withdrawal of von Gneisenau's detachment to Hilsbach. Page 79
5. How would you dispose of the three divisions of the 2nd Corps after withdrawing from the ridge? Pages 84 and 119–120
6. Draw up general directions for advance of Second Army to the Saar, and, co-operation in battle, if necessary, of the First Army. Page 90
7. How would you move the 7th Corps from Trêves to line Wadern-Saarburg? Page 92

7a. How would you disposal the 3rd, 5th, and 6th Cavalry Divisions as a screen? Page 96

8. Draw up dispositions for the advance of the Second Army to the line Neunkirchen-Zweibrucken, and subsequent deployment. Pages 98 and 101–102
9. Formations of 13th and 14th Divisions on the march. Pages 105–106
10. Formation of 9th Brigade on the march. Page 108–109

10a. Give directions for reconnaissances to be carried out by 11th and 13th Cavalry Divisions, and indicate the points to be visited. Pages 109–110

11. As commander of 14th Division, what would be your action on learning at Guichenbach that the Saarbrucken Ridge had been evacuated? Page 112
12. As commander of 14th Division what would be your action on reaching the ridge? Pages 113–114
13. As commander of 14th Division, what would be your action on learning that the enemy was retreating? Page 117
14. As commander of 2nd Corps, how would you have occupied the Spicheren position? Pages 129–131
15. Arrange for occupation of Drathzug and defence of the railroad by II/74. Page 136
16. As commander of 14th Division, give directions for the attack of the French position. Pages 135–136 and 159–160

16a. How would you have disposed of your four batteries? Page 136

17. As commanding II/74, what would have been your action when III/39 began to fall back? Pages 137–138

18. As commander of 14th Division, how would you have supported attack of the 74th in the Rotherberg? Page 141
19. As commander of the 2nd Corps, how would you have dealt with the Prussians at 2.30 pm? Pages 145–146 and 222
20. As commander of 13th Division (advanced guard at Wehrden), how would you have acted on hearing the caution and receiving the reports quoted? Form up your advanced guard. Pages 149 and 209
21. How would you have carried out the counter-stroke at 2.30 pm? Page 152
22. As General von Goeben, draw up a plan of action to relieve the pressure on the troops holding the Rotherberg and Gifert Wood? Page 163
23. Draw up the 2 battalions (8 companies) of 48th Regiment in attack formation. Page 163
24. What should have been the object of the six batteries on the Galgenberg? Page 168
25. Make dispositions for an attack on Toll House, Golden Bremm, and Baraque Mouton, indicating line to be followed by F/77. Page 172–173
26. Describe how you would have employed the next aiming battalion. Page 183
27. State how you would have met Bataille's counter-stroke after the French infantry had abandoned the N.W. portion of the Spicheren Heights. Page 189
28. How would you have supported the Prussian infantry on the Heights? Pages 193–194
29. How would you have disposed of the 6 battalions which had just arrived on the Ridge? Page 198
30. How would you have protected the exposed flank, and have formed the troops for the attack of the Spicheren Wood? Page 199
31. Describe how you would have drawn up the 55th Regiment as a rear guard. Page 206
32. Form up advanced guard of 13th Division for the attack of the Kaninchenberg. Page 209
33. State what you would have done, as commanding one of Bazaine's divisions, when you heard the sound of cannon to the front. Page 218
34. How would you have employed the Prussian cavalry during the battle? Page 238

FURTHER READING

A guide prepared by Duncan Rogers

Official histories

France, Army, État Major, Section Historique, *La Guerre de 1870/1, publiée par la* Revue d'Histoire, *rédigée à la Section historique de l'État-Major de l'Armée* (Paris, 1901-13, 22 vols)

Germany, Army, Generalstab, Kriegsgeschichtliche Abteilung, *Der deutsch-französische Krieg 1870-1871*, 5 vols)

General histories of the War

Ambert, J., *Gaulois et Germains. Récit militaires* (Paris, 1883-85, 4 vols)

Hiltl, G., *Der französische Krieg von 1870 und 1871: nach den besten Quellen, persönlichen Mitteilungen und eigenen Erlebnissen geschildert* (Bielefeld, 1913)

Lehautcourt, P., *Histoire de la Guerre de 1870-71* (Paris, 1893-1908, 15 vols)

Lehautcourt, P., *Guerre de 1870-1871. Aperçu et commentaries* (Paris, 1910)

Lonlay, D. de, *Français et Allemands, histoire anecdotique de la guerre de 1870-71* (Paris, 1888-89, 6 vols)

Pflug-Harttung, J., *Krieg und Sieg 1870-71, ein Gedenkbuch* (Berlin, 1895)

Rousset, L., *Histoire Générale de la Guerre Franco-Allemande (1870–1871)* (Paris, 1910, 2 vols)

Rousset, L., *Les Combattants de 1870–71* (Paris, 1891, 2 vols)

Scheibert, J., *Der Krieg von 1870-71. Auf Grund des deutschen und französischen Generalstabswerkes und zahlreicher neuerer Quellenwerke* (Berlin, 1906)

Operations in Alsace-Lorraine

Bonnal, G.A., *L'esprit de la guerre moderne: La Manoeuvre de Saint-Privat, 18 juillet-18 août 1870* (Paris, 1904-12, 3 vols)

Picard, E., *1870. Perte de l'Alsace. La guerre en Lorraine. Sedan* (Paris, 1907-10, 5 vols)

The Battle of Spicheren

Anon., *Bataille de Spickeren envisagée au point de vue stratégique, traduit de l'allemand par M. Weil* (Paris, 1872)

Anon., *Erlebnisse in den Tagen v. 2.-9. August 1870. Von e. Saarbrücker* (Eckartsburg, Barmen, 1871)

Anon., *Führer zum Spicherer Schlachtfelde durch Saarbrücken, St Johann und Umgebung* (Saarbrücken, 1884)

Anon., *Illustrierter Fremdenführer für die Besucher des Spickerer Schlachtfeldes* (Saarbrücken, 1895)

Anon., *Journée du 6 Août 1870 par un Lorrain. Frœschwiller-Forbach* (Paris, 1887)

Anon., *Skizze von der Schlacht bei Saarbrücken am 6. August 1870 nach dem officiellen Bericht* (Berlin, 1870)

Appleton, L., *Reminiscences of a Visit to the Battle Fields of Sedan, Gravelotte, Spicheren, and Wörth* (London, 1872)

Beck, Oberstlieut. E., *Die Einmarschkämpfe des deutschen Heeres im August 1870. Taktische Studien. 2e fascicule: Die Schlacht bei Spichern* (Teschen, 1873)

Bleibtreu, C., *Die Eingangskämpfe bei Spichern* (Stuttgart, 1903)

Cardinal von Widdern, G., *Kritische Tage. Theil 1, Die Initiative und die gegenseitige Unterstützung in der deutschen Heeres- und Truppenführung. Bd.3, Die Krisis von Saarbrücken-Spicheren. Heft 1, Die Kavallerie-Divisionen während des Armee-Aufmarsches : 1. bis 7. August 1870* (Berlin, 1898)

Cardinal von Widdern, G., *Kritische Tage. Theil 1, Die Initiative und die gegenseitige Unterstützung in der deutschen Heeres- und Truppenführung. Bd.3, Die Krisis von Saarbrücken-Spicheren. Heft 2, Die Führung der I. und II. Armee und deren Vortruppen : 31. Juli bis 6. August* (Berlin, 1899)

Cardinal von Widdern, G., *Kritische Tage. Theil 1, Die Initiative und die gegenseitige Unterstützung in der deutschen Heeres- und Truppenführung. Bd.3, Die Krisis von Saarbrücken-Spicheren. Heft 3, Die Befehlsführung am Schlachttage von Spicheren und am Tage darauf 6. und 7. August 1870* (Berlin, 1900)

Castagny, Gén. de, *Réponse à la brochure du général Frossard, en ce qui concerne la division de Castagny pendant la journée de Forbach* (Paris, 1870)

Claretie, J., *La France envahie (juillet à septembre 1870): Forbach et Sedan. Impressions et souvenirs de guerre* (Paris, 1871)

Cornet, N.-J., *Une Quinzaine à Spickeren après la bataille du 6 août 1870* (Verviers, 1870)

Frossard, C.A., *Rapport sur les Opérations du deuxième corps de l'armée du Rhin dans la campagne de 1870* (Paris, 1871)

Germany, Army, Generalstab, Kriegsgeschichtliche Abteilung, *Kriegsgeschichtliche Einzelschriften Heft 18: Das Generalkommando des III Armee Korps bei Spicheren und Vionville* (Berlin, 1895)

Goltz, C. Freiherr von der, *Die Operationen der Zweiten Armee bis zur Kapitulation von Metz* (Berlin, 1873)

Grouard, A., *Woerth et Forbach* (Paris, 1905)

Herrmann, K., *Die Invasion der Franzosen in Saarbrücken im August 1870* (St Johann-Saarbrücken, 1888)

Hoffmann, P., *Chronik der Gemeinde Stieringen-Wendel mit Berücksichtigung der Kriegsereignisse am 6. August 1870 bei Stieringen, Spichern und Forbach* (Oberginingen, 1905)

Hucher, Lt Col., *Troisième conférence d'histoire. 1870. Spicheren* (Limoges, 1921)

Kläber, H., *Die Preussische Artillerie in der Schlacht bei Spicheren am 6. August 1870* (Berlin, 1898)

Krieg, T., *Constantin von Alvensleben, General der Infanterie : ein militärisches Lebensbild* (Berlin, 1903)

Krosigk, H. von, *General-Feldmarschall von Steinmetz : aus den Familienpapieren dargestellt* (Berlin, 1900)

Kunz, Major H., *Wanderungen über die Schlachtfelder von Saarbrücken und von Metz. Ein Reisebericht* (Berlin, 1896)

Lattorf, v., *Denkmäler u. Erinnerungszeichen auf den Schlachtfeldern bei Saarbrücken* (St Johann-Saarbrücken, 1877)

Ley, Prof Dr, *Zur Erinnerung an die Juli- und Augusttage 1870* (Saarbrücken, n.d.)
Maistre, P.A., *Spicheren (6 Août 1870)* (Paris, 1908)
Metman, gén., *Réponse à M. le gén. Frossard. Bataille de Forbach-Spicheren* (Paris, 1872)
Montaudon, gén., *Réponse à M. le gén. Frossard. Bataille de Forbach-Spicheren* (Versailles, 1871)
Pelet-Narbonne, G. von, *Verfolgung und Aufklärung der deutschen Reiterei am Tage nach Spicheren (7. August 1870) : zugleich eine Richtigstellung und Vorausgabe zum zweiten Auflage der Schrift: Die Reiterei der Ersten und Zweiten Deutschen Armee in den Tagen vom 7. bis zum 15. August 1870* (Berlin, 1901)
Quincampoix, J., *La vérité sur Forbach* (Besançon, 1908)
Röchling, C., "Meine Erlebnisse in Saarbrücken 1870" in *Universum* VIII. Jahrgang, 1891/92
Römer, J., *Die Vorpostengefechte bei Saarbrücken v. 18. Juli bis 5 Aug. 1870 u. die Schlacht bei Spicheren am 6. Aug. 1870* (Saarbrücken, 1873)
Ruppersberg, A., *Saarbrücker Kriegs-Chronik. Ereignisse in und bei Saarbrücken und St. Johann sowie am Spicherer Berge 1870* (Saabrücken, 1895)
Schell, A. von, *Die Operationen der Ersten Armee unter Steinmetz* (Berlin, 1872)
Schick, M., *Die Schlacht bei Saarbrücken am 6. August 1870* (Reutlingen, 1871)
Tendering, Dr F., *Die Schlacht bei Spicheren am 6. August 1870. Vortrag* (Saarbrücken, 1882)
[Various], *Selbsterlebtes 1870/71* (Saarbrücken, 1894)
Vorberg, C., *Das Heldentum des Dampfes* (St Johann-Saarbrücken, n.d.)
Winn, C.A., *What I saw of the War at the battles of Speicheren, Gorze and Gravelotte* (London, 1871)
Zernin, G., *Das Leben des Königlich Preußischen Generals der Infanterie August von Goeben* (Berlin, 1895-97, 2 vols)
Zins, R., *La bataille de Spicheren* (Annecy-le-Vieux, 2001)

French regimental histories[1]

II Corps, 1st Division, 1st Brigade

Bertrand, Capt. A., *Historique du 3e bataillon de chasseurs à pied* (Saint-Dié, 1900)
Papot, E., *Souvenirs d'un volontaire de 1870. 3e bataillon de chasseurs à pied: 10e de marche* (Châlons, 1871)
Batault, Lt., *Historique du 22e régiment d'infanterie (1774-1889)* (unpublished manuscript, Archives Historiques de la Guerre)

II Corps, 1st Division, 2nd Brigade

Landais, Capt., *Honneur et Patrie! Historique du 76e régiment d'infanterie depuis 1677 jusqu'en 1873* (Paris, 1874)
Fresnel, Cmdt. du, *Un régiment à travers l'histoire. Le 76e, ex-1er léger* (Paris, 1894)
Vilarem, Capt., *Historique du 77e régiment d'infanterie, ex-La Marck, ex-2e léger* (Niort, 1901)

1 Only major regimental works have been listed. French regiments published a profuse number of pamphlet-type publications which contain only a modicum of information, these have been omitted from this list.

II Corps, 2nd Division, 1st Brigade

Jeanneney, Capt., *Glorieux passé d'un régiment. 8e d'infanterie (1562-1899)* (Paris, 1899)

Ceccaty, Lt. de, *Historique du 23e régiment d'infanterie (1656-1893)* (unpublished manuscript, Archives Historiques de la Guerre)

II Corps, 2nd Division, 2nd Brigade

Devaurieux, gén., *Souvenirs et observations sur la campagne de 1870 (armée du Rhin) … d'aprés mes notes personnelles prises au jour le jour comme lieutenant au 66e régiment d'infanterie* (Paris, 1909)

Galdemar, Capt., *Historique du 66e régiment d'infanterie (1672-1821)* (unpublished manuscript, Archives Historiques de la Guerre)

Anon., *Historique du 67e régiment d'infanterie (1672 à nos jours)* (unpublished manuscript, Archives Historiques de la Guerre)

II Corps, 3rd Division, 1st Brigade

Noret, *Historique du 2e régiment d'infanterie (1569-1873)* (unpublished manuscript, Archives Historiques de la Guerre)

Molard, Capt. J., *Historique du 63e régiment d'infanterie (1672-1887)* (Paris, 1887)

II Corps, 3rd Division, 2nd Brigade

Amiot, Cmdt., *Historique du 24e régiment d'infanterie* (Paris, 1893)

Amiot, Cmdt., *Historique du 24e régiment d'infanterie. Ephémerides et anecdotes* (Paris, 1894)

Coste, Sous-Lt. E., *Historique du 40e régiment d'infanterie de ligne* (Paris, 1887)

II Corps, artillery & engineers

Uzac, Capt., *Historique du 5e régiment d'artillerie de 1720 à 1893, comprenant l'historique du 5e régiment d'artillerie à cheval de 1794 à 1814* (privately published, 1893)

Publication de la Réunion des officers, *Historique du 15e régiment d'artillerie* (Paris, 1875)

Anon., *17e régiment d'artillerie. Historique* (unpublished manuscript, Archives Historiques de la Guerre)

Azibert, Cmdt. et al, *Historique du 2e régiment du genie* (Paris, 1893)

Cavalry Division Valabrègue

1st Brigade

Féraud-Giraud, Capt., *Historique du 4e regiment de chasseurs jusqu'au 15 mars de l'année 1888* (unpublished manuscript, Archives Historiques de la Guerre)

Courtez-Lapeyrat, Capt., *Historique du 5e regiment de chasseurs* (Paris, 1888)

2nd Brigade

Cossé-Brissac, Lt. R. de, *Historique du 7e regiment de dragons (1673-1909)* (Paris, 1909)

Allenou, Capt., *Historique du 7e regiment de dragons (1673-1890)* (unpublished manuscript, Archives Historiques de la Guerre)

Gabriel, l'abbé, *Dieu, Honneur et Patrie. Histoire du 12e regiment de dragons* (Verdun, 1882)

German regimental histories
First Army

VII Corps, 13th Infantry Division, 25th Brigade

Gescher, L., *Geschichte des 1. Westfälischen Infanterie-Regiments Nr. 13 während des Feldzuges gegen Frankreich 1870/72, nebst einer kurzen Uebersicht über die Jahre 1872/79* (Münster, 1880)

Blume, W. von, *Geschichte des Infanterie-Regiments Herwarth von Bittenfeld (1. Westfälisches) Nr. 13 im 19. Jahrhundert* (Berlin, 1910)

Breyding, E. von & O. von Kortzfleisch, *Geschichte des Füsilier-Regiments General-Feldmarschall Prinz Albrecht von Preussen (Hannoversches) Nr. 73 : 1866-1891* (Berlin, 1891)

VII Corps, 13th Infantry Division, 26th Brigade

Krafft, H., *Geschichte des Infanterie-Regiments Graf Schwerin (3. pommerschen) Nr 14 bis zum Beginne des Jahres 1900* (Berlin, 1901)

Blomberg, O. von & S. von Leszczynski, *Geschichte des 6. westfälischen Infanterie-Regiments Nr 55, von seiner Errichtung bis zum 2. Sept. 1877* (Detmold, 1877)

Meysenbug, H. von, *Erinnerungen eines alten Fünfundfünfzigers aus der Zeit des deutsch-französischen Krieges der Jahre 1870/71* (Berlin, 1910)

VII Corps, 13th Infantry Division, divisional troops

Rudorff, G., *Geschichte des westfälischen Jäger-Bataillons Nr. 7 von seiner Errichtung bis zur Jetztzeit* (Berlin, 1897)

Anon., *Geschichte des 1. Westfälischen Husaren-Regiments Nr. 8* (Berlin, 1882)

Schreiber, C., *Geschichte der fünften leichten Batterie Westfälischen Feld-Artillerie-Regiments Nr 7 (Avantgardenbatterie der 13. Division) während des deutschen Krieges gegen Frankreich im Jahre 1870/71* (Münster, 1872)

Hamm, A. & K. Moewes, *Geschichte des 1. Westfälischen Feld-Artillerie-Regiments Nr 7* (Berlin, 1891)

VII Corps, 14th Infantry Division, 27th Brigade

Rintelen, W., *Geschichte des niederrheinischen Füsilier-Regiments Nr 39 während der ersten fünfundsiebenzig Jahre seines Bestehens 1818-1893* (Berlin, 1893)

Nedden, A. zur, *Geschichte des I. Hannoverschen Infanterie-Regiments Nr 74 und des vormaligen Königlich Hannoverschen 3. Infanterie-Regiments : 1813 bis 1903* (Berlin, 1903)

VII Corps, 14th Infantry Division, 28th Brigade

Richter, W.R., *Geschichte des 5. westfälischen Infanterie-Regiments Nr 53 während der ersten fünfundzwanzig Jahre seines Bestehens (4. Juli 1860 bis 4. Juli 1885)* (Berlin, 1885)

Leuckfeld, H., *Geschichte des 5. Westfälischen Infanterie-Regiments Nr 53* (Berlin, 1910)

Conrady, E. von, *Die Geschichte des 2. hannoverschen Infanterie-Regiments Nr 77 : Die ersten 25 Jahre 1866 bis 1891* (Berlin, 1892)

Schimmelpfeng, H., *Geschichte des 2. Hannoverschen Infanterie-Regiments Nr. 77 (1866-1913)* (Oldenburg, 1913)

VII Corps, 14th Infantry Division, divisional troops

Anon., *Geschichte des Hannoverschen Husaren-Regiments Nr. 15, jetzigen Husaren-Regiments "Königin Wilhelmina der Niederlande (Hannoversches) Nr. 15"* (Wandsbek, 1903)

VII Corps, corps troops

Hoffmann, J.O., *Geschichte des Westfälischen Pionier-Bataillons Nr.7* (Berlin, 1888)

VIII Corps, 15th Infantry Division, 29th Brigade[2]

Lehfeldt, R., *Geschichte des Füsilier-Regiments Graf Roon (ostpreussischen) Nr 33* (Berlin, 1877)

VIII Corps, 15th Infantry Division, 30th Brigade

Neff, W., *Geschichte des Infanterie-Regiments von Goeben (2. Rheinischen) Nr 28* (Berlin, 1890)

Charisius, R., *Bei den 28ern 1870-1871. Kriegserinnerungen* (Düsseldorf, 1896)

Heinrich, M., *Die ersten 25 Jahre des 4. magdeburgischen Infanterie-Regiments Nr 67* (Berlin, 1885)

Anon., *Bis in die Kriegsgefangenschaft. Erinnerungen aus der Zeit des grossen Kampfes von 1870-1871. Von einem 67er* (Berlin, 1893)

VIII Corps, 15th Infantry Division, divisional troops

Weber, L., *Geschichte des Rheinischen Jäger-Bataillons Nr. 8 von seiner Errichtung 1815 bis zum Jahre 1880* (Berlin, 1880)

Kinzenbach, F., *Mein Kriegsjahr 1870-1871. Erinnerung eines Kriegsfreiwilligen im rheinischen Jäger-Bataillons Nr.8* (Bremen, 1881)

Deines, A., *Das Husaren-regiment König Wilhelm I. (1. rheinisches) Nr. 7 : Von d. Formation d. Stammrgts bis zur Gegenwart* (Berlin, 1904)

Eltester & Schlee, *Geschichte der Rheinischen Feldartillerie bis zu ihrer Teilung in vier Regimenter 1. Okober 1899 insbesondere des Feldartillerie-Regiments v. Holtzendorff (1. Rheinisches) Nr. 8* (Berlin, 1910)

VIII Corps, 16th Infantry Division, 31st Brigade

Wellmann, R., *Geschichte des Infanterie-Regiments von Horn (3tes Rheinisches) Nr 29* (Trier, 1894)

Schroetter, R., *Geschichte des 7. Rheinischen Infanterie-Regiments Nr. 69* (Berlin, 1885)

VIII Corps, 15th Infantry Division, 32nd Brigade

Seton, J.L., *Notes on the operations of the North German troops in Lorraine and Picardy, taken while accompanying principally the 40th or Hohenzollern Fusilier Regiment* (London, 1872)

Sauerwein, A., *Die Vierziger in Frankreich : Geschichte des deutsch-französischen Kriegs vom Jahre 1870/71, mit besonderer Berücksichtigung des Hochenzollernschen Füsilier. Reg. N. 40* (Trier, 1874)

2 I.R. 60 is one of the very few Prussian regiments to lack any detailed history for 1870.

Liebeskind, P., *Geschichte des Füsilier-Regiments Fürst Karl Anton von Hohenzollern (Hohenzollernschen) Nr. 40 : unter Benutzung der Regimentsgeschichte von Major Kosch und Einfügung der Geschichte des Feldzuges 1870/71 von Oberst Gisevins, ehemaligen Offizieren des Regiments* (Berlin, 1896)

Fabricius, J., *Geschichte des 4. Thüringischen Infanterie-Regiments Nr 72 in den Jahren 1860 bis 1878* (Berlin, 1879)

VIII Corps, 16th Infantry Division, divisional troops

Bredow, K. von, *Geschichte des 2. Rheinischen Husaren-Regiments Nr 9* (Berlin, 1899)

VIII Corps, corps troops

Schüler, *Geschichte des Rheinischen Pionier-Bataillons Nr.8* (Berlin, 1883)

Ibing, K., *Geschichte des Rheinischen Train-Bataillons Nr.8 in Ehrenbreitstein* (Berlin, 1905)

3rd Cavalry Division

6th Cavalry Brigade

Rückforth, *Geschichte des Kürassier-Regiments Graf Geßler, rheinisches Nr 8* (Berlin, 1910)

Kusenberg, O., *Geschichte des Rheinischen Ulanen-Regiments Nr 7 : 1815-1890* (Berlin, 1890)

Epner, K., *Geschichte des Ulanen-Regiments Grossherzog Friedrich von Baden (Rheinisches) Nr 7* (Berlin, 1902)

Braun, *Das Rheinische Ulanen-Regiment Nr.7 im deutsch-französischen Kriege 1870/71* (Berlin, 1909)

7th Cavalry Brigade

Boehn, H. von, *Geschichte des Westfälischen Ulanen-Regiments Nr 5* (Düsseldorf, 1890)

Anon., *Erlebnisse des 1. Hannoversches Ulanen-Regiments Nr.13 während des Krieges 1870/71* (Hannover, 1871)

Seydewitz, F. von, *Die ersten 25 Jahre des Königs-Ulanen-Regiments (1. Hannoverschen) Nr 13* (Berlin, 1897)

Second Army

III Corps, 5th Infantry Division, 9th Brigade

Lichtenstein, W., *Geschichte des königlich preußischen Leib-Grenadier-Regiments (1. brandenburgischen) Nr 8 : 1859-1882* (Berlin, 1883)

Dallmer, V., *Geschichte des 5. Brandenburgischen Infanterie-Regiments Nr 48* (Berlin, 1886)

III Corps, 5th Infantry Division, 10th Brigade

Müller, H., *Geschichte des Grenadier-Regiments Prinz Carl von Preussen (2. Brandenburgisches) Nr. 12 : 1813-1875* (Berlin, 1875)

Hopp, F., *Das Grenadier-Regiment Prinz Carl (2. Brandenburgisches) Nr. 12 in der Schlacht bei Spicheren am 6.VIII.1870* (Frankfurt-an-der-Oder, 1904)

Berkun, H., *Geschichte des Infanterie-Regiments von Alvensleben (6. Brandenburgisches) Nr 32 : 1860-1897* (Berlin, 1899)

III Corps, 5th Infantry Division, divisional troops

Anon., *Geschichte des Brandenburgischen Jäger-Bataillons Nr.3 während des Feldzuges 1870/71* (Berlin, 1877)

Heydebreck, C., *Das Dragoner-Regiment von Arnim (2. Brandenburgisches) Nr. 12. : Geschichte d. Regiments v. seiner Formation bis z.Jahre 1908* (Berlin, 1908)

Stumpff, K. von, *Geschichte des Feldartillerie-Regiments General-Feldzeugmeister (1. brandenburgischen) Nr 3* (Berlin, 1900)

III Corps, 6th Infantry Division, 11th Brigade

Kirchhof, G.H. & R. Brandenburg, *Das 3. brandenburgische Infanterie-Regiment Nr 20 in den Feldzügen 1866 und 1870-71* (Berlin, 1881)

Lehmann, R., *Kriegserinnerungen eines 20er Füsilier aus dem Felde 1870-1871* (Rathenow, 1891)

Isenburg, F., *Das brandenburgische Füsilier-Regiment Nr 35 in Frankreich 1870 bis 1873* (Berlin, 1875)

Ehrenberg, H., *Feldzugserinnerungen eines 35ers, 1870-1871* (Rathenow, 1889)

Reitzenstein, *H. von, Erinnerungen und Aufzeichnungen aus den Kriegsjahren 1870/71 als Compagnie-Chef im Brandenburgischen Füsilier-Regiment Nr. 35 jetzigen Füsilier-Regiment Prinz Heinrich von Preußen [Brandenburgisches] Nr. 35* (Rathenow, 1897)

III Corps, 6th Infantry Division, 12th Brigade

Wörmann, A. & P. Beyer, *Fortsetzung der Geschichte des 4. Brandenburgischen Infanterie-Regiments Nr.24 (Großherzog von Mecklenburg-Schwerin) von 1870-1873* (Neu-Ruppin, 1873)

Jahn, H., *Aus Deutschlands grossen Tagen : Erlebnisse eines 24ers im deutsch-französischen Kriege* (Braunschweig, 1895)

Bubbe, J., *Kriegs-Erlebnisse aus den Feldzügen 1864, 1866, 1870/71, ehemaliger 24er* (Neu-Ruppin, 1897)

Becher, P., *Geschichte des Infanterie-Regiments Friedrich Franz II. von Mecklenburg-Schwerin (4. brandenburgisches) Nr 24* (Berlin, 1908, 2 vols)

Gentz, G., *Geschichte des Infanterie-Regiments General-Feldmarschall Prinz Friedrich Karl von Preußen (8. Brandenburgischen) Nr 64* (Berlin, 1897)

III Corps, 6th Infantry Division, divisional troops

Kraatz-Koschlau, M.T. von, *Geschichte des 1. Brandenburgischen Dragoner-Regiments Nr 2* (Berlin, 1878)

III Corps, corps troops

Wollmann, E., *Geschichte des Brandenburgischen Pionier-Bataillons Nr. 3 (Minden, 1888)*

Schreiber, W., *Geschichte des Brandenburgischen Train-Bataillons Nr.3* (Berlin, 1903)

5th Cavalry Division

11th Cavalry Brigade

Anon., *Erlebnisse des 1. Hannoversches Ulanen-Regiments Nr.13 während des Krieges 1870/71* (Hannover, 1871)

Seydewitz, F. von, *Die ersten 25 Jahre des Königs-Ulanen-Regiments (1. Hannoverschen) Nr 13* (Berlin, 1897)

Schweppe, G., *Geschichte des oldenburgischen Dragoner-Regiments Nr 19 ehemalig groszherzoglich oldenburgischen Reiter-Regiments* (Oldenburg, 1899)

12th Cavalry Brigade

Hiller von Gaertringen, H. & K. von Schirmeister, *Geschichte des Kürassier-Regiments von Seydlitz (Magdeburgisches)* Nr. 7 (Berlin, 1890)

Koblinski, E. von, *Aufzeichnungen aus der Geschichte des Altmärkischen Ulanen-Regiments Nr 16* (Berlin, 1882)

13th Cavalry Brigade

Thielen, H. von, *Geschichte des Magdeburgischen Husaren-Regiments Nr 10 : 1813-1888* (Hannover, 1888)

Rohr, H-B.. von, *Geschichte des Magdeburgischen Husaren-Regiments Nr 10 : 1813-1913* (Berlin, 1913)

Ardenne, A. von, *Bergische Lanziers. Westfälische Husaren-Regiments Nr.11* (Berlin, 1877)

Eck, H. von, *Geschichte des 2. westfälischen Husaren-Regiments Nr 11 und seiner Stammtruppen von 1807-1893* (Düsseldorf, 1904)

Schlieffen-Wioska, H. von & R. Mackensen von Astfeld, *Hundert Jahre braunschweigische Husaren* (Braunschweig, 1909)

Mackensen von Astfeld, R., *Braunschweiger Husaren in Feindes Land : Erinnerungen aus der Kriege 1870/71* (Berlin, 1914)

Divisional troops

Rogge, P., *Geschichte des Feldartillerie-Regiments Prinzregent Luitpold von Bayern (Magdeburgischen) Nr 4* (Berlin, 1898)

Colditz, R. von, *Geschichte des Feld-Artillerie-Regiments von Scharnhorst (1. hannoverschen) Nr 10* (Berlin, 1891)

6th Cavalry Division

14th Cavalry Brigade

Schmiterloew, B. von, *Geschichte des brandenburgischen Kürassier-Regiments (Kaiser Nicolaus I. von Russland) Nr 6 von 1842 bis 1876* (Brandenburg/Havel, 1876)

Restorff, F. von, *Geschichte des Kürassier-Regiments Kaiser Nikolaus I. von Russland (Brandenburgischen) Nr. 6* (Berlin, 1897)

Bothe, H. & K. von Ebart, *Geschichte des Ulanen-Regiments Kaiser Alexander von Russland (1. Brandenburgisches) Nr.3. Vom Jahre 1859-1879* (Berlin, 1879)

Glasenapp, G. von, *Geschichte des Schleswig-Holsteinschen Ulanen-Regiments Nr 15 von seiner Stiftung bis zum Tage des 25jährigen Bestehens* (Berlin, 1894)

15th Cavalry Brigade

Ardenne, A. von, *Geschichte des Zieten'schen Husaren-Regiments (Berlin, 1874)*

Anon., *Erlebnisse Angehöriger und ehemaliger Angehöriger des Husaren-Regiments von Zeiten* (Rathenow, 1910)

Terno, E., *Fünfundzwanzig Jahre : Erinnerungsblätter aus der Geschichte des Husaren-Regiments Kaiser Franz Joseph von Oesterreich, König von Ungarn '(Schleswig-Holsteinisches)' Nr. 16* (Kiel , 1891)

Christiansen, J., *Unsere 16er Husaren. Blätter zum Ruhmesglanze des Regiments. Bilder von den Schlachtfeldern vor Metz und Nachklänge von der Denkmalsweihe bei Rézonville* (Schleswig, 1902)

BOOKS IN THIS SERIES:

1. *The Battle of Majuba Hill The Transvaal Campaign 1880–1881* John Laband (ISBN 978-1-911512-38-7)
2. *For Queen and Company Vignettes of the Irish Soldier in the Indian Mutiny* David Truesdale (ISBN 978-1-911512-79-0)
3. *The Furthest Garrison Imperial Regiments in New Zealand 1840–1870* Adam Davis (ISBN 978-1-911628-29-3)
4. *Victory Over Disease Resolving the Medical Crisis in the Crimean War, 1854–1856* Michael Hinton (ISBN 978-1-911628-31-6)
5. *Journey Through the Wilderness Garnet Wolseley's Canadian Red River Expedition of 1870* Paul McNicholls (ISBN 978-1-911628-30-9)
6. *Kitchener The Man Not The Myth* Anne Samson (ISBN 978-1-912866-45-8)
7. *The British and the Sikhs Discovery, Warfare and Friendship c1700–1900* Gurinder Singh Mann (ISBN 978-1-911628-24-8)
8. *Bazaine 1870 Scapegoat for a Nation* Quintin Barry (ISBN 978-1-913336-08-0)
9. *Redcoats in the Classroom The British Army's Schools For Soldiers and Their Children During the 19th Century* Howard R. Clarke (ISBN 978-1-912866-47-2)
10. *The Rescue They Called a Raid The Jameson Raid 1895–96* David Snape (ISBN 978-1-913118-77-8)
11. *Hungary 1848 The Winter Campaign* Christopher Pringle (ISBN 978-1-913118-78-5)
12. *The War of the Two Brothers The Portuguese Civil War 1828-1834* Sérgio Veludo Coelho (ISBN 978-1-914059-26-1)
14. *Forgotten Victorian Generals Studies in the Exercise of Command and Control in the British Army 1837–1901* Christopher Brice (editor) (ISBN 978-1-910777-20-6)
15. *The German War of 1866 The Bohemian and Moravian Campaign* Theodore Fontane (ISBN 978-1-914059-29-2)
16. *Dust of Glory The First Anglo-Afghan War 1839–1842, its Causes and Course* Bill Whitburn (ISBN 978-1-914059-33-9)
17. *Saarbruck to Sedan The Franco-German War 1870–1871 Volume 1* Ralph Weaver (ISBN 978-1-914059-88-9)
18. *The Battle of Lissa 1866 How the Industrial Revolution Changed the Face of Naval Warfare* Quintin Barry (ISBN 978-1-914059-92-6)
19. *The Zulu Kingdom and the Boer Invasion of 1837–1840* John Laband (ISBN 978-1-914059-89-6)
20. *The Fire of Venture Was in His Veins* Major Allan Wilson and the Shangani Patrol 1893 David Snape (ISBN 978-1-914059-90-2)
21. *From the Atacama to the Andes Battles of the War of the Pacific 1879–1883* Alan Curtis (ISBN 978-1-914059-90-2)
22. *The Rise of the Sikh Soldier The Sikh Warrior Through the Ages, c1700–1900* Gurinder Singh Mann (ISBN 978-1-915070-52-4)
23. *Victorian Crusaders British and Irish Volunteers in the Papal Army 1860–70* Nicholas Schofield (ISBN 978-1-915070-53-1)
24. *The Battle for the Swiepwald Austria's Fatal Blunder at Königgrätz, the climactic battle of the Austro-Prussian War, 3 July 1866* Ernst Heidrich (ISBN 978-1-915070-49-4)
25. *British Military Panoramas Battle in The Round, 1800–1914* Ian F.W. Beckett (ISBN 978-1-915113-84-9)
26. *Onwards to Omdurman The Anglo-Egyptian Campaign to Reconquer the Sudan, 1896–1898* Keith Surridge (ISBN 978-1-915070-51-7)
27. *Hungary 1849 The Summer Campaign* Wilhelm Ramming, Christopher Pringle (editor) (ISBN 978-1-915113-80-1)
28. *Line in the Sand French Foreign Legion Forts and Fortifications in Morocco 1900–1926* Richard Jeynes (ISBN 978-1-915113-83-2)
29. *The Republic Fights Back The Franco-German War 1870-1871 Volume 2* Ralph Weaver (ISBN 978-1-915070-50-0)
30. *Controlling the Frontier Southern Africa 1806–1828, The Cape Frontier Wars and The Fetcani Alarm* Hugh Driver (ISBN 978-1-915113-78-8)
31. *The Battle of Magersfontein Victory and defeat on the South African veld, 10–12 December 1899* Garth Benneyworth (ISBN 978-1-915113-79-5)
32. *Too Little Too Late The Campaign in West and South Germany June–July 1866* Michael Embree (ISBN 978-1-804513-77-4)
33. *The Destruction of the Imperial Army* Volume 1: The Opening Engagements of the Franco-German War 1870–71 Grenville Bird (ISBN 978-1-915113-81-8)
34. *Kitchener* The Man Not the Myth Anne Samson (ISBN 978-1-804513-84-2)
35. *From Ironclads to Dreadnoughts* The Development of the German Battleship, 1864–1918 Dirk Nottelmann & David M. Sullivan (ISBN 978-1-804511-84-8)
36. *The Destruction of the Imperial Army* Volume 2: The Battles around Metz Grenville Bird (ISBN 978-1-804511-85-5)
37. *More Work Than Glory* Buffalo Soldiers in the United States Army, 1866–1916 John P Langellier (ISBN 978-1-804513-34-7)
38. *The Spioenkop Campaign* The Battles to Relieve Ladysmith 17–27 January 1900 Robert Davidson (ISBN 978-1-804513-31-6)
39. *The Destruction of the Imperial Army* Volume 3: *The Sedan Campaign 1870* Grenville Bird (ISBN 978-1-804513-32-3)
40. *The Destruction of the Imperial Army* Volume 4: *Sedan, Strasbourg and Metz* 1870 Grenville Bird (ISBN 978-1-804514-59-7)
41. *Memorandum on the Prussian Army in Relation to the Campaign of 1866* Lieutenant Colonel W.E.M Reilly (ISBN 978-1-804516-27-0)
42. *Black Week: The British Army and Defeat in Anglo-Boer War 1899-1900* Quintin Barry (ISBN 978-1-804511-86-2)
43. *War in the East. A Military History of the Russo-Turkish War 1877-78* Quintin Barry (ISBN 978-1-804517-30-7)
44. *The First Schleswig-Holstein War 1848-50* Nick Svendsen (ISBN 978-1-804517-36-9)
45. *The Hundred Thousand Sons of St Louis* Ralph Weaver (ISBN 978-1-804517-37-6)
46. *Bismarck's First War: The Campaign in Schleswig and Jutland 1864* Michael Embree (ISBN 978-1-804517-38-3)
47. *The Honvéd War. Armies of the Hungarian War of Independence 1848-49* Nigel James Smith (ISBN 978-1-804514-60-3)
48. *Radestzky's Marches. The Campaigns of 1848 and 1849 in Upper Italy* Michael Embree (ISBN 978-1-804517-42-0)
49. *The Campaign on the Loire 1870-71: Orléans and Le Mans* Quintin Barry (ISBN 978-1-804517-82-6)
50. *The British Empire's Regulars 1880-1914: Soldiers of Britain, India and Africa* Wendell Scholander (ISBN 978-1-804515-62-4)
51. *The Last Throw of the Dice: Bourbaki and Werder in Eastern France 1870-71* Quintin Barry (ISBN 978-1-804517-78-9)
52. *Three Weeks in November. A Military History of the Swiss Civil War of 1847* Ralph Weaver (ISBN 978-1-804518-49-6)
53. *The Battle of Wörth August 6th 1870* Lieut.-Col. G.F.R. Henderson (ISBN 978-1-804517-90-1)
54. *The Battle of Spicheren August 6th 1870* Lieut.-Col. G.F.R. Henderson (ISBN 978-1-804518-50-2)